CANADA AND THE REAGAN CHALLENGE

The original edition of this book was published in the Canadian Institute for Economic Policy Series.

NEW UPDATED
EDITION

CANADA
AND THE
REAGAN
CHALLENGE

CRISIS AND ADJUSTMENT, 1981-85

StephenClarkson

James Lorimer & Company, Publishers
Toronto 1985

ISBN 0-88862-791-2 cloth
        0-88862-790-4 paper

Cover design: Don Fernley
Cover photo: Scott Grant, Government of Canada

Canadian Cataloguing in Publication Data

Clarkson, Stephen, 1937-
 Canada and the Reagan challenge

Includes bibliographical references and index.

1. Canada — Relations — United States.
2. United States — Relations — Canada. I. Title.

FC249.C42 1985   327.71073   C85-098331-2
F1029.5.U6C43 1985

45,486

James Lorimer & Company, Publishers
Egerton Ryerson Memorial Building
35 Britain Street
Toronto, Ontario M5A 1R7
Printed and bound in Canada

6 5 4 3 2 1   85 86 87 88 89

This new edition is dedicated to the first edition's godfather, the Hon.
   Walter Lockhart Gordon:
chairman of the Royal Commission on Canada's Economic Prospects
   (1957),
cabinet sponsor for the Watkins Report, Foreign Ownership and the
   Structure of Canadian Industry (1968),
chairman of the Canadian Institute for Economic Policy (1978-84) and
   éminence grise behind its thirty-one studies,
a man of business and of government who has contributed more than
   any of his compatriots in public life to the exploration of Canada's
   many national problems and to the proposal of policies for their
   solution,
a Canadian of unflagging determination and inspiring optimism.

Contents

Preface to the Second Edition

The thirteen original chapters of the first edition have been left intact except for the correction of some typographical errors. Despite perfunctory protestations from the U.S. ambassador to Canada, the authenticity of the documents on which the analysis of the 1981 crisis was based (chapter 2) has been confirmed — tacitly by senior members of the embassy staff and practically by the search carried out in the Department of State to identify how they were leaked. The response to *Canada and the Reagan Challenge* by professionals who need its analysis as background for their work and by students who use it in their research has been a heartening indication that the book was worth writing in the first place and is worth reissuing now that its stock is exhausted.

The reprinting of the book has given me the opportunity to write a final chapter having two purposes. The analysis of 1982 has been brought up to the end of the Trudeau era in 1984, under the main categories of economic and sovereignty issues used in the original edition. Secondly, I have attempted to provide a reader's guide to the Mulroney government. I appraise the assets that the new prime minister brings to the job, identify the changes he has made in the bilateral process, and ask what prospects he has for successfully accomplishing his objective of recreating a "special relationship" with Washington.

The research for this epilogue was based on personal interviews, written documentation and collegial discussion. Seventy interviews were conducted in Ottawa, Toronto and Chicago, some 45 for the first time, some 25 as repeat interviews. The names of the interviewees are listed in the appendix with the exception of those who did not want to be identified. In coping with a continuing flood of documentation, I am indebted to the research assistance at various times of Lisa Feld, Kathleen Finlay, Andrew Mitrovica and Ann Xinidis. Gary Hufbauer in Washington, and Robert Martin, John Rouse and Paul Heinbecker in Ottawa were particularly helpful in supplying me with research reports and official documents. Over the course of the past two years I have spoken to several dozen groups in public lectures, in conferences, in colloquia and in seminars in Canada, the United States and Europe. While it is not possible to identify which ideas were garnered from which meetings or individuals, my understanding has deepened as a by-product of these exchanges with students, professionals, members of the interested public and colleagues. One such colleague who must be mentioned is John Kirton, a scholar of Canada's international role, with whom I have taught a graduate course and from whom I have learned a great deal in the past year. It is to Christina McCall to whom I owe the greatest debt, both intellectual and moral, in bringing this work to a happy conclusion.

S.C.
Toronto
Spring, 1985

Preface

This study was commissioned by the Canadian Institute for Economic Policy in August 1981 when news stories in the Canadian press emanating from Washington indicated that the American government was considering taking unprecedented retaliatory actions against Canada. The Canadian-American relationship appeared to have entered a new period of crisis. My assignment was to review the issues on the bilateral agenda that had become cause for serious conflict between the two countries.

Because what was at stake in so many of the issues had changed significantly from the Seventies, it was decided that I should conduct intensive interviews with the chief players on both sides of the border in order to find out *viva voce* how they viewed these issues and the resultant tensions that were straining the relationship. During the next ten months, two hundred Canadian and American government officials and businessmen were interviewed by me in both national capitals, two key provincial capitals (Quebec City and Edmonton) and three financial centres (Montreal, New York and Calgary), as well as in my home city of Toronto which is important as both a provincial and financial capital. In view of the sensitivity of the issues at stake, my interviewees were given assurances that I would neither quote their words directly nor attribute their thoughts indirectly unless these had been otherwise expressed either in a public forum or in print. In exchange for guarantees of anonymity, almost everyone I spoke to was willing to discuss frankly what seemed to them a matter of intense importance: the state of the Canadian-American relationship. With only a few exceptions, the names of all interviewees are listed in the Appendix. (Those not listed specifically were left out for professional reasons.) Interested readers will also find in the notes listed at the end of the book the documentation used and will realize how much I have profited from the labours and expertise of many of my academic colleagues who have given extensive study and thought to the individual policy problems that this study reviews in the context of the 1981 crisis.

By its size and nature, this study obviously cannot provide a detailed exposition of every aspect of the Canadian-American relationship. Its purpose is to analyze and review the major problems the two countries confront in the context of their new nationalisms — the reinvigorated centralism of the Trudeau government of the Eighties and the America-first assertiveness of the Reagan administration. The chapters that follow are directed primarily at the general Canadian reader who is overwhelmed almost daily by items in the morning news involving issues — emissions causing acid rain, factors affecting high interest rates, the deployment of nuclear missiles, counter-insurgency in Central America, layoffs in the automotive industry, changes in the price of oil — that directly affect relations between Canada and the United States for better or for worse. We all suffer from an overload of information which bombards us so incessantly that it becomes difficult to assess the significance of any single event, to decipher the pattern into which it fits, and to see how it relates to other factors. My aim in this study is to provide a framework within which the endless events affecting Canadian-American relations can be understood.

I write from the Canadian side of our long undefended border and I have had greater access to data from Canadian rather than American sources. Were I an American, the light cast on the same events would undoubtedly be different. I trust nevertheless that American readers will learn something from this analysis, just as Canadians derive great benefit from American studies of our mutual relationship. For students conducting research on specific aspects of the Canadian-American relationship, much of the information in these pages will rapidly become dated. I hope it will still have value as a coherent overview linking the various individual policy problems to a specific historical context.

In arranging my interviews I received inestimable help from Marshall Crowe, Peter Meekison and Judy Wish (for Alberta), Louise Beaudoin, André Dufour and François Lebrun (for Quebec), David Adam and Paul Fraser (for New York City), and Gerry Shannon (for Washington), while my visits to Ottawa were turned from business to pleasure by the warm hospitality of Jane and Geoff O'Brian. After my travelling was finished I benefited from correspondence with Willis Armstrong, Barbara Hodgins, Mitchell Sharp, Robert Turner and Raymond Waldmann. John Fredenburg of the U.S. International

Communication Agency in Ottawa, Audrey Gill, Policy Director of the Liberal Party of Canada, Jim Laxer, Research Director of the New Democratic Party, and Sheila Purse, Librarian for the Canadian Consulate in New York responded generously and expeditiously to my repeated requests for documentation. Robert Blair, Marsha Chandler, John Curtis, Don Daly, Gary Hufbauer, Mel Hurtig, Allan King, John Kirton, Bernard Picchi and Gil Winham kindly sent me published and unpublished works of theirs that I requested. Particularly useful during the course of my work were conferences and seminars organized by the Centre for International Studies at the University of Toronto and the Canadian Institute of International Affairs whose work on the Canadian-American relationship has been made possible by financial support from the Donner Foundation. Leave to carry out this work was graciously accorded me by my own institution, the Department of Political Economy, where Mary Rous and Mary Bochar were continually helpful in meeting my organizational needs.

Throughout the period of research and writing I was helped on a continuing basis by the meticulous research assistance of Kathleen Finlay. Kris Inwood prepared the statistical tables and graphs. John Donner and Annis May Timpson acted as fastidious readers and thoughtful commentators for the entire manuscript, as did James Lorimer and the Hon. Walter Gordon, chairman of the Canadian Institute for Economic Policy. One person who must remain unnamed, but not unthanked, helped unstintingly with factual research and textual scrutiny. For expert vetting of individual chapters and sections of the manuscript, I am particularly indebted to the comments of Paul Audley, Carl Beigie, François Bregha, Rod Byers, Elizabeth Dixon, Arthur Donner, John Grant, John Kirton, Fred Lazar, Don Munton, Ross Perry, Douglas Peters, Cranford Pratt, Abraham Rotstein and Brian Segal. Mary Harrison typed and retyped the manuscript with her customary dispatch, accuracy and good humour. Roger Voyer, executive director of the Canadian Institute for Economic Policy, was most cooperative in facilitating the entire project. But this study has profited most of all from the sustained concern, constant love and generous help of my wife, Christina McCall-Newman.

S.C.
Toronto

Part I

Conditions for Crisis

Conditions for Crisis

On October 28, 1980, the minister of finance, the Honourable Allan MacEachen, rose in the House of Commons in Ottawa to table a budget that contained — in addition to the routine juggling with taxation rates that normally attracts Canadians' attention on budget night — a startling document with the simple title, "National Energy Program." The NEP was, in effect, a broad economic strategy whose ambitious intent was threefold: the restructuring of the oil and gas industry in order to achieve energy self-sufficiency for Canada after a decade of OPEC-induced uncertainty, the restoration of financial primacy to a federal government dangerously drained by growing transfer payments to the provinces, and the increase of Canadian ownership levels in this predominantly foreign-controlled sector of the economy. Not the least unusual aspect of the NEP was that it represented the fulfilment of an election promise made by the Liberal party only ten months before. (Canadians may have been astonished, but they were also pleased. Six months later, after Petro-Canada, the state-owned oil company, had moved in the direction promised by the NEP by purchasing Petrofina from its Belgian owners, public opinion polls revealed that 84 per cent of the respondents supported the NEP's target of 50 per cent Canadianization of the industry by 1990.[1])

On November 4, 1980, just one week after the NEP was unveiled, Americans were startled by the size of the electoral mandate given to Ronald Reagan, the Republican presidential candidate with the radiant smile and the resonant voice who stood foursquare for the virtues of America's past. He promised to return in the Eighties to small government, free enterprise, balanced budgets, reduced crime, a firm foreign policy and an America of which Americans could once again be proud. (Americans may have been surprised by the extent of the Republican sweep, but they were on the whole pleased by what they had wrought. A year later, following the decisive victories Reagan had won in his budget jousts with Congress, his miraculous escape from an assassin's bullet, and the firm stance taken with foreign statesmen at summits in Ottawa and Cancun, Mexico, 54 per cent of Americans polled felt that America was "at least as respected throughout the world as it was one year ago."[2])

At the time, these two dramatic events, which made each nation feel unusually content with itself, did not seem fated to induce the most acute crisis in the Canadian-American relationship in living memory. After all, Energy Minister Marc Lalonde, the chief architect of the NEP, had aimed the program not at defying the United States but at shifting political power from Alberta and economic rents from the oil industry towards the federal government. Lalonde was not anti-American. In all the hectic months of planning the NEP, little thought had been given to what would be the reactions of the United States to this projected internal change in the dynamics of the federal system. For its part, the foreign policy thrust underlying the Republicans' neo-conservatism was directed towards pushing back the Soviet Union, not towards putting Canada in its place. In fact Canada, with Mexico, enjoyed pride of place in the world view of Ronald Reagan who had, during his successful election campaign, spoken glowingly about the need for the U.S. to build an almost mystical "North American accord" with its continental neighbours. Despite these good dispositions on either side, the two political thrusts embodied in the National Energy Program and the Reagan victory were sufficiently divergent in their directions that they presaged a potential confrontation between the two countries. The likelihood that a confrontation would escalate into a crisis had already been heralded in the Seventies by the incompatible trends developing within each political system and by the resulting instability introduced into the previously harmonious "special relationship." The confrontation between Washington and Ottawa following the NEP's announcement, and Ronald Reagan's election and the policy changes wrought since 1981 in bilateral relations, indicated that the Canadian-American relationship had undergone a severe crisis and shifted onto a new and treacherous path.

"Crisis" in political economy analysis has acquired its connotation from common usage. This originally referred to the critical point in the course of an illness at which the patient either succumbed or began to recover. In more current parlance, "crisis" applies to those emotionally charged events that can produce radical changes in a person's life. Historical and social analyses use the concept to denote an unstable period in a country's development when some decisive change is impending and a societal condition characterized by unusual stress which leads to some transformation in the system.[3]

For the purposes of this study of the Canadian-American relationship we will adopt a three-part definition of "crisis," requiring that each condition be satisfied if the term is to apply.

- First there must be a condition of *instability* in the relationship making it vulnerable to some dramatic change.
- Second there must be a period of excessive *stress* when high levels of tension among the protagonists endanger the continuity of the relationship.
- Third there must be sufficient *change* in existing attitudes, values or policy patterns for the crisis to have marked a historical turning point in the relationship.

Our objective in the introductory chapter is to examine to what extent the decade of the Seventies leading up to the NEP and Reaganism displayed the first condition of *instability*, making the Canadian-American relationship vulnerable to a crisis. Certainly the Fifties and Sixties had been a period of stability so firmly based that the various differences of interest that had brought Washington and Ottawa into conflict were amenable to resolution without observers rushing in with claims that a "crisis" existed. The relationship between the two countries was truly special by contemporary international standards. The extent to which "crisis" accurately describes the Washington-Ottawa confrontation of 1981 as the second, subjective condition of acute *stress* is the concern of chapter 2, which chronicles the diplomatic pressures that were exerted at the formal intergovernmental level by Washington on Ottawa. Whether we can say that Canadian-American relations went through a crisis in 1981 in the sense of the third condition of objective *changes* that have transformed the relationship is the question considered in chapters 3 through 11, which examine the nine major policy issues that have been most prominent on the bilateral agenda.

The Shaking of the Special Relationship

1

What diplomats and scholars now call special in the Canadian-American relationship was more an unspoken attitude characterizing the way the United States treated Canada, and the way Canada responded to the United States, than a body of rules governing how each country was to behave towards the other.[1] Under the Cold War pressures of the Forties and Fifties, when both countries' perceptions of the Soviet threat emphasized their common international goals and mutual economic needs, quiet accommodation characterized the way the two capitals dealt with each other. Ottawa acknowledged Washington's pre-eminence in the Western alliance, deferred to its foreign policy positions, reserved any objections it might have for friendly discussions behind the scenes, and assiduously avoided, in the words of the Merchant-Heeney Report of 1965, "raising a row in public."[2] In return for Canada's quiet and diplomatic approach to the U.S., Washington was conciliatory and indulgent towards Canada's needs, offering the Canadian military privileged access to strategic intelligence and granting Canadian industry privileged access to the Pentagon's defence contracts.

Privileged access also characterized the ability of American corporations to set up so many subsidiaries in mining, manufacturing and distribution in the Canadian economy to the point that Canadian-owned firms in many sectors found themselves operating at a disadvantage in their own market. The economy's structure had largely been determined under the aegis of C. D. Howe, the dominant economic minister in the Liberal governments of the Second World War and the Cold War era. Along with most politicians, bureaucrats and businessmen of his generation, Howe saw no meaning in the nationality of capital and therefore no reason to resist the flow or to affect the form of foreign investment. American tariff barriers prevented the maturation of Canadian manufacturing industry by excluding its finished products from its neighbour's mass market. At the same time Canadian tariffs had attracted foreign-controlled branch plants that turned Canada's economy into a miniature replica of the American. Notwithstanding those barriers, the truncated Canadian economy remained largely open and dependent in the sense that its pace of development was determined by the demands of American industry for Canadian resources and by the supply of American manufactured goods sold to Canadian consumers. Canada's capital markets operated like an extension of the U.S. money markets. Canadian corporate tax policies were kept in general harmony with American practices.

So integrated was the Canadian economy in the American that proposed American legislative changes in the Sixties designed to correct U.S. balance of payments problems could have had powerful effects on the Canadian economy if Ottawa had not repeatedly requested and Washington as repeatedly granted exemptions, under certain conditions, for Canada from these measures. Conscious of Canada's military value as a bomber route to and from the Soviet Union and its strategic importance as a supplier of raw materials for U.S. industry, the Department of State kept a watching brief on Canada's interests in Washington, helping the executive to insulate Canada from congressional actions that could inadvertently damage the special relationship.[3] In effect, Canada was treated as a backyard neighbour rather than as a distinct foreign power for whom the United States needed an explicitly articulated foreign policy. The clichés repeated *ad nauseam* in political speeches about the thousands of miles of undefended border expressed a basic truth: a convergence of world views and a mutual satisfaction with Canada's economic and cultural integration had laid the foundations for an impressive stability in the Canadian-American relationship.

By 1965, when a bureaucratic attempt was made by the Merchant-Heeney Report to exalt the slogan of quiet diplomacy into a doctrine codifying Canada's American relationship, cracks had begun to develop in the special relationship's foundations. Many separate and smaller forces — cultural concerns, economic issues, political worries — were putting strains on a structure whose facade was still intact. None of these had as traumatizing an effect as American policy in Vietnam, which undermined Canadians' blithe confidence in the United States' Cold War leadership and revealed the American economy's inflationary mechanisms to be a threat, not a support, to its partners' industrial goals. In addition, civil unrest and repeated outbreaks of urban riots shattered the image of America-the-beautiful. Nothing was more indicative of which way the wind was blowing than the violation of the norms of quiet diplomacy by Lester Pearson, the Nobel Peace Prize winner turned prime minister, in his speech at Temple University in 1965 that criticized the American bombing of North Vietnam. Lyndon Johnson expressed his presidential pique to the prime minister with characteristic bluntness: "You peed on my carpet," he growled.[4]

The first really open break in the special relationship did not come until August 1971 when, without warning, President Nixon announced a series of draconian measures to shore up the American economy at the expense of its trading partners. The first shock of "Nixonomics" in Ottawa was the announcement of general measures which would have a direct impact on the Canadian economy: an import surcharge of 10 per cent and a tax device called the Domestic International Sales Corporation (DISC) to encourage U.S. multinationals to export from their American facilities to the detriment of their foreign branch plants. A further shock was the U.S. demand that Canada raise the value of its dollar above par and fix it there, even though the Canadian dollar had already appreciated against the American. The final blow was the realization that, this time, there were to be no exemptions for Canada. John Connally, the American treasury secretary, was as intransigent with protesting Canadian ministers as he was towards the irate French and Japanese. Canada was no longer special to Republican Washington: it had become a foreign country *comme les autres*.

The crisis of Nixonomics had shaken, but did not immediately terminate, the special relationship. Putting up a stubborn resistance, the Canadian government was able to stare down Connally's demands until the treasury secretary fell from presidential favour and the administration was diverted by more pressing matters. Efforts were made to define a course for Canada that would be less vulnerable to the arbitrary actions of American politicians. In 1972, Mitchell Sharp, secretary of state for external affairs, published a paper proposing that the Canadian government shift Canada's international strategy away from the trap of a self-perpetuating and deepening continental integration towards what he called the "Third Option," a strategy of lessening Canada's dependence on the U.S. by expanding its relations with other countries.[5] Mitchell Sharp's Third Option was never accepted by his cabinet colleagues as the consensus governing government strategy. As a result, the Seventies turned into a long period of uncertainty in which the special relationship apparently lingered on under the guise of still warm relations between the leaders in the two capitals. During this decade, external shocks (the OPEC crisis) and internal strains (provincial separatism in Canada, foreign policy disputes in the U.S.) put both countries under severe stress which also affected their bilateral relationship.

The Unstable Seventies

Once Richard Nixon had left the White House in disgrace in 1974, a semblance of normalcy returned to the Washington-Ottawa axis, first under the straightforward Gerald Ford[6] and then with the sympathetic Jimmy Carter. But the specialness of Canadian-American relations was more apparent than real. John Turner, as minister of finance, and Donald Macdonald, as minister of energy, could relate "one on one" with their counterparts in Washington. President Carter could call up Prime Minister Trudeau to exchange their largely amenable views of the international situation on their red telephones. But beneath the surface of summit niceties, basic shifts were taking place within the political economies of both countries, shifts that were to be expressed later as perceptible divergences in the definition of some of their major national interests.

In the United States, confusion and doubt had overcome the country in the aftermath of its Vietnam debacle and what it felt to be its abandonment in a time of crisis by its European allies. Once the failure of Carter's liberal humanitarian approach to international relations had been signalled by the indignities suffered when American diplomats were taken hostage in Tehran, a new surge of isolationist sentiment demanded that America go its own way, put its own interests first, and redress the balance of its perceived military inferiority to the Soviet Union. With the sense that America must assert itself in the world in response to the expanding power of the Soviet Union went the feeling that the United States must also act to defend its weakening corporate position. A new doctrine of protectionism took shape in amendments to the U.S. Trade Act, whose defence mechanisms were a response by Congress to a worsening American economy now pinched both by accelerating inflation and stagnating productivity. At the same time as the U.S. government gave itself greater powers to fight competing imports, it pushed ahead with a strategy to have the international community accept an investment code that would give multinational corporations the key to the city of all non-communist economies and so create further demand for American exports.

9

The move towards isolationism and protectionism was reflected within the U.S. government by a structural shift of power that had been going on for years within the institutions that affected Canada's interests. Following repeated changes of parties, each bringing new partisans into office, the State Department had lost a generation of knowledgeable bureaucrats. These were the career civil servants who had built the postwar international economic institutions alongside the mandarins in Ottawa with whom they had shared an internationalist ethos. As the State Department lost its expertise, it also lost its capacity to control the Canadian-American relationship within the U.S. government. Influence had moved within the executive towards the economic departments. When in 1962 a new bureau was established to monitor and defend the foreign commercial interests of the U.S., the Office of the United States Trade Representative was located not in the State Department but in the White House. It was the secretary of the treasury who had been in charge of Nixonomics, not the secretary of state.

The shift in international economic power within the U.S. executive was accompanied by a shift of power over international economic policy away from the executive branch towards Congress. Angered by the deceptions of the administration throughout the Vietnam imbroglio, and alarmed by the improprieties to which the presidency had shown itself so inured in the Watergate affair, American congressmen took it upon themselves to reassert their authority in areas of policy that the executive had for some years appropriated for itself.[7] This change occurred during a period when the American economy was apparently threatened both at home and abroad. At home, dollar-rich Arab countries seemed on the point of buying up large sectors of the economy. Abroad, competitors were putting into place an alarming network of legislation aimed at extracting more benefits from the branches of multinationals and so reducing the exports that the American economy made through U.S. transnational corporations. Talk about a new international economic order that would benefit the impoverished nations of the Third World seemed to presage further barriers to the free flow of American exports and investment capital. Business warned Congress that its technological lead in telecommunications and information services could be hamstrung by foreign governments' restrictions on trans-border data flow. In the Seventies, Congress became the centre of government responses to interest groups and regions apprehensive about their economic well-being. The concern of Congress was expressed in various pieces of legislation

10

designed to force the executive into a more aggressive defence of American economic interests abroad. The late Seventies was not a good time, in other words, for the United States to accept new claims to assertive autonomy by the formerly clinging cousin to the north for whom it had so long acted as military and economic guardian. The timing was particularly bad if Canada expected to revise without American objections the rules that had long governed its economic relations with the United States.

These rules, which had controlled the Canadian economy's distorted evolution throughout the twentieth century, had been largely "Made in U.S.A." The interconnection of Canadian and American capital markets had for decades forced Canadian fiscal and monetary policy to be made with a weather eye kept on Washington's fiscal and monetary actions. Even some of the major forces within the private sector of the Canadian economy were controlled from south of the border, either by their head offices or by the U.S. government applying legislation extra-territorially to those many Canadian corporations that were using American technology. By the late Seventies, the combined effects of the Canadian economy's unbalanced integration had produced a self-aggravating situation that was reaching critical dimensions. A permanent balance of payments disequilibrium resulted from a huge and mounting deficit in manufactured goods and necessitated a continued borrowing of foreign capital. Efficiency and innovation in the private sector were stifled by technological and managerial constraints imposed by the branch plant syndrome, and this held back Canadian productivity. Although expert reports called for dramatic new public policies, the federal government suffered from a deteriorating capacity to formulate remedial strategies or to implement them with concerted policies.

At the same time as Canada's central government was losing its power to manage the national economy, a process of federal decentralization that had gathered momentum in the Sixties continued through the decade, with the ten provinces attempting, in the light of Ottawa's failures, to formulate their own province-building strategies.[8] They modernized their bureaucracies and took big steps towards developing their regional economies under some form of state capitalism, whether through social-democratic nationalizations (as with potash in Saskatchewan and, later, asbestos in Quebec) or liberal-capitalist incentives for free enterprise mixed with government regulation (as in Alberta and Ontario).[9] The provinces all competed among themselves to offer incentives that would attract job-creating

11

foreign investment. As they developed their resources, they became further integrated in, and established more active political relations with, the adjacent regional economy of the United States — B.C. with the Pacific Coast states, Alberta with the midwest, Ontario with the central states and the military industries, Quebec and the Atlantic provinces with the northeast. The more effective the provinces were in their regional policy making and the more the Canadian common market became balkanized by barriers to internal commerce, the less Ottawa appeared capable of imposing national coherence on the economy's development.

The weaker the federal government became as a directing force in Canada's political economy, the stronger grew the demands that it take action to reverse a trend that had developed in parallel with federal decentralization: the tendency towards dependent continental integration. In 1968 the Watkins Report, commissioned by the Pearson government to investigate, under the aegis of former finance minister Walter Gordon, the structure of foreign investment in Canada, brought out its recommendations for a state trading agency, a national venture-capital development corporation and a change in competition legislation to favour industrial rationalization.[10] Two years later, the Wahn Report was issued by the House of Commons Standing Committee for External Affairs and National Defence, a tri-partisan group that proposed various additional methods to achieve an overall target of 51 per cent Canadian ownership of the economy.[11] After two more years, the most comprehensive of all the investigations of the foreign control question, the Gray Report, was published by the government. It called for a screening agency to monitor the performance of foreign direct investment in the economy so as to help reduce its costs and increase its benefits to the Canadian economy.[12] These federal documents were supplemented by a substantial literature generated by such provincial inquiries as the Ontario Select Committee on Economic and Cultural Nationalism, and the Royal Commission on Book Publishing.[13] In addition, an increasing flow of political economy studies on specialized aspects of Canadian dependency (from the hiring practices of universities to the play selections made by regional theatres) kept swelling the public awareness of what came to be seen in intellectual circles as the emerging crisis of the Canadian state. Canada's survival as an independent entity in North America was at stake.

The federal government took several initiatives in a piecemeal fashion in order to deal — sometimes reluctantly, sometimes effectively — with these emerging concerns. The Canadian Radio-Television Commission (CRTC) was created in 1968 with a broad mandate for cultural rescue of the air waves. A venture capital holding company called the Canada Development Corporation was established in 1971. A new screening mechanism, the Foreign Investment Review Agency (FIRA), was set up in 1973, and a Crown corporation, Petro-Canada, was parachuted into the energy sector in 1975. The combined impact of these institutions was hard to gauge. Since they did not fit into a coherent economic strategy, they went their several ways, often at cross purposes. The decline in the late Seventies of the federal Liberals' capacity to govern could be measured by their inability to develop a comprehensive industrial strategy for the economy which could bring into balance the conflicting demands for the expanded export of staple resources and for the launching of a new manufacturing capacity.[14] It was small wonder, then, that with its federal-provincial conflicts and its agonizing over the future of Quebec, Canada in the Seventies had not been able to define its national interests vis-à-vis those of the United States.

The one institution that had a formal responsibility in the Canadian-American relationship had been traumatized since 1968. The Department for External Affairs, which had been the most prestigious ministry in the days of Lester Pearson, had been largely incapacitated by what it considered the hostile and haughty treatment it had received at the hands of Pearson's successor, Pierre Trudeau, and his foreign policy adviser, Ivan Head. External Affairs became a foreign office merely filing reports from the rest of the world, not a master agency able to orchestrate Canada's multifaceted relationships with its most important interlocutor, the United States. At the same time, the Prime Minister's Office did not formulate an American strategy of its own. Quebec separatism preoccupied the government's leadership energies. Pierre Trudeau's fight with Quebec and with several other provinces over constitutional and economic issues kept Canada looking inward at its federal-provincial problems throughout the decade.

While the Liberals' hold on federal power weakened, the Progressive Conservatives' attacks on the failing Liberal administration re-emphasized the tendency to national disintegration. The initiatives the federal government had taken towards establishing national energy and investment policies must be undone, the Tories said: Petro-Canada should be privatized; FIRA should be de-fanged. As they developed their successful campaign to unseat the Trudeau government, the Conservatives appeared to have grasped the mantle of

C. D. Howe and adopted a stance of frank, pro-business continentalism.[15]

Unlike Ronald Reagan's Republicans in 1980, Joe Clark's Progressive Conservatives were elected in 1979 despite their program, not because of it. Once sworn into office, the new Conservative cabinet found that its election promises were too unpopular to be implemented. Petro-Canada had to be perpetuated; privatization had to be forgotten; the state's intervention in energy policy and other areas was too necessary to business, too popular with the public to be abandoned for the sake of Milton Friedman. When John Crosbie, the new Tory minister of finance, flew a kite about continental free trade, it was clear from the public's reaction that the Progressive Conservatives' neo-continentalism had not found resonance in the Canadian body politic. The Progressive Conservative government was too beset with the need to decide its internal policies to work out a new American strategy for Canada. Conservative American policy did not go beyond establishing personal relations at the summit level. Joe Clark struck up a good relationship with Jimmy Carter, and Flora MacDonald, his secretary of state for external affairs, got on well with her counterpart, Cyrus Vance.

This warm summitry veiled the instability of the Canadian-American relationship resulting from the conflicting political and economic pressures which had produced so much uncertainty within each state. Of the unresolved and contentious bilateral issues at the end of the Seventies, nine were particularly important as harbingers of trouble for the Eighties.

- In energy matters conflict and irritation had flared up repeatedly as Canada reduced its exports of oil from 30 per cent to 2 per cent of American import needs and restrained the increase in exports of natural gas.

- Foreign investment policies in Canada were a continuing American concern, as the Foreign Investment Review Agency began to operate, while the United States exerted pressure on Canada to accept an international investment code being developed at the Organization for Economic Cooperation and Development (OECD). This found Canada resisting its partners' desire to have it agree to the principle of "national treatment," non-discrimination against foreign capital.

- The Auto Pact, once thought to be the model for future Canadian-American integration via sectoral free trade, produced mounting deficits for Canada's trade balance in manufactured products. But the U.S. government refused to accept revisions to the agreement that would give Canada what it considered its fair share of the available jobs, investment and research funds. At the same time, amendments to American trade legislation and American resistance to Canadian objectives in the multilateral trade negotiations raised growing concerns in Ottawa about American protectionism.

- The construction of a northern pipeline to bring Alaskan oil and gas to American markets bedevilled Canadian-American politics throughout the decade. The Canadian proposal to provide a land bridge for Alaskan oil, so as to prevent the dangerous shipment of oil by tanker along the British Columbia coast, was rejected. The Carter administration then put tremendous pressure on Ottawa to accept a gas pipeline to Alaska. Once the treaty was negotiated and signed, it was Canada's turn to wax impatient since Washington did not move to implement the agreement.

- In multilateral bodies concerned with economic questions, the agenda remained heavily loaded with issues left unresolved because of the administration's inability to bring under control the inflation which was destabilizing the economies of the OECD countries.

- No sooner was one environmental issue satisfactorily coped with than another raised its ugly head. The Great Lakes Water Quality Agreement of 1972 represented a triumph of cooperation, but when it became clear that industrial emissions transported by air from the United States were poisoning the lakes and rivers of some of central Canada's best tourist regions, the American government's willingness to cooperate markedly diminished: the costs of cleanup would be high and would fall mainly on American taxpayers, while the benefits would be mostly felt north of the border. Canadian pollution of American border states was enough to cause annoyance but not action. Despite President Carter's undoubted support for environmental conservation, the Garrison Diversion Unit was muted but not killed, so threatening disastrous consequences for Manitoba's Red River basin.

- Fisheries and boundaries, the perennially contentious bilateral issue over which wars had earlier been fought, proved highly conducive to bilateral tension once the two countries extended their offshore sovereignty claims to 200 miles. A draft treaty was

15

laboriously negotiated and given moral support by the White House, but its ratification was delayed indefinitely in the Senate because of vociferous opposition among New England fishermen.

- The federal government's few moves in the cultural policy field — withdrawing *Time* magazine's privileged position in the Canadian magazine market and making advertising on American border TV stations non-deductible for Canadian corporate tax purposes — caused disproportionate anger in Washington where the media lobbies pressed relentlessly for retaliation against Canada's violation of the American principle of the free flow of information.
- In the North Atlantic Treaty Organization, the practice of détente by the West in the face of continuing Soviet deployment of more advanced missile systems raised European concerns about the value of the U.S. military guarantee and forced Canada to reconsider the relevance of NORAD.

As the time of the Carter administration drew to a close, it was clear that in many important domains Canada's interests now differed from those of the United States. No longer could the Canadian-American relationship be judged just by the friendliness of the American president or the American public towards their northern neighbour. Throughout the spring of 1980, unprecedented outpourings of goodwill towards Canada marked the American response to the Canadian embassy's role in the smuggling of six American diplomats out of revolutionary Tehran. Yet in the autumn of 1980, Canada's foreign minister painted in black tones how strained the relationship actually had become. "In a sharp condemnation of U.S. policy towards Canada," the *Toronto Star* reported, "External Affairs Minister Mark MacGuigan has warned normal relations between the two countries 'may no longer be possible.' "[16]

Nine years after Nixonomics was introduced no one could say what constituted "normal relations." The special relationship of quiet diplomacy days was certifiably dead. The fabric of each society was being torn by serious political and economic strains. Lacking coherence in their own policies, each country's impact on the other became dangerously unpredictable. What would emerge as a new normalcy could not be foretold. It was difficult to estimate whether the assertive new centralism of Pierre Trudeau's government elected in 1980 could coexist peacefully in North America with the assertive new conservatism of Ronald Reagan's Republican regime. If they came into conflict, Canada's neo-centralism and America's neo-conservatism could explode into opposing nationalisms.

16

Divergent "Nationalisms" in North America

There is strong reason to question whether any government presided over by Pierre Elliott Trudeau can properly bear the label "nationalist." The hallmark of Trudeau's carefully defined political philosophy has been a single-minded crusade against the social and economic distortions caused within his own society of Quebec by what he viewed as parochial nationalism. He had developed his political commitment to federalism in his first career as a maverick intellectual, fighting first the right-wing conservatism of the Union Nationale led by Maurice Duplessis and then the left-wing separatism of nationalist intellectuals who came together under the banner of the Parti Québécois, led by René Lévesque. His economic thinking was formed at Harvard and the London School of Economics during the postwar flowering of liberal internationalism. One of his most important intellectual mentors in the evolution of his economic thought was Albert Breton, whose theory of nationalism as a retrograde rationalization for the selfishness of the middle class had been developed in collaboration with Harry Johnson, the most ferocious of the many Canadian economists who were ideological and intellectual critics of what was termed in Canada "economic nationalism."[17]

The Liberal Party of Canada, whose leadership Trudeau assumed in 1968, had itself already rejected the nationalist program proposed for it by Walter Gordon, the *éminence rose* of Lester Pearson's first ministry. The nationalist measures contained in Finance Minister Gordon's first budget of 1963 had been beaten back by the outraged protests of business, led by such powerful figures as the then president of the Montreal Stock Exchange, Eric Kierans. Later, the predominantly anti-nationalist forces within the Liberal party's cabinet and the Liberal government's bureaucracy prevailed not just over Gordon but over Kierans himself. Kierans's experience as Quebec's minister of revenue revealed to him the distorting economic effect of the American government's extra-territorial control over the operation of American-owned branch plants in Canada. By 1968 Kierans was an expressed nationalist in the federal cabinet of Pierre Trudeau, but he found the environment in which he worked too hostile for his ideas and resigned in frustration.

The allegedly nationalist measures taken during the Seventies were half-cocked concessions to pressure coming as much from the New Democratic Party as from the Liberals' own minority nationalist wing. This series of inconsistent actions showed from how much indecision the leadership of the Canadian government suffered during these years.

Time magazine lost its privileged status, but *Reader's Digest* was allowed to remain in business, on the unusual grounds that, while American-controlled, it was Canadian-owned. The Canada Development Corporation was established with public funds to repatriate control of Canadian business, but was allowed to operate like any private corporation with its eye on the continental market. The Foreign Investment Review Agency was put in place, but successive ministers of industry, trade and commerce made it clear that they conceived their mandate to be the encouragement, not discouragement, of foreign investment in the economy. Looking at the Trudeau government's record from 1968 to 1979, there can be little room for doubt that, from the prime minister through the cabinet to the upper and middle ranks of the federal bureaucracy, nationalism was consistently resisted by the federal government, whether it was French-Canadian separatism or English-Canadian demands for economic and cultural protection.

Two factors account for the startling transformation of the Liberal government's orientation between May 1979, when it lost power, and February 1980, when it returned to office. First was the emergence of a new nationalism in certain sectors of the Canadian business community. In all parts of the economy, nationalist refrains, which a decade previously had only been sounded by dissident academic choruses, were now being heard from some of the most successful and aggressive business leaders in the country. Robert Blair, president of NOVA, an Alberta corporation, co-chaired a task force that called for preferential treatment for Canadian-owned companies in gaining access to the contracts for the enormous energy projects being planned for the next two decades.[18] John Shepherd, chairman of Leigh Instruments, urged that Canada develop a national industrial strategy based on specialization in order to break out of the vicious circle of technological dependence which he felt was the direct product of Canada's branch plant manufacturing structure.[19] Jack Gallagher, chief executive officer of Dome Petroleum, deliberately placed the contracts to develop new drilling and production platforms and ice-breaking tankers for the company's Beaufort Sea operations with Canadian rather than foreign firms. Raymond Royer, president of Bombardier's mass transit division, denounced the purchase by Calgary of German light rail vehicles for its subway system; the city awarded the contract to the Siemens-Duwag consortium without calling for bids from Canada's three competitive LRV manufacturers. Having equipped the Montreal Métro and contracted to do the same for Mexico City, Bombardier was aware of the need to maintain a secure domestic industry in order to create a base from which to grow internationally. A similar awareness was shared by Lavalin Inc. of Quebec, the engineering firm that presided over the construction of the James Bay hydroelectric facility, a feat that made it a world-class engineering firm.

It was no coincidence that the new corporate nationalists were speaking from boardrooms that had direct connections with either the energy industry or markets dependent on government procurement. These businessmen had experience with the ways in which the major industrialized countries provide covert protection for their own companies, despite their official endorsement of free international capital flows. Conscious of the limits of the Canadian economy from which they eyed world markets, they had transcended the narrow and defensive protectionism that formerly characterized the soft sectors of the economy, calling instead for government cooperation in the development of an outward-looking industry that nevertheless would be supported and secure in its own national base. The change of tone was symbolized by the Toronto Empire Club's invitation to NOVA's Robert Blair, the architect of the Alaska Natural Gas Transportation System and the progenitor of the new petrochemical industry in Alberta, to address its membership. From a podium more used to resounding with the anti-government, pro-American litanies of the Business Council on National Issues, the Canadian Petroleum Association or the Canadian Manufacturers' Association, Blair preached "that positive nationalism is a virtue . . . a necessary prerequisite to our putting the country of Canada forward as a real nation."[20] This new thrust in the business community, which took a positive view towards government intervention, found a response in the second transmogrification — a drastic revision in the thinking of the Liberal party after it went into opposition in 1979.

As leader of the opposition preparing to retire from politics, Pierre Trudeau made two crucial decisions when he and his former cabinet colleagues were trying to accustom themselves to becoming a shadow cabinet and looking across the aisle of the House of Commons at the government benches. Following the advice of his chief of staff, Jim Coutts, he appointed his most trusted cabinet colleague, Marc Lalonde, to be the opposition spokesman on energy, and made Herb Gray the opposition spokesman on finance. These were appointments that would change the public face of the Liberal party. Gray's views on Canada's need to overcome the costs imposed on the economy by truncated branch plants had not altered since the early Seventies, when

19

he had presided over the authoritative government report, *Foreign Direct Investment in Canada*, commonly known as the Gray Report. His new prominence in the shadow cabinet was to help revive explicitly nationalist thinking at the party's decision-making centre. A left-leaning nationalism was also being articulated by the extra-parliamentary party's core of policy activists who were militating for a reorientation of Canadian liberalism along more progressive lines in order to make a fresh and reformist appeal to the public at the next election.

Marc Lalonde was not a nationalist. His career had parallelled Trudeau's in combating Quebec separatism, first as principal secretary to the prime minister, then as minister of health and welfare and finally as minister for federal-provincial relations in the last Trudeau cabinet. When he took over the shadow cabinet portfolio of energy, Lalonde had the leisure for the first time in over a decade to do some of his own thinking, rather than rely on the briefs of his senior bureaucrats. Working with policy activists drawn from the Liberal party's ranks, he quickly realized the decisive role that energy could play in resolving a dual problem that had long preoccupied federal politicians: the growing power of the provinces and the declining financial capacity of the central government.

When the Clark government was defeated over its budget early in December 1979, the Liberal party found itself running an election campaign with its recently retired leader hastily resurrected as messiah once more and it had to scramble quickly to produce an election platform. The rethinking that had been done under the aegis of Gray and Lalonde in the caucus committees during the previous few months was brought to fruition by a platform committee of MPs and party activists who gave top priority to energy policy and industrial strategy as the basic thrust for the party's campaign stance. Thus it was no accident that Trudeau's electoral speeches heralded a renewed commitment of the Liberal party to interventionism and an assertive centralism. The Liberals on the stump promised to launch a broad energy policy aimed at self-sufficiency, higher Canadian ownership levels, more industrial benefits for Canadian industry from mega-projects, and a price of energy maintained below world levels. Trudeau also committed his future government to expand the scope of FIRA's activities and to renegotiate the Auto Pact's disastrous imbalances.

That these policy proposals were not simply electoral rhetoric became clear when the new Liberal government's cabinet was sworn in with Marc Lalonde as minister of energy, mines and resources and

Herb Gray as minister of industry, trade and commerce, and when the throne speech was delivered in April with the electoral promises now entrenched in the government's official legislative program. The Liberal government was declaring a new centralism in its governing objectives, a determination to reaffirm the power of the national government by claiming a greater share of the projected increases in Canada's energy revenues and greater control over the development of those strategic fuels, oil and gas, for Canadian economic development. The new centralism implied that the government was determined to play a larger role in directing the economy. Although greater government intervention in the economy would necessarily have a great impact on an industry overwhelmingly owned and controlled by American companies, there was no thought among the architects of the new Liberal strategy that their plans would lead them to a confrontation with Washington. Such features of the NEP as the target of 50 per cent Canadian ownership, which were later to be denounced by the *Wall Street Journal* and by enraged oil executives as nationalist and anti-American, were seen by their designers as necessary to achieve the centralizing goal of gaining greater revenues for Ottawa. These policy makers did not reckon on the possibility that, by the beginning of 1981, the party in control of the White House would be the most nationalist that had come to power since Teddy Roosevelt's Republicans in the 1900s.

● ● ●

Ronald Reagan's militant conservatism appeared to foreigners a shocking change from the mild humanitarianism of Jimmy Carter, but the America-first chauvinism of the former Californian movie star was more in harmony with the feelings of Americans who felt beleaguered in the world than were the beatitudes of the displaced Georgian peanut farmer. The foreign policy declarations that Reagan had made in the past — "we now enter one of the most dangerous decades of western civilization"; Cuba should be blockaded in reprisal for the Soviet invasion of Afghanistan; if the Soviet Union were not "engaged in this game of dominoes, there wouldn't be any hot spots in the world" — indicated a black-and-white view, uncomprehending of the complex power relationships that had replaced the bipolar world of Reagan's imagination.[21]

Ronald Reagan was serving notice on the world that America's decade of instability and indecision was over. A simplistic and self-serving moralism claimed that, if a strong America was needed to "restore the margin of safety" for the free world, the United States could be expected to be less generous in its dealings with the international community. Very little was known about how the new government in Washington would perform in directing relations with its foreign interlocutors. Apart from Secretary of State Alexander Haig and a handful of State Department alumni, Reagan's transition team had no foreign policy expertise. Under congressional questioning, the new president's candidate for deputy secretary of state revealed he did not know where Zimbabwe was. This new team of international innocents believed in closing "the window of vulnerability" by re-establishing U.S. military supremacy, confronting the Soviets, making the world safe for U.S. multinationals, and restoring the United States' world leadership role with gun boats sent to defend American interests wherever they might be threatened. Professional analysts of the Canadian-American relationship could be forgiven for showing some reluctance to predict how "special" Washington-Ottawa relations would be under the new Republican regime.[22]

The American and Canadian governments had been at loggerheads many times before over one issue or another without any crisis arising. The spat over the Cuban missiles in 1961, the arguments over the duty remission policies for the Canadian automotive industry in 1964, the criticism of the guidelines for American multinational corporations proposed in 1968 had, like many another issue, been resolved without the disputed issues escalating into a full crisis between the two governments. Now that a recentralizing, assertive, state-capitalist government on the banks of the Rideau Canal had set its sights on restructuring its energy industry, and that a remilitarizing, straight-capitalist administration had taken power on the banks of the Potomac River, future disputes might be less easy to reconcile. The ideological changes of both governments signalled the end of a long period of national uncertainty and the start of a more self-confident assertion of each country's interests. The two systems had moved into a potentially antagonistic stance that only needed a serious issue to bring their relationship under severe stress. It is ironic, as we shall see in chapter 2, that the stage of acute crisis in the relationship was triggered by the action of Canadian business operating in faithful compliance with the Reaganite doctrine advocating free flows of capital.

1981: Crisis in the Capitals 2

Neither the announcement of the National Energy Program, which expressed the renewed centralism of the Liberal government in Ottawa, nor the election of a sabre-rattling Republican administration in Washington, was sufficient to cause a crisis to break out in the Canadian-American relationship. These events of October and November 1980 were logical culminations of antithetical tendencies that had been growing in each country, but they did not in themselves inaugurate a critical period of tension. What provoked the Americans' anger, bringing the Canadian-American relationship to a state of crisis, in the second, subjective sense of acute stress, was a spate of takeover attempts of American businesses by Canadian companies. A few, like Seagrams, were seeking control of entire U.S.-based firms; some, like Dome Petroleum, were responding to the incentives offered in the NEP by moving to purchase the Canadian operations of American transnationals.

Although the tender offers by Dome, Canadian Pacific and Seagrams respected the letter of free-enterprise Reaganism, they violated the spirit of American business nationalism. The American oil companies, finding their Canadian possessions under attack, screamed in outrage when they found out that the NEP had changed the rules of a continental game they had been playing profitably for decades. They called on Washington to force Ottawa to restore the status quo ante NEP. The new Reagan team of free enterprisers discovered in the interventionist actions of the Canadian government an ideological heresy challenging the free-market values on which their own program was based. In supporting the practical complaints of their businessmen, they launched a campaign to bring Ottawa to its ideological senses and political knees, calling on it to abandon its *dirigiste* policies that contradicted the thrust of the United States' international economic program. Canadian government resistance to U.S. pressure resulted in

23

a period of confrontation between the neighbouring states which continued through four seasons, from the spring of 1981 to the winter of 1981-82. That the confrontation amounted to a crisis in the subjective or psychological connotation of the term can be seen by the extent to which the issues at stake between the two governments threatened basic values which each side considered crucial to its system's survival.

There can be no question that the National Energy Program immediately became an issue on the bilateral agenda. Ten days after the Honourable Allan MacEachen announced the NEP in his budget, a group of American officials flew to Ottawa to express their shock and disappointment. The program was "shattering." They could not exaggerate their "bitterness and outrage" at the prospect of such "withdrawal from the world."[1] On the day of this meeting of American officials with the Canadian deputy minister of energy, November 7, 1980, Jimmy Carter was still president of the United States. The meeting was a typical event in the recent history of the Canadian-American relationship, in which one government alerted the other to its concern over the impact of its partner's proposed legislation on its own interests, be they corporate or cultural, economic or ecological. Six weeks later, on December 17, further discussions were held, this time in Washington. Peter Towe, Canadian ambassador to the U.S., read an official text indicating that the United States should not have been surprised by the NEP which had been announced in the throne speech earlier in the year and which was more a consummation of previous policy developments in the energy sector than a new departure in government policy. For their part, the Americans listed their objections. Although Canada had signed a declaration at the OECD upholding the value of the non-discriminatory treatment of foreign capital, the NEP constituted a departure from its basic principle of "national treatment."* The NEP would have expropriatory effects, particularly in the 25 per cent back-in.† The schedule of controlled price rises envisaged for oil and gas relative to world levels would give Canada an unfair competitive advantage and constitute a subsidy for

---

* A country accords "national treatment" if its policies are exactly the same in their treatment of foreign-controlled as of nationally-controlled companies.

† What was known by the Americans as the "back-in" was the provision in Bill C-48 that, in each oil or gas development on Canada lands such as the huge Hibernia find off Newfoundland, the Crown would take by right and without compensation a 25 per cent equity interest to be held by some public corporation like Petro-Canada on behalf of the Canadian people.

Canadian industry while, at the same time, lowering the rate of exploration and so reducing Canada's contribution to the goal of the International Energy Agency — the industrialized countries' organization that was attempting to respond to the OPEC cartel — to reduce western dependence on OPEC oil. Then on January 30, Secretary of State for External Affairs Mark MacGuigan met his newly appointed counterpart, Alexander Haig, in Washington. In response to Canadian pressure to have the long-delayed fisheries treaty signed, Haig assured MacGuigan that settling the matter was a high priority for the U.S. government. The possibility of changing the Auto Pact was also discussed.

These exchanges between officials showed that the American government took substantial exception both to the rationale underlying the NEP and to the practices it proposed, but they did not indicate that the Canadian-American relationship was anywhere near a crisis situation. It took a totally unexpected series of events in the private sector for a normal bureaucratic exchange to escalate into an explosive international confrontation. The crisis was not experienced with equal intensity by each protagonist at the same time. In its early stages Washington became agitated while Ottawa kept its cool. When the Reagan administration turned to consider retaliation, the Canadian government started to panic. After the Americans exerted strong pressure and achieved major Canadian concessions, they pushed for more gains only to cause the Canadian government to bridle. While many factors came into play during the twelve-month period of strain — from acid rain and interest rates to NORAD and border broadcasting — the following chronicle will focus on the two issues on which the Americans centred their attack on Canada, the NEP and FIRA. From published information, personal interviews, and the confidential Canadian and American documents to which the author had access, the dynamic of the four seasons of the Canadian-American crisis can be reconstructed to identify the players, the agendas and the interactions, in short: the anatomy of the crisis.

Spring: Crisis on the Potomac

On January 19, Canadian Pacific Enterprises made a tender offer to get control of Hobart Corporation of Troy, Ohio, of $32.50 for each of Hobart's outstanding shares. Under an administration so committed to the teachings of Milton Friedman, the action of a private corporation following the dictates of the market's invisible hand should have raised little attention, since it presumably illustrated that capital was flowing

25

from less efficient to more efficient centres. But Friedman's theory of latter-day capitalism does not explain the politics or psychology of latter-day capitalists — at least not of those capitalists who had just helped elect Ronald Reagan. The chief executive officer of Hobart Corporation was Reagan's finance chairman for Ohio. He went straight to the White House and the Congress with his rage and called on the representatives whose election he had helped finance to get protection from CP's offer. "Should we stand idle and watch our economy come under the control of foreign investors? . . . Should Congress permit American companies to stand vulnerable to the sort of raid underway by Canadian Pacific, reaching out from all of the protections of fortress-Canada?" he asked.[2] Some members of Congress apparently thought not. On January 27, Senator Tower (Republican, Texas) introduced S-289, a bill to amend the Securities Exchange Act of 1934, to require foreign companies to conform to the same margin requirements as American companies attempting takeovers. The same day Congressman Brooks (Democrat, Texas) introduced a similar amendment, HR-1294, in the House of Representatives. In the event, Hobart found an American company, Dart and Kraft, to act as its "white knight" by buying it out and so forestalling the CP takeover.

Two months later the pattern of the CP-Hobart takeover bid was repeated. JES Developments, Inc., a Delaware corporation and a wholly-owned subsidiary of Joseph E. Seagram and Sons, Inc., a New York corporation, itself wholly owned by Seagram Company Ltd., a Canadian corporation, offered $2.1 billion for all the common stock of St. Joe Minerals Corporation, the 258th largest industrial firm in the U.S. according to the ranking of the *Fortune* 500. The board of St. Joe resisted the tender offer and set its Washington lobbyists into motion to do what they could to fight the takeover. On March 26, St. Joe's lawyers wrote to James Watt, the secretary of the interior, invoking the Mineral Lands Leasing Act (MLLA) of 1924, section 1, which stipulated that reciprocity must exist in the leasing of coal, oil and gas on lands owned by the federal government: "Citizens of another country, the laws, customs or regulations of which deny similar or like privileges to citizens or corporations of this country, shall not by stock ownership, stock holding, or stock control, own any interest in any lease acquired under the provision of this transfer." On the grounds that Canada's Foreign Investment Review Agency aimed to prevent foreigners acquiring control over Canadian industry, and because the new National Energy Program would only grant production licences to corporations having a Canadian ownership base of not less than 50 per cent, St. Joe petitioned that "Canada be declared a non-reciprocal country based on the denial of similar or like privileges to citizens or corporations of this country under FIRA." Conjuring up a spectre of "the disruption of minerals and petroleum production necessary for the welfare and defence of our country," St. Joe's lobbyists urged James Watt to suspend Canada's current reciprocal status immediately.[3] The day before, Congressman Emerson (Republican, Missouri) had introduced HR-2826 proposing a moratorium on the MLLA. Eventually Seagrams withdrew its offer after St. Joe found an acceptably American white knight in Fluor Corporation.

Demands for retaliatory protectionist measures against Canada came swiftly. Congressman John Dingell (Democrat, Michigan), for instance, had not been upset by the NEP when the program was first announced, but when the French government-owned company, Elf Aquitaine, and the Canada Development Corporation worked out a deal to split Texas Gulf's American and Canadian assets between them, he called for prompt action before another Canadian government-controlled firm "picks the bones of a U.S. corporation." Politicians on Capitol Hill became angry. They did not know much about the details of the cases and often had their facts wrong, but that did not matter. They only cared that American companies were being "kicked in the knee" by Canadians. Furthermore, they were being kicked unfairly, since the Canadians could borrow 100 per cent of the takeover costs from their banks, whereas American companies had to operate under a 50 per cent margin requirement. The unfairness was compounded by the existence of the Foreign Investment Review Agency, whose procedures effectively prevented American companies from making retaliatory takeover bids against their Canadian suitors. To add insult to injury to aggravation, the National Energy Program was discriminating in favour of Canadian oil companies and, so the Americans claimed, reducing the asset value of American companies' Canadian subsidiaries in the energy field. This let the Canadians pick off American subsidiaries at "firesale prices." This concatenation of injustices — so went the line of Capitol Hill — was due to the rabid nationalism of Pierre Trudeau who was fanning the flames of anti-Americanism in order to try to hold his disenchanted followers and his strained federation together. The Canadians were changing the rules in mid-game, shutting out the Americans, reducing American investment unfairly by getting American companies on the cheap. All the fears that had been raised in the early Seventies about Arab oil money coming in to take over American industry were revived; but this time it was the North that threatened.

The hysteria in Washington was fuelled by the egregious special pleading of the takeover targets. The level of foreign control in U.S. mining was 5 per cent, in Canadian mining it was 40 per cent; foreign control of the oil and gas industry in the U.S. was 18 per cent, compared to 65 per cent in Canada. But the screams of outrage and predictions of disaster that emanated from chief executive officers, lobbyists, the business press and Congress were louder and more apocalyptic than those heard from Canadian economic nationalists in the previous twenty years. In the spring of 1980, Canadians had been celebrated by Americans as the heroes of the Western world for rescuing six American diplomats from Tehran. A year later Canadians were made out to be like the hordes of Genghis Khan descending from the north to plunder innocent American enterprise. No matter that the furor was over a non-issue. Most of the takeover attempts were rebuffed. While the boards of directors may have wept crocodile tears, their shareholders profited handsomely from the upward bidding of their assets. In the seven years since its inception, FIRA had not noticeably prevented American investment in Canada. Nor did the NEP make foreign operations in the Canadian energy sector unprofitable. The failure of the Canadian government and the interested Canadian corporations to correct the allegations and half-truths that were circulated around the Washington rumour mill helped fan the fabricated issue into a real political crisis. An inaccurate story was allowed to grow and, with it, congressional demands for action.

Under pressure from business and the legislature, the new Reagan team did not adopt the traditional buffer stance taken by previous administrations which tended to insulate Canada from the parochial aggressivities of Congress. Canada came to the Republicans' attention as an issue at the time when they were taking hold of the reins of office and clarifying their policies. The NEP and FIRA, when pointed out by the takeover targets, appeared as prime examples of what the Reaganites had come to power to eliminate — obstacles to the free flow of capital and trade, a flow that was crucial to their plans for the resuscitation of American business through free-market forces. Far from dismissing business complaints about the takeovers and the NEP on the grounds of the United States' special Canadian relationship, members of the Reagan cabinet and their crusading subordinates

28

became convinced of the symbolic importance of the Canadian case. If they were to push back the protectionist barriers of the European Common Market, if they were to convince Japan to grant fair access for American exports, they could not let Canada get away with a further move away from the principles of internationalism. This time Canada was not to be taken for granted. On the contrary, Canada became a showcase for Reaganism's international economic policy, a test to show the world that the new administration was going to be tough with its partners and insist that they play by the formal rules as established by such bodies as the General Agreement on Tariffs and Trade (GATT).

As the new Reagan team learned the ropes in the first months of 1981, its response to the National Energy Program and its dealings with Canada on other matters showed it to be an aggressively free-enterprise administration that had not yet decided how to handle its neighbour to the north. At one moment it was diplomatic; at another it talked tough; later still it would retract its words, only to make more demands. A summary of the two capitals' interactions from February to May 1981 indicates the confusions of the American approach.[4]

• *February 20:* Richard Smith, chargé d'affaires at the U.S. embassy in Ottawa, sent a letter to Mark MacGuigan and Marc Lalonde which objected to some trade and investment aspects of Bill C-48 which was to implement the NEP. He rebutted the Canadian position that the NEP did not violate Canada's international commitments with the OECD to provide "national treatment" for foreign capital.

• *February 26:* Canada's response to Smith's letter about "national treatment" repeated Ottawa's position that it had clearly reserved its right at the OECD to take measures affecting foreign direct investment that it believed necessary, particularly in industries with high levels of foreign control.

• *March 5:* Alexander Haig sent Canada a formal note opening with the flourish of traditional diplomacy — "The Secretary of State presents his compliments to His Excellency the Ambassador of Canada" — and going on to itemize a long list of the administration's concerns about the National Energy Program, some of whose measures it called "unnecessarily discriminatory." The case against the NEP led to an explicit threat: "Should the balance of concessions be disturbed the United States would be obliged to consider how a new balance might be achieved."[5] "In effect," as David Crane paraphrased the note, "the U.S. government wanted the NEP buried."[6]

• *March 6:* The White House announced its intention to scrap the East Coast fisheries treaty. Ottawa was astounded.

• *March 7:* President Reagan fired the U.S. delegation to the United Nations Conference on the Law of the Sea.

• *March 9:* Haig's note of March 5 was formally withdrawn, apparently because it was thought to be too peremptory, coming as it did just before the bilateral summit.

• *March 10-11:* President Reagan met Prime Minister Trudeau in Ottawa on Reagan's first official visit abroad as president. Secretary of Commerce Malcolm Baldrige and U.S. Trade Representative William Brock met Herb Gray, minister of industry, trade and commerce, and Ed Lumley, minister of trade, to warn them of their concerns about the NEP and FIRA.

• *March 11:* William Brock sent Herb Gray a letter summarizing his policy concerns on trade, investment and energy matters and indicating the U.S. government's intention to request formal consultations with the Canadian government under article 22 of GATT.

• *April 3:* The State Department sent a second toughly-worded letter, this time to Ambassador Towe at the Canadian embassy in Washington, requesting written assurances that Canadian firms would only get equal opportunity — not preference — in contracts for the megaprojects under the National Energy Program. Three days later this letter, too, was withdrawn, apparently because it was also seen to be unacceptably intemperate in its tone.

• *April 6:* Myer Rashish, under-secretary for economic affairs at the State Department, chaired a meeting with Canadian officials in Washington, but the various departments of the administration had not managed to achieve a united front. "We were unable to get agreement to give the Canadian Embassy a formal paper at that time," wrote an American participant critical of the State Department's performance. "Until the last minute we understood that Rashish would give the Canadians a piece of paper called 'Canadian energy policy, talking points' but that paper was never used either."[7] Ambassador Towe reiterated assurances that Canada's international agreements would not be violated. Canada wanted national treatment for Canadian suppliers, not preference. Rashish pressed for changes in Bill C-48 to remove this ambiguity and to provide compensation for the "back-in."

30

• *April 9:* William Brock and Malcolm Baldrige wrote to Herb Gray providing examples of their concern about the operations of the Foreign Investment Review Agency and concluding with a veiled warning: "We are concerned that failure to deal with these types of problems could lead to FIRA becoming a significant irritant in our bilateral relationship."

• *April 10:* Herb Gray met Brock and Baldrige in Washington to review the American complaints.

• *April 27:* Richard Smith of the U.S. embassy wrote to Ted Lee, director of the U.S. Bureau in the Department of External Affairs, reaffirming the U.S. position on the back-in: "Because of the prospect that it would give rise to claims of expropriation without compensation, I consider this to be one of the most sensitive and potentially disruptive issues growing out of the NEP."

• *April 29:* Ambassador Towe briefed Myer Rashish in Washington about the changes that Marc Lalonde was about to announce in Parliament concerning Bill C-48.

• *May 14:* The Canadian government had decided to make two concessions to the Americans which it did not feel would compromise the thrust of the NEP. Marc Lalonde announced that "ex gratia" payments would be made as part of the Crown taking a 25 per cent interest in existing oil "plays" on Canada lands. Concerning tendering on megaprojects, the wording of Bill C-48 was amended to remove the ambiguity: Canadian companies would not have preference over foreign companies. The same day, Ambassador Towe wrote to William Brock outlining these two concessions to American pressure.

• *June 1:* Appeasement failed. The Canadians having given an inch, the Americans demanded a mile. Brock replied to Towe, welcoming the changes, but responding that the ex gratia payment was inadequate compensation since it did not take account of the true commercial value of the assets of which the Crown was taking a 25 per cent share. He warned: "We continue to have serious concerns about other elements of the NEP which Minister Lalonde did not address."

For the first season of the crisis, American pressure had gradually grown, targeting first the National Energy Program and then the Foreign Investment Review Agency with which the NEP had been rapidly linked by business lobbyists and congressmen. The Canadian response had been a mixture of polite stonewalling with what were considered minor concessions to give the Americans some feeling their grievances had been accommodated. The attitude in Ottawa was complacent and superior: the "California cowboys" needed time to learn their jobs; their objections were too sweeping to be acceptable; Canadian public opinion in any case supported the government on the NEP; once the Canadian takeovers dropped from the headlines and American executives stopped crying wolf, the issue would disappear.

Summer: Scenarios for Retaliation

Unfortunately for Ottawa the takeovers did not stop, so the issue did not disappear. In May, NuWest Group Ltd. of Calgary bought 7.2 per cent of the shares of Cities Service Co., the twentieth-largest U.S. oil company, an approach that Cities Service fought off with bitter determination. In June, Dome Petroleum Ltd. spent $1.68 billion to buy control of Conoco Inc. temporarily and to force it to sell off its controlling interest in Hudson's Bay Oil and Gas Co. Ltd. The same month, Allied Corp. sold its Canadian oil and gas operation to Husky Oil Ltd. and Drummond Petroleum of Calgary. In July, Hudson's Bay acquired Cyprus Anvil Mining Corp. of Vancouver from Amoco CYM Corp., which Standard Oil of Indiana had acquired. FIRA had not allowed Standard to keep Cyprus Anvil, thus putting it on the market for Canadian acquisition. At the same time, Husky Oil bought many of the Canadian assets of Shell Explorer Limited, a subsidiary of Shell Oil Co. of Houston. Canadian Pacific Enterprises then stunned the U.S. business community with its $1.1 billion purchase of the American-owned Canadian International Paper Co. And then Seagrams made a second attempt of its own, offering to take over Conoco, the ninth-largest oil company in the U.S. Like Hobart, St. Joe and Cities Service, Conoco did not want to be bought by Canadians, however much Seagrams had Americanized itself over the years. Conoco found its white knight in DuPont, but only after an epic takeover battle that, in the process of bidding up Conoco's shares from $73 to $98, had revived Canadian takeovers as a political issue.

Once again the actual truth of the charges had little to do with the issue. Bronfman was an American citizen; Seagrams was, for all intents and purposes, an American company. But the takeover victims kept on protesting loudly, and the storm revived in Congress as politicians cried for blood. On July 8, William Brock told a joint hearing of the Senate Finance and Banking Committees that he intended to get tough with the United States' trading partners. "The

Administration will strictly enforce United States laws and international agreements relating to international trade. . . . We will insist that our trading partners live up to the spirit and the letter of international trade agreements, and that they recognize that trade is a two-way street.''[8] On July 9 the *Wall Street Journal* advised Reagan to give Trudeau a tough lecture. ''The prime lesson ought to be that you can't promulgate the kind of xenophobic national energy program that Canada is currently pressing without driving away foreign capital and reaping a backlash from the nations you are turning against.''[9]

By the time Prime Minister Trudeau flew to Washington on July 10 to discuss the forthcoming economic summit, positions were hardening. The American president and his entourage wanted to extract more changes to the NEP and FIRA from Canada. The Canadian prime minister and his entourage had come to press the United States to support the notion of global negotiations on the North-South dialogue. Each side was unhappy with the response of the other. Clear signals that middle-level officials under William Brock and Malcolm Baldrige had lost their patience and were searching for other weapons were made following Trudeau's pre-summit visit to Washington. ''The U.S. Administration is not going to stand by and do nothing. Canada has been firing salvo after salvo. At some point, Americans are going to react,'' an unnamed insider told the *Globe and Mail*.[10] During the economic summit meetings in Ottawa from July 20 to 22, the American economic ministers, Baldrige and Brock, again met their Canadian counterparts and put on more pressure. The Canadians pointed to the concessions on Bill C-48 that had been made in May. The Americans responded that this wasn't enough. They needed more movement by Canada ''to get Exxon off their backs.'' Unhappy with the Canadian government's response to its continuing objections to FIRA and the NEP, the Reagan administration turned to the option of retaliation.

Business still demanded action and so did Congress. By August 1981, seven bills had been introduced into Congress concerning the margin requirements; one bill had been introduced to impose a nine-month moratorium retroactively on Canadian acquisitions of more than 5 per cent of the stock of a U.S. energy company; and two further bills had been introduced to make Canada a non-reciprocal country under the Mineral Lands Leasing Act. The administration did not feel that the agenda established by the proposed congressional bills was particularly promising. The bills to deny Canadian companies access to leases on federally-controlled lands under the MLLA of 1920 would only play into Ottawa's hands, since it would staunch the drain of energy capital from the Canadian to the American west. A bill to have foreign companies controlled by the same margin requirements as governed American firms in financing takeovers was less dramatic but equally inoffensive to Ottawa. Finance Minister MacEachen had already called in the presidents of the Canadian banks on July 29 to request a reduction of allowable credit for Canadian takeovers of foreign companies, in order to ease the downward pressure on the Canadian dollar which had resulted from the rush of repatriating takeovers in the spring. The bill before Congress to impose a moratorium of nine months on Canadian takeovers of American companies was thought to be a mere nuisance that had no serious prospects of becoming legislation.

An interdepartmental group was set up in Washington to examine what possibilities were available for putting pressure on the Canadian government to make significant concessions on the NEP and FIRA. William Brock had warned Herb Gray back in March that the U.S. was considering asking for "formal consultations" with Canada about Bill C-48 under the General Agreement on Tariffs and Trade, but the prospect of taking the issue to an international forum was not one to run shivers down the spines of Canadian diplomats. More forbidding were the other economic weapons that were being considered in the Department of Commerce and the Office of the United States Trade Representative:

- The U.S.-Canada automotive agreement, already a major problem for Canada, could be used to put serious pressure on Ontario.
- Harassment of Canadian exports at the border could injure sensitive targets that would then press Ottawa to make the required concessions.
- Putting impediments in the way of the Defence Production Sharing Arrangements could worsen Canada's already growing deficit in military production.
- Blocking certain Canadian exports on the ground that they were unfairly benefiting from cheaper energy was considered.
- Most serious of all was the opening of a case against Canada under section 301 of the U.S. Trade Act of 1974. This authorizes the president to retaliate against any other nation that "engages in discriminatory or other acts or policies which are unjustifiable, unreasonable and which burden or restrict United States commerce," or which "impose unjustifiable or unreasonable restrictions on access to supplies of food, raw materials or manufactured

or semi-manufactured products which burden or restrict United States commerce.'' With wide discretion to impose duties, import restrictions or other costs, the president under section 301 could act first and take evidence second.[11]

During July and August official Washington was both preoccupied with postulating scenarios for retaliation and moving to increase the level of anxiety in Ottawa by stepping up the level of psychological pressure. To do this, the Reagan administration continued to exploit the media. Articles in the press transmitted information judiciously leaked to raise the level of tension. The *Wall Street Journal* quoted ''one official'' in Washington as saying that Canada was considered a test case by Washington. '' 'If the U.S. allows Canada to get away with its new policies,' he asks 'what about Mexico? It's not something we can just sit by and not fight.' ''[12] The *Financial Post* reported that a survey was being made of U.S. companies with interests in Canada to determine what impediments they were suffering as a result of nationalist legislation in Canada. This was a questionnaire sent to the *Fortune* 500 by the Department of Commerce in order to gather data for a possible retaliatory move against FIRA.[13]

The fine line separating brainstorming from fantasizing was easy to cross. One official was reported to have told a Canadian, ''When Chile nationalized our copper, we could cut off our aid. But we don't give aid to Canada . . .'' Indicating his experience may have been gained more with subversive activities in Latin America than the complexities of the Canadian case, he went on to sketch a scenario of destabilizing the industrial base in the Liberal party's strongholds of Ontario and Quebec. ''If we pass the word to Wall Street that Canada is not a good place to invest, the Canadian dollar will fall, inflation rates will rise, and the standard of living will decline,'' went the reasoning. Once the Canadian people understood that the NEP and FIRA were responsible for this, a groundswell would develop to make the government ripe for defeat.[14] One proposal endorsed by William Brock was to read Canada out of the club of industrialized countries. On the grounds that Canada was acting less like a developed than a Third World country in its hostility to foreign investment, Brock made it clear that he was not going to invite Canada to a trilateral event that had been proposed during the Montebello Economic Summit: a meeting of Japan, the U.S. and the European Community on trade matters.

By the end of August the word in Washington being relayed to Ottawa through the Canadian press was: ''It's not a question of *if* but *what* action will be taken.''[15] Once the prospect of retaliation had been mooted, the locus of crisis shifted from the American business press and an angry Congress to the Canadian capital.

Fall: Collapse on the Rideau

The fact that dossiers on retaliation were being examined at the U.S. trade representative's office and that data on FIRA were being systematically collected at the Department of Commerce, had indeed registered with officials on the banks of the Rideau Canal. Ottawa, which at first had not taken seriously the warnings coming from the Canadian embassy about congressional anger, now developed a case of severe panic. Once the word got out that Washington had become serious about retaliation, the mood in Ottawa shifted from confidence to apprehension. Senior officials nervously talked about the United States' virtually unlimited possibilities for retaliation. They pointed out how vulnerable Canada was with its national unity crisis and its severe current account deficit. The U.S. could poach in Canadian waters, playing on federal-provincial divisions. The Liberal government could not afford to give the impression of not being able to manage the Canadian-American relationship.

Since the trade of diplomacy hangs on the ability to talk and negotiate, it was the threat of exclusion from the "club" of developed countries that seemed to carry most weight among Canadian officials. A new level of uncertainty was created as bits and pieces of information were relayed by private diplomatic channels and public press reports. The anxiety level within the Privy Council Office and External Affairs rose perceptibly: Ottawa was no longer in control of the situation; the practices of FIRA and the goals of the NEP were suddenly threatened. The U.S. administration was invested with almost mystical powers. Reagan was far worse than Nixon had been because he was a master manipulator of the media. Clearly — so went the consensus that had built up at the Tuesday morning interdepartmental breakfasts held at External Affairs — it was time to back down and buckle under. Ottawa had already signalled through the finance minister's message to the banks that it wanted to slow down the rate of Canadianization in the private sector. By the end of August the decision had been made that no "second shoe" would be dropped in the public domain: the NEP would not be applied to other sectors of the economy in the all-embracing new industrial strategy that Herb Gray's speeches had been heralding since the throne speech of April 1980. As for the expansion of FIRA, also announced in the throne speech, Gray's confident speeches about this development had become markedly muted by the summer of 1981. No one knew what to do since no one knew what the Reaganites would do. And for good reason: the Reagan administration didn't know itself. Ottawa had decided to back off before Washington had even loaded the guns whose use it had been considering.

The main reason that the guns weren't loaded was the U.S. administration's realization that they would backfire. Acting on the Auto Pact would bring howls of protest from American parts makers who supplied the Canadian market. Blocking Canadian goods at the border would contradict the ideological thrust of the Reagan administration, which had been attacking protectionism with considerable fervour. Taking Canada to GATT might prove an embarrassment, since Washington was disregarding the recent GATT judgment against the American domestic international sales corporations. The mood in Washington was undeniably nasty. Officials who had had to deal with Canada were angry at what they felt was its intransigence. They wanted to retaliate, but, as expressed in the cowboy cliché that ran around Washington, "We don't want to shoot ourselves in the foot." *Fortune* magazine quoted a senior policy maker's explanation of the problem: "Anything we've come across so far would hurt us more than them."[16] As another official put it, retaliation had to be carefully targeted — they did not want to hurt Alberta, whose government was a supporter of the American position on the NEP — and its effect had to be limited. An acceptable retaliatory action had to be retractable, reciprocal and not linked with other issues. Ironically, the extent of Canadian dependence on the American economy was furnishing it with a degree of independence from retaliation. This partial invulnerability did not prevent the administration from intensifying its verbal barrage and increasing its demands.

An examination of the events of the autumn of 1981 suggests that the U.S. administration did not realize that it had already achieved its long-term objectives of preventing Ottawa from carrying out its planned extension of FIRA's capacity and developing the NEP into a broad industrial strategy. Not having found any workable retaliatory weapon, it nevertheless proceeded to badger Ottawa for more and more concessions. The chronicle of the autumn's bilateral dealings shows how the pressure escalated.

• *September 8:* At a high level meeting of U.S. and Canadian officials in Washington, Ambassador Towe briefed the Americans on the Alberta-Ottawa energy accord. The U.S. side presented a list of the retaliatory possibilities being currently considered, and made it clear that "in view of public and industry pressure caused by the recent spate of Canadian takeovers or attempted takeovers of U.S. companies, they would have to make some concrete gesture from among the possibilities." Myer Rashish, U.S. under-secretary of state for economic affairs, said that pressure was building "for action against Canada in response to what is perceived as unfair treatment of American investments." David Macdonald, deputy U.S. trade representative, warned that the U.S. was heading for a GATT action. Marc Leland, assistant treasury secretary for international affairs, said that the NEP's Petroleum Incentive Program (PIP) grants were a big problem and that Lalonde's ex gratia payments did not meet American concerns about the back-ins, which were considered to be expropriations without adequate compensation. Macdonald warned that the U.S. government "may have an obligation to publicize the risks of investment in Canada." The Americans appeared to be overplaying their hand because the Canadians inferred that nothing would make them happy. As a participant from Energy, Mines and Resources reported, "given the current intransigent stance being taken at least at the senior officials level of the U.S. Administration, it is difficult to see how further concessions on the NEP, unless they were in key policy areas, which we would not want to change, would improve dramatically bilateral relations."[17] The Canadian officials said that Bill C-48 was cast in bronze and that no changes were possible.

• *September 10:* An inspired article in the *Washington Post* quoted Raymond Waldmann, assistant secretary of commerce for international economic policy, as saying that the U.S. government was "finger-twisting": tough retaliatory sanctions against the Canadian government were being considered.[18]

• *September 16:* Finance Minister MacEachen met Treasury Secretary Donald Regan in Washington and gave him the Canadian government's private assurance that there would be no "son of NEP"; an industrial strategy based on Canadianization would not be pursued. Despite this pledge, the meeting was considered unfruitful by the administration, as the *Wall Street Journal* reported.

• *September 17:* Prime Minister Trudeau met President Reagan at Grand Rapids, Michigan during the dedication celebrations of the Gerald Ford museum. The "back-in" aspect of the NEP took thirty-five of their forty-five minute discussion. Trudeau defended the back-in as an extension of the previous leasing regime in Canada. No consensus was reached, and the president asked Alexander Haig to look into the issue. Haig later met Brock, Baldrige, Donald Regan and the newly-appointed ambassador to Canada, Paul Robinson, in order to plan the administration's next move.

• *September 22:* A senior Washington official went public. Myer Rashish attacked Canadian energy and investment policies in a speech in New York, warning that they were inviting U.S. retaliation with risks of irreparable damage to the bilateral relationship. "Mr. Rashish, in the most sweeping public condemnation of Canadian-ownership programs by a top U.S. official," the *Globe and Mail* reported on its front page, "referred to 'the perception, virtually rampant in Washington, that . . . relationships are sliding dangerously towards crisis.' "[19]

• *October 9:* To prepare the way for what was clearly hoped would be a decisive breakthrough by Treasury Secretary Donald Regan, Secretary of State Haig sent Secretary of State MacGuigan a "Dear Mark" letter communicating "my increasing concern that our two countries are heading toward a confrontation." The situation was "urgent and extremely serious." Hence Mr. Regan wanted to come to Ottawa on October 13 for another meeting before Bill C-48 passed into law. "The President's primary objective is to avoid a circumstance in which the United States and Canada find themselves in a situation where actions lead to counteractions with serious damage to the overall relationship. I am personally convinced that this outcome can be prevented, but it will require a dedicated and concentrated effort on both sides, and, frankly, I fear that time is running out. . . . I fear that if we cannot make progress in these discussions, the situation will almost certainly become much more serious, and management of it far more difficult."[20] If there had been any doubt in the minds of the protagonists, the Canadian-American relationship had now been officially declared to be in a state of crisis.

• *October 13:* Treasury Secretary Regan, accompanied by three officials, flew to Ottawa to meet Allan MacEachen and Mark MacGuigan. The Canadians were invited to lunch at the U.S. ambassador's residence. Regan said he needed some concessions to be able to report to Congress. Ambassador Robinson claimed that FIRA's tentacles were expanding, and laid out a double demand. "The U.S.A. would like a formal statement from the Government of Canada on not extending FIRA. . . . [and] a public statement like MacEachen's speech of July 29 to the effect that there would be no 'son of

NEP.' "[21] MacEachen reminded Regan that he had already assured him in Washington that there would be no new NEPs and that Bill C-48 could not be amended. Regan responded, "The oil companies are particularly concerned with the back-in." MacGuigan offered to talk about more adequate compensation payments but not about full asset value being paid. Grandfathering (exempting the currently operating firms) was not possible.

The other main issue raised was the original concern about the purchasing requirements for bids for megaprojects. Ambassador Robinson again put the American case: "We believe that the companies on the megaprojects would pay Canadian firms a 30 per cent premium to avoid trouble. If we knew that CIRB [Committee on Industrial and Regional Benefits] would be handled fairly there would be no objection." MacEachen pointed out that there had been no grievances with regard to the Alaska gas pipeline, although the procurement problems were almost identical. Ernest Johnston of the State Department insisted that transparency (complete divulging of tender information) was crucial: "without transparency the bidders would not be able to get equity."[22] Ian Stewart, deputy minister of finance, cited statistics that showed the actual problem was that procurement went to U.S. firms more than to Canadian ones because companies fixed their contracts with known suppliers without competitive bids. Raising the question of whether there would be any end to the Americans' demands, MacEachen said the Canadians would need some understanding that any proposed changes would actually satisfy the United States.

• *October 21:* David Macdonald, deputy U.S. trade representative, spelled out how extensive were the American demands to a committee hearing in the House of Representatives. On the purchasing requirements of Bill C-48, the U.S. "is pressing for a procedure which assures non-discriminatory national treatment for all bids, provided no justification is required if Canadian suppliers are not chosen." On the Petroleum Incentives Program (PIP), which replaced depletion allowances with grants giving an incentive to Canadian-controlled firms, "the United States is asking that subsidies be provided on a non-discriminatory basis." On FIRA, "the United States is seeking a complete elimination of these requirements [which entail performance commitments]." Further, "the United States is seeking a change in the FIRA process to permit all takeovers that do not increase total foreign-owned assets, so long as the purchaser is not objectionable on grounds such as moral turpitude."[23]

40

• *October 30:* Robert Cornell, deputy assistant secretary of the treasury, flew to Ottawa for another meeting with Ambassador Towe and Under-Secretary of State for External Affairs Allan Gotlieb. Gotlieb commented that the excessive American rhetoric had reduced, not increased, Canadian flexibility. He repeated that the back-in was not expropriation, so that compensation payments were not appropriate. While Canadians were prepared to discuss these matters, there was an "exceedingly slight" area for manoeuvre on the NEP. Cornell said his government could not contemplate many months of dialogue. Gotlieb responded there was no possibility of doing it in a few weeks. Cornell insisted that discussions were not adequate: "They would have to produce solutions and they would have to do so quickly."[24]

• *November 5:* Mark MacGuigan sent a "Dear Al" letter to Alexander Haig in another attempt to lay the back-in to rest. "We recognize that several large U.S. oil companies have been immediately affected by the Crown Interest but so have a number of Canadian companies. Frankly, we are perplexed as to why this should be perceived as such a seminal issue leading to a crisis in our relationship."[25] He attached a five-page, single-spaced memorandum entitled "Canada Lands and the Crown Interest," clearly hoping that a detailed exposition of the Canadian case would finally remove the American objections.

• *November 12:* Allan MacEachen delivered his second budget, and with it a clear response to Washington's fall season of finger twisting. In the accompanying budget document, *Economic Development for Canada in the 1980s*, was the public statement Ambassador Robinson had been demanding on the NEP and FIRA. First, the possibility that the NEP would be a model for Canadianizing other industries through a new industrial strategy was denied.

> The special measures being employed to achieve more Canadian ownership and control of the oil and gas industry are not, in the Government of Canada's view, appropriate for other sectors.[26]

Second, the government swallowed the promises on FIRA it had reaffirmed following its election.

> In the Speech from the Throne in the spring of 1980, reference was made to three specific measures . . . which involved changes to the Foreign Investment Review Act. For the time being, no legislative action is intended on these measures.[27]

Washington had succeeded in pushing Ottawa to forswear its economic development options based on an interventionist role for government. The budget document was the outward and visible sign of the summer's inward and spiritual collapse over the long-term economic issues. Only the NEP and the existing FIRA remained intact — but they did not long remain unattacked.

Winter: After Appeasement, More Demands

Without having taken a single concrete action, Washington had managed to spike Ottawa's economic development options. The Reagan administration had made no retaliatory move other than to threaten possible actions and to make demands for Canadian concessions. Ottawa had responded twice, first in May with relatively minor concessions on the National Energy Program, then in the November budget with an abandonment of its initial determination to intervene more actively in the establishment of an industrial strategy to resolve the grievous problems of the Canadian economy.

But Washington was still not satisfied. On December 4, William Brock sent an extraordinary letter to the Canadian embassy. It started by referring to the numerous Canadian-American meetings over the past year and expressing his "appreciation for the growing understanding shown by your Government over the course of these bilateral consultations." Brock went on to bestow a condescending pat on the back.

> Let me begin by restating the fact that the U.S.A. especially welcomes the commitments made by the Government of Canada that there will be no expansion of FIRA's mandate or extension of the policies embodied in the NEP to other sectors. We believe that these pronouncements represent a positive step in meeting *some* of the concerns of the U.S.A. Government.[28]

He also expressed appreciation for the assurances that megaproject sponsors would not be coerced into sourcing from Canadian firms, but went on to warn that he would be watching Ottawa's every move in the future.

> I want to emphasize that we will be monitoring closely the activities of CMIRB* and would object to the imposition by CMIRB of any requirement that companies report on or justify their use of foreign goods and services.

---

* Committee on Megaproject, Industrial and Regional Benefits, also called CIRB.

The preliminaries dispensed with, Brock came to the heart of his message: a demand for more concessions on FIRA and the NEP.

> As you know, there remain a number of very serious objections on our part to the Canadian Government's current and proposed investment, energy and industrial policies . . . So far U.S.A. Government action in response to these policies has been limited to consultations, despite great pressures from the private sector and through Congress. *We cannot, however, continue simply to discuss matters without substantial movement both on the FIRA and on the NEP.*

Next followed a pro-forma recognition of Canada's right to make its own policy.

> Let me emphasize at the outset that we are not opposed to the Canadianization objective of the NEP and the screening of foreign investment by the FIRA per se. We do not question the sovereign right of Canada in these respects.

Having approved the principles of the NEP and FIRA, Brock went on to explain why they were unacceptable in practice.

> Our objective throughout our bilateral consultations has been to seek modification of the methods being employed by your Government in the pursuit of these objectives . . . We are most concerned about the following discriminatory and inequitable measures associated with the operation of the FIRA and the NEP . . . It is most important that the first two practices be *eliminated*, and that the others be *eliminated or modified* as appropriate.

The two FIRA practices to be eliminated then followed:

> 1. Trade-related performance requirements such as undertaking to purchase Canadian goods and services, to reduce imports or to export specific quantities or percentages of production.
> 2. Restrictions on foreign firms seeking to distribute their own products in Canada.

Six more features of FIRA's actions were included for elimination or modification: undertakings to relocate activity to Canada from other countries; undertakings to transfer patents to Canada at less than fair price; absence of clear guidelines concerning FIRA's requirements; new performance requirements in indirect takeovers; length of time required to get approvals; low threshold of assets to trigger FIRA reviews. Brock clearly felt no compunction about dictating detailed changes to the administrative processes of Canada, whatever its "sovereign right" might be.

On the NEP, those measures to be "eliminated or modified as appropriate" included the absence of grandfathering provisions and the absence of payments proportionate to the asset value of the Crown interest; the Petroleum Incentive Payments' discrimination against foreign firms; the requirement of 50 per cent Canadian ownership and control for production of oil and gas on Canada lands; the requirement that Canadian ownership be considered in obtaining access to natural gas export licences and natural gas bank benefits.

Finally, Brock gave an admonition:

> Given the growing pressure within the U.S.A. for a response to the problems raised by the above issues, I would hope that your Government would be in a position to respond to the points raised at the earliest possible date.

The Canadian government was furious. This communication was too much even for it to swallow. On December 10, Mark MacGuigan told Alexander Haig during a multilateral meeting in Brussels that Brock's letter was strange and excessive. On December 16, Canada's new ambassador to the United States, Allan Gotlieb, replied to Brock that he was "both surprised and disturbed at the scope and tone of your letter." It was what diplomats call a stiff note. For one thing, Brock's letter called into question the whole process of consultations. Referring to the visit by Donald Regan in October, Gotlieb said Canadian authorities had gathered that "the U.S. Administration appreciated in particular that [the NEP and FIRA] were and are designed to achieve legitimate Canadian objectives."

> With regard to the NEP, both the SSEA [Secretary of State for External Affairs] and the Minister of Finance stated to Secretary Regan that "grandfathering" of the Crown interest position and payment of proportionate asset value for the 25 per cent Crown share would strike at the heart of the legislation and were, therefore, not possible. We thought this position was well understood, and I am troubled that your letter could have the effect of negating the advances which we thought had been made at that time.[29]

Gotlieb expressed appreciation that Brock did not oppose the NEP's objectives but went on to note that

> in seeking changes in such programs as the Petroleum Incentive Program and Crown lands production requirements, you are singling out those aspects of the NEP which are central to its Canadianization objectives and critical to its success.

With regard to Brock's critique of FIRA, Gotlieb responded equally firmly.

> The Canadian Government does not share your point of view on these issues. In addition, I should note that these practices, as well as some of the others with which you expressed concern, are basic to the operation of the Act and have been in effect since the inception of FIRA in 1974.

The former under-secretary of state referred to the November budget's renunciation of the prospect of applying the NEP to other sectors of the economy and giving FIRA additional powers. Canada had bent over backwards to accommodate U.S. demands: "You seem to have taken insufficient account of the genuine efforts made by the Canadian government over the past year to meet your concerns." Gotlieb's message was clear: the U.S. should put up or shut up; if it felt so inclined, it could take Canada to court.

> Nonetheless, where differences of opinion remain, the issue boils down to whether Canadian law and practice are consistent with international law and other commitments Canada has entered into multilaterally with other governments. . . . The Canadian authorities would consider it entirely appropriate and non-confrontational if recourse were had to international dispute settlement mechanisms to resolve outstanding issues.

Ottawa had drawn the line in confidential print. The same day that the official reply was dispatched, another bilateral "contact group" meeting of top-level officials convened in Ottawa to draw the line in confidential parlay. The Canadians gave their counterparts the same message as Gotlieb had given Brock. A long memorandum written by the meeting's U.S. notetaker Richard Smith, minister in the U.S. embassy in Ottawa, reported the discussion's highlights and pithily revealed the exasperation and anger felt by the Canadians in the light of the Brock letter.

De Montigny Marchand, the acting under-secretary of state for external affairs, opened the meeting. "This one is on a subject, back-in, that we feel has been flogged to death. It is a key feature of the NEP and the GOC [Government of Canada] is frankly having difficulty understanding your problems with it." He went on to affirm, "We are open to arguments that we are not acting fairly, but you have not been convincing. You are throwing out accusations, but your evidence is unconvincing." Micky Cohen, deputy minister of energy, mines and resources, "expressed the view that everything that can be said has been said. He said he accepts the sincerity of our view but fundamentally disagrees with it. He said GOC has thought long and hard about this and is fully convinced that back-in is not unfair or retroactive — any more than a tax change is.'' William Jenkins, the deputy under-secretary of state for economics, added that ''Canada doesn't accept the charge that it is not living up to high standards and finds statements that it is no longer worthy to be a member of the [international] club to be highly offensive.'' Marchand went on to remark ''on 'nasty habit' USG [United States Government] has of making linkages, e.g., holding Canada hostage on trade talks.'' Later he reiterated his anger. ''Marchand intervened to say . . . that the USG stop calling us 'bad citizens. Our honour has been impugned and it should stop.' ''[30]

The Americans remained unabashed. Joseph F. Dennin, deputy assistant secretary of commerce, said that ''given our inability to change each other's views, GOC shouldn't be surprised by positions we put forward in communications like the Brock letter, in Congressional testimony, and in advice to businessmen.'' Robert D. Hormats, assistant secretary of state for economics and business affairs, ''expressed the view 'that Canada over-reacted to Brock letter. If Brock letter reflected frustration, it is because it is there. The letter was an honest presentation of our views. The Gotlieb letter in response will raise hackles in Washington.' Cohen responded that the Brock letter had done that in Ottawa.'' Marchand and Jenkins agreed: ''Brock letter was political dynamite in Canadian context. Marchand added that such letters have a way of leaking. Jenkins said, 'We had to reply in exactly the same vein.' ''[31]

The Canadians were also bitter about the Americans' never defining a fixed ''bottom line.'' Marchand pointed out that one reason for disappointment with the Brock letter was that ''points covered in the Regan meeting [in October] came bouncing back under the signature of a minister.'' ''Cohen said it is worth recalling Canada's unfortunate experience with past attempts to accommodate U.S. concerns. He noted that last spring, in response to appeals on our part, he and minister Lalonde successfully pressed for politically difficult changes affecting language on procurement and introducing the 'ex gratia' payments. 'This was costly for us — and six months later it's like it never happened.' He added GOC 'once bitten' is 'more than twice shy'.'' Bernard Drabble, associate deputy minister of finance, underlined the political costs of the concessions Canada had already made. ''Drabble said that Canada has been listening and responding to

U.S. views . . . for example, certain elements in the budget document moved in our direction despite substantial political difficulty, e.g., FIRA review, no new NEPs.''

The mandarinate had been pushed to the wall and had decided to fight back. They had been treated like colonials but had not acted like compradors. They recognized that in trying to accommodate the superior power, they had given away a large part of the shop. Now that they were being squeezed for more, they were not craven. In this prolonged, exhausting dispute, the Brock letter had become the last straw. It brought the crisis to a climax from which the Canadian side emerged weaker in policy (Canada had agreed to forgo its economic policy options) but stronger in resolve (Ottawa had defined a bottom line of its own below which it would not be pushed).

December 16 did not mark the end of this time of troubles but it was a turning point in the tension. On January 5, 1982, in a letter to the Canadian mission in Geneva, the United States requested consultations with Canada regarding FIRA under article 22 of the General Agreement on Tariffs and Trade. This meant that bilateral discussions would begin without arbitration. Herb Gray called the complaint normal and non-confrontational. The U.S. could have asked for an immediate ruling by a GATT panel but opted for the less dramatic route of formal talks. The next stage, a formal request that the GATT Council create a panel to examine FIRA and rule on its conformity with international trade rules under article 23 of GATT, was taken at the end of March.[32] Even if the court upheld the complaint, it was unlikely that its ruling would contain punitive sanctions. The U.S. government had shifted its campaign against Canada from a bilateral campaign of threats to a multilateral approach through international agencies.

The winter of confrontation had come to an end with the Canadians angry. Although they had given way on the major fronts of the NEP and FIRA, Washington had kept escalating the pressure to the point that its demands lost credibility. The U.S. had won the battle for what were realizable targets, but had pressed on for total surrender. In the end it seemed that it was the Canadians who, in resisting excessive U.S. demands, could claim the real victory by saving the NEP and FIRA. In the summer of 1981 Ottawa had been paralyzed at the prospect of American retaliation. The Canadian government had devised no scenarios that would help it think through what the Americans could realistically do and what could be done in response. Nor was there a clear perception of how to exploit the disorganization, the internal conflict and the uncertainties that characterized the U.S. administration. Speculation about retaliation was enough to shift power back to the anti-nationalist forces within the federal bureaucracy and to make the Liberal government abandon the commitments it had made to the Canadian electorate and had reaffirmed in its throne speech. When the Americans persisted into the winter with further concrete demands, the Canadians' hackles rose at last. The atmosphere in Ottawa had changed from paralysis to stubbornness. Though Ottawa did finally stop its retreat and set up a line of defence, it was only after abandoning so many major weapons that it had few strategic reserves left with which to handle its worsening economic problems.

The commotion in Congress during the spring of 1981 and the administration's determination to force Canada to make changes in the NEP and FIRA precipitated such prolonged tension that the interactions of 1981 can legitimately be called a crisis in the sense of our second psychological condition of acute stress. The Reagan administration's goal of expanding the zone of its free-market ideology was threatened by the interventionism it saw the Canadian government perpetrating. Its sense of control over the international environment was reduced and its level of tension with its northern neighbour increased. It found itself working under evident time pressure to get Ottawa to back down before the new Canadian energy legislation was enacted. On the Canadian side, a psychosis of crisis did not develop until retaliation became a serious possibility. Though it came later in Ottawa, the crisis atmosphere was more pervasive and more acute than in Washington. Fundamental national objectives involving the system's survival were at stake; tremendous concern about possible American actions reigned in the capital; and senior government officials displayed high levels of stress and considerable anxiety about the future, in particular concerning their ostracism from the "club" of the industrialized countries. That both sides were in crisis can be seen from the strained tenor of their meetings and the stiff language of their not-so-diplomatic correspondence. The policy goals and objectives of both teams of players were threatened by the actions of the other side and by the uncertainty that resulted from the unsettled dispute.[33]

The Canadian takeovers of American companies in the spring of 1981 had sparked an authentic international crisis, a period of extreme stress which was rooted in the political and economic instability that had reigned in the Seventies within and between both countries. This time of troubles was also to mark an important turning point in the two states' previous history of generally tranquil and tolerant interaction. If the psychological crisis of 1981 also brought about a fundamental change in the Canadian-American relationship, we can say that it represented a crisis in its third aspect of a historic turning point that results in a new set of circumstances, a change in the relations among participants, an outcome whose consequences shape the future of the actors.[34] To determine the extent of the objective changes in the Canadian-American relationship that resulted from the 1981 confrontation, it is necessary to examine each of the main policy areas on the bilateral agenda. These issues are addressed in the next nine chapters.

Part II

Continental Economic Issues

Continental Economic Issues

Whether the psychic crisis of the early Eighties also marked a historical crisis or turning point in the Canadian-American relationship is a question that is easier to answer as time elapses and provides a better vantage point for observers to judge the import of 1981's events. In the final analysis, the confrontation of 1981 will prove to have marked a significant turning point only if the Canadian-American relationship has changed.

Time alone is not enough. In addition to a temporal perspective on 1981, we need to have some means with which we can detect and determine shifts in that intense, heterogeneous and multidimensional set of endless interactions known as the Canadian-American relationship. The complexity of the relationship has long eluded the best conceptual efforts of North American scholars. Various concepts and theories have been put forward — functionalism and integration, duopoly and dependency, imperialism and continentalism — but none has succeeded in pinning down this evasive quarry.[1] Rather than tackling these issues of meta-analysis, this study will assess whether the relationship changed as a result of the events of 1981. To do this, it will focus on its principal policy components.

In Part II we will consider the five economic issues that figure most directly on the bilateral agenda. The National Energy Program represented an unprecedented effort to change the ownership pattern and control mechanisms of an industry, and because Canadianization impinged directly on major U.S. corporate interests, it became a highly contentious issue between the two governments. The NEP also raised a question which the United States government found objectionable to its own international investment policies; the Foreign Investment Review Agency gave Washington a convenient target to attack on this issue. Canada came under attack by protectionist American trade policies, both U.S. non-tariff barriers to imports and the retaliatory devices against other countries' export promotion that were being developed under the slogan of "reciprocity." In the area of resource integration, the level of controversy was less intense, though such megaprojects as the Alaska natural gas pipeline had raised very high stakes for both countries. Finally, on the level of the two economies' macroeconomic relationship, the question of high interest rates and massive Canadian borrowings of American capital gave this dimension of the continental system a heightened intensity. The next five chapters present an examination of the main developments in each of these areas in order to ascertain the extent of change that the relationship underwent in the course of the 1981 confrontation and its aftermath.

The National Energy Program and Canadianization

3

On October 28, 1980, when Ronald Reagan had started the last week of his campaign, promising to resuscitate the American economy with the vague magic of supply-side economics and to bolster it with a new but equally ill-defined North American accord, the Canadian minister of finance, Allan MacEachen, brought down his first budget in the House of Commons. Lurking in MacEachen's dense text was a time bomb that would shake existing North American accord to its foundations. The explosives were set out in a six-page section innocuously titled "National Energy Program," which reiterated much of what leaders of both Conservative and Liberal governments had been declaring for years: Canada should achieve self-sufficiency in oil production and should increase the degree of Canadian ownership in the petroleum industry. The long list of complex measures contained in the accompanying budget document, *The National Energy Program*, went beyond a mere consolidation of the various initiatives that had been taken by the federal government over the previous decade in response to the world oil crisis precipitated by OPEC, the Organization of Petroleum Exporting Countries, in 1973. The NEP proposed to introduce a much greater degree of government intervention in the energy industry. Through its measures the government would be able to influence the pace of development of both oil and gas, to order the drilling of wells on federal lands, and to fine-tune the industry in response to conjunctural changes.

For an energy-exporting country, self-sufficiency in oil within a decade was not a pipe dream. By international standards the NEP's goal of 50 per cent Canadian ownership of the petroleum sector by 1990 was moderate, although the means that had been chosen offended the industry. Yet a shiver of incredulity passed through the thin ranks of the country's nationalists. They could scarcely believe that a Liberal government, whose policies since the Second World War had

55

entrenched the economy's resource dependency on the American industrial machine, now intended to repatriate control over the petroleum sector. When it became clear through the winter of 1980-81 that the government was putting its new rhetoric into legislative reality, such long-time critics of Liberal continentalism as Tommy Douglas, former leader of the federal New Democratic Party, and James Laxer, former leader of the NDP's radical Waffle faction, rallied to support the government's program. "Canadianization" became, like "patriation," a new and popular word in the Canadian political lexicon, a hopeful concept that affirmed the country's ability to run its own affairs.

In the early months of the NEP's existence, its most controversial aspects appeared to be the pricing, taxing and revenue-sharing provisions, which precipitated an aggravation of the long-standing conflict between the federal government and the provincial government of Alberta, Canada's major oil-producing jurisdiction. Alberta's reaction — cutting back oil supplies to the Canadian market — triggered ten months of federal-provincial brinkmanship as the two governments tested each other's strength and will. But by September 1, 1981, the two governments had finally reached an agreement on a schedule of price increases for oil and gas, a standoff on how much each government would tax the industry, and an allocation of administrative responsibility which left Alberta in charge of implementing the new Petroleum Incentive Program within its own boundaries.

The American Question Mark
There remained a more intractable problem. Looming over the uncertainties in the prolonged federal-provincial crisis that the NEP had brought to a head was the ominous question: Would Ronald Reagan's government concede to Canada the right to reorder its own energy affairs? At first, few people could tell. Since the designers of the NEP had been exempted from the normal bureaucratic constraints of interdepartmental consultations, the most knowledgeable America watchers in the Canadian government, the diplomats in the Department of External Affairs, had been kept in the dark. The Canadian embassy in Washington, the normal conduit for feeding American governmental concerns into the Canadian decision-making process, had only heard about the thrust of the NEP a couple of weeks before the budget speech released its actual provisions. Since the drafting process had been veiled behind the shrouds of budget secrecy, the normal prior

consultation with American officials had not taken place. The NEP hit Washington without forewarning. At first the official American reaction was registered through diplomatic channels. On November 7, just after the Carter administration had been defeated at the polls, a large interagency meeting of senior American officials was held with their Canadian counterparts to voice American alarms about the NEP's proposed violation of those principles governing the treatment of foreign investment that the U.S. government had long defended around the world. Officials in the Carter administration, who had enjoyed good relations with the Canadian government, were familiar with its energy policy dilemmas; they could be expected to register official objections without pressing too hard. Besides, they owed Canada a favour over delays in approving the joint Alaska gas pipeline.

No favours were owed Canada by the new Republican officials who swept into Washington in January 1981 on the coattails of the president elect. In this group there was no one to fill the "friend of Canada" role that Vice-President Walter Mondale had played in the Carter administration. Policy advisers in Reagan's entourage knew little about Canada and its sometimes subtle but substantial differences from their own political and legal traditions. As the Reagan team grasped the long-sought reins of power in the early weeks of 1981, it started to hear a cacophony of complaints about Canada's NEP from a number of oil company executives. They had funded Reagan's successful election campaign and now turned to the government, expecting it to defend their interests. Many objected that the value of their assets had been reduced up in Canada. They wanted Washington to get Ottawa to back off from its plans. At the same time, Congress was expressing anger at Canadian takeover attempts, which seemed to threaten the middle tier of the American oil industry in a wave of mergers.[1] As congressional lobbyists defended their clients from unfriendly Canadian takeovers, they used every means at their command, including loud attacks on the unfairness of the situation: Canadian companies, who were being enriched by the National Energy Program at the expense of American branch plants, were now coming south to pick off their parent companies.

The Reagan team not only heard the pleas of big business calling for action against the depradations of the NEP; it also saw in Canada's energy program a direct contradiction of its own economic philosophy. As part of his small-government ideology, Reagan had promised to speed Carter's deregulation of both oil and gas. Prices would be allowed to rise in response to the forces of demand and supply.

57

Declining domestic and insecure overseas supplies had been unable to match the growing demands of industry and consumers who had been protected from the discipline of world prices. Now national supplies would increase as exploration responded to the incentive of higher prices, while demand would be constrained as consumers adapted to the new reality of expensive fuels. With its mission to reinstate the supremacy of the free market, how could the Reagan administration be expected to condone its closest trading partner's embarkation on an energy program based squarely on the principle of greater government intervention in the marketplace with artificially fixed oil and gas prices? Surely Canada could not be allowed — in its own best interests — to undertake such a foolish venture. Surely, too, President Reagan, who needed to assert himself on the world stage as a forceful foreign policy maker, could not brook his closest and most dependent ally launching a program that was anathema to his economic philosophy. Canada's traditional acceptance of American policy leadership had to be re-established.

Historically, Canada had been happy to follow the policy lead given by the U.S. in energy matters. Indeed, the development of Canada's petroleum industry with minimum government interference had followed closely patterns developed in Texas and Oklahoma.[2] Furthermore, the policies that established the nascent Canadian industry had been executed mainly by American oil subsidiaries whose exploration and development in Canada were subsidized by American as well as by Canadian tax stimuli.[3] The multinationals that controlled the Canadian industry had recommended to the Borden Commission of 1958-59 the basic rationale that was incorporated in the National Oil Policy promulgated by the Diefenbaker Conservative government in 1961. This strategy was "national" in a very incomplete sense. It kept the area west of the Ottawa River as a protected market for Alberta oil which, though cheaper to produce than U.S. oil, was sold at above the Gulf Coast posted price. At the same time, Quebec and the Atlantic provinces were established as a captive market of the multinationals' more expensive Venezuelan supplies. Venezuela had lost its big market when U.S. oil import quotas shut out its exports. The State Department, concerned about political instability in Venezuela, wanted it to keep its market in eastern Canada. In exchange for not extending its oil pipeline to Montreal, Canada was offered an exemption from the U.S. oil import quota. Thus did the multinationals rationalize their branch plants' trade. The cost of importing this foreign oil could be offset by the revenue earned from selling to the locked-in market of the U.S. northwest the maximum possible volumes of what was thought to be a permanent surplus of prairie oil.

Throughout the oil-abundant Sixties, self-sufficiency was not seen to be important by Ottawa. Canada had integrated itself as a northern extension of the United States' continental energy system. In the early Seventies, American pressure on Ottawa to build a Sarnia-to-Montreal oil pipeline in order to increase self-sufficiency and so reduce North America's strategic vulnerability was actually resented. Both the federal and provincial energy departments had intimate, client-patron relationships with the industry: they depended on it for their information on the state of energy supply and demand, they acted as spokespersons for it within the councils of government, and they took care to consult closely in the making of policy. The National Energy Board which, from its inception, was extremely deferential to the wishes of the major gas exporters,[4] developed a close relationship with the Federal Power Commission, its counterpart regulatory agency in Washington, for the export of gas to the American market.

By 1970, Canada seemed unequivocal in its acceptance of the view that the United States' definition of its own strategic and continental needs should shape Canadian energy policies. In February 1970, the Nixon administration had articulated its approach to the problem of oil security in the Shultz Report, which the president had directed his secretary of labour, George P. Shultz, to produce. Shultz had warned that the oil-producing nations of the Third World might band together to extract a better deal from the West and recommended a search for "safe" sources of foreign supply, Canada being the safest of all.

> The risk of political instability or animosity is generally conceded to be very low in Canada. The risk of physical interruption or diversion of Canadian oil to other export markets in an emergency is also minimal for those deliveries made by inland transportation.[5]

As if in illustration of this analysis, the Canadian government agreed in September 1970 to the long-term export to the U.S. of 6.3 trillion cubic feet of natural gas. The Ottawa government wanted to increase its exports and to build political support for the Mackenzie River pipeline project.

The frank continentalism of the Shultz Report did not offend Ottawa. On the contrary, Energy Minister J.J. Greene was still complaining to the Independent Petroleum Association of America in May 1970 that he was deeply dissatisfied with the U.S. quota's limitation of Canadian oil imports. He called for "realistic trading

59

arrangements in respect of oil which would secure that Canadian oil enters United States markets on a normal commercial basis . . . an outcome [that] would be entirely consistent with the basic complementarity of resources and requirements in the two countries."[6]

Canada had clearly signalled its compliance to the United States, and American officials acknowledged this response. Speaking to an energy resources hearing of the U.S. Senate in May 1971, the president of the U.S. National Coal Association testified that "our government considers Canada our own for energy purposes." The next month President Nixon made a statement saying that a major solution to the U.S. energy crisis lay in importing vast quantities of oil, natural gas, hydro-power and water from Canada.[7] Canada's energy reserves were now known in the U.S. as "continental resources."

Ottawa's Centralizing Response to the OPEC Crisis

For Washington to assume that Ottawa would follow its policy lead in 1970 under conditions of abundance had made complete sense; for it to expect the same behaviour in 1980 under conditions of scarcity was naïve. In that decade Ottawa had learned some painful lessons and no longer accepted the notion that what was good for Exxon and the United States was necessarily good for Canada.

The supply of Canadian oil had started to decline in 1970, but the danger signals had been ignored. When the world oil crisis of 1973 saw international supplies threatened and interrupted, then prices doubled and redoubled, it revealed how exposed the National Oil Policy had left Canada. A new team of economists in the Department of Energy, Mines and Resources had already been rethinking the rationale for long-term commitments to oil and gas exports to the U.S. The resulting green paper, *An Energy Policy for Canada — Phase I*,[8] raised concerns about the coherence of federal policy. It was a tentative document, asking questions without taking positions. Should surplus Alberta oil production be redirected towards the Quebec market via a new pipeline to be laid from Sarnia to Montreal? Should price controls shelter the consuming provinces from the shock of the world price rises? Reductions of exports to the American market could conserve Canadian fuel for Canadian markets. Should taxes on the remaining exports help finance the enormous costs of importing oil at OPEC prices for eastern Canada? Should a national petroleum company be created to provide the government with a window on the industry and to expand the minuscule Canadian-owned element of the petroleum industry?

60

The chronology of the two years from December 1972 to November 1974 set out in Table 3-1 indicates how Canada tried to extricate itself from its continental energy relationship in oil.[9] These moves did not go unnoticed in Washington. The administration was angry: raising the price of Canadian crude exacerbated the U.S. balance of payments problems. Although Canada did not reduce gas or electricity exports, and although oil was sold on 30-day contracts so no contracts were actually broken, Congress too was furious: Canada's reduction of energy exports was hurting the U.S. Threats of retaliation were made, including the proposal to cut off the Middle East oil piped from Portland, Maine to Montreal. The tempest calmed when Donald Macdonald ultimately convinced the president's energy adviser, William Simon, about the reality of Canada's two basic problems. First, reserves were far lower than had been assumed by the Shultz Report, which had overestimated the ease of attaining continental self-sufficiency. The multinationals had also overestimated the volumes of oil that would become available at predicted prices. Canada could not supply a significant portion of American oil needs. Second, the eastern Canadian market was supplied by imported oil that had to be paid for at OPEC prices; if Canadian exports to the U.S. were to continue to offset these costs, they too had to be priced at world levels. By February 1974, Simon announced his support for the export tax, indicating the U.S. government's understanding that Canada could not be completely integrated in a continental energy plan.[10]

The next seven years witnessed further trauma in Canada's energy policy development. New discoveries were made of reserves in the inaccessible Arctic, although no "elephants" — huge oil and gas fields — were proved up in the commercially exploitable dimensions of Prudhoe Bay. Fear grew that shortages of natural gas might develop in Canada as they had in the U.S. A second, more definite federal policy white paper, *An Energy Strategy for Canada,*[11] was issued in 1976 to respond to these rapidly changing circumstances. A confusing debate grew ever more vehement between continentalists and nationalists, between corporations and environmentalists, between governments and native-land claimants. Groping their way, both provincial and federal governments levied new taxes, established new monitoring agencies, founded new Crown corporations, and promulgated new regulations.

Looking back at this bewildering maze of government action, it is possible to see four main thrusts in federal energy policy as it evolved through the decade. First came the priority of **freedom from oil**

TABLE 3-1
CHRONOLOGY OF CANADA'S RESPONSE TO THE OPEC CRISIS AND CONTINENTAL INTEGRATION IN OIL

1972

December
: A National Energy Board report on demand projections for Canadian oil indicated Canada would no longer be able both to satisfy Canadian demands and to export. Till then Canada had been exporting as much as possible.

1973

January
: Energy Minister Donald Macdonald announced that only "surplus" amounts of energy would be made available for export in order to preserve adequate supplies for Canadian needs.

February
: Macdonald announced oil export controls would be imposed in March, the multinationals having refused to guarantee they would meet domestic needs first.

March
: Crude oil export controls were imposed.

June
: Export controls on most petroleum products were instituted.

September
: A special tax of $0.40 per barrel was imposed on oil exports.
: The government announced its intention of extending the interprovincial pipeline to Montreal.

October
: Exports to the U.S. were reduced from 1.2 million to 1.025 million barrels per day.
: An energy supply contingency plan was established in the light of curtailed international production and selective embargoes.

November
: The export tax was increased twice to $1.40, then $1.90 per barrel.

December
: A bill to establish an Energy Supplies Allocation Board was introduced in the House of Commons.
: The prime minister placed before the House of Commons a proposal for a new national oil policy to establish a national market for oil with a single price, to create a national oil company, to extend the oil pipeline to Montreal, and to intensify research on oil sands technology.

TABLE 3-1 (continued)

1974

January   The two-price system was enshrined: Canada would have a controlled price, the U.S. would pay world prices for Canadian oil.

The Oil Import Compensation Program became effective to provide for a single crude oil price across Canada subject only to transportation and quality differences.

March   At a First Ministers' Conference agreement was reached on a price increase from $3.80 to $6.50 a barrel, effective April 1.

Mr. Justice Thomas Berger was appointed by the Government of Canada to report on the terms and conditions for a natural gas pipeline along the Mackenzie River.

November   The minister of energy, mines and resources announced his acceptance of the recommendation of the National Energy Board that exports of oil should be reduced to provide additional protection for Canadian requirements.

---

imports. The goal was called self-sufficiency in the green paper of 1973, rechristened self-reliance in 1976, defined again as self-sufficiency by the Progressive Conservative government in 1979, and then relabelled as energy security by the Liberals in 1980. Whether this meant that every drop of oil consumed in Canada should be produced in Canada was not always clear, but a substantial decrease in vulnerability to supply interruptions from overseas and an accompanying reduction of a huge debit item in the nation's balance of payments were fundamental, bipartisan objectives.

Second was the target of **greater participation by Canadians** in the industry. High levels of foreign ownership had been of little concern to public, politician or bureaucrat in the Sixties. The conventional wisdom of mainstream economists, that the benefits from foreign direct investment far exceeded the possible costs, was then widely accepted. Now a general disillusionment with the elixir of foreign investment set in. One after another, the high costs of foreign ownership alleged earlier by critics of the multinationals were verified. The Shultz Report had already demonstrated that "71% of the dollars

63

which U.S. companies brought into Canada in order to finance their expanded capacity returns to the United States in the same year."[12] In 1978, the Nova Scotia Light and Power Company won its case with Imperial Oil, successfully proving that Imperial had been using the mechanism of transfer pricing to siphon off profits — and so tax yields — from its Canadian entity to its tax-free subsidiary in Bermuda while keeping prices to consumers at higher than world levels.[13] In 1979, Imperial Oil again showed itself to be poorly serving the national interest when Exxon cut back on Canada's allocation of oil shipments from Iran which were diverted elsewhere by the parent firm. As the Bertrand Commission on oil company operations reported in 1981:

> Imperial, throughout most of the post-war period, was forced to take higher priced Venezuelan crude because this gave Exxon larger profit margins than did cheaper Middle Eastern crude. . . . However, the fact that Imperial paid more than arm's-length prices for crude did not protect it from supply instability. At times during the nineteen sixties, Imperial found itself having cargoes of crude arbitrarily diverted from it.[14]

More serious still, the industry as a whole had been seen to be less than reliable as the sole source of honest information about itself. In the early Seventies, when it was still pressing for increased export permits, it forecast future "elephants" would be found in the Mackenzie Delta and the Arctic, and gave the impression that its potential reserves of oil and gas were big enough to fuel North America for hundreds of years. By 1973, when it wanted prices to rise to the then escalating world levels, it claimed that supplies would be in peril unless greater "netbacks" — the industry term for price after transportation costs are deducted — were offered as a stimulus for exploration and development. Gradually, both public and government stopped believing the industry. With no credibility, it lost the political clout it had wielded in pre-crisis years. Its economic magic was also called into question. Far from bringing in foreign capital to develop Canadian energy resources, the multinationals turned out to be exporting more in the form of capital, interest and dividends than they were importing. The industry's net capital *outflow* from 1975 to 1979 was $2.1 billion.[15] In those cases where the oil companies were increasing their capital expenditures in Canada, they were diversifying out of energy, using their mushrooming cash flows to take over other unrelated sectors of the Canadian economy.[16] For every dollar of profit they made, the independent Canadian companies were reinvesting $1.36 in energy development, whereas the foreign-owned were

64

reinvesting just $0.60 of their revenue stream[17] — and this despite the fact that tax incentives were paying them $1.25 of every $1 of development costs.

A growing appreciation of what was wrong with foreign ownership was complemented by a series of government efforts to increase Canadian ownership. The multinationals had themselves insisted that the federal and provincial governments share the risk of such new frontier developments as the Syncrude tar sands plant by joining in as equity partners. Petro-Canada was brought into being as a public oil company in January 1976, assuming the federal government's assets in Syncrude and PanArctic. In August it took over Atlantic Richfield (Canada) and, two years later, Pacific Petroleum.

To accelerate the growth of Petro-Canada, new oil and gas land regulations were proposed in 1976 and implemented in 1977 to govern the leasing of properties for exploration on federal lands outside provincial boundaries. When exploration permits expired, Petro-Canada was given the right to buy a 25 per cent interest where the permit holder's equity was less than 35 per cent Canadian-owned. To scrutinize the equity holdings of permit holders and applicants, and to build up data on the ownership, control and capital movements in the industry, the Petroleum Corporation Monitoring Act was passed in 1977. Through its acquisitions Petro-Canada had become the second-largest natural gas producer and the seventh-largest oil and natural gas liquids producer in the country by the end of the decade. Repeated speeches and policy statements by federal energy ministers confirmed that Canadianization was not a passing fad. In 1976, for instance, Energy Minister Alastair Gillespie indicated to the Independent Petroleum Association of Canada that the emphasis on 25 per cent Canadian participation was intended to achieve a Canadian ownership target in excess of 50 per cent.

The third thrust of Ottawa's developing energy strategy through the Seventies was the assertion of **federal paramountcy** over resources as far as pricing and regulating were concerned. Ottawa was engaging a battle on two fronts. One of the main messages of the prime minister's December 1973 proposal for a new national oil policy, and of the many measures taken in 1973 to set prices, regulate export volumes and levy export taxes, was that Ottawa was going to wrest from the industry the power to control the pace of development in this vital sector of the economy. Increasingly, energy policy in Ottawa had become an integral part of federal macroeconomic policy.

In addition to declaring its right to regulate the industry, Ottawa was also taking on the producing provinces. Each time the price of oil went up, Alberta received more revenue and inflation was further stimulated. Ottawa, which was paying tax incentives to the industry, and only received one-quarter of the provincial share of oil and gas revenues, was losing financially as world prices rose. The federal government needed a greater fiscal return and wanted to regain its ability to manage the economy.[18] Elected as it was by the voters of the non-producing provinces in the industrial heartland of the country, the Liberal government lent a sympathetic ear to the spokespersons for central Canadian industry and consumers. They argued that Canada should exploit its comparative advantage in energy supplies by isolating energy prices from world market levels, thereby cushioning the consumer from excessive inflationary pressure at the expense of the producing provinces and the oil industry, who would otherwise have captured the windfall gains from higher price rises. As equalization of living standards between rich and poor regions of the country had long been a cardinal principle of federal economic policy, Ottawa's acceptance of a single, national price for oil required it to pay for the difference between the cost of overseas oil imported for eastern Canada and the price charged to consumers, a killing burden of $3 billion a year that was reflected in the mounting federal budget deficits through the decade. If the federal government was to make good this shortfall in its income, it had to attain a larger share of the tax revenues produced by future price increases. Reduced to its political essence, the third thrust of Ottawa's energy strategy was a drive to divest Alberta of some of its resource power. The tension between the federal and Alberta governments was not simply a product of partisan policy, but the result of a structural opposition between the central government and a province enjoying a near-monopoly over a strategic resource from which it was determined to extract full value. This was demonstrated in 1979 when the Progressive Conservative government failed, as the Liberal government had failed before it, to reach an agreement with Premier Lougheed on an acceptable schedule of price increases for oil and gas and a division of the resulting increased tax receipts.

Despite the Progressive Conservatives' deep hostility to the growing centralism of the Liberals' energy policies, the ultimate impact of the short-lived Joe Clark government was to commit the country to a still more centralizing direction in energy policy. The new Conservative government's contradictory efforts to "privatize" Petro-Canada in the summer of 1979 only served to increase the Crown corporation's popularity in the public eye as an instrument of federal government policy. Equally important for the future was the Liberals' appointment, in the summer of 1979, of Marc Lalonde as opposition critic for energy in the shadow cabinet. It was during his time in opposition, according to his own account, that Lalonde realized the central role that the petroleum industry could play as the trump card in the federal government's hand.[19] The former minister of federal-provincial relations and future minister of energy, mines and resources came to see in energy a potential to buttress the power of the central government vis-à-vis the growing power of the provinces. Lalonde, who had devoted his political career to combating Quebec separatism and who was remembered as a tough bargainer with the provinces when minister of health and welfare, saw the need for recentralizing economic power in Ottawa after two decades of its attrition.

Related to this thinking was the fourth thrust of government energy policy: extracting **industrial benefits** for Canadian manufacturers in central Canada from the huge megaprojects still to be built. The proper handling of the enormous energy projects whose construction was envisaged for the Eighties could provide a crucial impetus to help reverse the trend of deindustrialization that was threatening the manufacturing sectors of the Canadian economy. Capturing the industrial benefits from the future construction of colossal energy projects was a theme of government thinking already represented in the Gillespie Guidelines, that had set out principles for branch plant behaviour, and the Advisory Committee on Industrial Benefits of 1975.

Although Liberal party strategy during the 1979-80 election campaign, following the defeat of the short-lived Clark government, was to minimize policy pronouncements in order to keep the spotlight of public attention on the alleged iniquities of the Conservative budget, their campaign did give some attention to energy. In a major policy address to the Halifax Board of Trade, Pierre Trudeau promised not simply a price that would be lower than that forecast by the Conservative budget, but a 50 per cent target for Canadian ownership in the energy sector by 1980, an expanded Petro-Canada, and industrial development near energy sources.[20]

In its first Speech from the Throne, the new Liberal government promised a price of oil "based upon Canadian conditions and circumstances, and not upon the vagaries of a turbulent and unpredictable world market"; a petroleum price auditing agency to report to the government on "oil company costs, profits, capital expenditures, and levels of Canadian ownership''; reduced dependence on imported oil "by promoting conservation and by stimulating the production of new domestic energy supplies"; and the expansion of Petro-Canada and amendments to leasing provisions on federal lands to "provide new preferential rights for Petro-Canada and other Canadian companies on federal lands.''[21]

The government had not been silent about its intentions as it went about the business of turning campaign and throne speech promises into legislation. As anyone who had access to the front page of the *Globe and Mail* knew, Marc Lalonde had told an energy seminar sponsored by no less vitally interested a body than the American Stock Exchange, "Canadians must be partners, not just employees, in our future oil and gas industry." Foreign ownership was excessive and not performing adequately: nineteen of the top twenty-five companies producing oil and gas in Canada were more than 50 per cent foreign owned, and had accounted for 75 per cent of Canadian oil and gas sales, but were taking many times more capital out of the country than they were investing in new developments. "If Canadians are to be asked to pay significantly higher oil and gas prices over the next decade, they have a right to demand that they have an opportunity to participate in the resulting expansion of the energy industry.''[22]

To these clear declarations of governmental intent there seems to have been no American reaction. The American energy consultant Edward Wonder reported that the "objectives of the [NEP] came as no surprise, as its basic thrust had been apparent for several months.''[23] The policies contained in the NEP extended policies that had been discussed at length in government documents and had been put into legislation in some form or other over the previous seven years. Rather than presenting a major change of direction, the NEP was a consolidation and dramatic intensification of previous policies which attempted, in the light of a decade's experience, to achieve the four goals of energy security for Canada: greater Canadian entrepreneurial participation, price increases and tax shifts to capture more economic rent for the federal government, and more industrial benefits from the energy megaprojects for Canadian manufacturers. Despite the NEP's predictable character, the Reagan administration reacted as if the Seventies hadn't happened: the NEP was totally unacceptable.

Leaving aside the egregious special pleadings of congressional lobbyists and the exaggerated doom saying of oil company presidents, there were two major dossiers in the case that the new Republican administration developed against the NEP. Its price strategy raised real questions affecting America's *national* interest. Its Canadianization provisions impinged on American *corporate* interests.

Canadianization and U.S. National Interests

Canada's improved competitive position vis-à-vis the U.S. economy was one concern raised by the NEP's proposal to hold oil and gas prices permanently below world levels. As the National Planning Association saw it, artificial prices represented a subsidy that would give Canadian producers in petrochemicals, synthetic textiles and basic plastic products an international cost advantage. Since "these producers appear to be counting confidentially in their plans on having a strong comparative advantage in the costs of their hydrocarbon inputs," the prospect of American competitors raising cries of unfair practices appeared possible.[24] A second alarm produced by the price targets of the NEP derived from the revenue-sharing implications of the federal strategy. The proposed tax changes were aimed at capturing a greater share of the economic rents for the federal government. The federal/provincial/industrial share of the economic rents, which had been 8.8/50.5/40.7 in 1979, was to change to 24/43/33 according to the NEP. The money raised by new taxes would allow the Canadian government to engage in other industrial development activities — a constant concern in Washington which, as we shall see in chapter 5, keeps a watching brief on all rival governments' efforts to stimulate their own economic development. (It is interesting to note that Washington was already pursuing a similar policy on revenue sharing with regard to Alaskan oil: "the Federal government through other taxes was already collecting 36 per cent of the revenues from Alaska's Prudhoe Bay oil field [which is owned by the Alaska state government], leaving only 30 per cent to be collected by the state and 34 per cent netted back to the oil companies."[25])

Blunting the U.S. national-interest criticism of the NEP was an offsetting consequence of chronically lower Canadian prices. The price differential would encourage more drilling in the U.S. by both American and Canadian operators who would, as James Watt, secretary of the interior, told a congressional committee, "benefit the U.S. by shifting Canadian investment resources to the U.S."[26] The increased rate of discoveries of U.S. energy in the immediate future would be the corollary of a slower rate of growth for Canadian energy supplies.

Still, the intellectually strongest ground on which the Americans stood was a position they shared with most energy economists.[27] To maintain Canadian prices for "old" oil below world levels with a ceiling of 85 per cent of world levels (reduced to 75 per cent by the Ottawa-Alberta agreement of September 1, 1981), with the price of natural gas pegged at even lower levels, was fundamentally irresponsible behaviour by an important member of the International Energy Agency. From the point of view of the industrialized nations — for whom the IEA was a counter cartel to reduce the threat of OPEC — such deliberate pegging of domestic prices below world levels would necessarily inhibit conservation and discourage exploration and development in Canada, relative to the rates of conservation and development that would result from the discipline and incentive of world prices. As the only IEA country to subsidize consumer demand, Canada seemed to be taking a free ride. This objection lost its edge as the "new" oil — which tracked the world price with a 90-day lag — steadily rose as a proportion of total production. This was the oil discovered since January 1981, produced from the tar sands, from special or frontier projects, or realized by secondary or tertiary recovery out of "old" oil wells.

To the extent that U.S. national security also required Canada to be independent of imported oil, a price policy that would slow down the reduction of Canadian oil imports and the attainment of self-sufficiency was a bad thing. The prospect of oil imports continuing through the Eighties presaged a longer period of balance of payments difficulties and a weak Canadian dollar. A lower Canadian dollar, in turn, would make Canadian products more competitive with American.[28] This criticism, too, was blunted by Canada's vigorous oil substitution program, which included lower price ceilings for natural gas, subsidies for conversion to gas and electrical furnaces, and subsidies to gas distributors. As a result of these measures and of the economic recession, demand for oil fell an astonishing 6.7 per cent in 1981, which led forecasters to conclude that the trend to increasing oil imports had been reversed.[29] When oil from the Hibernia field starts flowing in the early Nineties, Canada can expect to have achieved self-sufficiency.

The basic thrust of this attack by energy economists was unanswerable — as long as the factor of ownership was ignored. But Canada was not like other energy-producing nations of the IEA in its industrial ownership pattern. Internationally abnormal levels of foreign ownership (74 per cent) and control (81.5 per cent) in the oil and gas industry had serious implications for the distribution of the benefits accruing from price increases.[30] The economists Scarfe and Wilkinson estimate that every dollar increase in the price of a barrel of oil in Canada results in increased payments to foreigners of at least $140 million per year. Although price rises also engender efficiency gains, they estimate that these gains are less than the drains of revenue to foreigners. In other words, the extremely high levels of foreign ownership in petroleum meant that Canadians were actually becoming worse off as a result of price increases.[31] Yet responsible membership of the IEA required a price rise. For Canada to realize the benefits that should accrue from price increases, the NEP would have to reduce the extent of foreign ownership of its oil and gas industry. But if the bulk of the foreign ownership was American, then the U.S. oil firms in Canada would feel the pinch. And if American corporations hurt, it would not take Washington very long to react.

The Crown Interest and U.S. Corporate Interests

Washington's position on the price policy of the NEP attacked the principle of a separate national price, but did not make too much of the actual practice. When it came to the defence of American corporate interests, it was not the principle but the practice that came under attack. For on the abstract point of Canada's aim of Canadianization, few in Washington demurred. A Canadianization goal of 50 per cent was accepted by top level American bureaucrats as a non-negotiable postulate, a broad political objective which made eminent sense in an industry that had such high levels of foreign control, especially when compared with an 18 per cent level of foreign control of the American petroleum industry. Those less knowledgeable about the realities and more vociferous about the iniquities of the NEP saw Canadianization simply as the shutting down of U.S. companies in Canada, with their investment assets being reduced unfairly.

The first point of unfairness, the bone that stuck in the corporate craw, was the stipulation that a 25 per cent carried interest was to be reserved to the Crown in every development right on Canada lands. This meant that Petro-Canada, or some other Crown corporation, would obtain a 25 per cent working interest in any lease prior to the authorization of production in a field on Canada lands. The American objection was not to the idea of the "back-in": to the extent that this provision "applied to new players in the game — they simply must plan accordingly."[32] But the carried interest was "applicable to all existing interests, however acquired."[33] It was the American participants in the Hibernia play, the large, potentially commercial oil find off Newfoundland, who raised a hue and cry over this provision.

Their first complaint was that Canada was discriminating against American capital; but it was quickly pointed out that the carried interest gave the Crown a mandatory one-quarter participation in every operation, Canadian or foreign. Indeed, as Jack Gallagher, chief executive officer of Dome Petroleum, plaintively wrote, "Dome, as the major explorer in the Arctic areas, is being penalized more percentagewise than any other company, including multi-nationals."[34]

If the measure was not discriminatory against American firms, it was certainly retroactive, and it was on this issue that Washington took its stand. "Retroactivity is a major concern to us," wrote Richard Smith, minister in the U.S. embassy in Ottawa. "When rules of the game are changed as radically as this, investors who had played by the previous rules and made significant finds should either be 'grand-fathered' [exempted from the application of the new regulations] or adequately compensated for their holdings which are taken under the new rules."[35] When, to show goodwill in response to U.S. objections, the Canadian government announced on May 14 that it would indeed offer compensation, the State Department scored a minor victory. Although Canada called the money an "ex gratia" payment, the U.S. felt it had forced Canada to concede the validity of its position. Canada had made a tactical error. As soon as the industry had calculated the value of the proposed reimbursement, it renewed its complaints and Washington renewed its pressure. The offer was a pittance; the compensation was inadequate.

Exploration is like a game of roulette, American officials would tell any curious observers with the patience to listen. You have to drill dozens of dry holes before you find producible quantities. All Canada was planning to pay was the equivalent of a quarter of the costs of drilling the wells that could be successfully developed. The compensation, which would only be paid when production actually started, was unrelated to the future value of the assets that had been found. Realists at the White House admitted that there was no way that Canada would pay one-quarter of the future assets represented by the Hibernia find. If, in oilmen's parlance, to be dipped is to be gouged, the American companies claimed that the new back-in idea was going to make them "double-dipped." Petro-Canada had already backed-in for 18.75 per cent of the play in 1978; now with the extra 25 per cent carried interest, it would have 43.75 per cent of the equity. They had, said the oilmen, been "hijacked," "expropriated," "nationalized," "socialized," "confiscated." What the oilmen were saying was quickly reiterated by the business press. What the business press proclaimed became the conventional wisdom of Washington.

Explanations of the rationale for the Canadian position did little to cool the rage of American politicians who had heard that "their" companies had been "kicked in the knee," but they did point out how easy it was for a Canadian-American crisis to result from Canada's pursuing its policies according to its own traditions and legal precedents. What has first to be understood about the difference between Canadian and American practice is that, while U.S. mineral rights are sold at auction, giving developers proprietorial rights, the mineral rights on Canada lands remain the property of the Crown. They are only leased out to those who want to explore on them for set periods, at the end of which the land reverts to the Crown which can establish whatever conditions it feels appropriate. Federal government land policies in the Sixties had been extremely weak. Foreign corporations accumulated massive banks of land with little chance for Canadians to participate in the ventures. After the twelve-year permit period was up, companies had three options. First, they could drop the project. Second, they could "go to lease," which meant giving 50 per cent of the land back to the Crown and, on the remainder, holding a lease valid only for five years unless production had been achieved. Third, they could get a special renewal of the exploration permit on conditions established by the government. In the Seventies, Alastair Gillespie, then minister of energy, had specified that companies having less than 35 per cent Canadian ownership would have to let Petro-Canada purchase up to 25 per cent equity interest as the condition for the renewal of the permit. Faced with a choice upon the expiration of their permit in Hibernia, Gulf and Mobil had opted for the Petro-Canada back-in as the lesser of two evils: had they gone to lease they would have lost the property entirely if, after five more years, they had not brought it to production — a technologically unfeasible prospect at the time. Mobil, the leading company, was not actually anxious to drill and had let Chevron farm into the property, paying for its share of the ownership by financing the drilling costs. Peter Towe, Canada's ambassador in Washington, could well lecture the American Gas Association that the carried interest provision was

> not a radical departure from the pre-NEP regime but a rationalization of a land reversion concept already entrenched in our Canada Lands exploration practices. The Crown share is not confiscatory or retroactive any more than your windfall profits tax or any other royalty or fiscal change which governments make affecting industry revenues.[36]

Though Ottawa's point was that any tax change is retroactive, in that it changes the rules of the game for players who had made their calculations of risk and return on the basis of the previous rules, Washington's position rested on the claim that the carried interest provision was so radical a change that it warranted grandfathering of the current players. Here, too, what seemed radical in Washington appeared mild in Ottawa. The economics of offshore development makes the exploration costs far less burdensome that industry public relations make them appear. Exploration costs, which are heavily subsidized by tax incentives at the rate of 70 cents per dollar for foreign-controlled and 93 cents per dollar for Canadian-owned and -controlled firms, account for but one-tenth of the total costs of bringing the oil to market; development of the finds constitutes the remaining 90 per cent. What is more, the interest taken by other countries' state oil companies is far more dramatic: in Norway, Statoil takes a 50 per cent interest in any block of land it does not already hold, and the British National Oil Company has first claim on a 51 per cent share of oil production and retains control of all joint ventures it enters with foreign-owned firms. As for changing the rules of the game, oil taxes have been raised frequently in the United Kingdom.

On balance it would seem that the American anger at the Canadian action over the back-in was not because it was out of line with international standards. Canada had been "one of the few non-OPEC nations other than the United States that has not moved to exert control through a strong public sector presence and heavy taxation of windfall profits."[37] That the NEP had belatedly moved to bring its rules into line with those in force in such eminently acceptable jurisdictions as Australia, Norway and Great Britain was not considered relevant by U.S. oil companies, who compared Canada's regulations not with those of other jurisdictions but with their own. Taking the same line, the U.S. government was defending the interests of a few of its oil firms whose future cash flow (along with the entrepreneurial risk) had been reduced — though far less than that of the two major Canadian players, Dome and PanArctic. But where Dome and PanArctic had to use what suasion they could as Canadian corporations, Mobil and Chevron had all the considerable weight of the American government to press their case for a better deal.

The back-in issue had the advantage for Washington of immediacy: the firms affected in Hibernia could see directly how their share of anticipated profits was going to be affected. But it also suffered from being somewhat petty: the future profits of some enormously profitable corporations were going to be reduced. Though some oil barons shouted confiscation and nationalization to their congressional cronies, there was no talk of the multinationals' being forced out of the play. Their take would be handsome, not astronomical, when the field was ultimately developed. What irked them most, though they did not admit this, was the prospect of a considerable Canadian governmental presence around their boardroom tables to keep an eye on their operations.

The Canadianization aspect of the NEP involved many separate changes in policy, but the American reaction to all its complexities boiled down to two major positions: Canadianization would harm the interests of American corporations in the oil and gas industry, and Canadianization was a blatant violation of the internationally accepted principle of "national treatment." Although Canadian spokesmen denied that their motivations were anti-American, nationalistic or socialistic — as the U.S. business press had kept intoning — there was little disagreement in Ottawa with the American understanding of the program's objective. It was designed to shift Canadian ownership and control from 30 per cent to 50 per cent in the course of the decade, at a rate of some 2 per cent per year. To do this it would use government regulatory power to discriminate in favour of oil and gas firms with high Canadian ownership ratings.

The American multinationals had not objected in the past, of course, to Canadian pricing and tax policies which had contributed substantially to the foreign-controlled development of Canadian petroleum; nor had they objected to the transfer to foreigners of the economic rent from Canadian resources whose development had been financed very largely by Canadian taxpayers through incentive programs and by Canadian consumers when paying for their fuel and gas. It had long been known that Canada's tax system had discriminated *against* Canadian-controlled firms. The Royal Commission on Canada's Economic Prospects had reported in 1957 that

(a) Canadians are at a disadvantage vis-à-vis the United States operators in the Canadian oil and gas field.
(b) Certain acquisitions and property costs are not allowed as deductions in computing taxable income.
(c) The method of computing depletion allowances is not as favourable in Canada as in the United States and, furthermore, it gives a substantial advantage to the large [mainly American] integrated oil companies as compared with the independent [mainly Canadian] producers.[38]

Canada had implemented a mineral incentives plan to rectify the problem, but the majors had been able to consolidate their dominance.

Finally, the NEP was seriously addressing this problem. The old system of depletion allowances, which favoured large, diversified companies from whose earnings the exploration costs could be deducted, would be phased out. In its place a Petroleum Incentives Program (PIP) had been "structured to encourage investment by Canadian companies and individuals"[39] by making direct payments for exploration. A small company without a cash flow from downstream activity would benefit as much as a giant. The schedule of incentives was weighted to favour exploration less on provincial lands, where the federal government received a smaller share of economic rents, than on Canada lands where the federal government took all the rent. The PIP grants did not exclude foreign developers as some claimed in Washington. All exploration on Canada lands qualified for incentive payments of 25 per cent of approved costs, but a high level of Canadian ownership qualified a company for a much higher PIP grant that reached 80 per cent of costs for a firm with more than a 74 per cent Canadian ownership rating. To counter the allegation persisting in Washington that non-Canadian firms had been sold out, Marc Lalonde insisted that the new regime was still attractive to foreign-controlled multinationals for whom, he claimed, a dollar's worth of exploration cost less in Canada (53 cents on Canada lands) than in the U.S. (67 cents in Texas). "Even with half a loaf," he quoted from Ralph Hedlin, a consultant critical of the NEP, "large profits can still be made by foreign owners in our oil fields."[40] Washington was not mollified by this kind of talk. The NEP presented the worst of all worlds for branch plants: taking away the entitlement to depletion allowances reduced their income stream, lessened their capacity to borrow, depreciated their asset value, and made them more vulnerable to takeover by firms that were getting the major incentive grants.

Other provisions that were not directly discriminatory worked in the same direction. The blended price policy that was designed to encourage exploration also worked against the interests of established multinationals. By setting the price of "old" oil (the production from already discovered wells) below that of "new" oil from wells to be discovered, the NEP was discriminating against the mature (mainly foreign-controlled) firms in favour of the young and potential (Canadian-owned) firms.

What made the multinationals feel under further pressure was the bald requirement that, following exploration, "A minimum of 50 per cent Canadian ownership — private or public sector — will be required for any production from Canada Lands."[41] Furthermore, a new management regime administered by COGLA, the Canada Oil and Gas Lands Administration, would require all companies holding interests on Canada lands to renegotiate exploration agreements. These would return 50 per cent of their lands to the Crown, opening up further possibilities for Canadian enterprise and simultaneously aggravating American feelings of injury. A Canadian Ownership Account, to be financed by special levies on oil and gas consumers, would ensure that the public sector had the muscle it would need to make the contribution expected of it "by acquiring several of the large foreign-owned firms." Although it was Petrofina and Elf Aquitaine, a Belgian and French company respectively, not two American companies, whose acquisition by Petro-Canada and the Canada Development Corporation were the first public sector takeovers to follow the NEP, the feeling persisted in Washington that the NEP was anti-American.

The American response to Canadianization was not to reject 50 per cent as a reasonable goal, but to challenge the means used to achieve that goal as unfair. One could hear all over Washington, and one could read every week in the business press, that American firms were being forced to sell out their holdings at "fire-sale prices," since their asset values had been deliberately driven down. No matter if the actual prices paid for the few firms that did change hands were all, as the Canadian ambassador insisted, substantially above these companies' pre-NEP share prices.[42] Analysts could see that the NEP would "reduce the value of their Canadian holdings making them more willing to part with their assets."[43] No matter if all sales that were made were between willing vendors and willing purchasers. No matter that more Canadian energy capital headed to the American market than to the Canadian. Conoco, which had tried to sell its Canadian interests in Canada before the NEP and had even offered them to Petro-Canada,[44] invoked the whole litany of complaints to drum up congressional sympathy in its fight to resist being taken over by Seagrams. No matter either that the shareholders of Conoco reaped an enormous increase in the value of their holdings as a result of this courtship by the Bronfmans' billions. No matter, indeed, that the process the NEP put into motion started to gather such momentum that the minister of finance had to call in the heads of the major Canadian banks and ask them to cool down the rate at which they were financing the Canadian repatriation of the oil industry. By July 1981, ten Canadian companies had spent $6.6 billion to acquire subsidiaries of foreign petroleum companies. The resulting strain on the current account balance and on the Canadian dollar impelled the government to slow down the speed at which its own policies were working. This was a signal to the multinationals that they were not expected to lay down their shares and capitulate. Canadianization could not absorb too many adherents at once.

It was the complaints of the takeover targets that raised the NEP to such a high public profile in Washington, but it was not the major oil companies who directed the attack on the Canadian government's position. The bulk of the multinationals seem to have accepted the advice to lay low in Canada and leave it to the Canadian independents to try to turn the NEP around. Some branch plants had instructed their American parents not to push Washington to press Canada too vigorously — Canadianization was very popular in Canada so any perceived U.S. bullying could provoke an anti-American reaction that might worsen their already delicate position. As for the attitudes of the multinationals' head offices, they seemed to take the NEP in their stride. They had been expropriated and forced into joint ventures under host control in all the best places in the world; the Canadian approach, by comparison, was moderate. It encouraged them to Canadianize, but did not force them out if they chose not to change.

For the oil giants known as "the Seven Sisters," Canada was a low priority problem in a world in which they were beset with real risks and serious problems. Those who were outraged were the executives of the smaller companies with continental horizons who seemed to regard Alberta as just another state of the union. They wanted their property rights as guaranteed by the Fifth Amendment.[45] Canada was giving them the message that their constitution did not apply in British North America, a message they found hard to accept.

Continuity or Change: An Industry Reclaimed

By the summer of 1982, some fourteen bills to implement the NEP had either been brought into law or were before Parliament. Faced with determined American resistance, both corporate and governmental, the Canadian government's largely successful imposition of its National Energy Program was a considerable achievement. In the summer of 1980 the odds were hardly in favour of such an outcome. The senior levels of the federal bureaucracy did not support the implementation of the energy program on which the Liberals had just been elected. The cabinet was split. The producing provinces were vociferously opposed, Alberta still taking a hard line on energy prices and revenue sharing. The petroleum industry, massively foreign-controlled as it was, could hardly be counted upon as an ally. Eighteen months later, the bureaucracy and cabinet were united and all the producing provinces except Newfoundland had entered into agreements with Ottawa to implement the NEP in their jurisdiction.

A number of different factors account for the survival of the NEP against domestic and American opposition. First, and not least in importance, was the policy-making process which gave the energy program a privileged position in the federal government, protecting it with the shroud of budget secrecy and removing it from the normal process of interdepartmental consultation which can be counted on to eviscerate any proposed program of its new policy initiatives. Even the Department of External Affairs was not informed until the last moment, so that considerations of American interests were not given primacy until after the policy was announced in final form.

Second, what made it difficult for the American government to intervene effectively once the policy was unveiled was the high state of tension that prevailed between Alberta and the federal government for another ten months. The energy question was in a state of continuing antagonism that was just as fundamental in Canadian politics as the concurrent federal-provincial battle over the amendment of the constitution. Just as the powerful multinational oil companies had been rendered politically impotent in the crisis atmosphere of 1973-74, when oil became a highly politicized issue in the light of OPEC's price escalation and supply cuts, so too the powerful American government found itself unable to get a purchase on the Canadian situation while Edmonton and Ottawa were engaged in a prolonged battle. The multinationals had left the lobbying to the Canadian independents. The State Department, too, had trusted that Canadian business pressure would turn the NEP around. But they had trusted in vain. And what both found hard to swallow was the great popularity of the NEP. "Canadianization" became a watchword of hope for the public which, in a Gallup poll, was found to be in solid support of the NEP's 50 per cent target by 1990 and in favour of a more accelerated process — 64 per cent of those surveyed favoured a 75 per cent Canadian ownership level by 1985.[46] Once the popularity of the NEP became clear, while that of the industry declined, the cabinet dug in. The energy minister's stubbornness was supported by his colleagues who realized that every U.S. threat of retaliation only served to produce more public support for Ottawa's tough policy stand.

Ottawa did give way on some points. In May 1981 it offered compensation for the back-in and amended the industrial benefits legislation to ensure competitive conditions for foreign suppliers. In July it asked the banks to help slow down the rate of takeovers. In February 1982 it dropped plans to give Canadian-controlled firms preference in gas exports. In April Marc Lalonde announced he would not proceed to give Canadian oil companies the power to force out their foreign shareholders.[47] But on the main thrust of the NEP, Ottawa had held firm.

Time worked against the American position. Once industry had realized that the NEP could not be gutted, companies started to adjust their corporate planning in the context of the new regulatory structure. In the first six months of 1981 the industry's domestic capital spending rose 20.4 per cent. In the same period, large domestic oil and gas companies increased their capital spending in Canada by 41 per cent, smaller Canadian firms increased theirs by 84 per cent, while large foreign-controlled companies cut back their spending by 17 per cent.[48] By September 1, 1981, when the Alberta and federal governments signed their agreement on price levels, revenue sharing and administrative responsibilities for the incentive programs, the petroleum industry had accepted the reality of the NEP as Canada's policy instrument even before it had gained passage through Parliament. Business continued to complain that it had been squeezed too hard. But, in the main, the oil companies had responded to the new stimuli by shifting more resources towards frontier exploration[49] and by working out arrangements to qualify for the incentives that favoured Canadian-owned operations.

> "We'll try as best we can to adapt to the Canadianization aspects of the National Energy Program," Imperial's chairman, Donald McIver, said in an interview. He cited exploration farm-outs to Canadian companies and joint venture arrangements with Canadian companies as increasingly useful for Imperial.[50]

When in October 1981 Suncor sold 25 per cent of its shares to the Ontario government, its parent, Sun Co., let it be known in Washington that it was satisfied with the deal. No angry speeches were made denouncing the onslaught of socialism on America's northern border. The NEP was working, and Washington had had grudgingly to adjust to its reality. William Brock's official letter demanding that the guts of the NEP be eviscerated (see chapter 2) had come too late. Washington continued to press for changes such as a "sunset" provision that would terminate the PIP grants once the target of 50 per cent Canadian ownership and control was reached, but Ottawa was barely worrying any more about American complaints.

This does not mean that the NEP's progress was by any means triumphal; but the main blow it received in its first tempestuous years came from an international, not a continental, direction. The dramatic fall in the world price of oil in 1982 was a change that invalidated the financial assumptions on which the pricing and tax levels of the NEP and the subsequent Alberta-Ottawa pact of September 1981 were based. The lower than anticipated netbacks actually received by the private sector forced both Alberta and Ottawa to lighten the tax loads and increase the incentives for the petroleum industry. The anticipated federal revenue for the five-year period 1981-86 fell by $25 billion to $36 billion, leaving the national government with 22 per cent of the oil and gas revenues compared with 32 per cent for the provinces and 46 per cent for industry.[51] Lowered projections of future oil prices caused abandonments, postponements or delays in the megaprojects on which policy makers had pinned their hopes. As a result, the coming on stream of Arctic and East Coast oil, the further extraction of synthetic fuel from the tar sands, and the ultimate achievement of self-sufficiency in petroleum may be delayed until the Nineties.

The more difficulty the NEP ran into, the fiercer became its critics and the greater was the pressure exerted on the government to abandon its basic principles. Such opponents of nationalist policies as the economist Donald Daly argued that the benefits were limited to a small group of civil servants, but that the costs of Canadianization were substantial, especially at a time when Canada suffered from a serious deficit in its current account and had to transfer output abroad to pay for the buy-back of previous foreign owners.[52] The lobby organization for Canada's largest corporations, the Business Council on National Issues, still pleaded to government "that the rigidity of the National Energy Program be eased, that the Canadianization rules be relaxed, that curbs on foreign-owned companies be softened."[53]

Such pressure might force further watering down of the NEP, but it was unlikely to alter the fundamental features of what was the most dramatic change to have emerged from the crisis of 1981 — the first major effort by a Canadian government to restructure a crucial foreign-controlled industry. Participation by Canadian capital in the most dynamic and potentially profitable sector of the economy had been opened up, and Canadian business had shown by its rush to take over or enter farm-in ventures with foreign multinationals that it was willing to profit from the new incentive program. During the NEP's first eighteen months, Canadian ownership of the industry had risen 6.7 per cent to 34.7 per cent, while Canadian control leaped 10.8

percentage points to 33.1 per cent.[54] At the same time, the formerly cash-rich multinationals appeared to have reversed their trend to take over other industrial sectors of the Canadian economy. Finding its cash flow squeezed, Shell Canada Ltd. decided to sell off its non-petroleum businesses acquired during the previous period of diversification into Canadian high technology industries.[55] The dual role of the Canadian state as regulator and as entrepreneur had increased dramatically. It cannot be argued that the NEP had isolated the petroleum sector from the continental economy. Indeed, the enormous investment by Canadian companies in American oil and gas plays had increased Canada's integration continentally. It can be concluded that government had taken over control of oil and gas development from the industry. While the bases for a large increase in government intervention were laid in the Seventies, the National Energy Program remained the most significant factor in this important shift affecting the power relationship within one sector of the two economies. Canada had established a powerful precedent that, when it judged an industry to be of strategic importance, it could intervene to reorient its development to serve what it viewed to be the national interest. The U.S. had signalled by its acquiescence that, press though it would on behalf of its corporations, it would give way to a Canadian government determined to pursue what it believed to be a reasonable and necessary course of action. Canada had re-established the right to interfere in its own affairs.

FIRA and Ottawa's Industrial Strategy Options

4

Throughout 1981 the Canadian government successfully withstood intense U.S. pressure to abandon the National Energy Program. The Liberals stood firm on their energy policy, citing the promises they had made during the 1980 election campaign and reiterated in the 1980 Speech from the Throne. In the same election campaign and the same throne speech, the same party had made similar commitments to expand the powers of the Foreign Investment Review Agency so that it could attack the problems associated with the poor performance of foreign-controlled corporations in other sectors of the economy. FIRA would review the functioning of established foreign-controlled industries and publicize foreign takeover applications, thus enabling Canadian firms to make counteroffers using government loans to bolster their bids. Instead of keeping these promises, the government backed down under strong U.S. pressure and shelved the whole program to strengthen the thrust of its foreign investment policy. In addition, Ottawa gave private assurances to the U.S., followed by a public declaration to Parliament, that the NEP was not a model that would be applied to other foreign-dominated industries in Canada in its promised industrial strategy. As a consequence of these two retreats, the Canadian government was left with an economic development paper so reliant on the forces of the imperfect Canadian marketplace and so accepting of the existing nature of the branch plant economy that it was warmly welcomed by the Reagan administration.

FIRA and the NEP were intimately linked in the U.S. attack on Canada's interventionist policies in 1981. That Canada had won on an energy issue while the U.S. prevailed on a foreign investment question says much about the priorities and capabilities of each government in their continuing interaction. Ottawa deemed the NEP to be crucial to its immediate economic and political goal to reassert its paramountcy over the provincial governments, whereas Washington had difficulty making a convincing case that Canadianization was a mortal threat to its own continental energy goals. When it came to investment policy, American politicians had a very clear bipartisan notion of their mission to clear the world's markets of obstacles to the free international flows of (American) capital, whereas the Canadian body politic was far from convinced in its own mind of the wisdom of expanding, let alone maintaining, the controversial process of foreign investment screening. Given this lack of a Canadian consensus, it may appear surprising that, in renouncing its proposal to broaden the scope of foreign investment review, Ottawa did not accede to U.S. demands for a de-fanging of the existing FIRA.

The Unnecessary Target

Observing the Canadian-American crisis of 1981 in which FIRA figured so prominently, one must ask to what extent any Canadian attempts to increase the returns and reduce the costs of foreign direct investment in the economy would make confrontation with the American government unavoidable. Because of the high levels of American ownership in key industries of the economy, almost any policies designed to affect the performance of Canadian branch plants would impinge on American interests. Would Canadian efforts to improve the functioning of the Canadian economy that had adverse effects on individual American firms provoke U.S. retaliation? Official American reaction would presumably depend not just on the extent of the alleged injury but on the validity of the Canadian case. There is no question that American experts on Canadian policy were well aware of a series of government reports recommending that measures be taken to restore to the Canadian economy some of the advantages of which foreign direct investment had deprived it.

In 1957, the Gordon Report sounded a gentle warning that high levels of foreign direct investment, with the resulting dominance of key resource and high technology industries, might not be in the best economic or political interest of Canada.[1] In 1968, the Watkins Report marshalled more data to demonstrate the inefficiencies of the "miniature replica effect" of branch plant operations which reduced competition by establishing oligopolies in the Canadian market. Prevented by American anti-trust law from merging into large, rationalized operations, branch plant manufacturers produced too many models in too small quantities to reach optimum efficiency.[2] Because the transactions taking place between units within the multinational corporation were private, the Canadian public could not easily find out whether it was being deprived of its fair share of taxable company profits by such well-known practices as transfer pricing, excessive charges levied by the head office for technology and managerial services, or abnormal imports from the home economy of items that might otherwise be supplied by Canadian companies that would have serviced the branch plant had it been an independent company. The Watkins Report recommended that data be collected to identify the dimensions of these problems. It also called for state intervention to establish Crown corporations that would become sources of venture capital for new enterprise and would act as state trading agents to facilitate international trade from which branch plants were precluded by market restrictions. The Wahn Report of 1970 reiterated this analysis but advocated a simple, yet dramatic, 51 per cent ownership target throughout Canadian industry to deal with the problem.[3]

Two years later the Gray Report consolidated the evidence, sharpened the analysis, and reformulated the policy recommendations for dealing with the mushrooming problems posed by the foreign-controlled sectors of the economy. The multinational organization institutionalized trade distortion through head office control over branch plant sourcing and by excluding branch plants from exporting into world markets. Because of their satellitic nature, branch plants were necessarily "truncated" operations, deprived of the R & D brains and manufacturing sinews of an integrated corporation, and left only with the functions of assembly and sales. Establishing key sectors such as rail and air transport or broadcasting and publishing where foreign ownership could not exceed specified low levels was an inadequate solution to the problem. Buying back majority control was a vain formula for buying more trouble. What the Gray Report recommended was a screening mechanism that, in the context of an overall industrial strategy, would allow the government to monitor the performance of the foreign-controlled sectors of the economy. It would press them to increase the benefits they yielded to Canada and negotiate with prospective new investors in order to improve the returns to Canada of the new investments they were proposing.[4]

While it is true that efforts to reduce the costs to Canada would likely reduce the benefits to the U.S. from the same foreign investment, it does not follow that such attempts would necessarily rouse the eagle from its roost. In the past, the Canadian government had taken quite dramatic steps that had adversely affected the acquired interests of certain American shareholders. In response to the

Broadcasting Act of 1968, the Canadian Radio-Television Commission had directed a reverse takeover of the broadcasting industry — a retroactive divestiture of American investments of long standing. On occasion, the sale of individual Canadian businesses in the uranium and petroleum industries to foreign interests had been prohibited. The creation of the Foreign Investment Review Agency in 1973 to determine that all foreign-controlled takeovers and (from 1975) the expansion of existing branch plants into new fields were of "significant benefit" to Canada, did not constitute a basic change in Canadian policy: the federal government had previously performed this kind of function on an ad hoc basis. FIRA was not the powerful institution proposed by the Gray Report to harness foreign investment to the national weal, because it was not linked to an overarching economic strategy. Rather, it was "intended to be a minimal response to political pressures for enhanced regulation of foreign investment . . . and the resulting process can best be explained as reflecting an exercise in symbolic politics."[5] As a symbol, it indicated that the government had moved in response to pressures from the nationalist side of the political spectrum. As a permanent government agency, it provided "a continuing, routinized, and pre-emptive mechanism to replace the earlier pattern of occasional government interventions that were more prone to generate conflict in relations with the United States because of their sporadic and *ex post facto* nature."[6] Under the guidance of some of its more anti-nationalist ministers — in particular Don Jamieson, Jean Chrétien and Jack Horner — it even became an agency to solicit rather than screen new foreign direct investment.

That FIRA had managed to reduce the level of conflict with the United States over investment questions could be seen from official American responses to it:

> I am pleased to be able to say that in the nearly two years that Phase I of FIRA has been in operation we have found no evidence that the Act is being used to discriminate among foreign investors to the detriment of U.S.A. firms. . . . We hope and believe that this evenhandedness in the administration of FIRA will continue (Deputy Assistant Secretary of State Richard Vine, January 1976).[7]

> L'Agence d'examen des investissements étrangers est une excellente chose. Elle clarifie les règles du jeu. Plusieurs hommes d'affaires se sont dit heureux de collaborer avec cet organisme. Jusqu'à maintenant nous n'avons pas à nous plaindre (Assistant Secretary of State Julius Katz, March 1978).[8]

> It was feared that FIRA might act as a barrier to new incoming investment in Canada. But rather it has applied its mandate — to assure

benefit to Canada in investment proposals. Its current approval rate of 90% is an indication of the quality of proposals it receives. I can understand how Canada relying as heavily as it does on outside investment feels the need for having such a mechanism to insure that its interests are identified and met (U.S. Ambassador Thomas Enders, May 1979).[9]

That FIRA was an unnecessary target for American-Canadian confrontation was the accepted view of American observers as the Seventies drew to a close: "U.S. official reaction has been more moderate than in the case of restrictions imposed by other countries on foreign investment, in part because the actions of the board established under the Act appear to be fair, even-handed, and non-discriminatory. Relative to recent treatment of U.S. direct investment by many other countries concerned about foreign ownership, Canadian behavior has to date been exemplary from a U.S. government viewpoint."[10]

What turned FIRA from a mouse to a monster in the eyes of Washington? Certainly it was no act taken by the Canadian government, since no change was made in the Foreign Investment Review Act. What moved FIRA from close to the bottom to second from the top of the United States government's list of grievances against Canada was the new vocabulary of Liberal politics in Canada in 1980 and the uproar in Washington about Canadian takeover bids in 1981. While discussions about strengthening FIRA's capacity to extract greater benefits from existing foreign direct investment in Canada had been going on in the opposition Liberal caucus during the fall of 1979, and while the issue was raised in the platform committee during the preparations for the 1979-80 election campaign, the first that the public heard about the renewed Liberal faith in FIRA was from the lips of the opposition leader himself on the campaign trail. "We want to expand and strengthen FIRA, not weaken it," Pierre Trudeau declared to the Toronto Ad and Sales Club at a luncheon speech in the Royal York Hotel on February 13.

> FIRA's mandate will be broadened to include the periodic review of all foreign firms of large size to assess the performance of these companies in such areas as export promotion and research and development.
> FIRA will also be required to publicize proposed foreign takeovers beyond a certain size once they have been submitted to the agency. This will encourage counteroffers from Canadian-controlled interests. More importantly, through government guarantees of bank loans, FIRA will help provide financial assistance to Canadian companies that want to compete for foreign takeovers or repatriate foreign ownership of assets.[11]

There was understandable scepticism about how genuine was Trudeau's commitment to a more nationalist shift in his party's direction. The main focus of his career as an intellectual had been to fight the notion of nationalism as a political movement, and the political impact of his anti-nationalism had been seen in the reluctance of his government from 1968 to 1979 to take more than symbolic steps along the road recommended by nationalist critics. Such doubts were confounded shortly after the election when the government revealed in the Speech from the Throne its intention that

> the Foreign Investment Review Act will be amended to provide for performance reviews of how large foreign firms are meeting the test of bringing substantial benefits to Canada. As well, amendments will be introduced to ensure that major acquisition proposals by foreign companies will be publicized prior to a government decision on their acceptability. The Government will assist Canadian companies wishing to repatriate assets or to bid for ownership or control of companies subject to takeover offers by non-Canadians.[12]

The appointment of Herb Gray to the Department of Industry, Trade and Commerce emitted a second signal that Trudeau had meant what he had said. Gray had been the minister responsible for the research and writing of the report on foreign investment that bore his name. Though demoted in 1974 from cabinet to the back benches, he had often attacked FIRA for its inadequacies compared to the comprehensive screening mechanism his report had recommended. As opposition critic he had helped develop his ideas into part of the party's platform. Now as minister with a direct mandate from his leader, reiterated by the Governor General in Parliament, he would surely have his chance to put words into action. His words certainly indicated that intent. In speech after speech throughout 1980 and 1981 Gray elaborated on his theme.

> The new government wants to expand the opportunities for independent Canadian-owned enterprise, especially in high-growth areas like advanced technology (Canadian Advanced Technology Association, April 1980).[13]

> [The government's commitment is] to ensuring that foreign-owned companies operate in accordance with Canadian industrial goals (Empire Club of Canada, April 1980).[14]

> If our industrial strategy is to be truly meaningful . . . the policy must address the very prominent foreign presence in our economy and the major effects that the presence has had and can in the future have for

efficiency, growth and the directions of industrial development in Canada (École des Hautes Études Commerciales, June 1980).[15]

The federal government is an active player in industrial development, not just a passive bystander. Our whole approach to national economic development is *activist* (Association of Canadian Financial Corporations, June 1980).[16]

The new measures are not intended to frustrate or unfairly burden the many foreign firms that are currently acting as good corporate citizens and contributing to the growth and development of the Canadian economy. They are directed at improving the performance of the Canadian economy (Canadian/Japan Businessmen's Conference, August 1980).[17]

We are examining the means available to the government to affect and improve the performance of, in particular, multinational firms in areas such as increased R and D, improved management, world product mandates, etc. (Niagara Institute, May 1981).[18]

There is no question that Herb Gray was taking pains to wave his red flag at the multinational bull. What was in question was whether he was equipped with a matador's sword. As the months passed, the promises (or threats) still did not materialize in the form of legislative action. The 1980 budget unveiled the National Energy Program, but neither a general industrial strategy nor legislation to strengthen FIRA. By the time that the alarms started sounding in Washington over the Canadian takeover of American industry, the Foreign Investment Review Agency was still the same institution that Americans had found so uncontroversial since the mid-Seventies. The Canadian government's failure to implement its undertakings might have indicated that FIRA was more likely to remain quiescent than emerge as a born-again monster. Having been an example of symbolic politics — dealing with only a small part of the expansion of foreign direct investment in Canada — FIRA had been turned by the rhetoric of the previous year into a symbol of the Canadian government's new attitude to foreign direct investment.[19] Since no comprehensive industrial strategy had been articulated, what the government had said in its throne speech and what the responsible minister had been saying from the podium had been understandably interpreted by Washington as the NEP-like path of economic development that the Liberal government wished to follow.

The American administration had responded immediately, though quietly, to the introduction of the NEP in October 1980. When the uproar over a series of Canadian takeover bids for medium-sized American corporations began to blow up a political storm in Washington, the lobbyists complained, as we have seen, that the NEP had unfairly been reducing the value of their branch plants' assets in Canada. The second string to their bow was the assertion that, in combination with the NEP, FIRA's review process prevented them from making retaliatory takeover bids against the unfriendly Canadian suitors. All of a sudden, Washington discovered a new FIRA, one that did indeed challenge the principles of American capitalism. It was much more than a paper tiger, and its powers were about to be strengthened by Herb Gray's much touted new armoury. In the space of a few weeks, the unnecessary target had become the major butt on which the Americans were drawing a bead. Although their alarm was about the as yet unborn son of FIRA, it was at the existing FIRA that they took aim.

The American Campaign
Washington's assault on FIRA in 1981 may seem inconsistent with its previous approval, but it did have a real basis in American political thinking. Throughout the Seventies there had been growing anxiety about the poor performance of the American economy — the decline in its productivity and the collapse of some industries in the face of competition by imports flooding in from Japan and the newly industrialized countries. This worry about U.S. trade was linked directly in the minds of policy makers with worry about international investment questions. American-controlled multinational corporations were establishing plants in countries like Mexico and Korea to exploit their lower labour costs and export the product back into the American market. It no longer appeared to be true that U.S. investment abroad automatically increased American exports; it increased U.S. imports at the same time. There was not only a concern voiced by the trade union leadership that American investment abroad was costing the U.S. jobs. Since the OPEC crisis of 1973 a new fear had arisen, that foreigners — especially the Arabs — were going to take over key sectors of the American economy. Specialists started to recommend that the United States should shift the whole thrust of its policy on both the investment abroad of U.S. capital and the inward investment in the United States of foreign capital. Hitherto, according to Fred Bergsten, an American expert on investment and trade policy,

> U.S. policy toward foreign direct investment had been simple, successful and supportive of U.S. interests: maintenance of open

markets to international investment in the United States by firms of other countries, and of open markets abroad for foreign investment by U.S. firms.[20]

U.S. political rhetoric assumed, along with traditional economic theory, that such investment responds to market forces and so increases global welfare, both that of the home and of the host country. Actual American policy had broken with free-market theory long since. Anti-trust legislation, anti-dumping laws, U.S. Trade and Buy America acts, special industry protection, all bespoke the reality that the free market was a mistress of dubious charms to American business. In the Sixties, Washington started imposing guidelines, first voluntary then mandatory, on its multinational corporations' activities abroad in order to increase their contribution to the American balance of payments in trade and capital.

Host countries had also recognized the doubtful relevance of traditional theory. They became active on the international investment scene, simultaneously wheedling and squeezing foreign investors to enter and adapt to their economies' needs. They offered incentives and subsidies to attract foreign corporations. In return, they required undertakings of performance to ensure they received value for their support. The resulting bargaining process produced ''an alliance of mutual advantage between the firms and the governments of host countries — with possible detriment to important economic interests of the home countries (notably the United States).''[21] Performance requirements of host countries who insist that most of a product be sourced in the host economy amount, Bergsten argued, to the functional equivalent of a very low import quota — a trade barrier that would otherwise be outlawed under the rules of GATT. Subsidies that are given in exchange for commitments to export a certain proportion of output similarly contravene the spirit of the world community's international trading agreements. ''In short, some of the basic elements of the international trading rules are being increasingly undermined by these host country investment policies.''[22]

U.S. government advisers expressed considerable frustration at the international community's unwillingness to heed American concerns. ''We have preached to the choir at the OECD, at Economic Summit meetings, in the GATT, and in the World Bank,'' said Gary Hufbauer, a former Treasury official. ''Unfortunately, the choir only pretends to listen.''[23] What was needed was a ''GATT for Investment,'' but as long as the United States was not able to impose tangible costs on its trading partners who deviated from the principles of free capital markets, the U.S. would get nowhere. In the context of this growing exasperation with its economic partners, Canada was announcing it intended to expand its foreign investment review agency's hitherto narrow jurisdiction. By 1980, U.S. foreign investment in Canada amounted to $45 billion or 21 per cent of total U.S. foreign direct investment abroad.[24] That the whole range of these assets might come under pressure enraged those in Washington who wanted to launch a new drive to liberalize world investment policy.

Once FIRA became the target of official American concern, its previously accepted features turned out to be intolerable. Quite apart from the American objection to the proposed expansion of FIRA's capacities, a three-pronged attack on the existing FIRA developed. It was claimed that first, FIRA would discourage investment; second, it imposed unfair requirements on potential investors; and third, it exerted extra-territorial jurisdiction over the actions of foreign corporations.

The "Investment Problem" and the American Double Standard

The most straightforward objection made by the American government (in harmony with what Canadian businessmen had long been saying) was that "the very existence of FIRA undoubtedly discourages many would-be investors."[25] FIRA was an obstacle to the free flow of international investment capital. The Canadian government did not take this "investment problem" very seriously, since all major industrialized countries have some mechanism for screening, licensing or controlling foreign direct investment. (Australia is the only other state to have established such an open and visible institution with the review of inward foreign investment as its sole function.) But the international prevalence of screening mechanisms did not prevent Reagan's ministers, as we have already seen, from demanding that changes be made in the way FIRA was administered. Echoing the complaints of businessmen and their lawyers, William Brock's letter of December 4, 1981 had demanded that action be taken to shorten the length of time it took FIRA to come to a decision on applications, to raise the threshold of assets that triggered a FIRA review thus allowing more takeovers of small businesses to take place without investigation, and to publish clear guidelines establishing the criteria FIRA used in its determination of whether an application promised "significant benefit" to Canada.

It was one thing for Canada's continental neighbour to advocate changes in the detail of an administrative mechanism: requests for apparently picayune alterations in laws or regulations, changes that can have very significant effects on their neighbour's interests, are the stuff of intergovernmental relations between Ottawa and Washington. It was quite another thing for the United States to be demanding that the Canadian kettle be polished to a high shine when its own pot was so flagrantly blackened. Although it is true that the United States has no formal agency like FIRA with which to screen inward investment flows, it is not true, as the U.S. claims when posturing in international bodies like the OECD, that the U.S. economy offers untrammelled access for foreign direct investment. Foreign investment doubled in the United States between 1972 and 1979, and statutes limiting the freedom of foreign direct investment in certain fields have proliferated. According to Gary Hufbauer, there has been a "slow but visible U.S. movement towards more interventionist policies" in the control of foreign investment.[26] The nine-volume government report, *Foreign Direct Investment in the U.S.*, published by the Department of Commerce in 1976, has documented the "number of U.S. restrictions which prohibit direct investment by nonresident aliens in enterprises engaged" in a long list of industries that have been declared off-limits to foreign investors.[27]

Foreign investment in the U.S. is directly controlled in the "national interest" sectors of the economy through prohibition, prohibition waived by reciprocity, limitations on stock ownership, or limitations on management participation. These national interest sectors include the maritime industries of shipping, shipbuilding and fishing; aviation, including air carriers; communications, including telegraph carriers, radio and television transmission and Comsat, the Communications Satellite Corporation; energy and natural resources (atomic energy, hydroelectric, gas and electricity utilities, mineral leasing, offshore oil and gas exploration); banking, including direct entry, indirect entry, acquisition of control over existing domestic banks, and international banking; private investment corporations and customs house brokerages; and defence where companies with as little as 6 per cent voting stock ownership or control by foreign interests are deemed to be under foreign ownership, control or influence, and thus ineligible for security clearance and access to military contracts. Emergency provisions of the Export Administration Act of 1969 and the International Emergency Economic Powers Act (formerly the notorious Trading with the Enemy Act) give the president wide powers to control the exports and property of foreign investors during times deemed critical to the U.S. Indirect control over foreign investment is further exercised by securities laws and regulations, which confront potential foreign investors with tremendous expenses of converting their financial reporting systems to conform with American requirements. Retroactive amendments to the Securities Exchange Act of 1934 have been introduced to block or reduce the rate of foreign takeovers of U.S. firms.

Most relevant to American complaints about administrative delays with FIRA are the administrative and judicial obstacles that U.S. anti-trust legislation puts in the way of takeovers. Under the Clayton Act, a foreign purchase or merger with an American firm is subject to anti-trust scrutiny lest the new venture lessens competition or creates a monopoly.[28] As a FIRA document remarked,

> it is important to note that Canadian investors doing business in the United States are at times harassed and frustrated by the highly legalistic nature of the U.S. regulatory system in which foreign takeover bids have been subjected to costly litigation and delays with respect to U.S. security, anti-trust, and state takeover laws. Congressional political pressures complicate this process further. In addition, the appearance of alternative U.S. buyers in the guise of "white-knights" should also be clearly noted.[29]

While the U.S. government has been pushing its trading partners to eliminate barriers to foreign investment, it has been moving at home in the direction of establishing screening mechanisms. Data-gathering legislation has put in place a number of activities which leave the American government poised to take more direct action:

- The Foreign Investment Study Act of 1974
- The International Investment Survey Act of 1976
- The Domestic and Foreign Investment Improved Disclosure Act of 1977
- The International Banking Act of 1978
- The Agricultural Foreign Investment Disclosure Act of 1978
- The Committee on Foreign Investment in the United States (established in 1975 to coordinate U.S. policy on inward investment)[30]

The Canadian government was not entirely mute in making these points. As Canadian ambassador to the United States, Peter Towe called attention to U.S. restrictions on foreign investment in occasional speeches. Allan Gotlieb, while still under-secretary of state for external affairs, raised the question of the American double standard with Treasury Secretary Donald Regan during the tense top-level meeting of October 13, 1981, but without apparent effect. Regan professed ignorance of the Canadian complaint and promised to look into it. A failure to acknowledge the economic nationalism of their own system generally has characterized the informed elite who deal with Canada — the officials, the editorial writers, the politicians. These key players have seemed unaware that at the level of the individual states there are further obstacles to foreign investment in energy and natural resources, railroads, securities regulations, banking and insurance, as well as actual statutes designed to delay takeovers. Table 4-1, drawn from a compendium compiled by Raymond Waldmann, later assistant secretary for international economic policy in the U.S. Department of Commerce, illustrates how widespread are state-level limitations on foreign investment.

Had the Canadian government been able to establish the Canadian objection to American restrictions on investment policy as a major countervailing factor in the 1981 confrontation, it might not have needed to absorb so much pressure to change its own practices, particularly when the real nuts-and-bolts issue for the Americans was FIRA's capacity to make American firms allow Canadian suppliers to compete for their branch plants' business. The question of "performance requirements" threatened American export interests, but the U.S. government raised the issue to the level of principle as an infringement of international investment morality.

Performance Requirements and "National Treatment"

The most serious of the three American charges was the alleged trade distortion effect of the undertakings that prospective investors made with FIRA in return for the approval of their proposals. These performance requirements, in the words of Robert Hormats, assistant secretary of state for economic and business affairs, took "the form of market-distorting Canadian sourcing requirements, export commitments, requirements to hire specified levels of Canadian management and labor, obligations to transfer patents and know-how to Canada without charge, and other commitments which run counter to generally accepted international practices."[31] The American attack was well grounded to the extent that FIRA negotiates with foreign investors to improve the package of benefits that every proposed venture yields the Canadian economy. Whether such commitments *distort* trade depends on what is considered normal in trading patterns. The Americans define the norm as the long-standing situation in which Canadian-

TABLE 4-1
U.S. STATE LIMITATIONS ON FOREIGN INVESTMENT

State	Land ownership & use	Corporations	Agriculture	Banking	Energy & fossil fuels	Commercial fishing & maritime	Insurance	Mining	Utilities
Alabama		•		•			•		•
Alaska		•		•		•	•	•	•
Arizona		•	•	•			•		•
Arkansas		•		•			•		•
California		•	•	•	•	•	•	•	•
Colorado		•		•			•		•
Connecticut	•	•		•		•	•		•
Delaware		•		•		•	•		•
D.C.	•	•		•			•		•
Florida	•	•		•		•	•		•
Georgia	•	•		•		•	•		•
Hawaii	•	•		•		•	•		•
Idaho		•		•			•		•
Illinois	•	•		•			•		•
Indiana	•	•		•		•	•		•
Iowa	•	•	•	•		•	•		
Kansas	•	•	•	•			•		
Kentucky	•	•		•			•		•
Louisiana				•			•		
Maine		•		•		•	•		•
Maryland		•		•		•	•		•
Massachusetts		•		•		•	•		
Michigan		•		•		•	•		
Minnesota	•	•	•	•		•	•		•
Mississippi	•	•		•			•		•

96

Missouri

Montana

Nebraska

Nevada

New Hampshire

New Jersey

New Mexico

New York

North Carolina

North Dakota

Ohio

Oklahoma

Oregon

Pennsylvania

Rhode Island

South Carolina

South Dakota

Tennessee

Texas

Utah

Vermont

Virginia

Washington

West Virginia

Wisconsin

Wyoming

Source: Raymond J. Waldmann, *Direct Investment and Development in the U.S.: A Guide to Incentive Programs, Laws and Restrictions, 1980-1981* (Washington, D.C.: Transnational Investments, 1980).

American trade largely flows between the subsidiaries and parents of multinational corporations: in recent years 56 per cent of Canadian exports to the U.S. flowed between entities of multinationals.[32] The market distortions caused by such non-arm's-length transactions have not been thoroughly documented by researchers, although a 1981 statistical investigation by Statistics Canada demonstrated that the propensity to import of foreign-controlled enterprises was almost four times as great as that of domestic companies.

> Even after excluding the largely foreign-controlled automotive sector, which had an exceptionally high propensity of almost 60 per cent due to the rationalization triggered by the Auto Pact, the remaining foreign manufacturers' import propensities were still more than double that for similar Canadian-controlled firms.[33]

These data confirm the suspicion that import-export transactions within multinational corporations are themselves distortions of what would occur in a market economy not dominated by foreign-controlled branch plants. American policy to encourage U.S. direct investment abroad is justified by the knowledge that trade advantages derive from equity control of foreign subsidiaries. Harvey Bale, assistant U.S. trade representative for investment policy, argued on July 8, 1981 before a U.S. Senate committee hearing:

> We believe that U.S. foreign direct investment has also made a contribution to employment in the United States through the link between exports and investment. Much of our trade with foreign countries originates with orders placed by the subsidiaries of U.S. companies located overseas. For example 75 per cent of our exports to the 300 largest companies in Canada originates from the subsidiaries of U.S. firms.

If the multinational corporations impose distortions on Canadian trade, then the actions of FIRA to secure performance commitments from new foreign investors can be seen as a means for overcoming artificial barriers imposed by head offices on subsidiaries and allowing greater efficiency through more rational use of existing national resources of labour and capital. As a FIRA document argues, the test of significant benefit to Canada "has been the elimination of artificial constraints resulting from foreign control and linkages so that, as far as is reasonably possible, the foreign-controlled enterprise will be free to behave as if it were Canadian-controlled."[34] What the Americans objected to was "the ability of FIRA to commit investors to maintain specific employment levels, to increase the level of investment or the export percentage of total sales [which] might well have adverse effects for U.S. interests."[35] In other words, to the extent that FIRA was successful in increasing the benefits Canada would derive from its foreign investment, the United States would cry foul. In crying foul, the U.S. made an appeal to the principles underlying accepted international agreements.

On the level of principle, the Americans argued that performance requirements violated Canada's OECD commitments requiring that foreign investors be given "national treatment" which was defined as "treatment under their laws, regulations and administrative practices consistent with international law and no less favourable than that accorded in like situations to domestic enterprises."[36] The OECD Declaration on International Investment and Multinational Enterprises specifically stated, however, "that this Declaration does not deal with the right of Member countries to regulate the *entry* of foreign investment or the *conditions of establishment* of foreign enterprises."[37] Since FIRA screened entry of new investment and the conditions of setting up foreign-controlled firms, the American case against the existing FIRA on the principle of national treatment appeared to be weak in theory.

When Canada's diplomatic actions at the OECD are considered, the American case became weaker still. As a condition of Canadian acceptance of the OECD Declaration, the then secretary of state for external affairs, Allan MacEachen, made a formal interpretative statement in which he noted the unparallelled level of foreign ownership and control in Canada, the existence of legislation such as FIRA "to ensure that foreign-owned corporations in Canada are responsive to Canadian domestic goals and priorities," and the government's intention to "continue its efforts to strengthen Canadian enterprises and to seek significant benefit to the Canadian economy from foreign investment."[38] When the OECD Declaration was reaffirmed three years later, on June 13, 1979, Flora MacDonald, the Conservatives' secretary of state for external affairs, reiterated that Canada's "right to take measures affecting foreign investors which it considers to be necessary in its particular circumstances" was the condition for Canada's reaffirmation of its acceptance of the declaration.[39] As Paul Heinbecker, a Canadian diplomat who participated in the negotiations of the declaration, reported

> I worked at the OECD for four years and I can say with confidence that interpretative statements both are taken seriously and are quite challengeable if they entail interpretations unacceptable to others. No

99

one, in fact, challenged the interpretation, in part at least because they considered it better to have Canada partly in than entirely out. They also were prepared to acknowledge that the circumstances prevailing in Canada, i.e. the degree of foreign ownership, were exceptional.[40]

When the State Department seized on the issue of national treatment to press its case against the discriminatory measures created by the NEP to achieve Canadianization of the petroleum industry, Canada pointed to the interpretative statements of 1976 and 1979. OECD decisions on national treatment support the Canadian view that the declaration "merely requires that Canada offer consultations on policies that derogate from the rule, not that Canada is bound to revoke existing nonconforming policies or to forego future policies with the same effect," as the United States maintains.[41]

Extra-Territoriality

The third American complaint was on a different point of principle, extra-territoriality. As the secretary of commerce and the United States trade representative wrote to Herb Gray,

> Company C, a non-Canadian company, purchased a U.S. company with a minor branch (six employees) in Canada. FIRA required "Canadian benefits" although no increase in foreign ownership had occurred. . . . [This is] typical of numerous other cases where Canada extends its jurisdiction beyond its borders. Although no increase in foreign ownership has taken place, FIRA has sought concessions from U.S. firms.[42]

Reviewing indirect takeovers, the purchase of a foreign-owned company operating in Canada by some other foreign company, had been part of FIRA's function from the beginning without raising American hackles. Now this was seen as Canada claiming a right to intervene in corporate mergers in the United States when an incidental effect of such a transaction was to change the parent of a firm in Canada. As a result, "even when there is no change in the activities, size, or any other aspect of the Canadian entity, FIRA asserts the right to review again the investment in Canada and perhaps seek new performance requirements, or even disallow it."[43]

What had brought the charge of extra-territoriality to the surface of Washington's consciousness was the legal case fought by Dow Jones against FIRA's decision to disallow Dow Jones's merger with Richard D. Irwin, Inc. to include its subsidiary, Irwin Dorsey Limited of Georgetown, Ontario, a small publishing house. Twice the cabinet disallowed the acquisition of Irwin Dorsey by Dow Jones. Dow Jones formally contested the jurisdiction of FIRA on the grounds that it was making an extra-territorial application of its powers. The government argued that the Foreign Investment Review Act was being applied only to the acquisition of the Canadian business, not to the American business of Richard D. Irwin, Inc. The trial division of the Federal Court of Canada ruled on June 10, 1980 in the government's favour. Dow Jones appealed the case, but the Federal Court of Appeals ruled against it. Nothing daunted, Dow Jones made representations to the Supreme Court to hear its case, but the court refused.[44] (That Dow Jones is also the proprietor of the *Wall Street Journal* is of note, given the virulent hostility expressed in the editorial pages of the *Journal* to FIRA and the NEP.)

In response to the U.S. government's charge that FIRA was acting extra-territorially in indirect takeovers, Herb Gray justified the practice by affirming that, without it, "a very large part indeed of the Canadian economy would be excluded from the scope of the Act, and the ability of Canadians to gain and maintain effective control over their economic environment would be greatly diminished."[45] He could have argued that reviewing indirect takeovers is not extra-territoriality at all because FIRA does not try to block the principal transaction taking place abroad. FIRA's decision about Renault's takeover of the Canadian subsidiary of American Motors has not prevented Renault's merger with American Motors in the United States. In contrast, when Campeau tried to take over Royal Trustco in 1981, the Federal Reserve Board threatened Campeau's bankers, who had branches in the U.S., with criminal sanctions because Royal Trustco had four branches in Florida. In an example both of U.S. control over foreign investment and of U.S. extra-territorial interference in Canadian investment affairs, the Federal Reserve wanted the principal merger transaction in Canada to be nullified even though it was taking place outside the United States.

Washington's challenge to Ottawa on the grounds of extra-territoriality was another example of the American double standard at work. As such it offered Canada an opportunity to put back on the bilateral agenda a major Canadian grievance that had lurked unresolved for decades. One of Canada's constant complaints in the Fifties and Sixties was the impact of such American laws as the Trading with the Enemy Act, which prevented Canadian subsidiaries of American companies from filling orders they received from countries like China with which the United States at that time refused to trade. In the administration of anti-trust legislation, American courts had frequently attempted to order Canadian branch plants to supply documents and data as if they were American nationals.[46]

In response to the agitation roused in Canada by such episodes, the official report of Ambassadors Merchant and Heeney in 1965 recommended that the American government restrict itself in its attempt to control the activities of American-controlled multinational corporations abroad.[47] The recommendation was made in vain. Although some understandings were achieved between the Canadian minister of justice and his counterpart (the Fulton-Rogers agreement of 1959 and the Basford-Mitchell agreement of 1969) concerning improved consultations between the two capitals, Washington did not withdraw from its position. The U.S. insisted it did have the right to direct the actions of foreign branch plants of U.S. companies. Although the United States has become more sensitive to Canadian concerns,[48] it put in place a series of guidelines and requirements in the Sixties that harnessed the branch plants of its multinational corporations to the greater cause of its balance of payments policy. The Canadian government has meanwhile moved to establish countervailing legislation which forbids Canadian companies from implementing foreign court rulings that would reduce competition in Canada.

As Canada has built up its defences against American extra-territoriality, the United States has extended its claimed jurisdiction over the international operations of its multinational corporations. American government officials preface their comments by claims of respect for Canadian sovereignty: "Both countries are entitled to make whatever laws they choose governing the behavior of companies within their jurisdiction."[49] But, on the grounds that both countries also "claim a legitimate interest in activities in the other which have effects in their own country," American officials have had no qualms about insisting that FIRA's teeth be pulled. While protesting that it accepted the principle of FIRA and respected Canada's sovereign right to legislate conditions for foreign investors, the United States in fact was challenging that right and claiming the power to demand changes in Canadian legislation. In neither protesting the principle of this action nor extending the agenda to the general issue of extra-territoriality, Ottawa lost an important chance to beat back Washington's branch plant diplomacy. Preferring to "let sleeping dogs lie," it let Washington press the case that the application of the Foreign Investment Review Act to indirect transfers was an improper exercise of Canadian sovereignty. Until such time as the United States renounces jurisdiction over the behaviour abroad of branch plants of

102

"its" multinational corporations, the issue of extra-territoriality will remain as a thorn in the side of the Canadian-American relationship.

From Bilateral Attack to Multilateral Adjudication

Even though the American case against FIRA did not turn out to be solidly grounded under any of its three rubrics, the administration was under strong domestic pressure to take action. It was not only the *Wall Street Journal* that expressed the unhappiness of American business. LICIT, the Labor-Industry Coalition for International Trade, had led the denunciations of trade distortion resulting from performance requirements imposed on American corporations. BIAC, the USA-Business and Industry Advisory Committee, had voiced strong opposition to Canadian investment policies at the OECD and sent letters to U.S. government leaders denouncing both FIRA and the NEP.[50] But Congress, the most important barometer of U.S. corporate reaction to Canadian investment policies, had become the main platform for criticism of Canada since the NEP was unveiled. Numerous hearings in 1981 addressed the impact of FIRA on U.S. companies and considered specific legislative proposals for retaliation. One bill, HR-1294, would require that foreign borrowers who used foreign banks to finance the purchase of U.S. equities be subject to the same 50 per cent margin requirements as were imposed on U.S. investors. Another, HR-4186, would amend the Mineral Lands Leasing Act of 1920 by placing a moratorium on foreign acquisitions for nine months as a way to retaliate against the NEP and FIRA.[51]

Although the administration found support against Ottawa in the congressional anger at Canada, it was caught in a dilemma. If the proposed congressional initiatives were passed, they would contradict the U.S. government's formal support for the free flow of international investment capital. Furthermore, any moves that would constrain the movement of Canadian capital into the U.S. economy would be contrary to the American desire to maximize investment in the U.S. Worse, these restrictions would please the Canadian government which would be delighted to have Canadian capital stay in Canada and contribute to the achievement of the NEP's goals. The administration, in Gary Hufbauer's judgment, "wanted to be seen as taking a strong stand against the Canadian moves," but could not "develop a suitable form of retaliation that would change the course of Canadian investment policy while remaining consistent with its non-interference philosophy."[52] The low level of Canadian direct investment in the U.S. economy — 0.45 per cent of non-financial institutions — gave

Canada a degree of immunity against U.S. retaliation on investment policy questions. This did not stop U.S. government spokesmen from pressing their campaign against the objectionable aspects of FIRA's practice. David Macdonald, the deputy U.S. trade representative, told a joint committee hearing of Congress on October 21, 1981 that the United States was seeking a "complete elimination" of performance requirements exacted by FIRA. The U.S. government was also pressing that FIRA "permit all takeovers that do not increase total foreign-owned assets," exempting indirect takeovers from its purview.[53]

After the 1981 confrontation had reached its climax with the Brock letter of December 4 and the Gotlieb response which indicated that the Canadian government would make no further major changes either in the NEP or in the existing FIRA, the Reagan administration abandoned its strategy of direct pressure and shifted its case to the international arena. On January 5, 1982 the U.S. requested consultations with Canada regarding FIRA under article 22 of the General Agreement on Tariffs and Trade. Following inconclusive consultations, the U.S. requested the Council of GATT to create a panel to examine FIRA and rule on whether its trade-related performance requirements were in violation of international trade rules. This move of the conflict from the bilateral to the multilateral arena appeared to signal a victory for Canada in its defence of the existing FIRA against American attack. In multilateral institutions such as the Council of GATT the onus is on the United States to convince its trading partners that more rigorous rules should be adopted. With so many other countries imposing performance requirements on foreign direct investors, it seemed unlikely that the GATT panel would rule against Canada — as Canada's advance agreement to abide by the ruling indicated. Despite sustained and severe American pressure that was supported by strong criticism of FIRA from business, provincial, legal and academic circles within Canada, Ottawa maintained FIRA intact. As it turned out, it was less important that the United States had failed to find an adequate retaliatory or international lever with which to press the Canadian government to gut the existing FIRA. More significant for long-term developments was Washington's success in forcing Ottawa to renege on its commitment to expand FIRA's powers as part of a new industrial strategy.

Continuity or Change: Economic Strategy

When the long-promised government document on industrial strategy was released with the budget on November 12, 1981, one paragraph referred to an undertaking in the previous throne speech to expand the Foreign Investment Review Act. "For the time being," read this new statement delphically, "no legislative action is intended on these measures until progress on the major initiatives already undertaken by the government has been assessed."[54] What these major initiatives might be was not stated. What was put into black and white — in response, as we saw in chapter 2 to strong American demands — was the commitment not just that FIRA would not be expanded to monitor established foreign-controlled industries, but that the NEP would not be a model for the Canadianization of other sectors of the economy:

> The special measures being employed to achieve more Canadian ownership and control of the oil and gas industry are not, in the Government of Canada's view, appropriate for other sectors.[55]

The American attacks throughout 1981 may have failed to force Canada to eliminate the energy and foreign investment programs that it had already drafted and implemented, but they succeeded in stopping dead in their tracks the plans that Ottawa was formulating to develop a comprehensive industrial strategy into which the new NEP and an expanded FIRA might fit.

American observers understandably had taken at face value Herb Gray's description in June 1980 of the industrial strategy that was being assembled under his leadership:

> To capitalize on Canada's energy base in order to build a world competitive industrial sector; to ensure that the Federal Government is an active player in industrial development rather than just passive referee; to strengthen Canada's research and technological capacity; to encourage independent Canadian enterprise; and, to expand Canadian control of the economy while increasing the benefits for Canadians from foreign investment already here.[56]

Seventeen months later the government's budget document, *Economic Development for Canada in the 1980s*, revealed that the NEP was to be the exception, not the rule. "Economic development" had significantly replaced "industrial strategy" as the key phrase. Interventionism had been abandoned and the forces of the market had been officially rehabilitated as the appropriate invisible hand to guide Canada's economic destiny. The theme of increasing Canadian control was replaced by the notion that more foreign investment was needed. Platitudes were offered up — "the management of change in the 1980s is of crucial importance to secure Canada's future prosperity" — but the choices between industrial and sectoral priorities which had to be made in such management were glossed over. When explained in private by the civil servants who had drafted the document, its rationale was revealed to be based on a faith that the market mechanism would develop Canadian staple resources in response to world demands. Canadian manufacturing would somehow manage to restructure itself after the implementation of the Tokyo Round's tariff reductions had cut away the economy's remaining protection from international competition. Support for industrial winners in advanced technology and high productivity services would come third in the government's priorities after resource development and resource-based manufacturing activity. Because the terms of trade had shifted in favour of resources and away from the traditional manufacturing areas, the government now appeared willing to let the former swim and the latter sink, wthout paying much attention to the consequences beyond providing a safety net for the shipwrecked.

It was clear at a glance that the nationalist school within the federal cabinet and bureaucracy had been routed. These were the advocates of an integrated set of complementary measures that would lay out a set of strategic objectives and attempt to orchestrate the various players — federal and provincial, domestic and foreign-controlled enterprise — to achieve the long-term goals. These included increased productivity in selected high technology sectors, a rationalized industrial structure freed from the market restraints imposed on branch plants, in short a capacity to exploit the domestic market demand for key products so as to export effectively into foreign markets. The victors were the free-market apostles, who had long dominated the main economic ministry, the Department of Finance, who staffed the policy-advising Economic Council of Canada, and who controlled the Ministry of State for Economic Development with strong support in cabinet. They viewed positively the decline of tariff protection and pinned their hopes on achieving free trade with the U.S. in order to gain access to the American mass market. Federal policy activity, according to the anti-nationalist school, was best left to making adjustments of the economic framework and to offering subsidies to cushion the effect of industrial adjustments in low-productivity, losing sectors.[57] The anti-nationalists had gained the ascendancy in the debate on industrial policy during the summer of 1981 when Ottawa had panicked about the threat of American retaliation. Supporting them intellectually was the community of economists who accepted the relevance to Canada of their free-market paradigms. Supporting them politically were the trade associations of big business (Business Council on National Issues), Canadian and American industry (Canadian Manufacturers' Association), and small and medium business (Canadian Federation of Independent Business), who were all opposed to the interventionism of the NEP and the regulation of FIRA.

Assessing the outcome of the clash over the NEP and FIRA in the context of the Canadian-American relationship, it would appear that Canada had won on the short-term issues of retaining the thrust of the NEP and the existing FIRA, while the United States had won on the long-term question of which direction Canadian economic policy would take. Washington had successfully diverted Ottawa away from "earlier indications that the discriminatory approach [the NEP] exemplifies might be used more broadly,"[58] as Richard Smith, chargé d'affaires at the U.S. embassy during the difficult first half of 1981, put it. While Smith might well have felt satisfied with the effect of his country's pressure, he could not rest easy, since the NEP harboured an embryonic industrial strategy which, if successfully pursued, would necessarily threaten U.S. interests.

Industrial Benefits from Megaprojects

The Canadian-American contention over the pricing and Canadianization aspects of the NEP had basically centred on ownership and how the economic rents from Canada's oil and gas would be distributed. Washington was no less concerned about a third dimension of Canada's energy policy which dealt with how the industrial benefits from energy projects would be distributed. Canadianization explicitly discriminated in favour of Canadian-owned and -controlled firms. When the U.S. government protested at this departure from the principle of "national treatment," Canada stuck to its guns, arguing that the energy situation was a unique case requiring special measures and that all energy-producing countries — including the United States of America — discriminated in favour of their own companies. On the important question of maximizing the industrial benefits to be gained from the large energy developments that were planned for the coming decades, the Canadian government was forced to back down from a policy of giving preferences in favour of Canadian firms to one aiming at equality in the treatment of national and foreign suppliers.

As in the area of tax incentives, Canadian policy on industrial benefits had developed haltingly, coming to grips reluctantly with the problem of reverse discrimination caused by the high level of foreign ownership in the economy. The tendency of a foreign engineering firm, when brought in to design a large project, is to conceive a plant whose specifications require machinery built in the design firm's home economy. This naturally engenders contracts for procurement of the needed supplies from home-economy suppliers with whom the design firm has had long-standing relations. No conspiratorial view of the multinational corporation is necessary to see how a vicious circle is created which denies to host-economy companies a fair chance to bid successfully for a share of the contracting. There is a long and convincing list of industrial development projects which have yielded far fewer benefits to the Canadian economy than the multiplier theory would have predicted because of the trade diversion effects of foreign control in project design, engineering and consulting. For Syncrude, the big tar sands plant, the American firm Bechtel was made the prime contractor and proceeded to conduct 43 per cent of all project engineering and administration — 8 per cent of total project costs — outside Canada.[59] Similarly, in offshore and frontier hydrocarbon exploration projects, 50 per cent of the equipment and materials being used were sourced outside Canada. Even in conventional areas Herb Gray claimed Canadian industry was getting short shrift: 100 per cent of engineering services for refining and processing conventional oil were being purchased abroad.[60]

Government policy had been slow to develop in this area. In 1966 the then minister of trade and commerce circulated to foreign branch plants a list of "guiding principles" of good corporate behaviour defining what good citizenship meant for foreign-owned firms. Included among these completely voluntary guidelines was the adjuration "in matters of procurement to search out and develop economic sources of supply in Canada."[61] At the same time, an Advisory Committee on Industrial Benefits was formed to monitor and encourage Canadian sourcing by all firms engaged in the development of major projects. The committee's work had some impact on the tar sands development. Partially as a result of its presence, Syncrude could claim that of the $1.9 billion invested, 80 per cent was sourced in Canada, though the loose definition of Canadian content (any supplier having an office in Canada) cast some doubt on such data.[62] In preparation for another major project, guidelines for applications to build a northern pipeline were proposed by the Departments of Energy, Mines and Resources and of Indian and Northern Affairs in 1970. They raised the question of Canadian content. The Northern Pipeline Act of 1978 included provisions to ensure that Canadian companies had a fair chance to bid for contracts in the supply and construction of the Alaska natural gas pipeline.

By the end of the decade these megaprojects had become a prime focus of government attention. Private-sector critics of government inaction over an industrial strategy noted that the megaprojects of over $100 million in size planned for the Eighties would require investments of some $120 billion, generating some $67 billion in opportunities for manufacturers, $48 billion of which could realistically be sourced through Canadian firms, given an appropriate industrial strategy.[63] At a time when the manufacturing sectors of the Canadian economy were suffering from a process of deindustrialization, the industrial benefits that could potentially accrue from the megaprojects represented a flare burning in an otherwise darkened tunnel. Since the bulk of the megaprojects would be in the energy sector, the Speech from the Throne of the newly returned Liberal government declared that

> Canada's resource base will be used as the basic building block of a vigorous industrial policy. A paramount objective of my Ministers is to develop economic policies that will provide jobs, spur growth, improve regional balance, and promote Canadian ownership and control of the economy.[64]

Spin-offs from megaprojects in the energy sector had become the government's industrial strategy in embryo.

Fourteen months later, in June 1981, a report was published by the Major Projects Task Force, a bipartite group of eighty senior business and labour representatives set up in 1978 under the co-chairmanship of Robert Blair, president of NOVA, an Alberta corporation, and Shirley Carr, executive vice-president of the Canadian Labour Congress. The Blair-Carr task force reported that out of $1 trillion that would probably be spent on capital investment by the year 2000, some $440 billion would be invested in megaprojects, 90 per cent of which would be for energy production and distribution and hydrocarbon processing. These projects, as Table 4-2 indicates, were well enough distributed both regionally and industrially to produce significant benefits throughout the economy if certain policies were adopted to maximize Canadian participation in all phases of the projects. The task force noted that participation of foreign-owned corporations in key areas of the projects was likely to result in fewer benefits to Canada than would be the case with substantial Canadian involvement in the same areas, and recommended that Canadian-owned firms should be chosen to play

TABLE 4-2
SUMMARY OF INVENTORY OF MAJOR PROJECTS TO THE YEAR 2000
($ millions)

Sector	% of Total Expen.	Total	Multi-Prov. or Undetermined	Atlantic	PQ	Ont	Man	Sask	Alta	BC	Yukon/NWT
Conventional hydro-carbon exploration & development	17.8	78,150	2,500	11,500					700	250	63,200
Heavy oil development	9.7	42,735						1,750	40,985	890	2,475
Pipelines	7.2	31,640	27,090	1,185							
Processing & petrochemicals	6.5	28,505		500	3,100	985		1,300	12,205	10,415	
Electrical gen. & trans.	45.3	198,855	620	29,870	66,335	38,435	10,375	3,160	20,250	29,710	100
Forest products	1.8	7,710		310	1,210	1,665			1,200	3,325	
Mining	4.5	19,935		1,010		4,100	500	3,965	3,230	5,625	1,505
Primary metals prod.	1.4	6,235		1,025	1,300	1,410	500			2,000	
Transportation	1.4	6,355		420	2,315	450			955	1,885	330
Manufacturing	3.1	13,380	8,575	400	175	4,080			150		
Defence	1.2	5,105	4,825	280							
Total		438,605	43,610	46,500	74,435	51,125	11,375	10,175	79,675	54,100	67,610
% of Total Expenditures			9.9	10.6	17.0	11.7	2.6	2.3	18.2	12.3	15.4

Source: *Major Canadian Projects, Major Canadian Opportunities: A Report by the Consultative Task Force on Industrial and Regional Benefits from Major Canadian Projects* (Ottawa: Industry, Trade and Commerce Canada, June 1981), p. 27.

key roles in future Canadian megaprojects.[65] Procurement policies should be established, it said, for management, engineering, procurement and construction, so that Canadian industrial and regional benefits from these projects would be maximized.

In August 1981, the federal government responded with the establishment of a system to administer the industrial benefits provisions of Bill C-48, the Canada Oil and Gas Act. An Office of Industrial and Regional Benefits (OIRB) was to be created within the Department of Industry, Trade and Commerce. Its terms of reference were a list of industrial benefits objectives and a set of guidelines for sponsors of major projects, aimed at improving the access for Canadian manufacturers and service companies to opportunities generated by projects within the Canadian market.

From the American perspective, this extension of the NEP into industrial spin-offs threatened U.S. corporate interests far beyond the oil and gas industry. Just as they claimed that Canadianization violated the principle of "national treatment," so did the industrial benefits thrust of the OIRB threaten to undermine the principles of free trade endorsed by GATT. The original wording of Bill C-48's industrial benefits provisions had been modelled on the parallel British legislation. British procedure had required operators to sign a memorandum of understanding that outlined their requirements, all purchases for which had to be reported to the Offshores Supplies Office which could report available opportunities to British manufacturers. British content in North Sea activities had increased through this method from 30 to 78 per cent. With this experience in mind, Bill C-48 required that exploration and development permits would both require the submission, for approval by the minister, of a plan for the employment of Canadians and for providing Canadian manufacturers, consultants, contractors and service companies with a chance to participate in the supply of goods and services. The U.S. administration responded extremely forcefully, claiming that the omission of the word "competitive" from the text indicated that the government was implicitly introducing a protectionist device to favour Canadian over foreign suppliers and so violate its commitments under GATT to allow free international competition. Under intense American pressure, Canada backed down. Canadian officials assured their American counterparts that the omission of the word "competitive" had been inadvertent and that all the government wanted was a chance for Canadian companies to have fair access to the megaprojects. As an earnest of their protestations, Bill C-48 was amended to read that

111

Canadian companies should have "a full and fair opportunity to participate *on a competitive basis* in the supply of goods and services used in that work program."[66]

The Americans were barely mollified. As the researchers for the National Planning Association saw it, the new bonanza of mega-projects was a zero-sum game: if Canada increased the opportunities for Canadian firms, this would ipso facto reduce the prospects for American competitors:

> Requirements that exploration and development projects on Canada Lands make maximum use of Canadian sources of equipment and services, coupled with a similar requirement imposed by Alberta, will create substantial opportunities for Canadian oil and gas machinery manufacturers and construction firms *but only at the expense of their U.S. counterparts.*[67]

Those guarding American interests had reason to worry. They had, first of all, a privileged position in the Canadian market that did not give Canadian competitors fair access; even a correction of this situation would necessarily affect U.S. trade opportunities. Establishing a fair competitive position for Canadian suppliers was one thing. Giving them preference was another. The Blair-Carr task force had recommended that Canadian tenders be given a 3 per cent preference. Although this recommendation had not been adopted by the government in establishing the Office of Industrial and Regional Benefits, the U.S. remained suspicious that protectionist ends were to be achieved by administrative means.

> We are anxious to assure that bureaucratic pressures and reporting and justification requirements do not in fact result in giving an unfair advantage to domestic over imported products. . . . [T]his is a serious matter, in which international undertakings such as GATT commitments and negotiated tariff concessions are at stake.[68]

Having won the point of principle, the American administration was determined to monitor the practice very carefully and be ready to react at the drop of an accusation by an American bidder alleging any discrimination in favour of a Canadian supplier. Knowing from the practice of their own customs officials how the administration of regulations can be used to hamstring foreign competitors of American business, the American officials remained on their guard lest the OIRB block U.S. suppliers with bureaucratic impediments.

With the disavowal of the NEP as a model for other industrial sectors, the retreat from the proposed expansion of FIRA to review foreign-dominated industries, and the otherwise laissez-faire approach of the November 1981 budget's economic development paper, the OIRB's mandate to improve the industrial spin-offs from major resource projects, which had appeared to be an industrial strategy in embryo, ended up as the government's industrial strategy by default. Even this partial strategy was in jeopardy by 1982. With the fall in the world price of oil and the rise in the cost of money, major energy projects such as the Alaska gas pipeline and the Alsands synthetic fuel plant had been delayed, while others such as the Trans-Quebec and Maritimes Pipeline had required massive government funding to keep in business. When energy prices climb to the point that these major projects are again viable, the question remains whether American trade policies will allow Canada to implement its industrial benefits plans. The serious impact of American trade ideology and practice on other aspects of Canada's economic development policies is a subject we turn to in chapter 5.

U.S. Trade Policy and Canadian Economic Prospects 5

With four days left in the 1980 election campaign, the leaders of both opposition parties singled out the distress of Ontario's automobile industry as the motif for the climax of their campaign. Ed Broadbent told his New Democratic Party followers that Canada needed a government that was willing to talk tough to the Americans in order to get a share of the $3.2 billion that would be invested in the auto industry, and of the 27,000 new jobs that this capital would generate by 1985.[1] In his last policy statement of the campaign, Pierre Trudeau promised that, if elected the following Monday, his government would initiate formal consultations with the American government to reduce the $3.1 billion deficit in the auto trade, expand duty-remission arrangements with foreign car companies, create an automobile investment division in the Department of Industry, Trade and Commerce, and negotiate with the Canadian subsidiaries of the Big Four automakers to increase their sourcing, their investment and their research in Canada.[2] Broadbent and Trudeau were voicing two perennial concerns of the Canadian industrial heartland: first, that Canada was getting a raw deal from the Auto Pact, which had been acclaimed at its signing in 1965 as a major step towards continental free trade, and second, that the government could do something about this inequity by putting pressure on the American government. From the safety of the opposition benches, Broadbent could continue after the election to decry the raw deal and demand action. Back in office, Trudeau's government could certainly come to grips with the dimensions of the crisis but would have considerably greater difficulty in achieving significant results.

The Auto Pact can be seen as an early case of the Canadian government extracting performance commitments from the subsidiaries of foreign corporations — the pact was signed a decade before FIRA was created. The Auto Pact was also a symbol for a broader question: could Canada achieve its industrial development objectives in the shadow of the United States' overwhelming dominance? We have seen how strongly the U.S. government objected to the proposed plans in the National Energy Program that Canadian contracting, engineering and manufacturing suppliers get fair access to their own market for the industrial benefits that the energy megaprojects would generate. Measures such as the NEP's procurement rules and FIRA's performance requirements, which were designed to compensate for the market-distorting restrictions imposed on the Canadian economy by its branch plants' dependence on U.S. parent companies, had been strongly attacked by Washington as violations of the internationally accepted GATT rules for the world economy, rules which the United States had been instrumental in drafting and dictating for the world following the Second World War. Washington's exploitation of its power over American multinationals in such matters as trading-with-the-enemy constraints, balance of payments guidelines, and anti-trust prosecutions had taught Canada that the nationality of its branch plants' parents did indeed affect their performance. Now Canada was taking steps to correct for the discrepancies between the textbook theories about how foreign capital performs under conditions of perfect competition and the casebook examples of how corporations from a dominant economy actually operate in a peripheral economy. But in attempting to define what was in its own economic interests — as opposed to what was in the interests of the resource-extracting and manufactures-distributing multinationals — Canada was running up against the power of the American state, one of whose functions is to defend those corporate interests abroad. In the NEP it came up against the interests of the U.S. energy corporations. The NEP and FIRA had, in addition, contravened American international investment objectives.

Both the energy and the investment controversies raised the most crucial issue of all for American international economic strategy — trade. Canadian sourcing of megaprojects would reduce American exports; performance requirements on new foreign direct investment might increase American imports. And trade was, in the final analysis, what mattered most to American politicians. American responses to the NEP, FIRA and the Auto Pact caused problems for Canadian energy and foreign investment policy makers. But more important still for Canada was the problem of trade. Whatever economic strategy Canada chose — whether market-directed and resource-project based, or interventionist and high-technology based — exporting into the American market was crucial to its success. Would the protectionist defences and offensive weapons of the United States' trade policy allow Canada to achieve its economic development aims? Trade policy lay at the heart of the new economic strategy that had evolved as a bipartisan consensus within the American political machine through the Seventies. This trade policy was a major block threatening the pursuit of Canada's possible economic options.

Canada in the Face of American Protectionism

American economic nationalism has long set the context and defined the limits within which Canada could operate. The abrogation by Washington of free trade with Canada in 1866 helped push the northern colonies to negotiate the terms of political and economic union enshrined in the British North America Act. Washington's refusal to renew free trade a decade later pushed John A. Macdonald towards the National Policy of 1879. Canadians in the twentieth century have tended to blame Republican administrations for the worst excesses of U.S. economic nationalism such as the Smoot-Hawley tariff of 1930, but, reflecting on trends before the Second World War, Harold Innis could see that "Canada will become increasingly dependent on the United States and the problem will become more, rather than less acute." Already American "monetary and tariff policies are largely the monetary and tariff policies of the North American continent, including Canada." The major problem he identified was the emergence of "governmental control on a large scale in the United States."[3]

Large-scale government control in the U.S. had evolved during the postwar decades as American politicians tried to manage the tension between supporting successful corporations' penetration of the international trading system and protecting declining sectors against foreign competition. By the Seventies, Washington had to encourage much of its productive capacity to adjust so as to maximize its comparative advantage in high technology industries. At the same time, it had to cope with the U.S. economy's loss of comparative advantage to the newly industrialized economies in many traditional industries, while responding to the pleas for help of its surviving labour- (and vote-) intensive sectors.[4] The American economy, which had previously been considered "closed" — so independent was it of international trade — was now becoming much more open as it interacted with the world trading community. In the decade of the Seventies, its international commerce had doubled as a share of its gross national product to 12 per cent. But at the time that its imports of

116

traditional manufactured goods were escalating, the U.S. was finding that a new generation of trade barriers was being placed in the way of its exports of the post-industrial products, such as information services, in which its comparative advantage now lay. Increasingly, American politicians became sensitive to their constituents' concern about the impact that imports from other countries with lower labour costs or higher government subsidy programs had on local enterprise. In response to demands for stronger defences against foreign competitors, Congress took major strides towards protectionism in the Seventies, at the same time as U.S. administrations were unabashedly pressing their commercial partners to liberalize their trade restrictions. In the 1974 Trade Act and the 1979 Trade Agreements Act, Congress refined the arsenal of weapons to be used against foreign products that were subject to progressively lower tariffs as a result of multilateral trade negotiations (MTN) at GATT over the years. American tariffs against processed raw materials and manufactured goods have been a traditional obstacle to Canadian industrial development. Nevertheless, by 1987 when the Tokyo Round of tariff reductions is fully implemented, 80 per cent of current Canadian industrial exports to the U.S. will cross the border duty free, and up to 95 per cent will be subject to tariffs of 5 per cent or less.[5] Despite these tariff reductions, the American market appeared to be more closed to Canadian products by the end of the Seventies than it was at the beginning. As tariffs declined, the American system of contingency protection became the prime threat to Canada's export strategy.

Even if American tariffs were reduced to zero, Canadian exporters would face a number of mechanisms which provide discretionary barriers — trade obstacles that are only imposed when certain conditions are considered to exist. These contingency measures create large areas of uncertainty, since their impact depends on how determined American businesses are to invoke them (a propensity that is likely to vary directly with their marketing difficulties), on how zealous American administrators are to find fault with the foreign importers (an attitude that is likely to vary directly with how bad are the relations between the U.S. and the country of origin at the time), and on how loosely the courts choose to interpret legislation requiring proof that the imports in question have caused injury to the complaining industry (a lenience that is likely to vary directly with the distress of the American economy). American contingency protection measures fall into two groups: those that protect U.S. firms from successful foreign products entering the U.S., and those that offer U.S.

companies redress against products that have received some kind of subsidy from foreign governments to enable them to penetrate the American market.

There are three principal measures that American business can use to defend itself against competition that invades its market.

Anti-Dumping   Since 1921, the Anti-Dumping Act has provided an instrument of defence against the import of products at prices below those charged in the exporter's economy if this causes economic injury. In dumping cases, the practical issue becomes how injury is defined and how causation is proven. U.S. anti-dumping practice has been criticized for its very loose and vague definition of injury and of "the degree of causation required before it could be held that such injury was by reason of the dumped imports."[6] The Kennedy Round of the GATT negotiations led to the adoption in 1967 of an international anti-dumping code, which gave a more precise definition to injury and causation as the principal factor in a dumping case. According to the Kennedy Round code, "dumping duties could only be imposed when the authorities were satisfied that the dumped imports were demonstrably the principal cause of material injury."[7] Congress defied GATT and in the 1974 Trade Act emasculated the code, giving a clear message to the Treasury Department (which had to decide if dumping existed) and to the International Trade Commission (ITC) (which had to decide if injury had occurred and if it was caused by the dumping): the vague Anti-Dumping Act should be vigorously applied in defence of American business. The MTN Tokyo Round watered down the 1967 code, bringing it into harmony with the weaker U.S. legislation, a "major backward step toward the very protectionism which the MTN was designed to guard against."[8] As Fred Lazar suggests, Canadian firms are likely to be seriously impeded in their efforts to export to the U.S., since they will probably have to price their goods below their Canadian market level if they are to overcome the U.S. tariff, higher transportation costs, and lack of brand-name familiarity or record of performance. Even before selling any goods, they can be harassed by a pre-emptive investigation requested by their U.S. competitors.[9] The protectionism represented by this anti-dumping legislation has been further extended for some industries like steel which have managed to have a trigger price mechanism established. This monitors the price of steel imports which, when priced below a certain level, triggers a dumping investigation.

Escape Clause Relief   Section 201 of the 1974 Trade Act provides a second line of defence against foreign products that compete successfully for the American market. Under this escape clause, the government can impose temporary quotas, tariffs or other restrictions if the International Trade Commission determines that an item is being imported in such quantities that it is a substantial cause of serious injury or threat to the domestic competitors. There is no need for a complainant to prove that the increase of imports has been a *major* cause of injury to the American competitor. Under GATT's article 19, import relief has to be related to tariff concessions made under a GATT trade agreement, but section 201 does not require that this connection be established: "increased imports alone are sufficient justification for undertaking an escape clause investigation."[10]

Unfair Trade Practices   Anti-dumping legislation and escape clause measures are sanctioned by GATT codes. Section 337 of the 1930 Tariff Act has no legitimacy under GATT. It gives a third way for American firms to obstruct imports on the grounds of unfair competition. Section 337 was mainly used to protect the property rights of American firms allegedly suffering from patents infringed by imported goods. As amended by the 1974 Trade Act and the 1979 Trade Agreements Act, the ITC's scope has been extended rather vaguely to all forms of unfair competition. Since the legal costs of the complainant are borne by the U.S. government, this action heaps potentially prohibitive costs on the importing competitor. As section 337 can also be used pre-emptively before a product has been imported, the mere threat of its use can impel potential buyers of imports to shift their purchases to American suppliers.[11]

Two types of contingency protection measures provide American business and government with weapons to be used against efforts made by foreign governments to improve their economies' capability of exporting into the American market.

Countervailing Duties   Section 303 of the 1930 Tariff Act allows the president to impose countervailing duties on products that have received a foreign government subsidy, no matter at what stage in the production process the subsidy may have been received. It was under section 303 that a countervailing duty was imposed on the importation of Michelin tires from Nova Scotia, even though the subsidy in question was the grant received by Michelin from the Department of Regional Economic Expansion, a federal incentive to have Michelin locate in a less developed area of the Canadian economy.[12] Section 303 was also used by the Treasury Department against the imports of a mechanism made by the U.S. branch plant, Honeywell, to prevent oil-tank vehicles from overfilling. Honeywell had received a grant from the federal Program for the Advancement of Industrial Technology, a bounty that, a U.S. competitor successfully argued, had allowed Honeywell to lower its costs. The 1974 Trade Act extended the application of this countervail from dutiable goods to goods imported free of duty — an enormous extension given the decline of tariff levels and the increase of government intervention in economic development programs.

There was no need for the complainant to prove that the foreign government subsidies had been the cause of injury to the complaining American industry, in contrast to GATT's article 6 which specifies that an injury test be applied. Section 303 also applied to a far wider range of subsidies than that authorized by article 6. In order to get the U.S. to include an injury test in its legislation, negotiations at the Toyko Round accepted a wider range of subsidies eligible for countervail. However, the subsequent amendment by Congress to the Tariff Act included an injury test so weak that "there are many U.S. observers who believe that all the U.S. law requires is some evidence of the existence of injury to an industry, and some evidence of a causal link between the dumping (or the subsidization) of the imports in question for the injury test to be satisfied."[13] Furthermore, "the Trade Agreements Act went well beyond the GATT subsidies code in offering U.S. companies greater opportunities for complaint against a wider range of foreign subsidies."[14] Since federal and provincial governments widely use the provision of capital, loans, loan guarantees, funding and forgivable loans as part of their economic development programs to compensate for higher construction costs and location disadvantages, a wide range of Canadian products are potential victims to countervail action initiated by U.S. business or government.

Retaliation Potentially more damaging is section 301 of the Trade Act governing unfair trade practices. This covers any policy of a foreign government that results in an increase in American imports. Since section 301 can be used to retaliate against any foreign government measure that reduces American exports, it has an offensive as well as a defensive capability of enormous significance. It was under section 301 that the American government retaliated against Canada for making Canadian advertising on American border TV stations non-deductible for income tax purposes, thus reducing U.S. exports of services.[15] Section 301 extends the type of retaliation that the American government can indulge in to virtually any area of Canadian policy.

If the criterion is what may reduce American exports or increase American imports, the American government has given itself extra-territorial authority beyond the previous limit of the activities of American-controlled subsidiaries. Quebec's economic strategy of using its cheap hydro power as the engine for industrial development is thus threatened by section 301 with eventual retaliation should it prove successful in developing either import replacements or exporting industries.[16] As Rodney Grey has written, "the excessive degree of arbitrariness or administrative discretion that seems implicit in the system" must be a major cause of concern to Canadians. "If the present U.S. countervailing duty system were frequently invoked by U.S. firms and vigorously administered, it could have a serious impact on Canadian industrial development programs."[17] Vicious circles of cause and effect are likely to be perpetuated. In attempting to compensate for the disadvantages of its small markets, Canadian federal or provincial governments set up programs to encourage industries to achieve the economies of scale resulting from world-size operations. To exploit the economies of scale, these plants must necessarily export part of their product. Countervailing duties or other retaliatory measures taken by Washington can tax away the subsidies that have been expended to develop viable Canadian industrial activity.

Advocates of a more judicious use of government procurement to benefit Canadian industry would have a more compelling case were it not for section 301. The drawback to government procurement policies is that the more effective they are in capturing benefits for Canadian manufacturing, the greater will be the negative spillover effect reducing American exports.[18] In other words, the more successful Canadian government procurement programs are, the higher is the potential for interdictive attacks by the United States government.

Contingency protection measures do not by any means exhaust the trade policy instruments used in the United States to Canada's commercial injury.

Export Subsidy Though the U.S. is prepared to retaliate against foreign governments' export subsidies, it is not shy about providing its own exporters with tax stimuli. DISCs, the domestic international sales corporations, receive export subsidies from the tax system for American corporations producing in the U.S. and selling the goods abroad. Despite Canadian protests, despite a formal ruling that the

121

DISC program was in breach of the export subsidy prohibitions of GATT's article 16, and despite MTN pressure on this problem during the Toyko Round, the United States has felt free to continue the use of DISC.

Government Procurement Policy   We have seen how vehemently the U.S. objected to the NEP's proposed legislation to give Canadian firms preference in bidding for megaproject contracts. Washington's indignation against federal and provincial procurement preferences showed a double standard at work. In over thirty-five state governments in the U.S., Buy America legislation has instituted preference levels of 6 to 12 per cent for American over imported products purchased by the state governments. Government procurement policies were a major focus of the Tokyo Round's attempt in the late Seventies to reduce the hidden protection of non-tariff barriers. The fact that these negotiations were aimed at trade liberalization did not prevent the American government from passing in 1978 the Surface Transportation Assistance Act (STAA) which gave subsidies to municipalities for modernization of their urban transit systems, provided their purchases were assembled in the U.S. Despite the high U.S. content of Canadian urban transportation equipment, the STAA's Buy America provisions have seriously cut back Canadian sales in the American market. As the minister of trade, Ed Lumley, argued, the Americans were cutting off their nose to spite their face, since STAA led to purchases of Japanese or German equipment assembled in the U.S. but with lower American content than the highly competitive Canadian alternative.

> Today, Canadian transit equipment invariably has a significant percentage of U.S. content. Even before Buy America legislation was implemented, this was the case. For example, Hawker-Siddeley of Canada subway cars sold to the Massachusetts Bay Transit authority before the enactment of STAA had about 70% U.S. content. . . . Other examples are the urban buses produced by GM Diesel of Canada and Flyer Industries in which American content comprises from 50% to over 60% of these Canadian-made vehicles.[19]

Rodney Grey has illustrated the problems that American protectionism presents the Canadian explorer.

> A Canadian proposing to export to the United States must consider a number of barriers or impediments, or contingency measures, which may be put into play to limit his market penetration. For example, if he

has received any subsidy from the federal or provincial governments he may be exposed to a countervailing duties proceeding. . . . If, in order to overcome the disadvantage of higher transport costs than his U.S. competition faces, or in order to establish his product in the market, the Canadian producer cuts his export price below his comparable price in the Canadian market, he may face anti-dumping proceedings. If his product can be held to have infringed a U.S. patent owned by a U.S. competitor, the Canadian producer may find himself before the International Trade Commission, acting as a special court to deal with patent infringement by imports. If the Canadian producer is competing in the market for telecommunications equipment, for rail or urban transit equipment, for electrical generating and transmission equipment, or for structural steel for highway bridges, he may find that there are Buy-American provisions that effectively preclude his selling to American Governments, unless, of course, he decides to build production or assembly facilities in the United States.[20]

Efforts to reverse the process of deindustrialization in Canada through the application of federal and provincial carrot-and-stick policies to industry may bear fruit in one sector or another. Since there is a general consensus, both among professed nationalists and committed anti-nationalists, that protectionism is no longer viable and that satisfactory solutions can only be found by gaining new access to world markets, the question raised by the battery of American protectionist legislation remains: Will successful attempts to overcome Canada's economic problems be stymied at the border? The question cannot be sidestepped by conjuring up visions of trade diversion in the tradition of John Diefenbaker's promised shift of 15 per cent of Canada's American trade to Great Britain or Mitchell Sharp's less specific Third Option. The proponents of a state trading corporation (STC) argue that this kind of institution could allow Canada to export some $10 to 14 billion worth of additional manufactured goods and capital projects representing a 15 per cent increase in Canada's present exports.[21] Even though American legislation envisages the creation of U.S. state trading corporations, the U.S. could retaliate against a Canadian STC, arguing, on the grounds of sections 337 and 301, that it constituted an unfair trade practice — an action that would become more likely, the more successful the Canadian STC appeared. Even if the Trudeau government had decided to keep its election promise and set up an STC, such trade expansion would do little to mitigate the ill effects that American countervailing retaliation could wreak on those two-thirds of Canadian exports that go to the United States market.

On balance, it is hard to conclude that time is not working against the Canadian position, since the impact of American tariffs and non-tariff barriers alike is to pull successful Canadian business south of the border where it can operate without the uncertainties they create for export planning from Canada. Alfred Powis of Noranda could have been speaking for Northern Telecom or Bombardier when he said "We cannot get into the U.S. market from Canada in those copper products because of the tariff structure. Therefore if we really want to operate in the U.S. market, we have to locate our plants there."[22] As Grey points out, the longer this situation exists, "the Canadian firms who really want to compete in the U.S. procurement market will establish factories in the U.S."[23] Bombardier has already found it necessary to set up a branch plant to assemble mass transit trains in Vermont.

In effect, contingency protection that has been partially legitimized by GATT favours large countries that subsidize import substitution and penalizes small countries whose subsidies can be perceived as export incentives. By the end of the Seventies, after decades of congressional amendment, the extent of American protectionist legislation had become truly daunting for its weaker neighbour. Whether Canada proposes to exploit some comparative advantage, as in petrochemicals, in order to profit from a potential industrial winner, or whether it decides to take remedial action to improve the performance of an industrial loser such as automobile production, the battery of contingency protection measures that has been put into place in Washington makes the prospect for success of either strategy of government intervention extremely problematic. The consequence is to put Canada at the mercy of American goodwill. Whether the United States leaves Canada room for industrial development remains a question to be decided by U.S. politicians of the moment and the administrators of these draconian non-tariff mechanisms.[24] Yet by the end of the Seventies, Canada's international commercial situation was sufficiently parlous that some kind of trade-related economic development strategy seemed urgently needed.

Canada's Free Trade Options

If the manufacturing sector lies at the heart of any industrial society, then Canada is in serious trouble, as almost every assessment of its economy confirms. The Standing Senate Committee on Foreign Affairs wrote in 1978:

> Canada has a deficit in manufactured products with every country with which it trades and in every major commodity grouping. Canada also takes a higher proportion of its imports in manufactured form than other

major countries — 74 per cent as compared to 60 per cent for the United States and 32 per cent for the European Community. . . . And the situation is deteriorating . . . the proportion of the Canadian work force engaged in manufacturing declined from 24 per cent in 1960 to 22.5 per cent in 1973, a decline not paralleled in other industrial trading countries during the same period.[25]

The House of Commons Special Committee on a National Trading Corporation wrote in 1981:

While we need not repeat the sobering litany of trade challenges facing Canadians, let us stress that Canada is on the verge of ceasing to be a serious contender in many key trade areas.[26]

Bruce Wilkinson's review for the C. D. Howe Research Institute of Canada's position in the changing world economy has noted that:

- In nearly half of Canada's manufacturing industries, protection remains virtually the same, or has increased.
- Canadian labour earnings are higher, relative to U.S. earnings, than warranted by Canadian productivity, relative to U.S. productivity.
- Capital is being used much less efficiently in Canada than in the United States.
- The vulnerable, labour-intensive industries that survive through high levels of protection have expanded in Canada.
- In 1975, R & D as a percentage of GNP was still lower in Canada than in any other developed nation for which data were available.
- "Canada's manufacturing sector is not in a strong position . . . because the rapidly changing world situation has meant that what may have been satisfactory in earlier years is no longer so."[27]

Canada's trade deficit in manufactured end products — those goods requiring high levels of processing — is continuing its disastrous plunge. From $3.1 billion in 1970 it reached $17.8 billion in 1980.[28]

In a period when Canada's industrial health was failing, the standard policy prescriptions — tariffs to protect the local market and a secure mass market — were becoming less available as time passed. As the Standing Senate Committee on Foreign Affairs (SSCFA) put it in its third volume on Canada-United States relations, the Tokyo Round has, in effect, left Canadian industry in the worst of both possible worlds — with tariffs too low to be an effective protection and, at the same time, still without free access to a huge assured market as enjoyed by its competitors, the European Community, Japan and the United States.[29]

125

Long an advocate of generalized free trade as the ultimate solution to Canada's economic problems, the SSCFA argues that, since the Canadian and American economies are becoming increasingly interdependent, the failure to formalize this reality through a free trade agreement confers on Canada "the disadvantages of an unprotected market and forgoes the positive advantages possible under a bilateral free trade arrangement." By not biting the bullet now, "Canada will increasingly feel the costs without any of the benefits of free trade."[30]

There are two types of approaches to the notion of free trade with the U.S., an economic prescription to remedy Canada's woes that is as old as the country itself. One is an all-embracing agreement that abolishes all restraints on trade. The other is a more limited agreement that liberalizes commerce between selected sectors of each economy. There has been extensive theoretical debate on the former and some real experience with the latter approach. The actual record with partial free trade via the Auto Pact or farm machinery and the prospective problems raised by free trade in petrochemicals provide helpful evidence for considering the validity of an across-the-board solution.

The Auto Pact and Sectoral Free Trade
In 1980 when the Canadian government wanted to extract more concessions from the American car manufacturers, the economic context of an industry-wide crisis made the prospects of turning the campaign rhetoric of party leaders into industrial benefits considerably less promising than they had been in the mid-Sixties. When the automotive products agreement was negotiated in 1965, the North American car market was protected from world competition less by tariffs than by consumer preference for large cars. Following the rapid escalation of fuel prices in the Seventies, consumer demand shifted to smaller cars, forcing the North American manufacturers to compete for their own markets not just with their traditional European rivals but with the far more productive Japanese car industry. A process of internationalization was radically transforming what had previously been a North American automobile fortress. In an effort to cope with their low-cost competition, the Big Four were turning to the low-wage, newly industrializing countries like Mexico as the sources for their automotive parts. To attract greater employment in the automobile work force, such American states as Ohio, Pennsylvania, Michigan and Tennessee have enticed foreign car assembly plants with loans, interest rate subsidies and tax abatements offered in exchange for job-creating performance requirements.

126

The United States-Canada Automotive Agreement of 1965 had originally been greeted by economists as a triumph of economic reason over political passion, proving the superiority of free trade over protection as the way of the future. Imports from the U.S. jumped in the first five years from 3 per cent to 40 per cent of the Canadian market for North American cars, while exports of Canadian-produced vehicles rose from 7 per cent to 60 per cent of Canadian production. The operation of the Auto Pact was thought by Carl Beigie, then an economist at the Irving Trust Company of New York, to have shown for one sector how great the benefits can be from gearing Canadian production "to the entire North American market rather than to a small domestic market isolated by tariff barriers at home and abroad."[31] By the end of the Sixties the logic of the continental market seemed to have triumphed. Gone were the inefficient, short runs of the Canadian miniature-replica plants. In their place were expanded output and higher productivity. New jobs were created as the Big Four invested for an expanding market. Things initially went so well for Canada that the United States soon pressed for a revision of the pact which had produced a temporary deficit in the American balance of payments with Canada in automobiles and was blamed for the loss of American jobs.

The political pressure that Congress was able to put on U.S. car manufacturers was only one factor in reversing these trade figures. There were economic reasons to explain why the American automotive trade deficit with Canada was transformed into a growing and enormous surplus. The Canadian dollar, which was unpegged from its fixed rate of 95.9 U.S. cents, rose in the early Seventies to 105 cents. In the same period, the United Auto Workers achieved their goal of parity in wage levels between the two countries. As a result, Canadian automobiles became more expensive, while U.S. imports of cars and parts were relatively cheaper. By the end of the Seventies even Simon Reisman, one of the civil servants involved in negotiating the original pact, had to admit in his royal commission report that the costs far exceeded the benefits that had been achieved for Canada in the agreement. The large deficit in the balance of payments had become chronic, as Table 5-1 shows. The branch plants' head office activity, which had always been severely truncated, lost even more managerial decision-making authority to Detroit. The pact had not reduced Canada's regional disparities in industrial activity. Ontario captured almost all the employment it yielded; even Quebec, the second most industrialized province, felt deprived of its fair share of the auto industry's industrial benefits. There had been no improvement in Canadian ownership levels; rather, the number of Canadian parts companies had declined. Even the impact on Canadian-American relations had been negative: the agreement's inflexibility had not allowed a creative adaptation to the changing economic situation so that shrillness and complaints characterized the intergovernmental dialogue.[32]

Published figures for the trade deficit in automobiles and parts understated the true picture by some $500 million: dividends of over $100 million, special tooling and other automotive charges for over $100 million, and R & D charges of from $200 to $300 million were further costs resulting from the location of the subsidiaries' head offices in the United States.[33] Research and development expenditures illustrated in a particularly graphic way the extent to which Canada had been deprived of its fair share of the benefits from the automobile industry: of the $2 billion spent between 1971 and 1975, "minimal" amounts had been expended in Canada, even though the Canadian branches were billed some $300 million per year for the privilege.[34] The parts deficit, too, could be attributed to the way that the automobile multinationals distributed the benefits between Canada and the United States: $1.7 billion of the $2 billion parts deficit was made up of in-house transfers within the companies themselves.

From the Canadian viewpoint the issue boiled down to the question of equity. Canadian consumption of cars had grown, but Canadians were not getting their fair share of the opportunities created by their buying power. Between 1972 and 1976, Canada's share of the North American market had increased over 2 per cent from 6.7 per cent to 8.9 per cent, but its share of the value added had stagnated at under 7 per cent. In a nutshell, "Canada's poor trade balance in recent years has resulted from the failure of the industry to respond to Canada's relatively larger share of the North American market."[35] The already bad situation was tending to get worse. The industry's Canadian manufacturing capability was poor, its parts companies were weak, and its relatively lower wages were providing no stimulus to investment. Everything indicated that the perpetual deficit would grow. Understandably, in February 1980 politicians such as Pierre Trudeau and Ed Broadbent insisted to their supporters that Canada must renegotiate the Auto Pact's terms. But Canadian voters who put their faith in such undertakings were due for a disappointment. Negotiations might take place, but there was little hope that consultation would result in improvements.

128

TABLE 5-1

CANADA-U.S. TRADE IN AUTOMOTIVE PRODUCTS, 1971-1980

($ millions)

	1971	1972	1973	1974	1975	1976	1977	1978	1979	1980	10-year Total
Canadian exports of											
Motor vehicles	2,472	2,712	3,074	3,461	3,802	4,762	6,095	7,210	6,704	6,638	46,930
Parts	1,388	1,708	2,050	1,915	2,036	2,876	3,539	4,274	4,188	3,215	27,189
Canadian imports of											
Motor vehicles	1,254	1,476	1,994	2,439	3,003	3,148	3,824	4,227	5,529	4,491	31,385
Parts	2,387	2,807	3,440	3,922	4,483	5,405	6,805	7,986	8,488	7,395	53,118
Balance of Trade											
Motor vehicles	+1,218	+1,236	+1,080	+1,022	+799	+1,614	+2,271	+2,983	+1,175	+2,147	+15,545
Parts	−999	−1,099	−1,390	−2,007	−2,447	−2,529	−3,266	−3,712	−4,300	−4,180	−25,929
Total	+219	+137	−310	−985	−1,648	−915	−995	−729	−3,125	−2,033	−10,384

Source: Department of Industry, Trade and Commerce, *Commodity Trade by Industrial Sector with the United States, 1966-1980*; and Ross Perry, *The Future of Canada's Auto Industry*.

Canada's position in the negotiations leading up to the 1965 pact had been one of strength. Following the Bladen royal commission of 1962 on the state of the automobile industry, the Canadian government had experimented with duty-remission schemes for waiving duties on imported components in return for the auto companies' agreeing to increase both their exports to the U.S. and the proportion of Canadian value added (CVA) in their production. In the early Sixties the government felt it did have an option besides a negotiated deal with the American industry: restricting access to the Canadian market and building a fully Canadian car. It was this credible alternative, along with the American government's reluctance to enter a trade war with Canada at a time when it was pushing for world-wide trade liberalization, that helped Canada achieve its goal — limited free trade hedged by safeguards that protected employment levels. Canada had refused to include replacement parts in the pact for fear that its inadequate companies could not stand the competition. When in 1968 the treaty came up for the automatic review anticipated in the agreement, Canada still refused to open replacement parts to free trade and refused to change the employment safeguards. In these safeguards, which were written into the letters of understanding that the car companies signed with the Canadian government, the Big Four had committed themselves to maintain a certain level of assembly activity in each vehicle class and to keep the CVA in the vehicles at 60 per cent. The result of these commitments "was to guarantee a level of Canadian production of automobiles and original-equipment parts as a proportion of Canadian consumption of automobiles."[36] In short, the safeguards' effect was to maintain the employment level in assembly line activity. Although it was able to resist American pressures for change, Canada could not itself get the changes it wanted. The U.S. Senate Finance Committee was watching suspiciously over the shoulders of the car companies who, as a result, did not accede to Canadian pressure for a commitment to increased levels of CVA. In subsequent years, talks were engaged on a number of issues, mostly without success for either side. The exception was a committee of statisticians who resolved the argument about the conflicting data that both sides produced to bolster their arguments. August 1971 marked the nadir of the relationship in the automobile sector when, after fruitless negotiations, President Nixon was on the point of abrogating the whole pact — only being dissuaded from such a drastic step by an impassioned intervention from the State Department an hour before the fatal step was to be taken.

After 1972 the American government stopped pressing. The balance of trade had swung in its favour. Since there is no sunset provision that would terminate the pact, it continues even though both countries have conflicting goals, the United States wanting freer trade and Canada increased production, employment and an improved balance of payments. The more the U.S. government presses to change the pact, the more Canada feels that the United States is out to hurt it. Rumours that the car companies are under pressure from Washington rekindle the banked fires of Canadian apprehension.[37] When the Americans were running a deficit, they saw the safeguards as the principal irritant in the Canadian-American relationship. Now that the shoe is on the other foot, Canadians view the clause of article I in the pact referring to participation of both countries in the industry on "a fair and equitable basis" as a formal commitment that Canada's share of production, employment, investment and research should be proportional to Canada's share of the market — a claim that the Americans deny has the status of a guarantee.

Frustrated in their attempts to improve their share, the governments of Canada and Ontario have turned to unilateral action. In 1978 a joint Ottawa-Ontario grant of $68 million was awarded to Ford of Canada to locate a $535 million engine plant in Windsor. The same year a duty remission scheme was announced as part of an agreement between the federal government and Volkswagen, whereby Volkswagen would get exemptions from duties in exchange for commitments to export. Washington took exception to both the subsidy and the remission scheme and, on August 4, 1978, initiated bilateral negotiations pursuant to article IV(A) of the Auto Pact and the 1976 OECD statement on international incentives. In launching this complaint, the U.S. was conveniently ignoring the subsidies and performance requirements negotiated by several individual states who sought from foreign car manufacturers the same kind of benefits to the local economy that Ontario had attempted to secure for central Canada. Far from being a model of tranquil free trade, the "North American automotive industry furnishes the most prominent example of bilateral Canada-U.S. tension stemming from investment incentives."[38] Agreement proved impossible once again, and the talks were suspended in 1979, only to be reopened by Herb Gray in 1980 on the strength of the campaign commitment made by Trudeau in February. It was the Americans' turn to stall: they pleaded negotiations with Japan as their excuse. Already in 1978 the Canadian Senate's report on Canadian-American trade opined that there was "very little leverage available to Canada for persuading either vehicle manufacturers or the U.S. government to modify the situation."[39] Canada had, in other words, lost its freedom to make policy for its own automobile industry and had no protection against the institutional barriers to trade represented by the multinational corporations.[40] With the unemployment rate in the automobile industry running at 13.7 per cent in Michigan and 10.4 per cent in Ohio, compared with 7.4 per cent in Ontario (in January 1981), there was little American desire to negotiate when Herb Gray met U.S. Trade Representative William Brock in February and April of 1981. Not only were there basic philosophical differences separating the two sides about the proper economic strategy to be taken, but also the United States was not inclined to revise the pact in Canada's favour when the U.S. industry was in such deep, possibly mortal, distress.

Worse from Canada's point of view, the Reagan administration's response to its crisis with Japan has been to make an assault on the integrated nature of the North American car industry. By negotiating a special U.S.-Japan deal on May 1, 1981, in which the Japanese government required its automakers to reduce their exports by 7.7 per cent from 1.82 million vehicles in 1980 to 1.68 million in 1981,[41] the U.S. government has left Canada doubly in the lurch. The Canadian market came under greater pressure to absorb the cars that Japan had agreed not to export to the U.S.; as the weaker economy, it was less able to defend its interests in the negotiations it subsequently opened with Japan. In disregarding the effects on Canada of its separate deal with Japan, the American government has shown little concern about the impact its actions have had on its allegedly closest friend and ally — even when the damage it has caused mainly hurts its own companies which dominate the industry in Canada.

Through the Auto Pact, Canada's automobile capability is intimately tied to this mature parent-controlled industry. In boom times Canada may break even, but in bad times its deficit falls to alarming depths. While neither side wishes to terminate the bilateral pact that keeps the Canadian industry as an appendage of the American parents, the American car industry is internationalizing so rapidly as to make the Auto Pact irrelevant. It would appear that another cyclical crisis is building, similar to but more severe than that of the early Sixties. Royal-commission advice not to rock the boat becomes less acceptable. Increasingly, governments will be pressured to turn towards the more radical solutions that other observers are proposing: Canadianization of the parts industry; world product mandates for the

132

branch plant parts companies; even an all-Canadian car for the Nineties. Assuming that the pressures for change build up and that the United States remains unwilling to treat Canada as a continental partner, the prospect for unilateral Canadian surgery on its ailing auto industry will be forced onto the political agenda. As the share of Japanese imports rises to 50 per cent of the market, the UAW will press for a strict limit on Japanese imports, a heavy import surcharge, or a draconian Canadian-value-added requirement to force local production — all moves that would put Canada in violation of its GATT undertakings. Given the high levels of foreign investment in the industry, given the stubborn resistance of the Japanese to the notion of manufacturing in Canada, given the United States' determination to capture for itself all of those investments that Japan may make in North America, given Ottawa's long-standing reluctance to rescue the industry with a higher level of protection, and given the resource-development thrust of the government's 1981 economic strategy, there is no serious prospect of Canada shifting belatedly onto the Swedish path of building competitive national automobiles. As Ross Perry argues, it may be time to recognize the logic of sectoral "free" trade and get out entirely from the car-building business.[42]

When in 1978 Simon Reisman wrote that "despite the hopes and aspirations of the originators, the Auto Pact had failed to provide the stimulus or inspiration to beget similar agreements in its image for the enhancement of international specialization and efficiency in the massive trade between Canada and the U.S.A.," he was being too sanguine.[43] There is another industrial sector that has proven free trade has not succeeded. In contrast to the automobile industry, Canada's farm machinery market benefits from no safeguards and is completely open to American imports, whereas the United States is much more restrictive in granting access to its market for Canadian tractors and after-market parts. Canada's lack of protection since 1944 has done nothing to close the productivity gap, increase research and development, or reduce foreign ownership. At the same time, the Canadian trade deficit in farm machinery increased from under $100 million in the early Fifties to $200 million in the early Seventies, and reached $670 million by 1977.[44] It is hard to see why the U.S. would grant Canadian manufacturers the same free access to its farm machinery market as American manufacturers have enjoyed in the Canadian market, given the advantages which flow to the U.S. from the status quo. Canada would have to play tough and introduce reciprocity provisions in its tariffs to achieve any correction of this imbalance. But reciprocity implies moving away from the free trade model with possible costs in other sectors where a free trade agreement is an objective on the Canadian side.

The Petrochemical Industry's Hope for Access

While international comparisons in the automobile industry may put Canada to shame as the only major car market without an indigenous car (Sweden, with one-third the market size, has managed to produce two successful automobiles), Canada's automobile industry had few viable options left. The industry was dominated by an oligopoly of U.S.-owned branch plants. The independent parts makers were uncompetitive, only surviving behind tariff protection. In short, Canada in the early Eighties had no comparative advantage to exploit. The government had got what it had asked for in 1965 — assembly-line jobs — only to discover a decade later that it should have been aiming for research, management and new technology. By the Eighties, it was having to negotiate with its hands tied behind its back, its only remaining card being the vestiges of the old protectionist system. By contrast, the Canadian petrochemical industry in the early Eighties was in the process of transformation from defensive inefficiency to aggressive competitiveness. As late as the mid-Seventies the Canadian petrochemical industry was characterized by small facilities that produced at high cost without reaping economies of scale for a small market that was, because of the massive imports of consumer goods, only one-twentieth the size of the American market. The trade deficit in petrochemicals was $500 million in 1977.[45] By 1980, investments by American branch plants, Canadian Crown corporations and private-sector companies had doubled the industry's capacity and achieved a trade surplus of $63 million. By 1985, industry production is expected to double again, primarily because of projects planned in Alberta.[46] This would represent some 10 per cent of North American needs, far surpassing Canadian domestic demands.

The industry has made a gamble in moving to world-scale technology, for its markets are not assured. Despite construction costs 20 per cent higher than those of American producers on the Mexican Gulf,[47] the combination of guaranteed feed stocks from natural gas, a depreciated Canadian dollar and lower energy prices has allowed Canadian petrochemical producers to overcome their higher capital costs and to envisage vaulting the American tariff as well.[48] Since the tariff remains a significant barrier in petrochemical commerce, American protectionism looms as a dark cloud on the industry's horizon. At a time when the industry's ability to export is soaring,[49] its counterpart in the United States is becoming more protectionist. At the most recent GATT negotiations the U.S. industry showed increased opposition to the Canadian objective of maximum tariff reduction feasible under the United States Trade Act. "Canadian interest in the U.S. market was of little concern in the United States," where industry opposition "became increasingly visible and strident."[50] The clout of the U.S. petrochemical lobby could be measured by the fact that the Tokyo Round resulted in higher, not lower, tariff protection for the American industry.[51]

For Canada, and the western provinces in particular, the stakes are high. Free trade for derivative petrochemical products would yield large industrial benefits. Compared to fuel refining, whose output contains between 10 and 15 per cent value added, the value added at the primary petrochemical stage is about two to five times the value of the basic raw material. Free trade already exists for these primary feedstocks, though they are vulnerable to non-tariff barriers. Primary petrochemicals provide the feedstock for the several dozen derivative petrochemicals whose production yields higher employment per unit and where value added amounts to four or five times the value of the hydrocarbon raw material. American tariffs escalate the higher the degree of processing and the greater the level of value added. It is these derivative products that are currently subject to high U.S. tariffs in the face of which it is doubtful that Canadian exports can be sustained. At the third stage of production come the fabricating industries which convert derivative petrochemicals to final consumer products. Here the value added ranges from ten to twenty-five times the original hydrocarbon value, and the employment effects are the highest.[52] Testimony before the Standing Committee on Foreign Affairs of the Senate of Canada left little doubt that free trade in derivative petrochemicals was strongly desired both by the industry and the Alberta government which, frustrated in its objective at the Tokyo Round, now favoured a free trade agreement with the United States in the petrochemical sector.[53]

Further testimony revealed there were few grounds for expecting the United States to be eager for such a deal. In the opinion of Julius Katz, former assistant secretary of state for economic and business affairs, "basically, I think the petrochemical industry in the United States would not welcome increased competition." Since the benefits would accrue largely to Canada, there would not be a "sufficient balance of interest to make such an agreement possible in petrochemical products alone."[54] According to Lawrence Krause of the Brookings Institution, the American industry would object that Canadian feedstock prices were unfairly low.[55] Having exerted its political muscle to increase tariff protection, the American petrochemical industry was unlikely to accept free trade without Canada making concessions that would offset any positive benefits that might accrue from the deal — access to Canadian fresh water supply, for instance.[56] Tying tariff reduction to increased exports of natural gas might have been attractive to the U.S. in the mid-Seventies but would now have little leverage in the context of a gas glut and high Canadian export prices. Unless Canada was willing to make a basic concession, such as abandon the NEP, it looked by 1982 as though the status quo remained "the only alternative consistent with the NEP."[57] Free trade remained a chimera in winning as in losing industrial sectors. If Canada had a potential winner, the United States was not about to open its doors and welcome the invigorating challenge of free-market competition that Reaganomics theoretically espouses. If Canada had a chronic loser like automobiles, the United States was not inclined to help its weaker cousin get back on its feet.

The poor prospects of free trade arrangements in particular sectors do not rule out the possibility of a broader approach to continental free trade. Indeed the SSCFA report considers that "only a broad approach to free trade, with a sharing of benefits and costs across many industries, holds the prospect of success . . . [that] would give the petrochemical industry the boost it needs."[58] There are two levels to the continuing discussion of the significance of free trade to Canada. In the ivory tower, academic economists still allocate large portions of their energies to analyzing the benefits and costs that would result from various scenarios of free trade between Canada and its major trading partner.[59] The consensus of mainstream economists such as the Wonnacott brothers favours trade liberalization as a general approach, with special emphasis in Canada's case on the productivity gains that they claim would result from exploiting the greater economies of scale that Canadian manufacturers would enjoy if they could count on the American market for their products.[60] Sceptics in the profession like Bruce Wilkinson doubt that productivity gains would be significant, since scale is only one, and not necessarily a major, factor in determining Canada's poor performance.[61] Reflecting on the example of the European Community (EC), Wilkinson points out that the United Kingdom's experience has not fulfilled the economic returns promised by the proponents of British entry. Schwindt reports that, for the critical assumptions of free trade proponents (the eradication of tariffs automatically increases competition and has extremely positive effects on economies at or below the plant level), "the experience of Western European economic integration does not provide [supporting] evidence."[62]

Policy analysts, who deal in the world of practical politics, voice strong scepticism about free trade as a viable solution. Rodney Grey, who was a chief negotiator for Canada at the Tokyo Round, argues that free trade is of limited relevance to the concrete problems facing Canada in North America, if by free trade is meant a global, comprehensive and "final" solution to the problem.[63] More practically, there are substantial political and economic considerations that make the proposal unlikely to "fly." Just to take one of the SSCFA's political assumptions is to show how far-fetched is its program: the Canadian government would have to obtain a negotiating mandate from the provinces to be prepared to surrender on the bargaining table such items as provincial protectionism, provincial marketing boards, and procurement programs favouring made-in-the-province products.[64] As long as federal-provincial relations are characterized by continuous confrontation, a high degree of alienation in Quebec, and provincial governments trying to build up their regional economies in competition with each other, conditions on the Canadian side will not be exactly propitious for initiating a free trade approach to the United States.

At the federal level, informed observers consider that the United States would require that Canada, in return for exemptions from U.S. protectionist legislation, would have to give up all the industrial policy tools to which the U.S. has been objecting. These would include federal subsidies to stimulate regional development, prices of energy set below world-market levels, tax discrimination to favour Canadianization, performance requirements on new foreign investors, and rules to allow Canadian manufacturers access to contracting for Canadian megaprojects. In short, the price for admission to the American market would be the economic policies needed to put Canadian industry in a position to compete there. The economic dilemma has a political parallel. Though free trade proponents claim that Canadians need fear no loss of their sovereignty, the conditions that the U.S. would exact would divest Canada of control over its own economic development policies. Having been caught twice in the quicksands of the American treaty negotiation process in the attempt to reach agreement over treaties on fisheries and the law of the sea (as we will see in chapter

10), Canadian diplomats are unlikely to relish the prospect of engaging in an endless game for which the ground rules never stay the same and for which the outcome would remain uncertain for years.

On the American side, the Seventies' congressional trend towards protectionist politicians zealously supporting the complaints of their own industrialists hardly suggests that the political spirit is willing to undertake a magnanimous act of statesmanship that could threaten dozens of individual economic interests. While Rodney Grey sees some precedent for appealing to the American interest in Canada's having a strong economy,[65] closer analysis leads A. R. Moroz to the view that, "for sound economic reasons, the United States will not enter a preferential bilateral free trade agreement with Canada."[66] Simply put, there are insufficient benefits for the U.S. in the kind of arrangement that Canada would be prepared to accept. The Standing Senate Committee on Foreign Affairs admitted that interest among American opinion leaders was low: "bilateral free trade is an issue many American business leaders have not thought closely about."[67] There is no indication of a potential consensus building in American politics to favour undertaking a project that would hold some risk that the United States' other trading partners might retaliate against it for making such a massive exception to the principle of most-favoured-nation treatment. On the contrary, the consensus that is building irresistibly in Washington is the drive to bring American protectionism to a new stage of development under the code word of reciprocity.

Continuity or Change: Reciprocity as a New Trade Threat

In deciding whether the Canadian-American confrontation of 1981 marked a turning point in the field of trade policy, we must remember that Canadian complaints about U.S. protection are as old as Sir John A. Macdonald's National Policy. American economic nationalism has always set the context for the stunted development of the Canadian industrial structure. It was during the Carter administration that the finishing touches were put to the American system of non-tariff, import-restricting barriers, which we noted earlier. This said, it seems clear that Washington has moved, under the Reagan administration, beyond a simple defensive protectionism based on multilateralism towards an offensive foreign-trade stance based on a bilateralism that is even more threatening to Canada's economic well-being. Lip service is still paid by administration officials to the trade doctrine which accords pre-eminence to the GATT rules for international economic trading behaviour, but the United States has lost its hegemony in GATT following the rise of Japan and the European Community.

Evidence of this declining power is the United States' frustration and anger at its inability to force its trading partners to play by the liberal rules that would favour American exports. Despite repeated American protests, both Japan and the EC keep out lower-priced American agricultural produce with non-tariff barriers or price support programs. An equally strong American grievance is directed at EC telecommunication agencies which are partially or wholly government owned or controlled and which limit market access for U.S. exporters of telecommunications equipment and information services.[68] Remaining unaware of their own violations of the principle of national treatment for inward foreign investment, their own trade-related subsidy programs that are channelled through the states, their own government-supported research and development efforts for high technology via military spending, and other local examples of their own offences against the liberal trade credo, American politicians have built up a strong head of steam about the inequities from which U.S. corporations suffer when trying to trade abroad.

Since the system of contingency protection against incoming imports has not managed to get foreign governments to desist from their illiberal practices, the emerging consensus in Republican Washington is that there is a need to develop a strategy to defend American exports against foreign protectionism. The notion is as simple as it is biblical: the United States must exact an eye for an eye, a tooth for a tooth; or in other, more modern, words, there must be a level playing field on which to engage. Washington must insist that its corporations get substantially the same market access in each partner's market as the U.S. grants that country in the United States.[69] Having lost its control of international trade through multilateral institutions, Washington is thinking of exerting direct pressure on its partners to force them, one by one, to play the trade game by its rules. United States legislation in trade and investment matters is to be the model on which other countries should harmonize their policies and remake their economic system.[70] If the U.S. could impose the American dollar currency as the basis for the world's foreign exchange system, surely it could impose liberalized trade, especially in agricultural produce and information services, in a new pax Americana.

The central objective of the Reagan administration's new foreign trade and investment policy was to force the same access to Japan's markets as Japan enjoyed in the United States. But reciprocity was to be superimposed over — it did not supplant — the old import defence system. As Ambassador Brock, the U.S. trade representative, put it, perhaps unconscious of the contradiction between preaching liberalization and practising protection,

> our antidumping, countervailing duty and similar structures are designed to neutralize or eliminate trade distortive practices which injure U.S. industry and agriculture. We regard these laws as *essential to maintain the political support for a more open trading system.*[71]

In the unpredictable partnership of the administration and Congress, the former is encouraging the latter to arm it with legislation with which it can "scare the hell out of the Japanese." Whether or not the Japanese are burned by the omnibus bill drafted by Senator Heinz (S-207), Canadians should certainly be chilled by the dramatic extension of retaliatory action that it proposes. In Heinz's explanation, "non-reciprocal market access and non-national treatment are grounds for a complaint and presidential action, *whether they involve a GATT violation or not.*"[72] The already powerful section 301 of the 1974 Trade Act would be expanded to embrace not just violations involving services but foreign direct investment as well. Senator Danforth's proposed bill (S-2094) would make it an offence to deny the U.S. "commercial opportunities substantially equivalent" to those offered by the U.S. — in the megaprojects for example. Retaliatory action in the new bills need not be limited to the equivalent product, investment or service sector raised by the complaint. In other words Danforth proposed that a tooth would now be vulnerable for revenge on an eye; an eye for a tooth. What Congress considers to be the administration's traditional reluctance to take retaliatory action against its trading partners in recognition of diplomatic, military or other political factors will be further reduced by the proposed new legislation which will enable committees of Congress to initiate section 301 cases in the absence of presidential action.[73] As sentiment in Congress grows that American corporations are being unfairly dealt with, it is likely that some broad legislation of this type will be passed.

What is also probable is the enactment of some more narrow acts such as the Telecommunications Competition and Deregulation Act of 1981 (S-898). The bill proposes that the importation of foreign telecommunications equipment only be allowed from countries that afford fully reciprocal rights to U.S. telecommunications companies.[74] Such a bill could be used to keep out Canadian high technology exports such as Telidon on the grounds that Americans are only allowed to own 20 per cent of Canadian cable television companies.

How this legislation is actually used when it is in place remains to be seen, but a significant straw in the wind is the first presidential ruling on a section 301 complaint concerning a services case. This was President Reagan's recommendation to Congress late in 1981 that a mirror bill be passed to retaliate against Canada's Bill C-58 which made Canadian advertising on U.S. border television stations non-deductible from corporate taxation. Canada's action was judged an unreasonable restriction of U.S. commerce. The message of the recommendation is clear: reciprocity will be seriously pursued by both the executive and the legislature.

This evidence of the American approach to blasting its way into the export markets of the world indicates that 1981 did mark a significant change in the evolution of U.S. trade policy as far as Canada is concerned. That change has not been towards free trade by a greater accommodation that could embrace sweeping exemptions for Canada from the bite of import-restricting contingency protection measures or export-promoting reciprocity legislation. On the contrary, 1981 witnessed a move towards a legislative framework for a higher level of confrontation which explicitly seeks to make an example out of Canada, as a lesson to the world community on how Washington proposes to achieve its own very unique definition of reciprocity. At the very least, 1981 ushered in a period of great uncertainty in Canadian-American trading relations. It is not just that the current agenda of contentious issues is particularly long: Canada's customs valuation methods are an issue in the light of agreements made in the Tokyo Round; so are Canada's duty-remission programs which reduce import duties, for instance, for Volkswagen in return for commitments for import substitution or increased exports; Canada's agricultural export corporation, CANAGREX, will create opposition from U.S. farmers with whose wheat exports it will compete; Washington is concerned about new anti-dumping and countervailing duty regulations being adopted by Canada; U.S. pharmaceutical companies are considering a complaint against Canada's patent law; the licensing of trucking companies is a further issue; the many industrial incentives leading to world product mandating and import substitution "promise a rich vein of trade disputes," in Andrew Samet's and Gary Hufbauer's phrase.[75] Such specific disputes are the bread and butter of the two capitals' normal relationship. What is new is the uncertainty bred of the vast powers and broad discretion that are being lodged in the U.S. presidency and its regulatory agencies.

The Eighties have raised broad questions that will only be answered as precedents are set or negotiations attempt to clarify the wide grey areas that have been introduced. Will any limits be placed on the kinds of federal, provincial or municipal subsidy that American officials can target as unfair to their competitive status? Will any recognition be given in the definition of the notion of reciprocity to the different sizes of the two economies? to the Canadian propensity to import from the United States, which is far greater than the U.S. propensity to import from Canada? to the enormous returns which American direct investment in Canada yields its beneficiaries? to Canada's legitimate needs to defend its beleaguered cultural industries? to the principle that Canadian citizens should not be affected by legislation over whose formulation they have no democratic powers? Uncertainty is not only the characteristic of the Canadian-American trade in manufactured products under Reagan. Even the area of raw materials export — long the rock on which the Canadian-American commercial relationship has stood — is not free from uncertainties caused by changing policy perspectives, as we shall see in chapter 6.

The Alaska Pipeline and Continental Resource Integration

6

In September 1981, Mitchell Sharp, commissioner of the Northern Pipeline Agency, made another of his many trips to Washington to wring assurances from senior officials in the administration that they would press Congress to support the Alaska pipeline project, of which he was the Canadian coordinator. At issue was another but more paradoxical energy issue which had troubled the Canadian-American relationship throughout the Seventies and which still remained a source of tension in 1981. The project was an American one, code-named ANGTS for the Alaska Natural Gas Transportation System, but the angst it caused was disproportionately felt among Canadian policy makers. The specific question was whether the United States government would keep the commitment it had made to Canada that it would get the Alaska gas pipeline built. Ministers in the Canadian cabinet opined that it would be disastrous should the pipeline not be constructed: How could we ever trust a deal made with the Americans again, they wondered aloud.

To those observing the fray, this crisis appeared more like a teapot tempest. Canada was exercising what political muscle it had in Washington, pressing the U.S. government to do what was much more obviously in the United States' long-term interest than Canada's — build a pipeline to bring Alaska gas to the U.S. market. The pipeline seemed of only marginal significance to Canada. The contradiction implicit in this position reached patently absurd proportions. Having exerted itself to establish a *national* energy program that was designed to disentangle Canada's energy system from its continental context, the same department of the same Canadian government was pushing the Americans to make a major move towards the further continental integration of energy marketing in North America along the lines long established for Canada's other resources, which will be examined later in this chapter. Canada had become caught in skeins it could no longer unravel and the knots were largely of its own tying.

143

The Alaska Gas Pipeline

The trend towards a continental integration of gas marketing had become firmly established twenty years earlier; by the late Fifties, the TransCanada and Westcoast pipelines were delivering Alberta and British Columbia gas to both sides of the border in central North America and on the Pacific coast. The history of the Alaska pipeline itself goes back before the OPEC crisis to 1968, when the largest field ever discovered in North America was found in Prudhoe Bay on Alaska's northern coast.[1] This was a real "elephant," promising 10 billion barrels of oil and 27 trillion cubic feet of gas. At that time world prices were still low, petroleum supplies seemed assured, and the U.S. was imposing quotas against the import of Alberta's surplus oil. Scarcely a year later, the Shultz task force was commissioned in response to the administration's strategic concern about its growing reliance on oil imports. Alaska's oil reserves became highly attractive, and this raised the question of how best to get them south.

There were three possible ways to bring the Prudhoe Bay oil to market: tankers shipping the fuel through the Northwest Passage, a pipeline pumping it up Canada's Mackenzie River valley, and a trans-Alaska pipeline system (TAPS) sending oil across the Alaska mountains to be shipped by tanker to markets on the American west coast and in Japan. While the multinational oil companies favoured the TAPS proposal, the Canadian government reacted strongly against this possibility. It would increase competition with Alberta's oil exports, and the environmental hazard of oil tankers navigating off the British Columbia coast raised very strong political concerns. Since there was some hope that commercially exploitable quantities of oil would be found in the Mackenzie River delta, the federal cabinet understandably concluded that a Mackenzie River pipeline would give it the best of all possible worlds: a route that was environmentally preferable to TAPS, a boost to the Canadian pipeline construction industry, a chance to increase the supply of Canadian oil from the Mackenzie basin, and a bargaining lever with the United States to continue Alberta's oil exports. Before any environmental, engineering or economic studies had been done of the project, Jean Chrétien, minister of Indian affairs and northern development, made a speech favouring a pipeline right of way for the United States across Canada. During the election campaign of 1972, the prime minister announced that a highway would be built up the Mackenzie River in the hope that this would influence the United States government to favour the land-bridge proposal — and coincidentally win a Liberal seat in the North. Although the United

States government decided, in the panic of the OPEC crisis and the resulting patriotic support for energy independence, to take the TAPS route, a pattern of expectations had been established: Canada was ready to accommodate American interests in a land bridge.

The choice of the trans-Alaska route for oil did not determine the means to be used for bringing Prudhoe Bay's gas south to market. Under pressure from the Canadian government, two competing groups of companies merged in 1972 to form Canadian Arctic Gas Pipeline Limited. This consortium comprised a staggering alliance of oil interests: the three largest companies involved in Prudhoe Bay (Atlantic Richfield, British Petroleum and Exxon), the three largest companies exploring in the Mackenzie delta (Imperial Oil, Gulf and Shell), three Canadian pipeline companies (TransCanada PipeLines, Alberta Gas Trunk Line and Alberta Natural Gas), gas distribution utilities with 85 per cent of the Canadian market, and several large American gas pipeline companies.[2] It was a consortium that was planning on a continental scale to bring northern gas to southern markets regardless of national boundaries. It was, by all accounts, an invincible alliance, and in 1974 a sudden shift in the perceived gas situation in Canada — the National Energy Board concluded that gas shortages would get worse if no pipeline were built — increased pressure for rapid completion of the Mackenzie valley project.

Nevertheless three events shattered the Mackenzie valley pipeline's aura of inevitability. A gas pipeline parallel to the TAPS oil pipe was proposed by El Paso, giving the United States government a better negotiating position vis-à-vis the Canadian proposal. Alberta Gas Trunk Line defected from Canadian Arctic Gas to form a smaller consortium called Foothills which proposed a rival, all-Canadian line to take Canadian gas to Canadian markets through its so-called Maple Leaf Project. All of a sudden the continental giant had to contend with a nationalist Jack. The third crucial action of 1974 was the Canadian government's concession to pressure from the New Democratic Party, which held the balance of power in the minority government and which opposed the Mackenzie River pipeline. Along with citizen groups such as the Canadian Arctic Resources Committee and the Committee for an Independent Canada, the NDP had demanded an inquiry be made into the proposal. In March 1974, when Canadian Arctic Gas filed its application, the government commissioned Judge Thomas Berger — a former leader of the New Democratic Party in British Columbia — to conduct a thorough investigation of the proposal. When the National Energy Board started its hearings on the Canadian Arctic Gas proposal,

145

the results still seemed preordained, but citizen-group interveners won precious delays in the process. Meanwhile Foothills made a new proposal that was to supersede the Maple Leaf line: a pipeline down the Alaska highway that would be much more efficient than the El Paso proposal because transportation costs would be lower even though capital costs would be higher. The ''Alcan'' highway route completely avoided the Mackenzie River valley together with its environmental and political difficulties.

Time was running out for the Canadian government because delays that had slowed down the decision-making process in the United States were coming to an end. In response to President Ford's request for more power to decide the issue over the heads of the Federal Power Commission (FPC) which had been studying the Arctic Gas proposal since 1974, Congress passed the Alaska Natural Gas Transportation Act in late 1976. This gave the president the power to review the FPC decision, while reserving to Congress the final judgment. By early 1977 an atmosphere of great urgency had built up. (Gas shortages in the U.S. were so severe that winter that 2 million workers were laid off. If Canada did not make a decision, and the United States went ahead with the trans-Alaska gas pipeline as it had previously for oil, Canada would not be able to bring its Mackenzie delta gas to market.) In January, a formal U.S.-Canadian treaty was signed, binding both sides not to interfere with oil and gas flowing through pipelines on their territory to customers in the other country, and by the summer of 1977 the U.S. Senate had ratified the treaty. In February, one judge of the Federal Power Commission issued a 430-page document favouring the Arctic Gas proposal, rejecting the Alcan system entirely and rating the El Paso line as feasible but inferior. Three months later, on May 2, 1977, the FPC issued a final, but split decision, two commissioners recommending the Alcan route, two the Mackenzie valley route. The next week Judge Berger brought out the first volume of his report and sent a shock wave across Canada. Having spent three years painstakingly investigating the probable impact of a pipeline in the Mackenzie valley on the life and economy of the different native peoples in the north, he passionately pleaded — to great public support — that the Mackenzie pipeline not be built for a ten-year period while more research was done and while native land claims for political and economic rights in the north were settled. For all intents and purposes the Arctic Gas proposal was dead. In theory, the Canadian government could have rejected the construction of any pipeline, since gas shortages were receding by mid-1977, but the Foothills proposal had

146

received support from environmentalists as the lesser of the possible evils and it was favoured by the National Energy Board's judgment that was brought down in July.

In addition, the Canadian government was under tremendous pressure. Since the U.S. Alaska Natural Gas Transportation Act had set a deadline of September 1, 1977 by which a decision had to be made, El Paso would presumably get the nod if the land bridge over Canada had not been secured by that time. In August, Prime Minister Trudeau announced Canada's support for the Alcan line. Despite the lack of adequate data, a fast decision had been made in response mainly to American urgings and to a hope that, with the Canadian economy in bad shape, a project of this size would provide many jobs and a boost to the whole economic system. Canada-U.S. negotiations were started in August to produce a formal agreement between the two governments. Tough bargaining sessions led by James Schlesinger, secretary of energy, and Allan MacEachen, president of the Privy Council, led to an agreement which President Carter and Prime Minister Trudeau made public in Washington on September 8.

There was considerable doubt that Canada had struck a good bargain. Indeed, "so great was the eagerness of the Trudeau government to conclude the agreement because of its expected boost to the Canadian economy that it weakened the position of the Canadian negotiators in the final round of bargaining."[3] Canada dropped its preference for a route closer to the untapped Canadian reserves of the Mackenzie valley. In return the United States assumed part of the burden of paying for the Dempster spur line that would connect these Canadian gas fields to the main pipeline. Despite the negotiators' lack of knowledge about the infrastructural and environmental costs of the project, Canada agreed to put a $30 million ceiling on property taxes in the Yukon, to forgo a throughput tax on the land bridge, and to build the pipeline before the land claims of the Yukon Indians had been settled. In effect Canada had guaranteed the United States access to Alaska gas at far lower cost than the El Paso line would have delivered it. The victory of Foothills over the Arctic Gas consortium represented a defeat of American and eastern Canadian corporate interests by smaller western newcomers to the petroleum game, and it promised certain gains to Canada, such as pipeline engineering capability with somewhat greater Canadian control. The fact that Canada had bent its decision-making system to the urgencies of Washington's deadline did not prevent a further process of delay during which Canada was to act more American than the U.S. president.

The Pre-Build

When Canada agreed to the joint construction of the Alcan pipeline, it reaffirmed that its energy policy was built on a contradiction. In the same period during which it was redefining the economic significance of oil and gas as *energy* (a vital input to the Canadian economy that had to be husbanded for the national market), natural gas was also being treated as a traditional *staple* (a resource to be exported at maximum possible rates to more developed economies in return for which Canada could buy manufactured products).[4] In the late Seventies, when the national energy policy was gestating, the export component of the national oil policy had been phased out. The country's petroleum policy was national in its thrust, but its gas policy returned to a continental orientation because the exportable gas surplus had expanded. The continental thrust of Canadian gas policy was itself caught in a contradiction. In its haste to capture the industrial benefits from the construction of a pipeline that would accelerate the channelling of its resources for integration in the continental market, Canada pushed so hard that it risked injuring even its continental interests. To implement its part of the Alcan agreement, the government introduced a bill that was passed by Parliament in February 1978 as the Northern Pipeline Act. Two months later, one of the most senior and experienced former members of the cabinet, Mitchell Sharp, was appointed commissioner of the new Northern Pipeline Agency.

Meanwhile an atmosphere of indifference succeeded that of urgency in Washington. It took until 1979 before the United States government had established a supervisory body equivalent to Canada's Northern Pipeline Agency. Even then, Congress was still delaying the legislation that was essential for the pipeline to be built.[5] While Americans delayed, the Canadians prepared. The Northern Pipeline Agency negotiated an agreement with the Alberta government for federal-provincial cooperation in environmental, social and economic surveillance of the project. Installation of the bureaucratic structure produced pressure to act. This pressure found strong support among the members of the Independent Petroleum Association of Canada who needed markets for the gas whose supply now exceeded the existing demand. That the "gas bubble" had largely been induced by the policies of the Alberta and federal governments, which had created an artificial surplus crisis, was not generally appreciated.[6]

By the summer of 1978, the Northern Pipeline commissioner recommended a new course of action to the Canadian government. It should "pre-build" the southern part of the Alcan line in order to

148

export more Alberta gas to the American market. While there was a long-term risk that the complete pipeline might not be built, or at least not for a long time, Mitchell Sharp's position was that not pre-building would anger business and the Albertan and American governments. Even though the Canadian government was given President Carter's assurance by letter that the pipeline would be built and a joint resolution of Congress indicated the legislature's commitment to the project, it was a hard decision to make. The National Energy Board had determined that Canadia did have an adequate gas surplus and in December 1979 had authorized the export of sufficient gas to justify the pre-built pipeline. Despite the opposition of the ministers of finance and energy to the idea, the government decided to authorize the project and amended the pipeline legislation which had stipulated that construction could not begin until financing had been guaranteed for the whole project.

This was a move more contradictory to than consistent with government goals. If the main objective of the Canadian government in signing the Alcan pipeline agreement had been a massive short-term stimulation of the economy, then authorizing the pre-building of the smaller southern section only partly achieved that objective. The increased export of Alberta gas reduced the sense of need among some American politicians for the total Alaska Natural Gas Transportation System, making eventual construction of the whole project less likely. If self-reliance was the guiding principle of Canadian energy policy, as the federal white paper on energy policy of 1976 had indicated, building a pipeline to connect Alberta's supplies with American markets was hardly an indication of consistency. If the Alaska pipeline were further delayed or did not get built, Canada had made an implicit commitment to keep supplying its own accessible natural gas to the U.S. for an indefinite period.

One needed considerable credulity to accept the industry's arguments. It maintained that the only way to assure future supplies of energy from frontier areas, which would cost more to develop and be more expensive for the eventual consumer, was to export the present low-cost supplies at the relatively low prices then prevailing. The argument was also put forward that exporting more gas would be good for the Canadian balance of payments. Even those who argued that Canada would be earning diplomatic points by doing the Americans this favour were hard put to prove their case. By the fall of 1981 the impression that had stuck in political Washington was that the U.S. had done *Canada* a favour by buying more of its gas at prices that had doubled in the previous year.

Far from earning credit for Canada, the whole pipeline issue tended to increase Washington's level of irritation with its neighbour who was continually pressing the administration to hasten the project along. Although President Carter had formally promised his government's support, such pledges did not oblige the Americans to do anything specific. The expected industrial benefits on which Canada had staked so much depended on two sets of decisions being made in the United States. The first was a series of legislative actions that Congress had to take in order to make the Alaska Natural Gas Transportation System feasible. This "waiver package" would allow gas producers to hold equity in the project, a situation hitherto precluded by American law. It would permit the $6 billion gas conditioning plant that had to be built in Alaska to be included in the financing of the project. Most crucial of all, the American principle that billing could not start before delivery had to be waived so that the huge costs of the project could be financed by its sponsors' customers. By October 1981, the administration had assured itself of enough political support to introduce the waiver package into Congress, and by the end of the year the necessary legislation had been passed. Over four years after the American government had urgently pressed Canada into signing the ANGTS agreement, it had put its own legislation into place to allow the project to proceed.

Actual construction required financing, and financing was quite another matter. Whether the North American capital markets could manage to finance the most expensive development project of all time had been a subject for considerable debate. The United States Department of the Interior had reported to Congress in 1975 that the "capital markets should have the capacity to provide the needed funds to finance privately either of the several competing systems, provided the project is established as creditworthy and the returns offered on the investments are competitive." Yet two U.S. energy consultants hired by the State of Alaska argued in 1979 that the "Alaska Highway gas pipeline cannot be financed and built unless the United States government guarantees at least part of the projected debt. This judgment . . . is held almost unanimously by the natural gas transmission industry, Alaska gas producers, investment bankers, lending institutions, state and federal regulators, and concerned members of Congress."[7] President Carter had not indicated his willingness to enter into financial guarantees. During his visit to Ottawa, President Reagan had expressly stated that the United States would not leave Canada "in the lurch" over the pipeline. But as the months passed in 1981, it became obvious that there would be neither U.S. government guarantees nor U.S. government funds for the project.[8]

The only certainty by the middle of 1982 was that financing the project would take considerable time. The prevailing glut of natural gas ensured that progress would be slow. The impending deregulation of gas prices in the U.S. also indicated that domestic gas supplies would increase enormously in response to higher prices. Deregulation promised to make it more difficult for the pipeline sponsors to "roll in" the expensive Alaska gas costs, averaging it with the expected higher price to be paid by consumers for domestic supplies. The process of financing the pipeline would be intertwined with the regulatory process, since American regulatory decisions would be required at each stage. The Canadian and American companies' ability to satisfy their respective regulatory authorities would depend in turn on their capacity to obtain financing for the entire project, a prospect that had been delayed indefinitely by the fall in energy prices and the rise in the cost of borrowing scarce long-term capital. The pipeline that appeared so urgent in 1977, now seemed unlikely to be built before the Nineties. The boost to the Canadian economy that Canada expected as ANGTS's main benefit would not come from other megaprojects, which had also fallen victim to the fall in the world oil prices and the high cost of borrowing.

The brouhaha over the pre-build and the completion of the northern pipeline in 1980-81 was a crisis mainly of Canada's own making. The American government did not stage-manage the affair; nor did it threaten retaliation. Too anxious to please, Canada gave away its trump card — the natural gas in the ground — in return for indefinite delays in completing the pipeline it so badly wanted for macro-economic reasons. Faced with delays in Washington's political process, Ottawa had overreacted, pushing itself into a corner, reducing its leverage with the American government, and getting the worst of all possible worlds: more rapid depletion of its non-renewable resources, further integration into continental energy planning, postponed industrial benefits, and considerable ill will in Washington. The winners in Canada were the Independent Petroleum Association of Canada, whose members could increase their revenues, and the Albertan government, which increased its royalties; and in the U.S., American consumers who received the gas. Whether the Canadian consumer was a winner or a loser will only be known in retrospect when we know if the income received for conventional gas in the

Eighties was enough to develop adequate supplies of frontier gas towards the end of the century. The losers were the native people whose land claims had been set aside, and the Canadian government whose credit in Washington had been diminished. Since the early Seventies the Canadian government had shown itself too anxious to please for its own good. Its decisions had been hastily made without either sufficient data or adequate reconciliation with broader energy strategy thinking.

While the NEP has changed the constellation of power within the petroleum industry, it has not altered the basically continental orientation of Canada's gas companies, whether foreign-controlled or Canadian, whether privately held or public. Petro-Canada, Nova and Dome Petroleum are pushing for permission to proceed with the Arctic Pilot Project, a $3 billion undertaking to ship liquified natural gas by ice-breaking tanker to eastern Canada and so allow more western Canadian gas to be exported to the United States. Exports will probably rise to over half of Canadian gas production by the Nineties, when Canadian oil from Hibernia in the east and the Beaufort Sea in the north may also be abundant enough to ship to the American market. The paradoxical spectacle of a "nationalist" energy policy maintaining a continentalist orientation as a resource strategy appears to bear out Eric Kierans's epigram that Canada, while rich in resources, is poor in policy.[9]

Continental Resource Integration

The lack of a conscious strategy towards resources in Canada can be traced to the manner in which their development has taken place. The exploitation of Canadian staples for export in the twentieth century has historically been a response more to demands originating in the U.S. economy than to Canadian initiatives, whether public or private. American enterprise made the rules for the exploitation of Canadian resources. It mobilized the bulk of the necessary investment capital. It provided the engineering design and so captured the industrial benefits generated by the process of building the required facilities. Typically, American direct investment represented backward vertical integration by large resource-consuming companies wishing a secure source of raw materials for their production process. The price for Canada of having an assured market for its resources has been continual difficulty in having its resources processed before export, in getting a share of the engineering and industrial benefits, and thus in gaining the employment and other economic spin-offs that a country can normally

152

expect from the exploitation of its own resources. If the proportion of crude mineral exports to total mineral shipments abroad can be taken as an index of industrialization, Canada has become more like a developing country than an industrial economy over the years: crude minerals have risen from 49 per cent to 53 per cent of its mineral shipments since 1928-29.[10] The high level of foreign ownership — greater in Canadian mining than in Canadian manufacturing[11] — means that a high proportion of the economic rents deriving from the exploitation of these resources is either exported as profits to the foreign owners or reinvested to expand the foreign-controlled holdings in the economy.

What makes the resource sector even bleaker from the Canadian perspective is Canada's decline in its comparative advantage. This results from the rapid depletion of the economy's most accessible resources and the increasing competition from resources developed in Third World countries by multinational corporations financed in part from profits made by Canadian subsidiaries, in part by international development agencies.[12] The maintenance of Canada's competitive position now requires massive investment outlays to bring more inaccessible reserves to market at a time when huge investments are being planned for energy megaprojects and when those pressing for a reindustrialization of Canada's manufacturing economy stress the need for the diversion of available capital into high technology development. Although the macro-level prospects for Canadian resources are not rosy, the situation varies significantly from resource to resource.

Canada's Non-Renewable Resources

In *iron*, the prospects for change — and potential bilateral conflict — appear low. Canada is the fifth-largest producer of iron ore in the world and the largest source of foreign ore imported by the U.S. steel industry. Although Canada's exports to Japan and Europe have increased, they face competition from the higher grade reserves of Brazil and Australia. Canada's American market is protected from such foreign competition because of the high level of American ownership in Canadian ore mines, a participation that guarantees a market for the bulk of Quebec and Labrador's output.[13] Tension is less likely at the resource than at the manufacturing level, where the Canadian-owned steel industry is more efficient than its American competition and operates under the threat of American protectionist restrictions discussed in chapter 5.

Nickel has never been a point of serious dispute between Canada, the world's largest nickel producer, and the U.S., the world's largest nickel consumer. Canada supplies 76 per cent of American nickel imports. There are clouds on the horizon, however. There are vast reserves of lateritic nickel (not found in Canada) elsewhere in the world, and Inco has already made moves to expand its mining operations outside Canada. Manganese nodules on the ocean bed are a potentially important source of nickel in the long run, though costs of retrieval will be determined by the development of new technology for deep-sea mining and a resolution of big-power disagreements resulting from the revised Law of the Sea which we consider in chapter 10. Canadian federal and provincial governmental attempts to increase the economic rent from the mining of nickel are constrained by the high level of foreign ownership in the industry. The two major firms, Inco and Falconbridge, are effectively U.S.-controlled. If they come under too much pressure in Canada, they can shift their operations abroad both on land and under the sea.[14]

The prospects for Canada's *copper* industry — the third-largest producer in the world — are clouded more by competition from Third World sources than by tensions with the United States' industry, whose competitiveness has been reduced by tightened emission control standards introduced in the 1970s.[15] Canadian firms were exempted from the U.S. industry's appeal for tariff and quota protection by the U.S. International Trade Commission. It appears that only a further significant devaluation of the Canadian dollar would bring Canadian copper under attack from American interests on the basis of unfair competition. The absence of conflict that has characterized the continental copper relationship is likely to continue.

Canadian *potash* already accounts for 88 per cent of American potash imports. The second-largest world producer of potash after the Soviet Union, Canada exports 95 per cent of its potash production. Since American potash reserves have rapidly depleted, and since the U.S. government's alarmist reaction to the province of Saskatchewan's nationalization of half its industry has subsequently calmed down, Canada's thrust towards maximum continental integration of the potash market is not a source of conflict between the two countries.[16]

Asbestos is for Quebec what potash was for Saskatchewan: a resource in which it enjoys a near monopoly position in North America yet does not benefit from the economic rents available. Unlike potash, however, Canada supplies asbestos to several markets and so is not as dependent on the U.S. for its exports, even though 95 per cent of U.S. asbestos imports come from Canada. Also, in contrast to potash, to which little value is added before it is spread on the land as a fertilizer, domestic processing of asbestos has a large potential for job creation in the Quebec economy, since the bulk of the asbestos fibre is exported unprocessed. The long-drawn-out attempt by the Société Nationale de l'Amiante to nationalize Asbestos Corporation was a first step in this direction. As long as the supply of asbestos is not threatened or its price not unduly changed, this nationalization is not likely to be of more lasting concern to the United States government than was the establishment of the Potash Corporation of Saskatchewan. Basically friendly attitudes of Quebec nationalists towards the United States should ensure that disputes in this area are kept to manageable levels.[17]

Renewable Resources
The myth of the North American forests' inexhaustible supplies has provided both countries with much of their self-imagery. The productivity of these bountiful resources has fuelled much of their economic development for over a century. Unhappily the depradations of the lumber industry, which has paid little heed to the question of ensuring future harvests of trees, the devastation wreaked by forest fires (the area burned in Canada was five times greater than that harvested in Canada in 1980), and the destruction caused by insects have not been compensated for by the rigorous programs of wood husbandry and reforestation that characterize the industry in Sweden, the world's second-largest exporter. Despite the fact that the American industry is more than twice the size of the Canadian, the pulp and paper industry is relatively speaking far more important to Canada than it is to the United States, as can be seen by the export figures. The $12.8 billion of forest industry exports in 1980 represented 17 per cent of Canada's total exports. With forest product imports of $1.0 billion, the industry yielded the country's current account earnings of $11.8 billion — almost twice the contribution made to the balance of payments by iron, steel and non-ferrous metals combined.[18]

The two countries' mutual trade is highly complementary. The bulk of American imports of lumber, pulp and newsprint comes from Canada, which finds 63 per cent of its export market in the U.S. As Peter Pearse has written, "More than 84 per cent of all U.S. forest-product imports in 1975 were from Canada, while two-thirds of Canada's exports were to the United States (as is roughly the case for all Canadian exports)."[19] Table 6-1 shows how complete is the two countries' interdependence in this industry. The picture is not without its dark clouds. American forest production has increased dramatically and promises to grow further so that Canada will find its share of the

TABLE 6-1
FOREST PRODUCTS TRADE BETWEEN CANADA AND THE U.S., 1975
(%)

	United States		Canada	
	Exports to Canada	Imports from Canada	Exports to U.S.	Imports from U.S.
Lumber	28.5	93.6	76.1	94.4
Plywood and veneer	48.2	13.5	44.9	72.9
Pulp	2.2	97.5	54.6	72.5
Newsprint	—	99.5	78.0	—
Other paper and paperboard	27.7	44.1	40.5	96.0
Other forest materials [a]	12.6	49.6	78.3	99.2
All forest materials	18.5	84.3	66.6	89.2

[a] Including sawlogs and pulpwood.

Source: Peter H. Pearse, "Forest Products," in Carl E. Beigie and Alfred O. Hero, Jr., eds., *Natural Resources in U.S.-Canadian Relations*, vol. II (Boulder, Colorado: Westview Press, 1980), p. 427.

U.S. market continuing to erode. Although Canadian exports to the U.S. have risen gradually in absolute terms, U.S. imports as a proportion of U.S. consumption declined from 80 per cent to 65 per cent between 1950 and 1974.[20]

The Canadian forestry industry may be entering a period of internal strain because the profligate wastefulness of its forest companies and governments' blindness to their disregard for conservation have jeopardized Canada's potential to satisfy future levels of demand. But the bilateral relationship is not in crisis in this industry. Wood is not considered a strategic commodity in the same way as are oil and gas. Foreign and American ownership are high (U.S. interests account for 29 per cent of total ownership of pulp, 28 per cent of newsprint, and 19 per cent of other paper capacity), but Canadian ownership levels have increased significantly in the past decade.[21]

The major difficulty that Canada must anticipate on the bilateral front is growing protectionist pressures from U.S. producers and fabricators of highly manufactured wood products. Since the turn of the century, both countries have attempted to retain the maximum number of jobs that their forestry industry could produce by imposing export restrictions on the sale of unprocessed timber abroad. Canada won this tussle because of its comparative advantage at the time in this industry. Canada will continue to press for free access to American markets for all wood products. Even though the United States is in a position of net dependence on Canadian wood products, future trade patterns will be determined in this sector, as in so many other resource industries, by American import policy, which is to say by the power of the U.S. industry's protectionist lobby.

Although federal and provincial governments want to extend Canada's role as hewer of wood, they are resisting American pressure to become a continental drawer of water. Canada, which has less than 1 per cent of the world's population, has rivers that discharge nearly 9 per cent of the world's renewable water supply. With ten times the population and industry of Canada, the U.S. has only half its water resources, many of which are located in areas far from where the greatest needs exist. This is particularly true of the American sun belt, where growing demographic and industrial pressures and inadequate natural supplies will steadily increase the demand for a dramatic solution to a critical problem. Colossal diversion plans such as the North American Water and Power Alliance (NAWAPA) proposed by the Ralph M. Parsons Company in 1963 are on the drawing boards waiting for political support. These are designed to tap northwest Canada's vast water flows and redirect them to the American southwest.[22] As droughts and brownouts recur, demands for water imports from Canada will become extremely difficult to resist. So far they have been resisted not just by environmentalists but by provincial politicians who have constitutional jurisdiction over water. The province of Alberta is already foreseeing water shortages caused by the voracious thirst of tar sands and petrochemical developments.

Since Ronald Reagan's election, the NAWAPA scheme has been revived. Now estimated to cost $200 billion over 30 years of construction, it is projected to generate a surplus hydroelectric capacity equal to one quarter of present U.S. production. As one expert wrote in the summer of 1981,

> it is in my opinion the only concept advanced so far that will enable the lower reaches of western (American) rivers to achieve the salt balance necessary for the long-term health of western agriculture, on which the entire U.S., and indeed the world, has such dependence.[23]

Canada's capacity to respond to serious American pressure to launch

157

such a scheme is low. Under the auspices of the International Joint Commission, Canada shares with the U.S. in jointly managing the large lakes and river systems that the international border bisects, but it has not developed adequate scientific data on the possible consequences of massive water transfer schemes. It does not even have a thorough assessment of its present water resources or its future needs.[24] As a result, Harold Foster and Derrick Sewell feel Canada is ill-prepared to respond to concrete export proposals and ''is in a weak position in negotiating with the United States on such matters as . . . water export.''[25] Though an unwilling drawer of water for the U.S., Canada may find itself pressed harder into this role, a role for which some precedent has been developed not just in small water transfers that have already been allowed from Lake Michigan, but also in the construction of huge hydro projects from which American electricity markets are supplied.

Some argue that there is a major distinction between transferring colossal volumes of water from one watershed to another and transmitting the electricity generated by the hydro power in one watershed to the markets of another. The physical transfer of water has far more drastic ecological consequences for both the donor and recipient watersheds, whereas the ecological damage resulting from large hydroelectric projects is limited to the river system whose energy is tapped. The export of hydroelectricity can be viewed in this perspective as profiting from a renewable resource. Others maintain that the export of electricity, like the construction of pipelines or aquaducts, commits the energy exporter in perpetuity to service the needs of the importer. This argument goes on to maintain that, because energy is a strategic commodity, surpluses should be preserved as part of the national patrimony for use by future generations. When Canada, which suffers from so many comparative economic disadvantages in its colder climate, smaller market and higher transportation costs, exports its surplus energy to the United States, it is giving away its major comparative advantage to its chief competitor, selling off its birthright to future industrial jobs for a mess of present-day potage.

Such is not the position of either the Quebec or Ontario governments. One quarter of Quebec's total capital investment has been placed in Hydro-Québec, much of whose power is exported on short-term contracts to the eastern American states. The thirteen-year, $5 billion export commitments of hydro energy will justify the construction of a second James Bay facility, an objective that the Parti Québécois government has actively pursued and that the Liberal

158

opposition has supported.[26] Reluctant to place themselves in a position of dependency on their provincial neighbours, both Ontario and Quebec prefer to export to the south.[27] Whether Quebec can use the proposed second phase of the James Bay hydro project's long-term export contract to the eastern states as a bargaining lever to achieve other economic goals, such as better access for its products to the American market, remains to be seen. It is very difficult for a province to lever negotiations with independent power companies into concessions from the federal or state governments. Gratitude to Quebec for relieving their long-term electricity shortage will not translate easily into exemptions from American protectionism. On the other hand, anger at Ontario for considering the export of thermally generated electricity was used against Canada in the environmental negotiations between the two federal capitals, as we shall see in chapter 9. The long-term export of Quebec hydroelectricity is generally considered to be an environmentally preferable alternative to the construction of either nuclear or coal-fired thermal generating plants in the eastern states. The export of coal-fired Ontario electricity is seen by the coal-burning states of the Ohio River Valley as proof perfect of Ontario's hypocrisy in its campaign against their acid-rain emissions. Resource development, in other words, is not a one-edged sword; its policy implications are complex and by no means solely of advantage to Canada in increasing its suasion, political or economic, with the U.S. government.

Continuity or Change: The Relevance of the NEP

Set in the international competitive context, Canada's unquestioned strength as a holder of valuable resources does not seem to give it particularly tangible leverage vis-à-vis the United States to enhance either its resource exports, the processing of more resources prior to export, or, more importantly, access to American markets for its manufactured products. When Canada's dependence on the United States as a source for Canadian resource imports is balanced against American dependence on Canada for American resource imports, Canada appears more dependent on the U.S. than the U.S. is on Canada, since in most sectors Canada is heavily dependent on the U.S. market while the United States has access to other suppliers. The U.S. will undoubtedly remain Canada's biggest customer.[28] Canada will therefore remain vulnerable to American policies that affect the level of U.S. demand for imported resources.[29]

These considerations do not imply that the United States enjoys arbitrary control over Canada in the resource field. Having been bitten by OPEC, the United States is nervous about resource cartels of producer countries led by interventionist governments. Since Canada is both a producer and a consumer of resources, it is ambivalent about cartels. It was reluctant to associate itself with OPEC, though its entry into the uranium cartel should make the United States sensitive about how far Canadian passivity can be taken for granted. When the United States shut off foreign imports of uranium in 1964 to protect American uranium suppliers, the Canadian government responded by entering into a cartel with other uranium-producing countries. This action caused further tension between the two governments when American anti-trust court proceedings against the cartel's members who were subsidiaries of American corporations raised the further thorny issue of extra-territoriality. As Donald Macdonald, who was energy minister at the time, subsequently complained, "the judiciary in the United States has been encouraged to disregard Canadian sovereignty by the actions of the U.S. administration" in this case.[30]

While the United States continues to regard Canada's resources "as a secure source of supply, analogous to domestic production,"[31] Canada can be expected to continue in the policy directions adopted in the Seventies. One benefit that Canadian governments can be expected to press for, but which holds some potential for conflict with the United States, is further processing. Since the federal government amended the Export and Import Permits Act in 1974 to allow export controls to be implemented, Canada has created a policy instrument that can be used in the future whenever increasing American dependence on foreign sources gives Canada greater leverage to achieve further processing before export. In the meantime little progress can be expected. Mineral procurement security policies of some of the major industrial countries will expand mineral development in other regions and reduce Canada's competitive position and so its bargaining power.[32] As the federal government's discussion paper, Mineral Policy, explains, the apparently low tariffs on minerals in Japan, the European Community and the U.S. are misleading: "The true protective impact of tariff rates is much higher than suggested by the nominal rates, when the value added by a protected processing activity is relatively low."[33] The industrialized countries' protectionism increases the incentive for Canadian exporters to sell concentrates and increases the disincentive to establish new smelters and refineries. Canadian negotiators failed during the Tokyo Round to gain international support for their objective of tariff changes that would discourage foreign tariff barriers to more processed products. In addition, the threat of such American non-tariff barriers as import quotas, long an irritant in the bilateral relationship, is likely to be as important an obstacle to Canadian exports of lead, zinc, sulphur, pig iron and aluminum as it has been in the past decade.[34] Even normal government assistance policies to further the resource industries could make Canadian exports subject to countervailing American action of the type discussed in chapter 5. Thus, until the United States seriously depletes its resources, Canada, with its current favourable balance of trade in resources, has little bargaining power with which to extract more benefits from its resource relationship with the United States.[35]

Until the early Seventies, the return from all types of resource taxes and royalties, except for those on petroleum, generally made no net contribution to government revenues.[36] The Carter Royal Commission on Taxation had recommended that, on the grounds of equity, the tax holidays and depletion allowances accorded the mining industry be terminated so that resource companies contribute their fair share to the public revenues. In his study for the Manitoba government, Eric Kierans revived the classical economist Ricardo's notion of economic rent to argue that governments should capture, on behalf of the public as owners of the resources, the excess profits that the resource companies were earning.[37] Federal and provincial governments used these rationales to increase their resource taxes during the decade. But there is a constraint: the potential for companies like Inco to shift their activities to other countries puts an upper limit beyond which increased taxation would be counterproductive.

If the taxation instrument's potential to increase economic rents has been exhausted, governments can be expected to turn their attention to the question of foreign ownership, since in industries with a high level of foreign ownership, "if the rents are not extracted by domestic tax systems, Canadians end up paying foreign shareholders more to consume their own resources."[38] Foreign-owned firms' capacity to minimize profits, and therefore local taxes in Canada, by transfer pricing, management fees and other head office levies has been demonstrated by the foreign-owned sector of the Canadian mining industry, which averaged only 36 per cent of the Canadian-owned firms' rate of return during the five-year period 1972-76.[39]

Having bitten off the oil and gas industry, the federal government clearly feels that further Canadianization cannot be digested. Its 1981 white paper, *Mineral Policy*, explicitly makes the case against "NEPing" or strengthening policies to reduce foreign ownership levels in mining. Security of supply is less pressing an issue than in petroleum, it argues: Canadian-controlled multinationals give Canadians a greater presence in the mineral sector; the outflow of dividends and the diversion of investments is not as big a problem, since mining is less profitable than oil and gas.[40] Despite the increasing interest of foreign-owned resource corporations in exploration and development, and despite the decline of the Canadian-owned junior mining sector, federal policy promises to be passive on the question of ownership. Thus, for all the political heat generated by the Alaska pipeline issue, the crisis of 1981 did little to change the deepening integration of Canada's resource industries in the continental market. The consequences of similar integration of the Canadian in the American money markets for Canada's macroeconomic policy dependence is the concern of chapter 7.

The Macroeconomic Policy Context

7

Much of Canada's dependence results from the country's abnormal bilateral domination by the overpowering American system, but in its macroeconomic dimension Canada's dependency relationship with the United States is more normal by international standards. West German Chancellor Helmut Schmidt, who had denounced American interest rate policy at the Montebello Summit of 1981, claiming that rates were the highest they had been since Jesus Christ, was concerned that artificially high American interest rates were endangering the fabric of European society. The summit leaders had pressed President Reagan to soften his tight-money stance, but the president had assured his colleagues that U.S. interest rates would decline in a matter of months as American inflation fell. When interest rates did not fall with the deceleration of American inflation, Schmidt waxed angry in public. High American rates had attracted capital from Europe, forcing European banks to raise their rates of interest in order to defend their currencies and so threaten the economy with "the deepest recession since the middle Thirties." American pressure on Europe concerning anti-Soviet economic measures was a further cause for exasperation. "For my case, there is too much talk about so-called strategic questions in the military and political field, and too little talk and too little co-operation in the economic field," Schmidt said.[1] A week later, on February 25, Prime Minister Pierre Trudeau joined the chorus expressing the OECD countries' public unhappiness with the economic policy of the United States from which they were all suffering. The Canadian government, he acknowledged to a press conference, had been impatient for months with the high interest rates resulting from U.S. monetary policies.[2] That West Germany was complaining bitterly about the constraints caused by American economic policies suggests that some of the problems of Canada's dependence on the U.S. are shared by its more industrialized European partners. Even if Canada

163

has enjoyed good company in suffering Reaganomics, there is reason to question whether it needs to tolerate this dependency so passively.

Interest Rates and Deficits

The Canadian economy's satellitic nature is denied by few, though described in many different ways. Finance Minister Allan MacEachen's acceptance of anti-inflationary monetary restraint in his ill-fated 1981 budget was called by NDP leader Ed Broadbent "tagging along at Ronald Reagan's heels like some lost poodle following a wolf."[3] Somewhat less colourfully, the former deputy minister of finance, Robert Bryce, made the same point as Broadbent while disagreeing with his prescription. Canada could not unilaterally hold its interest rates below American levels since the price of the integration of its capital markets with those of the United States is "some restraint upon our freedom of choice in monetary policy."[4] The dilemma posed by Canada's dependence is not new. In 1938, Harold Innis noted that the interrelation of the two economies was so advanced that they were like Siamese twins — "a very small twin and a very large one, to be exact": American monetary policy was the monetary policy of the North American continent, including Canada.[5] Wynne Plumptre has documented Canada's steady loss of flexibility in monetary policy.[6] With the integration of both countries' capital markets and the maintenance of the Canadian dollar at a fixed rate of exchange, Robert Dunn observed "that Canadian monetary policy was largely determined in Washington and that attempts by the Bank of Canada to adopt a different policy were doomed to be frustrated."[7]

Canada's return in 1970 to a flexible exchange rate was meant to give its monetary policy greater independence vis-à-vis the United States and greater effectiveness as one of the government's tools for managing the economy. Indeed "the most recent research indicates that flexible exchange rates do not significantly weaken, and may even enhance slightly, the effectiveness of Canadian fiscal policy."[8] This margin of independence appears to have been forfeited in recent years by the Bank of Canada's and the federal government's approach to fighting inflation.

Despite strenuous criticisms of his stance, the governor of the Bank of Canada, Gerald Bouey, has single-mindedly held to a strategy of monetary discipline, ambitiously trying to control the supply of money in circulation, the exchange rate of the Canadian dollar and the rate of interest. Since 1975 the rate of growth of M-1 — a narrowly defined portion of the money supply — has been cut in half. The immediate goal of Bouey's tight-money policy has been to keep interest rates above the rate of inflation, on the assumption that increasing the cost of money will decrease demand and thus achieve the bank's basic objective: cause inflation to fall.

Since introducing this strategy, four major shocks have complicated its execution. Following the prior acceleration of inflation and incomes in Canada in the permissive monetary policy environment of 1971-74 when the Canadian dollar rose above par, a major and overdue devaluation of the Canadian dollar took place during 1977 (see Figure 7-1). While the cheaper dollar made Canadian exports more competitive on the world market, it also made Canadian imports more expensive, thereby increasing inflationary pressures in Canada. Since export industries were operating at capacity, Bouey felt that the inflationary effects of any further devaluation would far outweigh the potential gains in productivity that might result. A more recent shock has been the rise of U.S. interest rates in response to the Federal Reserve Board's conversion to monetarism — a reliance on tight

FIGURE 7-1
CANADA-U.S. EXCHANGE RATES

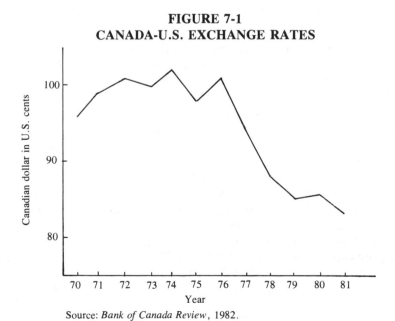

Source: *Bank of Canada Review*, 1982.

165

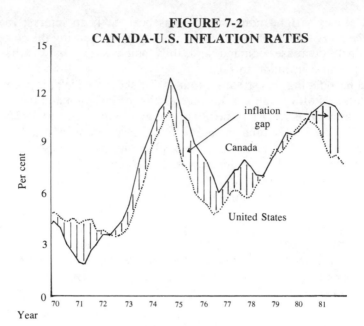

FIGURE 7-2
CANADA-U.S. INFLATION RATES

Source: Toronto-Dominion Bank, *Canada's Business Climate*, Spring 1982, p. 15.

control of the supply of money. High American interest rates strengthened the Bank of Canada's commitment to still higher rates. Maintaining Canadian rates of interest above American levels became the prime vehicle for protecting the dollar against devaluation pressures: high Canadian interest rates attracted short-term foreign capital which propped up the level of the Canadian dollar. The third shock bedevilling Canadian monetary policy is the "inflation gap" between the two economies (see Figure 7-2). This puts more downward pressure on the Canadian dollar. Since the bank is convinced that further devaluation would have catastrophic effects — further increasing inflation — it feels it must defend the dollar still more vigorously. Lastly came the massive export of capital in the first half of 1981, when some $9 billion was spent Canadianizing foreign corporations by takeovers.[9] This dramatically weakened the Canadian dollar in the summer of 1981, when American interest rates were soaring and when the Canadian prime lending rate reached its peak of 22.75 per cent.

What Arthur Donner called "Ottawa's exchange rate fixation"[10] — the commitment to prevent the dollar from falling below some

166

undefined level lest it trigger another inflationary cycle — has returned Canada to a situation close to the monetary policy dependence of the fixed exchange rate era, making Canadians more vulnerable to the vagaries of American interest rates which scaled unprecedented heights at the beginning of the 1980s. Had Ronald Reagan been able to deliver on his promise that interest rates would fall with the inflation rate, Gerald Bouey's problems might have been resolved. According to the new president's supply-side theory, large cuts in the taxation of marginal income would release private and corporate savings for prodigious, productivity-enhancing new investments. In actual practice, Reagonomics turned out to be based on a couple of contradictions. The tax cuts, to start with, were simply reductions of the planned increases in the 1981 budget. Reagan's tax receipts for 1982 were to be higher in real terms than those of 1981. Far more serious, the cutting of government expenditures that was necessary to achieve the secondary goal of a balanced budget turned into massive spending increases to meet another commitment, the expansion of the armed forces. When the president brought his message to Congress at the beginning of 1982, the fat was clearly in the fire. By his own admission the federal government's deficit would verge on $100 billion, though other observers of the American economy such as the Congressional Budget Office considered the estimate misleadingly low.

Even at $100 billion, the implications for American interest rates may be severe. Through the absorption of the available private pools of savings when the government borrows to finance its deficit, Reagan will force interest rates even higher, not bring them down as he had promised the summit leaders in July 1981.[11] Reagan has put all his chips on his untested and contradictory doctrine which preaches balanced budgets while escalating defence expenditures. Meanwhile the Federal Reserve Board has been pursuing a monetarist approach by sticking to a predefined target rate for the expansion of the money supply in its own attempt to bring down the rate of inflation. Unless the president can force the Federal Reserve Board to reverse its stance and increase the supply of money more rapidly, American interest rates will be under further pressure to rise. This in turn will force the Bank of Canada to keep the money supply tight and interest rates under upward pressure, both to combat inflation and to forestall the further devaluation that would result from Canadian savings shifting into American funds in search of a higher return. (Figure 7-3 shows how closely increases in long-term U.S. rates have been tracked by similar increases in Canada.)

FIGURE 7-3

LONG-TERM INTEREST RATES IN CANADA AND THE U.S.

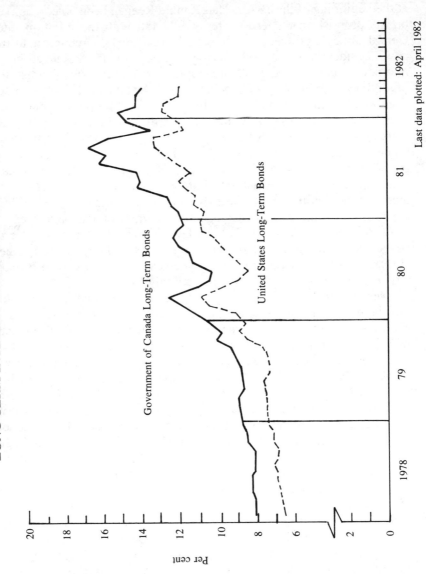

Source: Department of Finance, *Economic Indicators: Charts*, Ottawa May 7, 1982, p. 27.

The orthodox monetarist Thomas Courchene has criticized the Bank of Canada for artificially holding up both the exchange rate of the dollar and the rate of interest. While the Bank of Canada should continue to control the money supply (defined much more broadly than it is now), it should, he felt, allow both interest and exchange rates to be determined by market conditions.[12] In concurring with a further fall of the dollar, Courchene joined Arthur Donner, who argued that it is better to risk some inflationary pressure resulting from devaluation than to force the economy into a slump by maintaining high interest rates which serve not to depress prices but to accelerate bankruptcies, increase unemployment and prolong the recession, along the lines of the British experience under Margaret Thatcher.[13] Other economists joined the chorus of complaints. Policies of restraint cause great hardships by reducing production and increasing unemployment, without at the same time bringing down inflation, argued William Watson.[14] High interest rates were themselves inflationary, raising the cost of doing business and the prices paid by consumers, deterring investment, increasing foreign indebtedness, and worsening the balance of payments by artificially propping up the Canadian dollar, wrote Reuben Bellan.[15]

Because the Canadian and American capital markets are so closely linked, such critics of federal policies as the provincial premiers, who demanded that Canadian interest rates be dropped to stimulate employment in the provinces, had to face the implications of such a move's impact on the Canadian dollar, whose further depreciation would increase the burden of servicing their foreign debts. Analysis of previous capital movement showed that, for every 1 per cent shift in the differential between the two economies' rate of interest, $400 million of short-term capital moved across the border in three months.[16] According to Robert Bryce, there was $133 billion of interest-sensitive capital in Canadian banks that could take flight in the anticipation of lower interest rates or the devaluation that would ensue. In practice, everything would depend on the market's assessment of the aims of a new policy. A major devaluation forced by speculative pressure could start a vicious circle of higher inflation caused by higher prices for imports. Assuming that exchange controls are unworkable in such an open economy without the patriotism engendered by a wartime situation, John McCallum argued that a wage and price control program would be needed to accompany a policy that uncoupled Canadian interest rates from those in the U.S. Controls would break the price-wage spiral and give time for the dollar to achieve its natural level.[17] Others have noted that a more expansionary monetary policy, which lowered the rate of interest and the value of the Canadian dollar, would require a tighter fiscal policy — increased taxes or reduced government spending — to restrain the inflationary impact of these shifts. Bruce Wilkinson suggested that an interest equalization tax could be used to obviate the need for exchange controls as a disincentive for Canadian capital to flow south in search of higher American rates.[18]

The debate on uncoupling the interest and exchange rate was as heated and unresolved within the business community as among economists. William Mulholland, chairman and CEO of the Bank of Montreal, attacked Canada's tight money policies with their resultant "punitive" interest rates. "The gap between the supply of money and the amount that could be absorbed by non-inflationary economic activity contributes significantly, we believe, to the current high level of interest rates."[19] But major business organizations like the Business Council on National Issues (BCNI) argued that inflation is the first and worst enemy, so monetary restraint must be pursued. As its president, Thomas d'Aquino, prophesied to the Edmonton Chamber of Commerce, "To give in to demands to drive interest rates below their free market levels would result in loss of control of the money supply, acceleration of the trend of inflation, and disaster for the domestic economy."[20] The BCNI's invocation of the free market levels of interest rates appeared somewhat misleading, given that American rates were high as a deliberate consequence of administration and Federal Reserve Board policies and that Canadian rates were high because the government and the Bank of Canada had chosen to lock their monetary policies to the volatile American star. It was not American pressure that had tightened the knots of this dependency. It was Canadian government paralysis in the face of economic trouble. Disaster for the economy was what critics already saw in Canada's mushrooming foreign debt, the capital side of Canada's interest rate dependence.

Foreign Portfolio Capital

Canada's international debt has grown in recent years, not as a result of new foreign direct investment but because of huge sums borrowed in debt form on foreign, mainly American, markets by provincial governments and Crown corporations and by Canadian companies financing the repatriation of foreign-owned branch plants. (See Table 7-1.) As an issue in the Canadian-American relationship, the still growing indebtedness reinforced Canada's problem of dependence on American monetary policy. The growing payments required to service and redeem the debt put a downward pressure on the Canadian dollar, requiring the Bank of Canada to raise interest rates. This encouraged Canadians to borrow long-term capital abroad where rates were lower, perpetuating the vicious circle of cause and effect, a circle that would only be broken to the extent that the large users of capital expanded their export capacity. Even though federal and provincial fiscal policies have been tightened to reduce the burden of public debt payments, mounting interest rates have kept payments high. The more the foreign debt mounts, the greater become the costs of letting the Canadian dollar float down to some "natural" level, since it will take more devalued dollars to service and repay loans taken out in American currency — as Gerald Bouey told the premiers when they criticized his policy.

Foreign borrowing is not an evil in itself. At an early stage in an economy's growth, borrowing abroad can be justified as a means to produce the new investment that an immature economy cannot generate from its own savings. The massive borrowings made by Canada during the Seventies did produce a very large volume of physical capital outlays and a major expansion in corporate financial assets. But Canada is not a newly developing economy. As a wealthy society with a high level of savings it has no moral claim to so much of

TABLE 7-1
CUMULATIVE BALANCE OF CANADA'S INTERNATIONAL
INDEBTEDNESS
($ billions)

Year	Direct Investment	Portfolio Investment	Other	Total
1955	− 6.0	− 4.9	+2.9	− 8.0
1960	−10.4	− 8.0	+1.8	−16.6
1965	−13.9	− 9.8	+1.3	−22.4
1970	−20.2	−14.0	+5.8	−28.4
1975	−26.9	−21.0	+5.5	−42.4
1979	−33.0	−41.8	+5.3	−69.5

Source: Statistics Canada, Cat. No. 67-702, Bank of Canada *Review*, February 1981, and Donner, *Financing the Future*, Table A-1.

the available international capital. It is also argued that, even in a mature economy, foreign borrowing can allow faster economic growth than would be possible from the internally mobilized resources of the economy. This view assumes the economy is already working at full capacity, but Canada's huge borrowings in the Seventies took place when the economy had unused capacity and substantial unemployment. Capital imports tend to push up the value of the Canadian dollar and reduce exports.[21]

The final major argument used to justify an economy's growing foreign indebtedness is its need for direct investment. In actual fact, net foreign direct investment has been negative since 1975: Canadians have exported more capital than has entered the country from foreign sources. Foreign multinationals have disinvested from their branch plants; Canadian multinationals have increased their presence abroad. This has not stopped the foreign-controlled sector from growing, but the growth has taken place as a result of the reinvestment of profits generated within the Canadian economy. Even though the foreign-controlled sector grows from self-generated earnings, the drain on the balance of payments resulting from dividend and other service payments itself continues to worsen. Ironically, Canadianization — or buying back control of foreign-owned companies — increases the short-term drain, since high interest rates paid on the borrowed portfolio capital entail very high servicing charges on the foreign debt capital that is borrowed to finance the takeovers. (See Table 7-2.)

It is Canada's enormous deficit on current account since 1974 that best indicates its dilemma of international dependence (see Table 7-3). Simply put, the current account deficit, which averaged $4.6 billion from 1975 to 1979, is a measure of Canada's inability to pay its way in the world. The deficit of $23 billion accumulated over these five years indicated what Canada had had to borrow to make up the difference between what it earned in sales abroad and what it spent.

There was a public policy rationale for the increase in the deficit in the Seventies. The federal government made a conscious decision to prop up the economy in 1974-75, at a time when Canada's trading partners were suffering from the world recession. Federal policy aimed to cushion the impact of escalating world energy costs by subsidizing energy prices for Canadian consumers. Social policy decisions were made to index government transfer payments to individuals for family allowances, pensions, unemployment insurance and income supplements. At the same time, tax payers' obligations were sheltered by indexing from the impact of inflation. As inflation increased, the

172

TABLE 7-2
BALANCE OF CANADA'S INTERNATIONAL PAYMENTS
($ billions)

Year	I Commodity Trade Balance	II Interest and Dividends	III Other Services and Transfers	IV Net Foreign[1] Direct Investment	V Other Long-Term Capital Movement	VI Short-Term Capital Movement	VII Errors and Omissions	VIII Net Official Monetary Movements and SDR Allocation
1970	+3.1	-1.0	-0.9	+0.5	+0.5	-0.2	-0.4	+1.7
1971	+2.6	-1.1	-1.0	+0.7	-0.1	+1.0	-1.3	+0.9
1972	+1.9	-1.0	-1.2	+0.2	+1.4	+0.5	-1.5	+0.3
1973	+2.7	-1.2	-1.4	+0.1	+0.5	-0.6	-0.6	-0.5
1974	+1.7	-1.6	-1.6	—	+1.0	+1.3	-0.9	—
1975	-0.5	-2.0	-2.4	-0.2	+4.1	+1.6	-1.2	-0.4
1976	+1.4	-2.5	-2.7	-0.9	+8.8	+0.1	-3.7	+0.5
1977	+2.7	-3.7	-3.4	-0.3	+4.6	+0.6	-2.0	-1.4
1978	+3.6	-4.5	-4.1	-1.9	+5.3	+1.2	-2.8	-3.3
1979	+4.0	-5.3	-3.8	-1.3	+4.1	+7.8	-3.9	+1.9
1980	+8.0	-5.6	-3.9	-2.1	+3.5	+1.2	-2.5	-1.3

Note: [1] Excludes retained earnings and repatriated dividends and includes Canadian direct investment abroad and repatriated capital by foreign investors.

The inflow of capital (columns IV, V and VI) provided a short-term support to the Canadian dollar during the early Seventies. By the end of the decade the dollar was being weakened by direct disinvestment (column IV) and by the interest and dividend outflows (column II) needed to service the earlier borrowing.

Source: Statistics Canada, Cat. No. 67-001.

government's receipts grew less rapidly, just as government expenditures automatically increased. During this period major public utilities like Ontario Hydro and Hydro-Québec floated large loans abroad to finance their capital expansion programs. With the exception of such productive investments, the abnormal borrowing represented by the sustained current account deficits showed that Canada was consuming beyond its means.[22] Canada was financing social programs and consumption by going into debt abroad. In short, Canada, which had historically suffered from excessive dependence on the American economy, consciously spent itself into still greater dependency.

The public policy question that this situation raises is whether that macroeconomic dependence can be reduced. To see whether the current account can be brought into balance and then into surplus, one must look at its major components.

- Interest payments on debt already contracted cannot be reduced without the economy generating a surplus to retire that debt.
- Dividend payments can be expected to continue their upward trend after the 1981-82 recession unless there is a massive Canadianization to reduce the size of the foreign-owned sector of the economy. Under massive Canadianization, interest payments to service foreign debt would surpass dividend payments.
- For similar reasons, other service payments can be expected only to grow.
- The labour force which, under the combined impact of the baby boom and large-scale immigration, had grown fastest among all industrialized countries, has put heavy pressure on the economy to import capital in order to provide jobs.[23] The growth of the labour force will slow down, but it will remain twice as fast as the U.S. rate.
- Public borrowing is a factor over which the government should be able to exercise some control. A reduction of government expenditures, or an increase of receipts through higher taxation, could reduce the extent to which the government uses up the supply of private-sector savings and so allow private enterprise, provincial governments and Crown corporations to finance their needs within the economy rather than look to New York for their capital requirements.

In the final analysis, reversing the current account deficit, whose growth trend is indicated in Table 7-3, requires that Canada produce more than it spends. The formula is simple but its execution is

174

TABLE 7-3
CANADIAN CURRENT ACCOUNT
($ billions)

Year	(1) Current Account Balance	(2) Net Undistributed Earnings on Foreign Direct Investment in Canada	(3) Adjusted Current Account (1) − (2)	Adjusted Current Account as a Percentage of	
				GNP	Private Fixed Capital Formation
1970	+1.1	0.8	+0.3	+0.3%	+ 1.9%
1971	+0.4	1.3	-0.9	-1.0	- 5.3
1972	-0.4	1.5	-1.9	-1.8	-10.1
1973	+0.1	2.2	-2.1	-1.7	- 8.7
1974	-1.5	2.7	-4.2	-2.8	-14.5
1975	-4.8	2.5	-7.3	-4.4	-21.6
1976	-3.8	2.7	-6.5	-3.4	-16.9
1977	-4.3	3.3	-7.6	-3.7	-18.5
1978	-5.0	3.5	-8.5	-3.7	-18.9
1979	-5.1	4.1	-9.2	-3.2	-15.2

Sources: Statistics Canada, Cat. Nos. 67-001 and 13-001; Donner, *Financing the Future*, Table A-3.

TABLE 7-4
TRADE BALANCE BY COMMODITY CATEGORY
($ billions)

Year	Edible [a] Products	Crude [b] Materials	Fabricated [c] Materials	End [d] Products	Other	Total
1970	+0.8	+1.8	+ 3.0	− 3.1	—	+2.5
1971	+1.0	+1.9	+ 2.7	− 3.6	−0.2	+1.8
1972	+1.0	+2.0	+ 3.0	− 4.8	−0.2	+1.0
1973	+1.3	+2.9	+ 3.9	− 6.4	−0.2	+1.5
1974	+1.4	+3.7	+ 4.2	− 9.0	−0.2	−0.5
1975	+1.4	+2.8	+ 3.8	−10.3	—	−2.3
1976	+1.4	+3.2	+ 6.0	−10.0	−0.5	+0.1
1977	+1.3	+3.5	+ 7.9	−10.9	−0.4	+1.4
1978	+1.4	+2.9	+10.4	−12.4	−0.1	+2.2
1979	+2.1	+4.6	+12.4	−17.2	−0.5	+1.4
1980	+2.6	+3.4	+16.6	−17.8	+0.4	+5.2

Notes: [a] Live animals, food, feed, beverages, tobacco, etc.

   [b] Fibres, industrial vegetable products, pulpwood, ores, petroleum, natural gas, etc.

   [c] Leather, chemicals, metals, electricity, paper, etc.

   [d] Machinery, equipment, consumer goods.

Source: Statistics Canada, Cat. Nos. 65-202 and 65-203.

problematic, for the imbalance in Canada's trade pattern, which is already bad, is going to get worse. Canada's terms of trade are worsening.[24] Those goods in whose trade it enjoys a surplus have low income elasticities: their growth prospects are low since demand for them will not expand as the world economy grows. In contrast to raw and semi-finished goods, the manufactured goods on which Canada suffers a deficit of nearly $20 billion enjoy high elasticities: demand for them will grow, so Canada's import bill will get bigger. (See Table 7-4.) So will the demand for engineering and marketing services, computer programming, technology, films and television entertainment, and so on. The economic outlook is, in short, bad. The economy suffers from high levels of inflation and unemployment, while wage rates have increased faster than gains in productivity. Relatively high levels of protection have not been used strategically to generate world-competitive industries. Low levels of research and development lead to continued imports of technology, leaving Canada always lagging behind the technological level of its competitors.[25] As if this were not enough, Canada is facing competitive pressures from the newly industrialized countries, which enjoy much lower labour costs, at the same time as its potential markets in developed economies are being shielded by higher levels of tariff and non-tariff protection.

A long-term improvement in Canada's deteriorating trade prospects would require a major improvement in its competitive capacity resulting from a transformation of its manufacturing structure, a rationalization of inefficient branch plant sectors, an elimination of labour-intensive industries, and an expansion of world product leaders in new technologies that could open up new markets for Canadian end products. The very prescription, however, flies in the face of the constraints that have prevented these developments in the past: the extra-territorial application of American anti-trust laws prevents the rationalization by merger of American-controlled branch plants; the technological dependence of the manufacturing sector inhibits the development of an innovative industrial culture; the protectionist barriers in the United States, Europe and Japan militate against the ultimate success of promising Canadian ventures. And the powerful presence in the Canadian political system of the multinationals' viewpoint that is articulated by leading Canadian spokespersons in the legal fraternity, the business community and the media exerts strong pressures to dissuade government from embarking on a Japanese- or Swedish-style industrial strategy.

The thrust outlined in the National Energy Program — Canadianization of the energy industry together with the construction of energy megaprojects aimed at exporting Canadian hydrocarbons — will not be economic unless world oil prices rise again or interest levels fall dramatically. The repatriation of foreign-owned companies by Canadian capital has a direct, but negative, impact on the exchange rate in the short term. When a multinational corporation's head office converts the Canadian dollars it has received for its branch plant into foreign currency this depresses the value of the Canadian dollar. Under current Bank of Canada policies the priority given to defending the dollar requires the bank to raise the rate of interest and/or borrow short-term capital abroad to defend the currency. Given the existing large current account deficit and the debt-service costs of borrowing debt capital abroad, there are obvious limits beyond which a Canadianization program cannot be pushed, even though in the longer-term repatriation of control over resource corporations will lead to a decline in the payment abroad of dividends and service charges. As Arthur Donner notes, "Canadianization can only occur on a large-scale basis if the macroeconomic house is in better order."[26]

Undertaking the series of massive energy projects proposed for the next two decades will require a major adjustment of Canada's savings and investment pattern, since it is expected they will make up one third of Canada's investment needs. Although Canada has better "supply-side" policies to encourage the accumulation of savings for investment purposes than exist in the United States, it is estimated that 6 per cent of the $1.5 trillion of new capital formation that will be needed in the 1980s will still have to be financed by non-residents.[27] Were the megaproject strategy to succeed and Canada became a major exporter of oil and gas, the current account could be brought into balance. If it went into surplus, Canada would become a net exporter of capital. Such a scenario would allow the repatriation of control over the remaining foreign-controlled sectors of the economy and a dramatic decrease in the macroeconomic dependence represented both by the present alarming current account deficit and the Bank of Canada's high interest rate policy. Between the deep gloom of the present and the bright glow of the long-term future lie many unconfirmed assumptions and several difficult decades.

Continuity or Change in Macro-Level Dependence

There is little doubt that Canada's macroeconomic woes have been intensified as a result of the Reagan administration's monetarist obsession, but Canada is not unique in this general distress. What is specific to the bilateral relationship in this domain is the colossal increase in Canada's portfolio debt, which has resulted partly from the profligacy and investments of the Seventies and partly from the massive repatriation of assets in the energy sector in 1981. The long-term gain of containing economic rents within the country is being paid for with short-term pain by a dramatic depreciation in the dollar, astronomical interest rates and a stubbornly high rate of inflation. With Reagan, the nature of Canada's macroeconomic dependence did not change, but its passive acceptance by Ottawa had become more visible to the average citizen and more damaging to the economy's prospects.

Part III

Questions of Sovereignty

Questions of Sovereignty

In Part II we saw how the Reagan challenge has meant a serious change in all the economic issues of the bilateral relationship except for resource integration. In macroeconomic policy issues, Canada's helpless dependence on American monetarism has been aggravated by its headlong rush into greater portfolio debt. American pressure on Canadian policy towards foreign direct investment resulted in such a retreat that Ottawa gave up its potentially most promising option of a long-term industrial strategy to reduce its staple-export imbalances. Canadian efforts to develop a successful export capacity in high technology industries are jeopardized by Washington's trade policies, both in their defence against imports and in their overt retaliation against foreign export-promotion policies. The one area of some light in this generally gloomy picture of the shift in economic relations to Canada's detriment is the National Energy Program. While the NEP may be gravely weakened by the shift in world prices for oil and for capital, Canadianization can at least be seen as one policy that the Canadian government managed to implement despite vehement U.S. government and business opposition.

In Part III we turn to bilateral issues that have an economic component to be sure, but that impinge on other matters affecting the prospects or the quality of Canadian survival as a viable state in North America. Dependence, not sovereignty, characterizes the continental environmental relationship; acid rain and toxic waters are but two of an almost endless array of serious issues that can bring Canada and the United States into conflict (chapter 8). Efforts to negotiate formal treaties covering fisheries, the maritime boundaries and the international law of the sea have not proven successful as a means of resolving serious disputes (chapter 9). Various efforts to shore up Canadian cultural sovereignty in the past decade have created tensions in Washington, and the issues raised by the new information technologies promise to exacerbate these difficulties considerably (chapter 10). In the military field, Canada's multilateral relationship in NATO is inextricably enmeshed with its bilateral membership in NORAD; strategic and technical question marks litter this area of the changing relationship (chapter 11). Diplomatic relations with other countries are thought to give Canada some countervailing room for manoeuvre vis-à-vis its dependence on the U.S.; whether the Department of External Affairs can handle this trade-off is an important question in the overall puzzle. If, on balance, the change in these aspects of Canadian-American relations is significant enough for us to agree that 1981 did indeed represent a turning point in the relationship, we will need to consider what should be Canada's strategic view of the problem for the future, what capacity it has to implement a new strategy, and what chances it has for success. These will be the concerns of the concluding chapters.

Acid Rain and Environmental Dependence   8

When on March 10, 1981 President Ronald Reagan was seen by American TV viewers exchanging pleasantries with Pierre Trudeau on Parliament Hill, the cameras shifted to a small crowd of demonstrators carrying a bed sheet lettered with the message "Stop Acid Rain." Television stations across the United States were immediately flooded with inquiries: what is acid rain? Although the long-range transport of airborne pollutants was high on the agenda of this bilateral summit meeting and although Reagan was reported to have assured Trudeau, "We will not export our pollution, Mr. Prime Minister," the demonstrators' message may have had a far more important impact on affecting one of the most intractable issues in the Canadian-American confrontation than the president's verbal commitment on behalf of his government. The prime minister admonished the demonstrators, saying, "Hey, guys, when I go to the United States, I'm not met with these kinds of signs. You know, the Americans have some beefs against us too but they receive them politely. Now, how about a great cheer for President Reagan?"[1] Had he spoken less from a sense of diplomatic propriety than from an understanding of the urgency of the phenomenon known as acid rain, he would have congratulated the protesters and urged them to redouble their grass-roots political action, but on the steps of Capitol Hill.

Acid rain, or acid deposition, as it is more formally known, is a chemical soup of air pollutants, primarily sulphuric and nitric oxides, which is carried by the prevailing winds hundreds, even thousands, of miles from industrial and population centres before falling to the ground as dry dust or as acidified rain and snow. Possibly more dangerous than the acids, particles of poisonous heavy metals are also transported through the atmosphere. In turning North America's golden ponds into lakes that kill their fish, acid rain is doing more than destroying the myth of North America as natural wilderness. It is giving the most dramatic proof of what the prophets of technological doom have been warning when they inveigh against the evil effects of industrialization. Some of the damage Canada is suffering has been caused by Canadian polluters: Inco's smelter in Sudbury is the worst single polluter on the continent. But the recent discovery that the splendours of the Muskoka lakes are being irreversibly tarnished by acid rain coming mainly from the power generators of the Ohio Valley states — Pennsylvania, Ohio, Indiana, Illinois, Missouri, Kentucky and West Virginia — brings out in stark relief the meaning of two long-standing characteristics of the Canadian-American relationship, dependency and asymmetry. Acid rain is not the only environmental problem Canada confronts with its southern neighbour. Both the Garrison Diversion Unit and the Great Lakes Water Quality Agreement have major environmental implications — the former dangerously detrimental, the latter potentially beneficial — as we shall see in later sections of this chapter.

The economic dependence represented by the Auto Pact is not total: governments willing to pay the price can reduce the power of multinational corporations on their economy. By contrast, Canada's ecological dependence is unavoidable. Canada could in theory completely clean up its own sources of pollution, but its lakes that are downwind from the American midwest would still die. Air pollution cannot be stopped at the border. Whereas an ailing industry can often respond to remedial policies, scientists concur that the havoc wreaked by acidification is irreversible in lakes whose natural buffering capacity has been exceeded. Politicians are not scientists. Their sense of urgency derives from the priorities of their constituents. The voters of Muskoka may be convinced that their waters have become hazardous to the health both of fish and of humans, but if the voters of the Ohio Valley states are not affected by the emissions billowing from their generators' tall smokestacks, acidification will continue.

Environmental dilemmas are also characterized by a chronic gap between the changing state of scientific knowledge and the inadequacy of public policy: policy can never catch up to the needs identified by science. The Seventies saw a dramatic round of new legislation introduced in all industrialized countries to deal with the degradation of the environment, but these laws, which were meant to limit the short-range dispersion of pollutants, were inadequate to cope with the problem of their long-range transportation, particularly across an international boundary. Even the much-vaunted free market fails before the challenge of ecological dependency. When a political boundary separates the victims from the creators of pollution into two jurisdictions, there is little to stop a polluting industry from forcing people in the other political system to absorb the ecological costs of production. Polluters distort the workings of the theoretically free market by imposing on others the costs created by their steel mills, factories or generating stations. When these "externalities" are exported across a national boundary, it becomes even more difficult to fight the original polluters. The political issue raised by Canada's ecological dependence is how to get the United States to internalize the costs of cleaning up its own pollution.

Resolving this issue is made more difficult by the asymmetry of North America's pollution dependencies. The imbalance in the Canadian-American pollution relationship is not just to be found in the depressing data which show that the United States emits far more contaminants per year than does Canada — 20.2 million tonnes versus 2.0 million tonnes of nitrogen oxide, and 26.9 million tonnes versus 4.8 million tonnes of sulphur oxides.[2] Meteorology, the prevailing flows of weather, and geology, the varying capacity of the terrain to neutralize the damage, turn an industrial imbalance into an environmental crisis. Three to four times as much sulphur dioxide moves across the border from the United States to Canada as in the opposite direction.[3] The geology of the Precambrian shield makes the lakes of Ontario and Quebec particularly vulnerable to acidification. Experts argue as a result that the only long-term solution to the problem of acid rain is the concerted abatement of North American emissions.

The cost of an effective abatement program would understandably fall more heavily on the major polluter. "Such a strategy would add $5-7 billion each year to the cost of power generation, manufacturing and transport in the United States. The bill would be $350 million annually in Canada," according to Harold Foster and Derrick Sewell.[4] Canada's lesser contribution to the pollution means that its financial burden would be less, but it also means, as Don Munton points out, "that any unilateral Canadian effort to control acid rain would be relatively ineffective."[5] The political implication of this asymmetry is that the United States will benefit much less from Canadian abatement measures than Canada stands to gain from American reduction of emissions. Given the far greater costs faced by American industry, this imbalance explains, as Munton warns, "why the United States government would be considerably less enthusiastic, more prone to inertia, and, when moved, more cautious than the Canadian in the negotiation of environmental accords."[6]

185

How to overcome American resistance to stopping its trans-boundary pollution has presented Canada with an extremely difficult strategic problem. Since this is an international issue, it might be thought that Canada should have recourse to international law. After all, both countries signed the 1972 Stockholm Declaration on the Human Environment whose 21st principle proclaimed that, while states have the sovereign right to exploit their own resources, they have "the responsibility to ensure that activities within their jurisdiction or control do not cause damage to the environment of other States."[7] Canada and the U.S. were also both signatories to the Economic Commission for Europe's Convention on Trans-Boundary Air Pollution in 1979, but this first international accord dealing with acid rain did not provide for mandatory abatement, for its enforcement, or for compensation of the victims of other states' pollution.[8] As for the courts of international justice, the Trail Smelter case in the Twenties and Thirties created the precedent that a direct link has to be proven to join the claimed damage to a particular source — an impossible criterion of proof when there are multiple sources of acid rain. If recourse to international law offered no hope, Canada's next best strategy would be to persuade the United States government to commit itself voluntarily to stop polluting. For a government to do something it does not see to be in its own self-interest is to go against the nature of politics.

American Reluctance to Restrict Pollution

Research for the International Joint Commission had shown there was a serious problem of trans-border flows of sulphur dioxide between Ontario and Michigan. These were short-range pollution flows both between Detroit and Windsor (flowing mostly from Detroit) and between Port Huron and Sarnia (flowing both ways). By 1973, Ontario and Michigan had established a system for temporarily reducing pollution on one side of the border when air quality on the other side became unacceptable. Ottawa wanted to have this provincial-state program developed into a formal international agreement. The Nixon administration, which was busy impounding funds that had been allocated for the cleanup of the Great Lakes, had no desire to go beyond the quite tough Clean Air Act which was concerned with local air quality and sign an international air pollution agreement with an unacceptable price tag. All that resulted from the first round of bilateral talks was a memorandum of understanding between the Ontario and Michigan governments signed in November 1974, in which the province and the state agreed to move ahead with their program of cooperation and to ask their national governments to get the International Joint Commission to monitor the result.

When some American border states became concerned about pollution originating in Canada, pressure increased for a bilateral agreement. Concerns expressed in Congress from Montana and Minnesota about oil-fired thermal generating stations planned by Saskatchewan on the Poplar River and by Ontario at Atikokan led to a congressional rider to the Foreign Relations Authorization Act in 1978 requiring the Department of State to start negotiations for an air quality agreement with Canada. Meanwhile, the bilateral Research Consultation Group on the long-range transport of airborne pollutants was established with a mandate to prepare scientific assessments of the available research on acid rain. Informal discussions between the State Department and External Affairs led to the announcement on July 26, 1979 of a Joint Statement on Transboundary Air Quality by the two governments. This was a brief list outlining the "substantial basis of obligation, commitment and cooperative practice in existing environmental relations between Canada and the United States," the affirmation of "a common determination to reduce or prevent transboundary air pollution," and the intention to develop "a cooperative bilateral agreement on air quality."[9] Assurances given by the U.S. Environmental Protection Agency that American emissions were going to decrease were, however, exploded in February 1980 when the Carter administration launched a $10 billion program to reduce oil imports by converting 107 power plants to coal. Canadian negotiators felt they had been stabbed in the back: this "off-oil" policy would lead to some 400,000 additional tonnes of sulphur dioxide emissions. Emissions were also increasing as a result of the Environmental Protection Agency's relaxation of controls over existing coal-burning plants. The diffuse citizen-group interest in clean air was no match as a lobby in Washington for the coal-mining companies and coal-using utilities, particularly in the Ohio River Valley where the unemployment level among coal miners was high, and the general economy was in bad trouble.[10]

In effect the Carter administration was simultaneously proceeding in opposite directions. While emission levels increased, negotiations with Canada continued, bearing fruit on August 5, 1980 with the signature of a Memorandum of Intent that expressed "a common determination to combat transboundary air pollution," declared the intention "to develop a bilateral agreement which will reflect and further the development of effective domestic control programs," and committed both countries "to take interim actions available under current authority to combat transboundary air pollution" by the "vigorous enforcement of existing laws and regulations."[11] While these statements did acknowledge that each country's "air pollution laws, to the extent that they do or do not effectively deal with injurious transboundary pollution, have a de facto extra-territorial reach,"[12] they had little concrete impact on government action. Driven though it was by the need to shift from oil to coal, President Carter's administration did recognize the importance of ecological concerns by staffing the Environmental Protection Agency (EPA) with personnel committed to their agency's mandate. But in the same month that the Memorandum of Intent formally committed both governments to enforce existing laws vigorously, Ronald Reagan was entering the final phase of his successful campaign, one of whose themes was a critique of environmental regulations that imposed excessive costs on private enterprise. How much his administration would feel bound by a weak document signed by his predecessor was very uncertain.

The folk memory that while living with the Democrats is difficult for Canada, having to deal with the Republicans is worse had been based on Canadian experience with the trade protectionism of Republican administrations in the inter-war period and had been revived by Richard Nixon's aggressive unilateralism of August 1971. If the notion had not already existed for trade policy, Ronald Reagan's advance to power would have invented it for environmental policy. The president's reported assurance in Ottawa to Prime Minister Trudeau that the U.S. would not export pollution had a hollow ring, coming as it did from the man who had just withdrawn from the Senate the fisheries treaty (which provided for controlled management of depleting fish stocks) and blocked the United States' participation in the U.N. Law of the Sea negotiations (which were developing an international code for managing seabed resources) pending the administration's complete review of its maritime policy. Canadian government spokesmen expressed deep satisfaction with the Americans' reaffirmation that they would abide by the Memorandum of Intent, but they would admit in the next breath deep concern about the capacity of the EPA and the administration's intentions concerning the Clean Air Act. Attempts made in the Seventies to regulate industry's pollution levels had generated much of the business hostility to regulation that had propelled Reagan's Republican team to office. The Environmental Protection Agency fell victim to the new administra-

188

tion's dual thrust to reduce the size of government and to restrict the extent of regulation. A drastic change was made in its personnel. As part of the natural replacement of Democrats by Republicans, a whole new hierarchy moved in to replace the top three or four levels of officials in the agency. Everything the EPA had done under Carter was now under a cloud of suspicion. A new philosophy responded to the corporate view that anti-pollution rules had imposed an unduly heavy economic burden on some industries, lowering their productivity and international competitiveness. In a field where researchers were scrambling to develop techniques of measurement and standards of safety, the new environmental officers asserted that far more rigorous criteria of scientific proof would be needed to demonstrate that pollution was a genuine hazard. The guarantee that the EPA would not be able to police the existing regulations could be seen in the agency's budget cut of almost 26 per cent from fiscal year 1981 to $961 million in fiscal year 1983.[13] Within less than two years the headquarters' staff was to fall by 24 per cent to 8,465 employees, leading critics to charge that the Reagan administration was deliberately demolishing the environmental agency.[14] The EPA, which had been an ally of Canada in Carter's court, had become an adversary in Reagan's.

At the same time as Canadian observers watched the dismantling of the United States' environmental watchdog, they had to witness the byzantine process of review to which the U.S. Clean Air Act was subject throughout 1981 and 1982. The stakes were high. To meet American commitments in an eventual treaty on trans-boundary pollution, the United States government would have to win legislative authority to control the long-range transport of airborne pollutants — something the Clean Air Act had not originally been designed to regulate. Everything pointed in the opposite direction. The key Reagan appointee at the EPA, Kathleen Bennett, "had earned her stripes lobbying for corporate clients against EPA air pollution regulations." The attitude of administration officials had shifted diametrically away from that of the Carter group. "The present crop," Don Munton writes, "is loyal, firm, even aggressive, in its pursuit of de-regulation and government withdrawal from pollution control and research."[15] The administration's position was: more research, yes; emission reductions, no. A draft revision of the Clean Air Act prepared by the EPA was what one congressman called "a blueprint for destruction of our clean air laws."[16] In allowing states to set their own schedules and judge their own progress towards air quality standards, it would have allowed some states to reduce control requirements.

As summer passed to fall, still no administration position was formally announced. By December 1981, the administration resolved its dilemma by giving its informal support to a bill sponsored by Congressman Thomas Luken (Democrat, Ohio) to amend the Clean Air Act. The Luken amendments, which have been denounced by the environmentalist chairman of the House of Representatives Subcommittee on Health and Environment, Henry Waxman (Democrat, California), for envisaging "a virtual halt in the air pollution program," are strongly endorsed by John Dingell (Democrat, Michigan), the chairman of the House Energy and Commerce Committee, who is an ally of the automobile industry in its push for relief from emission controls.[17] The business community's pressure for deregulation is opposed by a force that political Washington also has to take seriously — public opinion. According to a Harris poll, 86 per cent opposed making the Clean Air Act less strict.[18] American public opinion had become Canada's main ally in the fight against acid rain, but it was an ally with whom Canada had had little experience in cooperating.

Politics: A Second String to the Canadian Bow

Traditional diplomatic consultations had achieved the Research Consultation Group, the Joint Statement on Transboundary Air Quality, and the Memorandum of Intent. At the same time as this quiet diplomacy had been proceeding, other voices, particularly in Ottawa's Department of the Environment, had been raising the question of acid rain publicly. In June 1977, Roméo LeBlanc, then minister of the environment, had described acid rain as an "environmental time bomb." John Fraser, the Conservative environment minister, had campaigned in 1979 to publicize the problem and press for a bilateral agreement.[19] His Liberal successor, John Roberts, increased the pressure, making high profile speeches in the United States, organizing press conferences for the American media, and toying with such undiplomatic language as "environmental aggression" to describe the Carter administration's expansion of coal-fuelled power generation. To the Air Pollution Control Association convention he said,

> Stated very bluntly, I see no reason why Canada's ecosystems — let me be blunter yet, Canada's people, tourist camp operators, fishing guides, commercial fishermen, loggers, other forest product workers, building owners and tenants and possibly our asthmatics or others with respiratory illnesses — should have to pay the price of keeping the electricity rates of those coal-producing middle-western states well below those now being paid along the United States eastern seaboard.[20]

Roberts's squeaky-wheel diplomacy was based on the premise that the American administration could be shamed into responding to Canada's needs. If the United States wanted good relations with Canada, it had to recognize that the environment was a very important concern for its northern neighbour and had to be handled as a joint problem, with both governments seeking joint solutions.

A few months after the Reagan administration had taken office, questions were raised in Ottawa about the effectiveness of this strategy. Was it a mistake to try to emphasize how much damage the U.S. was doing to Canada? Was is not likely that, the more acid rain was seen to be a *Canadian* problem, the less would happen? With the administration already angry at Canada about the NEP and FIRA, outspoken Canadian criticism in the American media of American government inaction appeared to increase the level of irritation among Reagan appointees who complained of the "pummelling" and "bludgeoning" they had been taking. That the constant and public pressing of the case may have been counterproductive was admitted by Roberts's parliamentary secretary, Roger Simmons: "We made the tactical error of telling them what they were doing to us. We found out they were not particularly interested in what they were doing to us."[21]

Public pressure from the environment minister in Ottawa may have scored some points in catching the attention of the administration in Washington, but he was no match for a business lobbyist from the Ohio Valley in actually affecting the policy process. The thrust of the campaign to discredit Canada's position could be seen in the Coalition for an Energy-Environment Balance (CEEB), a pressure group for utility companies, which ran a series of ads in the *New York Times,* the *Washington Post*, and the *Wall Street Journal*. A presentation by James Friedman, legal counsel to Cleveland Electric Illuminating Company, typified CEEB's Canadian-conspiracy theory that found receptive ears among Reagan appointees and was expressed in congressional hearings. The main points of Friedman's presentation were as follows:

- The context for the acid rain issue was the intensive Canadian program of energy resource and economic nationalism which aimed to keep Canadian oil prices well below the international market price and to discriminate against American energy companies. Beyond the NEP "is Prime Minister Trudeau's proposal for 'Canadianization' of the country's other industries. This program aims to reduce foreign ownership of Canadian industry [sic] from 70 per cent to 50 per cent by 1990."

- At the same time the Canadian government "has encouraged Canadian private businesses in an expansive takeover campaign of foreign investment in the United States." While the government was eliminating "historic investment opportunities in Canada, Canadian private enterprise is engaged in an unprecedented intrusion south of the border."
- With the intensive debate over the constitution and regional polarization reflected in the Liberals' low representation in the West, the federal government was seeking "external issues which might unify Canadian constituencies. The acid rain issue is clearly one of these."
- Other Canadian behaviour in the environmental field "does not necessarily match its rhetoric meant for consumption south of the border": Canadian 1981 exhaust emission standards for passenger cars allowed 3.1 grams of nitrogen oxides per mile, compared to the U.S. standard of 1.0 gram per mile.

In short, Canada's acid rain attack on U.S. coal-fired thermal generation, was "clearly traceable to carefully planned Canadian national energy objectives."[22] This blend of truth, half truth and erroneous assumption was far more palatable to the Reagan administration than taking large doses of Canadian indignation.

The conspiracy theory was one of the weapons used by the corporations and their spokespersons to deflect attention from and discredit the strong warnings periodically published by Canadian and American scientists. The research carried out by the bilateral Canadian-American technical groups had used the best available techniques and data. The groups' reports were subjected to peer review, were solid in substance, and confirmed the thrust of other studies done in Europe. Striking confirmation of the environmental crisis appeared on September 4, 1981, when the U.S. National Academy of Sciences' National Research Council issued a report ponderously titled *Atmosphere-Biosphere Interactions: Toward a Better Understanding of the Ecological Consequences of Fossil Fuel Combustion*. The study had been financed by the Department of the Interior and the Environmental Protection Agency and had been subjected to peer review. It found the circumstantial evidence linking power-plant emissions to the production of acid rain "overwhelming." Many thousands of lakes had already been affected and, "at current rates of emission of sulphur and nitrogen oxides, the number of affected lakes can be expected to more than double by 1990." Based

192

on the evidence examined, "the picture is disturbing enough to merit prompt tightening of restrictions on atmospheric emissions from fossil fuels and other large sources such as metal smelters and cement manufacture. Strong measures are necessary if we are to prevent further degradation of natural ecosystems, which together support life on this planet." Control of new electrical generating plants "would be insufficient to accomplish this, and thus restrictions on older plants must be considered."[23]

Confirmed in their resolution by the scientific warnings but stymied by the antipathy of the administration to diplomatic pressure, whether quiet or noisy, the Canadians directing the campaign on Washington tied another string to their bow. If external pressure was not going to work, then Canada's strategy should be directed to turning acid rain into a domestic political issue. If the people of the U.S. northeast demanded a solution to their dirty-air problems and got Congress to implement it, then Canada would reap the benefits. Although the U.S. would not take action just to protect Canada, it might be moved to prevent damage within its own boundaries. It was easy to make a tactical decision to modify the content of the Canadian message and the manner of its delivery, but the challenge remained enormous. Many American legislators were not convinced that U.S.-sourced sulphur and nitrogen oxide emissions were having an impact on the northeast. More generally, there was throughout the United States an "appalling ignorance and lack of concern for the acid rain problem."[24] The two factors of hope for Canadian strategists were the overwhelming support of public opinion for not weakening the Clean Air Act and an increased public awareness of the nature of acid rain. The Canadian embassy in Washington hired the legal firm Wellford, Wagman, Krulwich, Gold and Huff to act as its legal counsel in Congress, monitoring its complex legislative processes with reference to Canada's interests as environmental legislation evolved, and advising the embassy on whom to lobby and how to do it. The campaign to influence political opinion in the United States ranged from red-and-white Stop Acid Rain buttons given to U.S. tourists, to films, slide shows, booklets and dozens of speaking tours by Canadian scientists and politicians. Canada's fifteen consulates across the United States were called upon to support the program of consciousness raising. Tours of acid-damaged Muskoka were organized for American legislators, congressional staffers and journalists. Some $1 million was being spent to convince Americans of the seriousness of the problem, the largest effort Canada has made to attempt to shape the policy of another country.[25]

On October 6, 1981, a new step was taken in official Canadian intervention in the American political process. Four senior Canadian officials, including two assistant deputy ministers from Environment Canada, testified before the Health and Environment Subcommittee of the House of Representatives in a hearing on the U.S. Clean Air Act. Whether Canada gained or lost from the encounter is difficult to assess. Congressman Clarence (Bud) Brown, who was running for election as Governor of Ohio, made much of Ontario and Quebec's efforts to export more hydro- and nuclear-generated electricity, saying it would fit their marketing strategy to ask "for further controls on already financially troubled U.S. power plants."[26] Strategically, the hearing represented a victory for Environment Canada's push to take the issue of acid rain into the arena of congressional politics, a move still resisted by the Department of External Affairs as unwise. In the view of the Irwin Report on acid rain, expressed a year earlier, such "efforts at shaping public awareness and legislative opinion in the United States should be continued and, indeed, should become more assertive."[27] According to a citizens group, the Canadian Coalition on Acid Rain (CCAR), even such direct and official Canadian intervention in the American political process was not enough. "Canadians must not depend on the Canadian Government to persuade the American Government to solve the acid precipitation problem," it argued. In addition, "a powerful, organized effort in the United States by Canadian citizens is necessary if Ottawa's efforts are to succeed."[28] The CCAR did not just preach; it practised what it proposed by sending a Canadian to Washington to act as the lobbyist on behalf of its twenty-eight Canadian member organizations.[29] Representing these groups whose total membership comprised some one and one-quarter million Canadians, the CCAR's lobbyist has been able to engage in some grass-roots coalition building that a government official would have been unable to attempt — forming alliances with environmentalists around the United States, drawing attention to the link between the deterioration of drinking water in the Adirondacks and Canada's environmental problems, and helping to generate phone calls, letters and visits by concerned Americans to their congressmen.

The registration of the Canadian Coalition on Acid Rain as the first Canadian lobbyist in the U.S. working for a non-government, non-business citizens' organization marked another step forward in Canadian intervention, though the CCAR itself felt more important steps had still to be taken. "Canadians must hire United States legal counsel to undertake legal research, the development of legal strategy, the drafting of legislation, and litigation before the various courts and administrative agencies of the United States; Canadian citizens must retain American lobbyists to assist Canadian approaches to the Congress, to organize approaches to the White House, and to organize approaches to the American people."[30] Hiring counsel and retaining lobbyists to represent them in a foreign jurisdiction are not just expensive but also uncomfortable activities for Canadian citizens to undertake. Some government institutions representing a large proportion of the victimized Canadian population have decided to make such a commitment.

In the case of acid rain there were three major governmental players, each with a different focus to its efforts. The Department of External Affairs has concentrated on the quiet diplomacy of negotiation and attempted to coordinate the activities of all the other actors on the stage. As the line department directly involved with the issue, Environment Canada has provided the technical expertise of its scientific research work and the political edge that its ministers' public diplomacy has given to the Canadian case. At the provincial level, the Ontario government has been active from the beginning of bilateral discussions. Queen's Park has expended large sums on research through its own Ministry of the Environment, has let its environment minister indulge in public diplomacy (calling the Reagan administration's movement towards deregulation as "close to an act of hostility on a friendly neighbour"),[31] and has gone furthest along the road towards direct intervention in the American political process.

Although the Department of External Affairs opposes the participation by cabinet ministers and civil servants in American politics, Keith Norton, the Ontario minister of the environment, appeared on July 1, 1981 at a hearing chaired by Senator Moynihan of the Senate Committee on Environment and Public Works regarding the revision of the U.S. Clean Air Act. The Ministry of the Environment has hired a lobbyist, the former chairman of New York's Upstate Republicans for Moynihan (and a member of the board of directors of Lake Ontario Cement), to monitor congressional activities and so give the provincial government an ear close to the ground of American politics.

Most dramatic of all, Queen's Park spent a year to develop a legal case, retaining counsel in six states. This work bore fruit on March 12, 1981, when the ministry filed a brief before the Environmental Protection Agency in a case to prevent the EPA from relaxing sulphur dioxide emission limits for eighteen coal-fired generating stations in the Ohio Valley. Its substantial documentation indicated that the sulphur dioxide emissions of these generators in 1979 were already 55 per cent greater than the limit allowed under 1979 regulations of 1,194,700 tonnes. The proposed new total emissions would be 2,515,400 tonnes.[32] Three months later Ontario intervened before the EPA, supporting the suit laid by New York and Pennsylvania against fifty power stations in the midwestern states. Ontario has been playing every card in its hand. It has lobbied Walter Cronkite who has a summer house in Canada. It has lobbied in Los Angeles, taking the issue to Reagan's home state. It has cultivated allies among American environmentalists and U.S. travel agencies. It has hosted tours for U.S. state legislators and co-hosted with the federal government tours for U.S. journalists and congressional committee staffs. In short, Ontario has jumped wholeheartedly into the fray. Knowing that the damage to its lakes would continue whatever environmental controls were imposed within Ontario, the Tory cabinet has made a strategic decision to take its crusade directly into the United States. Whether these activities, those of the federal government, and those smaller efforts made by the Atlantic provinces will bear any fruit remains a very open question.

To judge by the formal activities and public statements of the Canadian and American governments up to mid-1982, negotiations towards an acid rain agreement had been brought to a standstill by the Reagan administration. The bilateral working groups set up under the Memorandum of Intent have filed interim reports, and negotiation sessions were held in June and November 1981, and then in February and June 1982. In reality, the Americans have stonewalled and stalled to the point that the Canadian negotiators have considered withdrawing from the process. At the June 1981 meeting nothing happened, largely because the Reagan administration had not yet produced its policy on air pollution. By the time of the November negotiations, there was still no official Reagan policy in sight. In February, Canada made its first formal proposal: to reduce SO_2 emissions in eastern Canada by 50 per cent if the U.S. took "parallel action." The American negotiators proposed instead a drawn-out approach that pointed in the right direction but would drag on for years. When, at the fourth negotiating session, the Americans rejected the Canadian proposal and continued to drag their feet, Environment Minister John Roberts stated to the press that the "implication of this stick-in-the-mud stance of the Americans is that we have to ask ourselves whether it makes any sense to have officials flying back and forth."[33]

As the Irwin Report noted, Ontario has already placed stricter

196

controls on Inco at Sudbury, and Ontario Hydro has committed the funds to reduce emissions from its thermal generators by 43 per cent during this decade. By contrast, "it appears that the United States is not approaching the problem in the same spirit."[34] While Canada presses for action, the United States claims that more research is needed. While Canada urges the United States to increase controls, the administration is decimating its pollution control agency, claiming it will get better results by allowing industry to police itself, and reducing government intervention.

Necessary though it appears to have been, Canada's dramatic break with precedent, and its involvement in American environmental politics, does not seem destined to bear early fruit. The consequence of Reagan's election is far greater pollution. The question of acid rain, which was not an issue in 1980 even among environmentalists in the United States, may have risen high on the agenda of American politics. A critical mass may be developing against the administration's move towards deregulation. Canada can take some satisfaction in having been a catalyst for this development, but satisfaction among the specialists will not bring back the dead lakes of Ontario and Quebec and the sterile salmon streams of New Brunswick. The environmental stakes are so high that being a catalyst is faint compensation for losing the struggle. Two other major environmental issues are instructive for strategists concerned about rescuing Canada from the increased emissions of the Reagan regime.

Garrison Diversion Project
As originally authorized in 1965, the Garrison Diversion Unit (GDU) would be one of the world's first major interbasin transfers of water. The proposal was to divert large volumes of water from the upper Missouri River into North Dakota where they would irrigate 1.5 million acres of semi-arid land and provide additional water for municipal, industrial and recreational use. Through the construction of dams and canals to provide water for irrigation, the waste waters would be diverted northwards through the Souris and Red Rivers, bringing with them unintended but irreversibly damaging effects for the ecology of Manitoba.[35] Manitobans were alarmed that the transfer of water from the Missouri drainage basin would raise the saline level of their river system, increase springtime flooding and, more dangerously, introduce foreign biota — fish, fish parasites and fish diseases — into Lake Winnipeg and the Hudson Bay drainage systems, accelerating the rate of decay in Lake Winnipeg, and seriously harming the commercial

and sports fishery there.[36] Prodded by Manitoba sentiment, the Department of External Affairs pursued the issue through official channels and customary procedures — it voiced Canadian concerns through a series of official notes (April 1969, October 1971, January 1973, October 1973) — advising Washington that the project would violate article IV of the Boundary Waters Treaty of 1909 and calling for a moratorium on the projected diversion. Although the State Department made friendly noises, assuring Canada that the project would not begin unless the United States met its treaty obligations, the department had no way of making good its commitment, since it had little influence within American politics over a development that was in the bailiwick of the Department of the Interior. While Canada trusted the niceties of protocol, North Dakota politicians used all the pork-barrel devices at their command to lobby for a project that spelt industrial development for a no-growth state. Congress did not officially learn about Canada's request for a moratorium until mid-1975, when, in another note, Canada asked the State Department to intervene with the "appropriate committees of the United States Congress and the relevant departments and agencies of the United States government."[37]

Manitoba agreed with Ottawa on a common strategy in 1974. Increasing disbelief among federal and provincial politicians from Manitoba that quiet diplomacy alone would save them from the Garrison project brought the issue into the public domain. Manitoba MPs, the Manitoba government, Manitoba MLAs and Manitoban municipalities voiced very strong political objections. Jeanne Sauvé, then minister of the environment, spoke out on the issue in the United States. On October 19, 1975, after an interdepartmental consensus had developed in Washington against the project, the U.S. agreed with the Canadian government formally to refer the Garrison issue to the International Joint Commission. Two years later the IJC reported that the project was a "biological time bomb."[38] The Garrison dams would create major environmental and resource damages across the Canadian-American boundary. It recommended a moratorium on all aspects of the project that would affect water flowing into Canada.

By the end of the decade the story seemed to have reached a happy ending. The project had been considerably reduced in scope, though even this smaller undertaking was still strongly opposed by Canada. That Canada had protested and that the IJC had supported Canada's concern does not prove that these diplomatic and institutional initiatives were the cause of the political success. On the contrary, as

Kim Nossal argues, the outcome in the Seventies was determined less by Canadian objections and by the IJC's findings than by domestic political opposition within the American system.

Three factors in the Garrison equation had changed when President Carter came to power. Firstly, the president himself was sympathetic to environmental concerns as was his secretary of the interior (it was the Department of the Interior that had promoted the project originally). Secondly, at the bureaucratic level, environmental agencies like the Council on Environmental Quality, the Environmental Protection Agency and the Fish and Wildlife Service brought strong criticisms to bear on the project. Thirdly, pressure was mobilized inside and outside Congress by non-governmental organizations like the National Audubon Society and by politicians from the neighbouring states of Minnesota and South Dakota. These forces battled to reduce and freeze the funds appropriated for the massive project. As Nossal concludes,

> The resilience of congressional and bureaucratic supports of the GDU in the face of staunch internal and external opposition suggests that in this case, the Canadian government needed allies judiciously placed within the amorphous structure of American government in order to protect Canadian interests. . . . Without the support of the United States president, key members of his cabinet, segments of both the Washington bureaucracy and Congress, it is doubtful that the government in Ottawa would have been able to avert the potential environmental threat posed by the GDU.[39]

Canada had given ammunition to the American forces opposed to Garrison.

But if Manitoba benefited from the waxing of progressive sentiments in the United States in the Seventies, it stood equally to lose from their waning in the Eighties. Under Reagan the Department of the Interior has regained its developmental thrust. The new Republican governor of North Dakota approached President Reagan for his direct support to keep the project alive, and the president authorized $4 million in the budget for fiscal year 1982-83, a sum in addition to the $9.7 million of accumulated unspent funds already available, for continued work on the already partially-built project.

In the GDU where Canada was the potential victim and the United States the villain, Canada had almost no leverage. It could impose no retaliatory costs on North Dakota. It had no economic deal to offer. The only card it could play was the moral suasion of the Boundary Waters Treaty and the United States' international obligations flowing from it. In this case, where the asymmetry of the pollution threat was complete, Canada remained entirely vulnerable to the vicissitudes of American politics. Even where the ecological dependence between the countries was more symmetrical, Canada's ultimate reliance on the vagaries of American politics was very similar. This has been the lesson of the struggle to clean up the Great Lakes.

Great Lakes Water Quality Agreement

Cleaning up the Great Lakes — the major water quality problem facing the two countries — offers some parallels with the fight against the long-range transport of air pollutants. Although on balance the United States causes much more pollution of the Great Lakes than does Canada, the asymmetry is less marked than in the case of acid rain: Canada does more polluting through the pulp and paper industry than the U.S. As a result, the considerable American reluctance to commit itself to the principle and the practice of cleanup could eventually be overcome by American interest in the reduction of Canadian pollution and in the joint management of a very important common resource. In contrast to the acid rain problem, the proximity of the polluting cities and industries to the poisoned waters prevented the polluters from effectively mobilizing political support for the continued disregard of the environmental effects of their operations. Unlike Reagan, President Nixon sensed that the environment made good politics and was prepared to accept the negotiation of an agreement. What further distinguished the politics of Great Lakes water was the initiative and pressure exerted by a coalition of the provincial government of Ontario with its state counterparts. Though the states were leery of the dangers of more centralization of power, the alliance pressed Washington to commit itself to the expenditure of the massive monies required for the construction of modern municipal sewage systems and treatment plants on the American side of the lakes.

Strategists on acid rain can draw some comfort from the fact that, when bilateral talks about the Great Lakes began at the ministerial level, the American side was not committed to accepting the cleanup recommendations of the International Joint Commission's recent report or to negotiating a water quality treaty.[40] There was much foot dragging, but they did agree to establish joint working groups to examine the problem. Meanwhile the province of Ontario planned and hosted a Great Lakes Environmental Conference of premiers and governors at which the governors, premiers and senior representatives of three Canadian provinces (Ontario, Quebec, Manitoba) and eight Great Lakes states (Michigan, Ohio, New York, Pennsylvania, Illinois, Minnesota, Indiana, Wisconsin), and representatives from the federal governments of the U.S. and Canada, met to discuss "common environmental problems" and the arrangements necessary to alleviate them. When President Nixon and Prime Minister Trudeau eventually signed the Great Lakes Water Quality Agreement (GLWQA) on April 15, 1972, many meetings had taken place at both levels of government between and within both countries. To gain the agreement Canada had had to give way on many points of both principle and practice. Ontario and Canada argued that, since half of the lakes belong to each country, the U.S. had the right to emit only half of the pollutants each lake received. Since there was less industry north of the border, and so fewer polluters, the standards of emission control would not need to be so severe in Canada. The United States took a universalist position, arguing that polluters on both sides of the border should be required to use identical control technology — thus preventing Canada from obtaining an economic advantage from milder and less costly controls north of the border. Canada accepted weaker wording than it wanted concerning the practical measures to be taken, for instance, on the control of phosphates, the standards to be set, and the implementation schedule for achieving them.

Signing the document did not make the American administration particularly eager to fund its implementation. In November 1972, Nixon impounded the federal funds allocated for municipal sewage treatment plants.[41] The International Joint Commission reported continually through the Seventies that the reductions in phosphorous loadings were not being met and urged the establishment of U.S. regulations on detergent phosphates. The American government had complaints of its own, alleging that Ontario's pollution standards were not as tough as those of the U.S. Public Law 92-500, while Canada argued that, since it was the lesser polluter, its standards did not need to be so rigorous. (Political practice in the U.S. system has pushed American legislation to focus on effluent standards rather than water quality standards. Because those who drafted U.S. regulations in the Seventies knew that their proposed regulatory standards would not come into effect until after industry had tested them in the courts, they tended to write in the toughest standards they could hope for, knowing that these would get watered down as a result of the inevitable court battles. Since Canadian bureaucrats do not live in fear of court action, they draft their legislation in the knowledge that implementation will take place in the light of private discussions between government and industry.)

Although the GLWQA was given its stipulated five-year review and signed in a new version in 1978, and although the International Joint Commission continues to monitor the quality of the waters, observers remain sceptical about the achievements so far. There has been a visible improvement with respect to certain pollutants such as phosphates in the Great Lakes, but this amelioration may be illusory. The battle has shifted from sewage and phosphates to industrial pollution via chemical poisons of which there are thousands that are as difficult to measure as they are dangerous to the water.[42] The public uproar over the Love Canal and Hyde Park crises gives substance to such forebodings. On the one hand, they show that, where the polluting cause is American but has an impact on American citizens, there is a basis for an alliance between Canadian and American citizen groups, a coalition that can be supported by the federal and provincial governments. And when public outrage is sufficient, even the U.S. Environmental Protection Agency under Republican management can be pressured into allocating more funds for cleanups.[43] On the other hand, the budget reductions of the Reagan administration threaten not only to eliminate the new laboratories whose research is required to detect and assess toxic chemicals, but also to dismantle the surveillance and pollution control enforcement effort, and to immobilize the drive to plan programs for environmental control.[44]

Continuity or Change: Darkening Skies

The clear implication of acid rain, the Garrison diversion project and the Great Lakes environmental cases is that Canada will not achieve its bilateral environmental goals by the suasion of international law, the research of the International Joint Commission or the remonstrations of the Canadian government. The extra-territorial impact of American pollution (and anti-pollution laws to deal with it) shows how little independence Canada enjoys when it comes to environmental matters. The bold steps taken by federal and provincial governments and by citizen groups towards directly intervening in the American political process implicitly recognize that behaviour consistent with true sovereignty has to be compromised in the greater interests of dealing with such problems. Given the asymmetrical nature of the long-range transport of airborne pollutants, given the lower sense of urgency within the American political system, given the low incentives encouraging the American government to cooperate, there are real limits to the influence Canada can have even as a direct political participant. The capacity of Canadians to mobilize support within the American system is significant but their ability to achieve results is low. Canadian governmental efforts have helped firm up a coalition of pollution-receiving states. Canadian citizen-group activity has helped form alliances with American groups sharing a common interest in enhancing the quality of the environment. Indeed, the Canadian effort has had considerable success in raising the profile of air pollution as a major issue since the advent of the Reagan administration. But this step forward has to be placed in the context of the step backwards represented by the victory of the Reagan team which is openly hostile to the idea of more effective emission controls and is in close alliance with the powerful economic interests that stand to gain by the weakening of environmentally sound regulations. The attitude and policies of the Reagan administration will lead to greater acidity in the lakes and lands of northeast North America as well as in the Canadian-American relationship.

The existence on either side of the border of groups with interests in conservation of resources does not necessarily mean, however, that they will cooperate politically. That Canadian and American fishermen share a common objective interest in the conservation of the stocks on which they rely for their livelihood has not prevented the fishery from remaining a traditional source of conflict between the two countries — a problem we consider next in chapter 9.

Fisheries, Boundaries, and Sovereignty at Sea

9

On March 6, 1981, four days before Ronald Reagan was due in Ottawa for his first visit to a foreign capital, the president withdrew without warning from the U.S. Senate the fisheries treaty that had lingered there for almost two years since officials from both countries had finally signed an agreement after relations had approached what commentators had called a fisheries "war." Though Canada had given ground and made concessions on numerous issues to gain American assent, Ottawa was satisfied with the proposed treaty which President Carter had forwarded with his strong approval for Senate consent. Now here was Carter's successor turning his back on the previous administration's commitment with Canada and officially annulling the intense efforts that had been made to reach a definitive accommodation on one of the historical issues of contention between the two countries. Was this, one of the first acts of a new administration that Ottawa viewed with some trepidation, a warning signal putting in question the whole Canadian-American relationship?

The next day, March 7, Ronald Reagan fired the American representative to the United Nations Law of the Sea conference, a far more complex, multilateral negotiation that had involved some 150 countries over seven years to achieve what was thought to be a final convention. The agreement had been won at the cost of heavy bargaining, the U.S. military having achieved its goals of free passage through certain international straits at the expense of the private sector, which had had to compromise with the insistent demands of the less developed countries. Canada had also had to make concessions, but felt it had done well in this laborious bargaining. Now here was the new American president spurning the notion of a world order achieved by international bargaining, jeopardizing major Canadian interests at the same time. Was this abrupt act a harbinger of how the administration would let its corporate interests determine its international positions — to Canada's detriment?

Many were ready to conclude that President Reagan's unilateral and provocative actions on the eve of his first official meeting with his North American neighbour cast more light on the real content of his campaign slogan about a North American accord than any of the platitudes produced for Congress on this subject by his trade representative's office. For those able to look beyond the "shoot-first-ask-questions-later" style of the new incumbent, these arbitrary actions had important lessons for Canada about the problems of trying to manage common resources by negotiating formal treaties with the U.S.

We have just seen in chapter 8 the difficulties encountered when Canada and the United States attempted to handle through the political process a shared interest involving disproportionate costs to one and disproportionate benefits to the other. Despite the existence of a long-standing treaty under which the International Joint Commission managed boundary-water disputes, the new ecological issues of water and air pollution had been tackled by making political agreements, not treaties. Canada had stood to lose most from American pollution against which it had no defences. It had won a success in the Great Lakes Water Quality Agreement when the states in the area put pressure on Congress and when the administration was responsive to concerns about the ecology. It had failed to reduce acid rain when inadequate state and local pressure was mobilized in Congress and when the administration had given low priority to conserving and preserving the environment. An alternative route to the joint management of common continental resources had been taken over the Alaska Natural Gas Transportation System as we saw in chapter 6, but the negotiation and signature of a formal Canadian-American treaty on the problem had not proven more expeditious. ANGTS had still remained vulnerable to the delays and vicissitudes of Washington's political process.

Because enshrining a policy in the form of a treaty does not exempt it from the attention of lobbyists or the intervention of Congress, the attempt to negotiate treaties with the United States has proven no more heartening a way to resolve common resource management problems, whether this has been attempted bilaterally or multilaterally. In the multilateral negotiations at the United Nations on the Law of the Sea, American objections have centred around the fact that the United States government would not have full control over the outcome of the process. In the bilateral negotiations on the fisheries and boundaries treaty, the process came to grief because the administration's actions and commitments were not seen to be sufficiently under the control of local interest groups.

Drawing Lines: Allocating the Fish and Drawing the Boundaries

Several factors make the resolution of fishery disputes particularly difficult. Nation-states claim jurisdiction over their coastal waters and have tried to extend these zones of national sovereignty far out into the oceans. From the traditional three-mile limit, Canada and the United States extended their control to twelve miles in 1970 and followed the international trend to a 200-mile claim in 1977. Whereas the extension of land boundaries into the sea was relatively uncomplicated while the three-mile limit was accepted, the extension of national jurisdiction to 200 miles beyond terra firma created enormous potential for overlapping boundary claims and therefore disputes between neighbours. Depending on how the boundary was drawn, vast areas such as the rich fishing area and potential petroleum resources of Georges Bank, off the coasts of Maine and Nova Scotia, could fall inside or outside Canada's or the United States' ownership. What further complicated the notion of national ownership was the claim that the fish spawned in the stream beds of one country belonged to nationals of that country even though caught on the high seas in the territorial waters of its neighbour. These claims had much to do with a further factor, the attempt to husband fish stocks by investing public funds in artificially nurturing the spawning grounds of commercially valuable fish. The notion of conservation itself has become a bone of contention between nations, Canada, for instance, claiming the need for its extensive boundary waters in order to control the dangerously rapid depletion of fish stocks. American fishermen have retained a free-market approach to the fisheries, claiming that an exhaustion of the stocks will automatically reduce the number of vessels in the fishery and so allow the fish population to regenerate itself. Even the question of governmental control over the individual entrepreneur has become a pertinent factor in international fishery disputes. The Canadian government has, for example, set restrictions on the number of vessels, the duration of the season, and the size of the catch available to Canadian fishermen.[1] While Canadian fishermen in the main accept this regulation by their state, their American counterparts fiercely resist the very notion of regulation. The opposing attitudes of Canadians and Americans towards the policies of management have brought to grief the last major effort to reach a bilateral accord in this traditional area of Canadian-American tension.

Settling jurisdiction over North American fisheries had been a component of treaties between the United States and Great Britain on

206

behalf of the British North American colonies since 1783. The round of negotiations that started in 1977 was prompted by a growing Canadian assertiveness that had been under way for over a decade. In response to mounting concerns that indiscriminate over-fishing by other powers was exhausting the fish stocks, Canada extended its coastal water limits, closed off whole areas like the Gulf of St. Lawrence, and developed an approach to fish-stock management based on a regulation of the catch. Since the fishermen of both countries had centuries-old interests in fishing off each others' coasts, the adoption of the 200-mile limit by both countries triggered considerable friction — both sides had overlapping claims in four boundary areas, one on the east coast, two on the west coast and one in the Beaufort Sea.

To provide time for the negotiation of a more comprehensive settlement that would resolve the fishing jurisdictions and demarcate the boundary lines between the two countries, a modus vivendi was agreed to by the prime minister and the president in February 1977 to continue the status quo "in accordance with existing patterns, with no expansion of effort nor initiation of new fisheries."[2] On August 1, President Carter and Prime Minister Trudeau each appointed a special negotiator — Lloyd Cutler and Marcel Cadieux, respectively — to achieve a comprehensive settlement of the maritime boundaries, the fisheries and the management of hydrocarbon resources under the sea in the disputed areas. By October the negotiators submitted their report recommending that the governments proceed in two phases. The first phase would establish a joint fisheries commission that would manage the fish stocks of mutual concern, develop arrangements for sharing hydrocarbons in boundary areas, and set up binding settlement procedures for disputes in these issues. The second phase of negotiations would, they recommended, focus on the delimitation of the boundaries, which should be easier if the principles of resource sharing had been agreed to.[3] Although both governments accepted these recommendations, negotiations dragged on, requiring another interim agreement to be made between the two countries to maintain existing patterns of the fishery "with no initiation of new fisheries and no expansion of effort."[4]

In spite of the fact that both governments signed these official Notes in 1978, the U.S. government could not, because of the 1976 Fisheries Conservation and Management Act, actually bind its fishermen to abide by their terms. U.S. fishermen could — and did — ignore and challenge the interim agreements. Regional fisheries councils like the New England Regional Fisheries Management Council issued regulations contravening the officially accepted status quo. American fishermen ignored the quotas for scallop and pollock, cod and haddock on Georges Bank. The United States government claimed in response to Canadian protests that it was unable to restrict its fishermen. Canada expelled American fishermen from Canadian waters; the United States retaliated in kind. On the west coast, when Canada delayed closing salmon fishing on its side of the Swiftsure Bank area, the U.S. barred Canadian salmon trawlers from U.S. waters. The conflict escalated. Canada abrogated the 1978 agreement altogether. Both countries closed their waters to the others' fishermen. The Canadian-American fishery war had broken out.[5] No shot was fired, no casualties were recorded, but the impasse was unprecedented in recent times.

Much of the difficulty in this dispute was directly related to what has been called "a state of virtual anarchy in fisheries jurisdiction in the U.S."[6] The National Marine Fishery Service in Gloucester, Mass. served as a kind of fisheries department but was only an agency of the National Oceanic and Atmospheric Administration, itself a part of the U.S. Department of Commerce.[7] Much of the authority over fisheries management was claimed by fishermen-run regional councils which did not feel obligated to respect agreements entered into by the federal administration when it did not have clear enough jurisdiction to enforce them.

What further exacerbated the difficulties of negotiating agreements between the two countries were the different attitudes prevailing on either side of the border. Sobered by the harsh effect that over-fishing had had on their traditional zones, Canadian fishermen had accepted the need for conservation if exhaustion of the fishing stock was to be avoided. Their American counterparts viewed the fishery as another frontier to be exploited, and possibly exhausted — as with petroleum, other resources would presumably be found. In the three years following the adoption of a 200-mile limit, the number of American scallop boats on Georges Bank rose from 38 to 130, while the number of boats licensed by the Canadian government remained at 77, their trips limited to 12 days dock to dock and their catch to 30,000 pounds of scallops. In this three-year period the American fishermen increased their share of the catch from 31 per cent to 51 per cent, although the total harvest declined 40 per cent from 17,816 to 10,638 meat-tonnes.[8] Similarly aggressive disregard for regulations by American fishermen led to similar results in other parts of the industry. In 1979-80 the U.S. commercial catch on Georges Bank was 39,586 tonnes, 135 per cent of the quota set by the New England Regional Fisheries Management

208

Council. In the same period, Canadian boats took 7,000 tonnes, one-half the Canadian quota for cod. With a total cod stock estimated at 150,000 tonnes on the Georges Bank, Canadian experts consider the stocks to be depleting at a dangerous rate.[9]

Pushed by the urgency of the fishery war, the negotiators dropped the issue of sharing hydrocarbon resources and, by the end of March 1979 had finalized four fisheries agreements, two dealing with the Pacific fishery and two with the East Coast fishery. The latter provided for a fisheries regime based largely on the negotiators' original recommendations. Both sides were to enjoy reciprocal access in perpetuity to all boundary stocks. Effective conservation measures were to be ensured by a detailed system of entitlements, access areas, joint management authorities and dispute settlement procedures. For the Atlantic area there would be a joint East Coast fisheries commission that would have the authority to establish the total allowable catch, the dates of the fishing seasons, the limitations on mesh size and other details governing fishing conduct.[10] Although the total allowable catch was not specified in the draft treaty, it did lay down the proportion of the total catch to which each side would be entitled for each stock, a share that was to be adjusted once the boundaries had been delimited. Linked to the fisheries agreement for the East Coast was a boundary adjudication agreement for the disputed Georges Bank area. Canada's claim to 35 per cent of Georges Bank on the basis of the equidistance principle in international law had originally been tacitly accepted by the United States, which had not challenged the exploration permits issued by Canada for offshore oil and gas drilling until 1969. When the U.S. extended its jurisdiction to 200 miles, it published a claim to all of Georges Bank, claiming special circumstances. A year later following a decision by the International Court of Justice on a boundaries dispute between Britain and France, Canada applied this ruling to the Gulf of Maine and claimed a further extension of its jurisdiction.[11] The adjudication agreement represented the first time that the two countries had agreed to refer one of their disputes to the International Court of Justice which was to draw the final boundary line.[12]

On April 18, 1979, President Carter sent the fisheries and boundary treaties to the U.S. Senate for advice and consent, noting they were "in the best interests of the United States." Further delay in resolution of these issues would, he said, "be detrimental to conservation of the fishery resources and could lead to serious irritants in United States relations with Canada."[13] Delay was nevertheless the Senate's response, as was refusal to consent. Just because Canada was a friend, Senator Jacob Javits told the Senate Foreign Relations Committee one year later when testimony was finally heard on the agreements, the United States should not ignore its own interests.[14] Defining American fishery interests for the Senate had been a task left to the fisheries industry, which had built up a vigorous lobby against the treaty over the ensuing year. And, as a volume edited for the Atlantic Council by Willis Armstrong reported, "when the process of treaty ratification got under way in the United States, the fishing interests saw to it that it hit serious snags of a highly political nature, sometimes on issues unrelated to the region or to fish."[15] The American Fisheries Defense Committee was established to defeat ratification. A professional lobbyist was hired in Washington. Senators Muskie and Kennedy, politicians traditionally seen as friends of Canada, were enlisted. In a nutshell, they claimed that the American negotiators had failed to accommodate the recommendations of the New England fishing interests, confronted as they were "with higher costs for boats, fuel, gear, and labor, and with more depleted nearby resources."[16] In short, Lloyd Cutler, the U.S. negotiator, "gave the store away to Canada."[17]

One month before the Senate hearings, the House of Representatives Subcommittee on Fisheries published a report recommending that the fisheries agreement be rejected since it was not in the interests of the affected sectors of the U.S. industry and was incompatible with the Fisheries Conservation and Management Act of 1976.[18] This legislation had been instrumental in politicizing the American fishery industry by involving non-governmental organizations like the fishing councils in the formulation and implementation of policy. The treaty's proposed joint commission for managing the stocks was a direct threat to the autonomy of the regional councils, whose powers had been buttressed by the 1976 act. In hindsight, the passage of the Fisheries Conservation and Management Act of 1976, not the extension of the 200-mile limit in 1977, can be seen as the watershed in Canadian-American fishery relations since it effectively removed from the executive branch the power to conclude international agreements.

When Senator Kennedy proposed during the April 1980 hearings that the treaty's duration be changed from an indefinite period to three years and that Canadian scallop entitlements be further reduced, the Canadian secretary of state was enraged. These amendments were, Mark MacGuigan said, "of a drastic, far-reaching nature. They would destroy the balance of the agreements which resulted from long and arduous negotiations in which both sides made significant concessions.''[19] He had been caught, as had many foreign ministers in many other countries before him, by the powerful role played by the U.S. Senate — and therefore by American interest-group politics — in unmaking the foreign policy which American diplomats had supposedly already made under the aegis of the State Department. MacGuigan understandably could say in indignation, ''we don't propose to renegotiate the details of a treaty that has already been negotiated.''[20] But brave words did not bring the treaty back to life.

The aftermath of the Senate's inaction was an increase of American over-fishing, to which Canada belatedly responded with increased quotas for Canadian catches on Georges Bank.[21] The consequence of the new president's withdrawal of the treaty from the Senate was an effective separation of the fisheries' imbroglio from the boundary adjudication agreement, to which the U.S. fishermen did not object and which had been ratified by the Senate. Prime Minister Trudeau made this uncoupling conditional on achieving a workable conservation scheme for scallops,[22] but the management plan proposed by the U.S. for scallop fishing offered little hope of reducing the conflict between Canadian and American fishermen or in protecting the scallop stocks.

One can sympathize with those Canadian diplomats who threw up their hands in dismay. They had negotiated at length and in good faith, consulting with and coopting the Canadian fishermen in the Atlantic and Pacific provinces. They found that the agreement they had solemnly signed with their counterparts on behalf of their government had not in fact been taken as a binding commitment. Having been burned, they were tempted to conclude that it was no use trying to make a deal with the Americans on anything. The conservative Atlantic Council also cautioned that ''When the U.S. negotiates with Canada with a view to concluding a treaty, the executive branch should be extremely careful to make sure of support by the Senate, so that Canadians are not confounded by rejection of something they thought was agreed'' — just as Canada should carry with it in negotiations ''the relevant provincial authorities.''[23] But even though the United States cannot be counted on to deliver when its representatives make a commitment, Canada can hardly avoid engaging in the diplomatic process in order to resolve bilateral issues, although it may need to be prepared to negotiate twice — once with the administration and later with the Senate. Getting the Americans to include senators in the process of negotiation so as to coopt the legislators in a "C.O.D. diplomacy" is a constitutional and political non-starter.[24]

Canada will obviously have to continue to negotiate at the government-to-government level. In many cases, it will be appropriate for the resulting agreements to take the form of treaties. The example of the New England fishermen upsetting the fishery treaty emphasizes the important role that local American politics plays in the bilateral relationship. It gives further support to the notion, so hard for the Canadian diplomat to accept, that Canada cannot afford not to intervene directly in the American political process. Had the affected provinces and fishermen's organizations entered into bilateral discussions with the politicians and fishermen's groups of the New England states, it is quite conceivable that the proposed treaty would have satisfied the American fishermen. Even if that had not been possible, a substantial mobilization of American interests that stood to lose from the bad relations caused by the Senate's delay, could have exercised countermanding pressure on the Senate Foreign Relations Committee so that the definition of the United States' national interest could have been broadened from the self-seeking concerns of a few hundred scallop fishermen to the overall interest of the United States in responsibly managing the jointly exploited resources of the ocean bed.

Canada is not the only country to suffer from the impact of local politics on the United States' position on the exploitation of the resources under the oceans. At the same time that Canada was experiencing problems in its negotiations in the U.S. over the fisheries agreements, the rest of the world was being held ransom in the United Nations by the power of the American mining lobby.

Closing Down UNCLOS
When President Reagan fired the American negotiators to the United Nations Conference on the Law of the Sea (UNCLOS) and threatened to abort a multilateral process that had been years in gestation and parented by 150 members of the world community, there was good reason for America's friends to be upset. Consternation among the world community was not simply a matter of protocol, though none of the United States' allies had been given prior notification of this abrupt and drastic action. As Nicholas Burnett of the *Washington Post* put it, "the way the changes were made has deeply hurt America's credibility in the world and raised troubling questions about the Reagan administration's conduct of diplomacy."[25] Canada had been too

recently a victim of an American vested interest's intervention in U.S. diplomacy to be as shocked as its international interlocutors, but it had just as much at stake as other countries for whom the proposed treaty on the Law of the Sea promised a hopeful new era of global resource sharing.

There was reason for the dismay that spread through the international community. In 1970 the United States had voted in favour of a resolution passed by the U.N. General Assembly that the rich seabed resources of minerals were the "common heritage of mankind" to be exploited only "in accordance with an international regime to be created."[26] The convention on the Law of the Sea would represent the largest body of international law ever established, covering a vast range of issues from seabed mining, marine navigation and sovereign rights over the exploitation of continental shelves to sharing the ocean beds' resources and sea-pollution control. Negotiators representing both Republican and Democratic administrations had participated in the UNCLOS meetings over the years, pushing for, and obtaining, major concessions from other coastal states considered to be vital to U.S. security interests, albeit at the cost of the American mining companies who had bitterly and loudly complained that they would have to give away the technology they had developed at vast expense. At the close of the 1980 UNCLOS session, the U.S. chief negotiator, Elliot Richardson, assured conference members that it was "all but certain" that the treaty would be signed in 1981.[27] Now the new administration had no qualms asserting that domestic politics should have primacy over the painfully constructed creation of multilateral diplomacy. As Reagan's new ambassador to the reconvened conference put it, "The people of the United States, through their electoral process, have expressed their preference for a variety of policies that affect the work of this conference. My country's political leaders cannot and should not ignore that mandate."[28]

The mandate that previous negotiators had exercised had achieved substantial gains which satisfied U.S. concerns for its most basic strategic interests. Prime among these was the preservation of freedom to navigate and fly over the high seas even within the new 200-mile exclusive economic zones, and in such straits as Gibraltar and other choke points that would otherwise fall within the twelve-mile limit over which all nations can exercise sovereignty.[29] It was these rights that put the Pentagon strongly behind the draft treaty.

> The U.S. Joint Chiefs of Staff are eager to have these navigation rights. With them, the U.S. Navy can steam uncontested through strategic

213

straits like Gibraltar and Hormuz. With them its submarines can remain under water was they pass through coastal seas that other nations are increasingly claiming as sovereign. 'Creeping jurisdiction' — the unilateral extension of territorial waters — has become a serious problem in the last 20 years. The treaty would lay it to rest, enhancing U.S. national security.[30]

There had to be a quid pro quo. In exchange for these military and commercial navigation rights, the U.S. had had to offer concessions on sharing the wealth of the seabed with the developing countries, who had insisted that the mineral-rich nodules were part of the world patrimony and should be mined by a collective organization with profits flowing to the poor countries as a major part of the New International Economic Order (NIEO). The U.S. had wanted free enterprise to exploit the seabed, since the bulk of the seabed technical expertise and organizational capability had been developed by American corporations within international consortia including Japanese, French, Canadian and German companies. Under Henry Kissinger, a compromise was eventually struck, envisaging a parallel system of exploitation in which private-enterprise consortia and a collective organization called The Enterprise would both have authority to mine the seabed.[31] This sharing would be overseen by a new International Seabed Authority (ISA) whose revenues "in the form of taxes, fees, and profits from its own operations, as agreed from the outset, are to be allocated to the poor countries of the world for development purposes."[32]

The dispute over seabed mining had assumed the proportions of what Melvyn Westlake of the London *Times* has called a "classic struggle between the world's rich and poor nations."[33] Whereas the underdeveloped countries saw UNCLOS as a crucial test of their progress towards a new economic order, the American position was dominated by the self-interest of the big mining companies. The reason why the Republican party's election platform of 1980 had said that the proposed Law of the Sea treaty had slighted American long-term security requirements was essentially that the mining industry had most powerfully expressed its opinion that the U.S. had been too "soft" in these negotiations. With the Third World countries in control of the ISA, the mining industry feared that the rules might ultimately be changed and so threaten the tenure of their holdings. Having invested hundreds of millions of dollars in exploring the ocean floor, the mining consortia would come up against unfair competition from The Enterprise, which would be dominated by Third World interests,

214

would have priority in choosing its mining sites, would be exempt from tax, and would have access to the American companies' seabed mining technology.[34] For their part, Third World countries known as the Group of 77 — an umbrella coalition of roughly 120 Latin American, Asian and African nations that had put up strong resistance to U.S. demands on seabed mining at the conference — expressed the opposite concern. The Enterprise would be completely dependent on the consortia for its knowhow. With a lag of some twenty years, "many third-world delegates are apprehensive about The Enterprise's chances of ever becoming an effective match for its private competitors."[35]

Beyond the industry's concern, the Reagan administration had a general objection to international agencies that unduly restricted economic activity.[36] The ISA might become an institutional precedent for similar international authorities over other commodities that could spread the OPEC disease.[37] The proposed treaty imposed heavy obligations on the United States to finance the International Seabed Authority as well as provide capital to launch The Enterprise.[38] The administration wanted to ensure membership of a sufficiently large group of nations sympathetic to the American position that unacceptable action by the ISA could be blocked. Worse, the administration felt that the treaty would allow the U.S. eventually to be pushed off the ISA's ruling council, since the treaty could be amended in twenty years by a two-thirds vote of the ratifying states without the U.S. Senate having any further say.[39] The U.S. negotiator, James Malone, insisted that the U.S. could not be bound by such a procedure, since amendments would effectively amount to a new treaty which would have to be submitted again to the Senate for approval.[40] While the draft treaty would allow U.S. mining consortia to proceed under certain conditions, it limited the rate of exploitation of seabed resources by setting production limits on the ocean mining of nickel, copper, manganese and coal.[41] At a time when domestic supplies of certain key minerals were dwindling, the administration took the view that an international seabed mining authority would erode the United States' ability to guarantee access to the raw materials essential to American security. As one official put it, "by placing the mineral-rich nodules under U.N. supervision and by limiting our right to exploit them, we may be losing a unique opportunity to help ourselves to much needed raw materials."[42]

The American desire to help itself at the expense of the world community threatened Canada's stake in the UNCLOS treaty. In sharp

215

contrast to the Reagan administration's attempt to achieve security *from* international regulation, Canada's large stake in the Law of the Sea lay precisely in achieving security *via* the reinforcement of international authority — first over mineral markets and second in international law. In both areas the Canadian interest conflicted with the American so that Reagan's threat to the Law of the Sea was a direct menace to Canada. Like the land-based mineral-producing countries in the Group of 77, who were afraid of competition from the subsidized recovery of deep-sea nodules, Canada had pressed for a control system that would not permit excessive seabed mining to cause world mineral prices to collapse. Real tension had developed between Canada and the United States over the negotiation of a nickel agreement. A formula for nickel production limits was agreed to in 1978; it incorporated concessions made to Canada but was not passed because of American pressure, much to Ottawa's resentment. Canada had not been happy with the ultimate nickel production formula but had accepted it in the context of the general give-and-take that had characterized the complex process of negotiations. Although both Inco and Noranda Mines, the Canadian companies involved in the international seabed consortia, shared the American hostility to production controls,[43] Canadian negotiators favoured a reduction of the limit in the new negotiations, in opposition to the American pressure for its increase.

If economic factors alone had determined government policy on the Law of the Sea, differences between Canada and the United States would not have been substantial. As countries with long coasts abutting potentially rich continental shelves, both supported the coastal states' exclusive right to manage fisheries and exploit the billions of dollars worth of oil and gas resources within their economic zones, which the American position defined as 200 miles and the Canadian as the edge of the continental shelf when this lay beyond the 200-mile limit.[44] Where the two neighbours came into conflict at UNCLOS concerning sovereignty at sea was not so much the Atlantic and Pacific, where both countries acted as coastal states with economic interests and where access to the fisheries and resources had been under separate negotiations as we have seen. It was in the Arctic Ocean (where Canada's claims had been challenged by the United States but would be buttressed by the new UNCLOS treaty) that Canada's coastal-state interests came up against the United States' maritime and military-power interests in free navigation and the right of innocent (unimpeded) passage.

From Washington's perspective, the Canadian government had

216

become uncharacteristically and aggressively independent on maritime issues in the North. In response to a national outburst of indignation over the defiance by the S.S. *Manhattan* of Canadian sovereignty in the Northwest Passage in 1969, the Canadian government had passed the Arctic Waters Pollution Prevention Act the following year, establishing a 100-mile pollution control zone in the Arctic waters and asserting the Canadian government's right and responsibility for controlling navigational standards in the area. Related legislation in 1970 extended Canada's territorial sea from three to twelve nautical miles and, since the entrance points to the Northwest Passage are both less than twenty-four miles wide, thereby closed the Passage as an international strait.[45] Understandable fears concerning the irreversible damage to the fragile ecology of the Arctic by oil spills had been aroused by such maritime disasters as the Torrey Canyon in 1967. While the Arctic Waters Pollution Prevention Act gave the Canadian government jurisdiction to police such threats, the strategic thrust of this legislation was to move towards establishing Canadian sovereignty over the waters of the Arctic archipelago.[46] Because Ottawa was not prepared to spend the enormous sums required on military hardware to enforce its claims to Arctic sovereignty, "the government had to pursue these claims through legal rather than military or para-military means."[47]

The United States had officially objected to Canada's unilateral Arctic actions, protesting that "international law provides no basis for these proposed unilateral extensions of jurisdiction on the high seas, and the U.S.A. can neither accept nor acquiesce in the assertion of such jurisdiction."[48] Although the United States objected, it did nothing to push back what it considered an illegitimate Canadian thrust towards the North Pole. For its part the Canadian government continued to build its case for jurisdiction, not by asserting a public claim to sovereignty but by following a two-pronged approach. In purely functional matters, it asserted its jurisdiction by issuing permits for exploration to companies seeking oil and gas in the Arctic. As these permits have not been challenged by the United States, they give Canada an increasing de facto claim to sovereignty in the Arctic waters. Since Canada was "lacking the requisite 'gunboats' to underpin its diplomacy," it also sought refuge, in Michael Tucker's pun, "in the canons of international law."[49]

It is easy to see why UNCLOS was crucial to Canada's Arctic policy. The draft treaty would acknowledge Canadian jurisdiction over its Arctic waters and Canadian control over the gateway to the

Northwest Passage. It would also give international recognition of the boundary line claimed by Canada to delineate American from Canadian waters off Alaska and the Yukon.[50] And it would give to the coastal state authority to enforce anti-pollution and maritime safety measures — a position the United States had opposed but that Canada had vigorously propounded.[51]

Given the divergence of interest separating Canada from its neighbour, it might be assumed that President Reagan's attempt to close down UNCLOS would have created a major new source of conflict between the two countries. On sharing and marketing ocean bed resources, Canada's interests lay clearly with those of the developing and resource-exporting countries.[52] Had the treaty process collapsed, Canada could still have continued to negotiate bilaterally with the United States to resolve conflicting claims over the common Arctic Ocean boundary, but with prospects of success limited by the Americans' current distaste for bilateral deals. Canada's response to the Reagan bombshell was accordingly quiet and diplomatic. As the chief Canadian negotiator, Alan Beesley, put it, "It is a time for us to convince the United States that it would be a tragic error of judgment on their part to reject the treaty."[53] There were American voices articulating a similar position. As Lincoln Bloomfield from M.I.T. argued,

> By granting a victory to those opposed to the plan so far, the Administration has increased the chances of a major defeat for broad U.S. strategic interests and an unravelling of the most complex — and hopeful — international effort in history to bring order out of political chaos . . . If the treaty is pulled up by the roots with a demand for even greater American benefits, the various compromises which sustain other U.S. vital interests are bound to unravel. The moderates who helped us will have been discredited, leaving the field to the extremists. Nothing could be more damaging to broad American interests in peace and stability, or to the dimming prospects for a practical world order to help manage those things we either must cooperate to share equitably or will wind up fighting over.[54]

The United States was in a strong position to fight for these resources. The mining industry had already lobbied successfully for domestic legislation that licensed U.S. miners to begin exploration by 1982 and exploitation of seabed resources by 1988.[55] While such action would violate the 1970 resolution of the U.N. General Assembly, it would give some protection for American consortia in the total absence of a treaty, although some argued that the firms would be unable to get insurance protection without the safeguards of an international seabed law.[56] Others argued that the trade-off of seabed mining concessions for navigation rights was not necessary: the U.S. could make bilateral deals with the coastal states involved in order to secure the access it wanted.[57] According to Congressman Breaux (Democrat, Louisiana), American mining companies did not need an international treaty to establish their legal rights. Under the 1958 Geneva convention, nations and individuals had the right to utilize the high seas. Since the number of nations that would be participating in mining operations was small, "It would be very easy to make bilateral agreements with other developed nations such as Great Britain, West Germany and France."[58]

The administration's prolonged nine-month policy review concluded that the United States should negotiate changes in the proposed treaty rather than scrap it entirely, since some form of treaty was in fact in the American national interest.[59] Despite pressure from some highly placed U.S. officials to drop out of the conference, Reagan announced on January 29, 1982 that the U.S. delegation would return to UNCLOS seeking substantial changes in the provisions concerning seabed mining.[60] The U.S. had been brought back to the bargaining table by the uncertain fate of the so-called mini-treaty between the U.S., Britain, France and West Germany, which would have exchanged reciprocal recognition of exploration licences and a mechanism to arbitrate overlapping claims among the great powers.[61] Concern within UNCLOS that these countries were moving to pre-empt the Law of the Sea treaty by setting up an alternative regime eventually led to France's refusal to discuss the pact while the conference was still in session. Britain and West Germany also remained committed to the conference, unwilling to jeopardize the process by signing a separate treaty.[62]

On April 30, 1982 the United States, in an isolated group with Turkey, Venezuela and Israel, voted against the adoption of the global treaty on the Law of the Sea which was to come into force one year after being ratified by sixty nations.[63] The concessions offered to secure acceptance by the U.S. and other wavering industrial nations had fallen far short of their demands. Third World delegates had maintained they should not hand back to the U.S. concessions obtained for concessions of their own. Even the Western countries in sympathy with the American position were "embarrassed by the naked self-interest that the Reagan administration [was] displaying and by its heavy-handed tactics."[64] The conference was willing to pay a price in order to obtain American concurrence, but the price was not unlimited.

219

Continuity or Change: Treaties and Politics

It is not new to have the Senate throw a wrench into the workings of bilateral diplomacy or to have the forces of American nationalism jeopardize the prospects of international organizations. But even if they were not historic firsts, the aborting of the fisheries treaty and the attack on UNCLOS did give a clear message about the way that the Reagan administration would treat its international partners. They helped precipitate an atmosphere of uncertainty and an attitude of distrust by Canada in its formal dealings with the U.S. that had been growing through the Seventies with the long impasse over the Alaska natural gas pipeline. They also reinforced the conclusion many had drawn from previous unhappy experience with the tricks that lie in the hands of American treaty makers.

If U.S. negotiators are not in reality plenipotentiaries for their country because the U.S. Senate is increasing the role that it plays in determining foreign policy, Americans can hardly complain if foreign governments, Canada included, respond by trying to intervene more directly in U.S. politics to redefine the public perception of the American national interest in treaties that are ready for signing. If the United States' international interlocutors cannot trust commitments made by U.S. negotiators, they will be forced to shift their attention not just to Congress but to interest-group politics and media management as well. The complexities of American politics make the task of other countries in dealing with the U.S. more complex. In an international matter such as the Law of the Sea, Canada will have to continue dealing simultaneously on a bilateral basis with the United States and working at the multilateral level through the United Nations convention. In a bilateral affair such as the fisheries, Ottawa will both have to deal formally with the U.S. administration and also engage in the process of interest-group politics to help generate the consensus necessary for another attempt at rescuing the fisheries from unregulated and competitive depletion. The passages are sure to remain rough but no worse than those facing Canada's culture and information industries — the problem we examine in chapter 10.

Cultural Survival and Telecommunications

10

"When someone says 'culture' I reach for my gun," Hitler's deputy, Hermann Goering, is reported to have said. When someone says "culture" in Canada, most people stifle a yawn. Canadians have just as much difficulty believing that the pervasive American presence in their lives is a threat to their cultural survival as a viable state as they do apprehending U.S. protectionism as a threat to their economic survival. If culture were an abstract question, merely a concern of some intellectuals, artists and bureaucrats, it would have little potential for prominence on the agenda of Canadian-American tensions. But culture is concrete, not abstract. It affects the way a people expresses itself as a society, defines its political community, articulates its aspirations, and formulates its demands for action to achieve these goals. The coherence of a state's culture is a crucial factor in a state's capacity to survive. Without a common cultural consciousness, the Polish people would never have survived centuries of partition among neighbouring powers to emerge again as a state stubbornly claiming its right to exist despite continued foreign domination. What some observers call Canada's unresolved identity crisis is not so much a psychological as a political, sociological and cultural problem. Politically, the lack of a recognized identity for Canadians can be seen in the alienation of the Québécois from confederation and in the hostility expressed by Western Canadians to central Canada. These political separatisms reflect the historical difficulty that Canada has had as a new nation in developing a culture whose mythology and folklore, whose literature and music, whose theatre and arts, whose education and communications systems could give its population a social glue strong enough to bind together its various regions, nationalities and ethnicities into a coherent whole.

Americanization — the transfer of American cultural and economic values abroad — is a problem that almost all societies have had to

221

confront in the second part of the twentieth century. "Cocacoloniza-tion" is seen to threaten the values that hold together national societies, by supplanting traditional values that were functional to the indigenous culture by foreign norms that have often proved destructive of the social fabric. Traditional nation-states developed their political structure around an already existing people who shared enough common linguistic, historical, geographical, even religious, values to consider themselves a nation. But Canada is not a nation-state *comme les autres*: its native culture was destroyed by the successive waves of mainly European settlers who brought with them cultural fragments that, outside French-speaking Canada, have not had the time or the tranquillity to be amalgamated into a self-sustaining culture. The heterogeneity of the population with English as its majority language yields some insight into the enormity of Canada's cultural problem. Had Montcalm defeated Wolfe on the Plains of Abraham, and had the *Canadiens* extended their dominance *a mare usque ad mare* to form an *Amérique du Nord française*, the continually subverting impact of American cultural assimilation would not have been as powerful a force. Far from being a protective mechanism as the French language was for Quebec, the English language in the rest of Canada became a means of cultural absorption by Canada's demographically, econom-ically and, therefore, culturally more powerful neighbour.

Two other factors — economics and changing technologies — explain why adequate cultural coherence remains so difficult to achieve. British North America developed into an extension of American cultural markets, first for books, periodicals and U.S. wire services, later for the electronic media. The continental marketing of the cultural industries — originally through the medium of print (books, magazines and newspapers), later through the electronic media (radio and telecommunications) — has had the effect of overwhelming all aspects of cultural life in Canada with non-Canadian, mainly American content. At each stage, the introduction of new technologies of communication has repeatedly undermined belated governmental attempts to resist not just cultural assimilation but also the economic impact of American domination of the processing and transmission of data on the Canadian information industry.

Broadcasting and Cultural Survival
With every new development in communications technology, Canada has had to confront a further challenge to its cultural viability. When the advent of radio led to the overwhelming dominance of the

Canadian airwaves by American stations, Prime Minister Bennett warned the House of Commons that "this country must be assured of complete Canadian control of broadcasting from Canadian sources, free from foreign interferences or influence."[1] After the Aird Royal Commission on Radio Broadcasting proposed a public broadcasting system in 1929, citizen groups under the leadership of Graham Spry's Canadian Radio League lobbied against the private station operators who rebroadcast American programs. Ultimately, a mixed, private-public system was created which attempted to let private broadcasting flourish within the framework of a publicly-owned system. The public Crown corporation, the Canadian Broadcasting Corporation, developed a radio network achieving "full coverage for the scattered population of an immense territory, and the use of broadcasting to foster national objectives."[2] The private system was made up of Canadian-owned and -controlled operators who achieved their goals of profit maximization from advertising by playing the American popular music cranked out by the U.S. entertainment industry.

Reviewing the cultural scene at the height of the Cold War in 1951, the Massey-Lévesque Report used military metaphors in two senses. "If we as a nation are concerned with the problem of defence," it wondered, "what, we may ask ourselves, are we defending?" Its answer was the "spiritual foundations of our national life," "the quality of the Canadian mind and spirit," "the roots of our life as a nation," its "spiritual legacy" — in a word its culture, which gives "a community its power to survive." But this culture was threatened by more than the Soviet menace. It confronted a tidal wave of technology, the "American invasion by film, radio and periodical." The problem was "that a vast and disproportionate amount of material coming from a single alien source may stifle rather than stimulate our own creative spirit."[3]

The issue raised by the advent of television was still the same as Graham Spry had put it two decades earlier: the state *or* the United States. Liberal and Conservative governments produced similar and equally contradictory responses, accepting a role both for the state *and* the United States. The public sector was expanded alongside private-sector TV by giving the CBC a television mandate but with insufficient public funding. The CBC was thus forced to generate supplementary revenue by copying and competing with the private broadcasters, who relied on American entertainment programming to attract the audience ratings on which their advertising revenue depended.

It is the power of these media that has created such concern among cultural policy advocates over the past decade, since they are aware that the country's political fabric depends on the strength of its cultural fibre. "Never have communications had a more important role to play in the development of greater national cohesion," wrote Alphonse Ouimet, former president of the CBC in 1979. "But, instead of bringing Canadians closer together, these wonderful new instruments of communication threaten to obliterate the remaining cultural distinctions between English Canada and the United States."[4] Ouimet thought the impact on French Canada was much less rapid, though in the long run the threat could be the same. In fact French culture in Quebec is already in serious trouble as can be seen in the collapse of Quebec film making.

> Broadcasting [said the recent president of the CBC] is *the* most powerful means by which modern nations and peoples share a common experience, learn about their national identity, learn about their culture, learn about themselves.[5]

The consumption of television is the dominant cultural activity of Canadians; the average adult watches twenty-five hours of television every week, more than three hours a day. But the national identity and culture that Canadians learn about in front of their TV screens is not Canadian. Ninety-six per cent of all drama available on English-language television is of foreign origin; 74 per cent of the time Canadians spend viewing English-language television is devoted to foreign programs. Foreign programming is overwhelmingly American.[6] Even though the CBC was established almost fifty years ago to make broadcasting a public service, Canada's broadcasting system has given increasing priority to commercial gain as its guiding principle. The result has been "a massive commitment of air time to programs, many of them American, that are irrelevant to pressing Canadian needs."[7]

American programs have been directly relevant to the profit needs of the private broadcasters. Already amortized by their huge American circulation, U.S. programs are imported into Canada for a fraction of their original cost. Their appeal to the viewing public conditioned by the media to the Hollywood star system is such that they generate more revenue from advertising than do Canadian programs whose relatively higher costs can rarely be recovered by commercial sponsorship. To produce an episode of the 1980 CBC drama *A Gift to Last* cost $300,000. To purchase an episode of *Lou Grant* for broadcast in Canada would entail $30,000, even though it was produced for $1

224

million in Los Angeles. The net revenues for a Canadian broadcaster per half hour of comparable American and Canadian programs in 1976 were $21,000 and $55 respectively.[8] Dumping is the sale of a product in foreign markets at a price below that charged in the home market. The commercialization of television in a country unprotected by barriers to cultural dumping necessarily means its Americanization. In the Seventies, the Canadian Radio-television and Telecommunications Commission's authorization of cable systems as virtually unregulated common carriers represented an integral transplantation of individual U.S. networks into Canada, neatly circumventing the CRTC's own Canadian-content regulations, which had attempted to force Canadian over-the-air television broadcasters to offer Canadian programming, especially during prime viewing time. In a sense, the barely regulated wiring of Canadian households to cable moved the American border 200 miles to the north. The CRTC is also sabotaging its own policies in radio. Since 1979 it has allowed cable systems to carry U.S. radio services, a concession that makes it difficult to force regular radio stations to follow the celebrated Canadian-content rules which so successfully boosted the Canadian music industry.

By the end of the Seventies, when a typhoon of new technology could already be seen approaching on the horizon, few could claim that Canadian culture had been made secure from the threat of assimilation. On the contrary, the plight of Canada's cultural industries was graphically and repeatedly described by interveners before the Federal Cultural Policy Review Committee. Canada is "an occupied country" culturally speaking, affirmed Vancouver's Cineworks. "We have an English-language television system which is substantially American," admitted A.W. Johnson, then president of the Canadian Broadcasting Corporation. "The Canadian music industry seems to be, for the most part, in the hands of foreign-controlled companies who have little interest in the development of the Canadian music industry," reported the Toronto Recording Association of Commercial Studios. "The competition from the imported book, in particular from the U.S., is so enormous that a large share of the market is unavailable to the Canadian book," was the view of the Association of Canadian Publishers.[9]

While the present was bleak for these cultural leaders, new technology promises worse to come. Optical fibre and broadcast satellites threaten what is already considered an untenable situation by bringing multi-channel American programming to every community of the land that can afford the modest cost of a dish antenna. The ability

225

of cable operators to point their antennae directly at a U.S. satellite is putting enormous pressure on the government to introduce in southern Canada the same kind of satellite-cable package using the already advanced domestic Canadian satellite Anik that has been established by CanComm in the North. Once again, the danger is that Canada will be using its own advanced technology to increase American programming at an exponential rate at the cost of reduced Canadian viewing of local programming. The prospect of pay-TV, which would move television from the principle of universal broadcasting systems to user-financed ''narrowcasting'' with consumers eventually having seventy or eighty specialized channels to choose from, could, in the opinion of CBC vice-president Peter Herrndorf, inevitably result in ''a substantial increase in the Americanization of the Canadian broadcasting system — because most of the new program services will originate in the U.S.''[10] U.S. pay services will be ''scrambled,'' requiring Canadian licensing to make de-coding available. This provides Canada with an opportunity to create a Canadian system that can carry Canadian advertising and generate income to be used for the production of Canadian programming.

Coming to an agreement on the international use of satellite broadcasting services will be particularly difficult. Direct broadcast satellites will compete with the transmission of television programs off the air and by cable. The implications for Canadian business are considerable. Until now Canadian industry's ability to advertise on Canadian television has been sustained by ''simulcasting'' — the CRTC's requirement that, when a Canadian network has bought an American program and sold it to advertisers, cable systems pirating that program from the American networks have to substitute the Canadian version with its Canadian commercials. This capacity of the Canadian networks to offer the Canadian market to their advertisers is threatened by the satellites' direct delivery of the American networks' programs, with their American commercials, into living rooms across Canada via dish receivers.

Canada can draw some moral comfort from article XI of the 1972 UNESCO Declaration of Guiding Principles on the Use of Satellite Broadcasting for the Free Flow of Information, the Spread of Education, and Greater Cultural Exchange. This statement embodies the principle that a state does not have to be subjected to programs broadcast from a foreign state without its consent. Canada, with Sweden, maintains that there can be no economic exploitation of markets in the area of spillover of one country's programs on another, while the U.S. defends the uninhibited flow of broadcasting as an international expression of freedom of information.[11] The UNESCO agreement gives Canada some diplomatic leverage with the United States. Nevertheless the pressures are great to open up the use of American satellites for continent-wide broadcasting. On October 22, 1981, the U.S. Federal Communications Commission (FCC) gave its approval to several applications by American satellite transmission companies for the provision of trans-border video services. For example, RCA American Communications, Inc. would be able "to extend presently authorized program service to new receiver points located throughout lower Canada via RCA Satcom satellites from a transmit point in Atlanta, Georgia"; Satellite Signals Unlimited, Inc. would be allowed "to extend its operations to provide service to Vancouver, Canada, and London, Ontario, via Canada's ANIK satellites. . . [T]he proposed service will provide a significant new competitive alternative in the distribution of television programming from the U.S. to Canada."[12] In its justification of its support for these applications the FCC showed a clear understanding of the economic benefits that would flow to the U.S. "This extension will result in additional revenues to the U.S. programmers and carriers. In addition, there is a potential for increased trade of U.S. video equipment and program material."[13] Without a coherent policy of its own, Canada will have great difficulty resisting American pressure to acquiesce to these direct broadcast operations, even though they would gut the Canadian television advertising industry of its economic base.

The past failure of public policy to achieve its goal of Canadian-content television, the future promise of new technologies that will intensify the pressures of Americanization, and the present sense of crisis expressed by leaders of the cultural community have brought Canadian cultural policy to a turning point. But the CRTC did not decide to put an end to the blind transplantation of American programming by cable. Nor did it license a pay-TV system that would strengthen domestic program production. Instead its 1982 decision to license a national, a performing arts, and three regional services has launched too many companies that will be forced by their competition for subscribers to rely on the increased importation of U.S. entertainment, as Patrick Watson and Robert Fulford point out.[14] Since so many precedents have been set by such operations as CanComm's provision of U.S. programming to Northern communities, and since the regulatory power of the CRTC has been crippled by unfavourable court cases, it is unlikely that satellite broadcasting will be regulated to allow Canadian programming fair access to this new means of delivery. Far more likely for the Eighties is an intensification of the assault by the electronic media which, in the words of CRTC chairman John Meisel, are the major "agents of denationalization and of the Americanization of our climate." These new media technologies using the development of satellite transmission threaten the "complete annihilation of what remains of a distinct Canadian culture, of its regional and other unique components, and, in the final analysis, of an independent Canadian state."[15] Another threat, closely linked to the first because it relies on satellite transmission, is still more basic since it will transform the nature of information itself.

The Challenge of New Information Technologies
The challenge that new satellite technologies offer cultural policy makers is how to prevent an already disastrous situation from deteriorating beyond recall. The policy challenge to Canada of the new techniques of processing and transmitting data is whether to interfere once again with natural efficiencies created by new technology in order to sustain the efficacy of Canada as a separate economy. Bernard Ostry has stated the problem graphically:

> Imagine a future in which information must be in machine-readable form to be disseminated widely. What would happen if only foreign corporations and governments were translating information into machine-readable form? How much information on Canada — its regions, its literature, its law, its history, its traditions — would Canadians receive? And in which of our official languages? Probably very little. In such a future, we would cease to know ourselves, and very quickly, cease to exist at all as a Canadian community.[16]

Whether it is the transformation of the existing electronic mass media or the impact of trans-border data flow on the information industries, the small number of experts who are grappling with the issues are warning that Canada must harness the new technology or else be engulfed as a cultural and political entity. But the very act of harnessing the information revolution to the national vehicle will necessarily lead to conflict with the dominant force that is marketing the new technology — the United States of America.

For a country whose economic well-being, cultural identity and political cohesion have been vulnerable to successive changes in communications technology, Canada is naturally sensitive to the implications of the new, explosive developments in telecommunications, data processing, computers and semi-conductors, and communications satellites. As Allan Gotlieb, Charles Dalfen and Kenneth Katz noted in 1974, "Electronic technology, by providing the means to accumulate, store, change, and transmit information on an unprecedented scale, has dramatically upset the process of balancing the nation's interest in controlling the flow of information with the national interest in deriving benefits from its increased availability."[17] While the United States sees these areas as technical and commercial problems, Canada, along with other Western nations and Japan, views the rapid changes in this area as events that will have not only economic effects but powerful political consequences.[18] In North America, the information flow from the Canadian perspective is

> more than a flow: it is an onrushing flood of information of overwhelming social, economic, and cultural significance. The problems that arise for Canada, in trying to derive maximum benefit from this outpouring of information and yet stimulate the development of its own cultural values, are exceptionally difficult and possibly unique in scale.[19]

In its review of this problem, the Clyne Report noted that telecommunications would form the infrastructure of the new industrial society of the twenty-first century now coming into being, just as twentieth-century Canada was shaped by building the national railroad in the 1870s and 1880s.

> To maintain our Canadian identity and independence we must ensure an adequate measure of control over data banks, trans-border data flow, and the content of information services available in Canada. If we wish to build a Canadian presence in world industrial markets then we will be required to encourage the growth of Canadian telecommunications industries that will be competitive in world terms.[20]

Trans-border data flow (TBDF) — the movement of electronic data across national frontiers through linked computer-communications networks[21] — has dangerous economic implications for Canada. A report released in 1978 estimated that if current trends continue, Canada would be importing $1.5 billion of its computing requirements from foreign sources by 1985. Translated into employment effects, this trade deficit would establish 23,000 data processing jobs abroad in order to meet Canadian information requirements by 1985.[22] The estimate was too conservative. By 1980 the trade deficit in computers and automated office systems had already reached $1 billion, and the Science Council expected it to climb to $5 billion by 1985.[23] Beyond

229

the adverse effect on the balance of payments and the labour market for high technology jobs, the acceleration of trans-border data flow will have repercussions throughout the Canadian economy, as a 1981 study by Price Waterhouse indicated.

- *Competitiveness of Canadian computer service industry:* "Large scale imports of computer processing or systems development services could threaten the viability of Canadian service bureaus and software houses. Their domestic market space might become inadequate."
- *Economic sovereignty:* "The centralization of decision-making at the headquarters of multinationals could make it more difficult for the governments of host countries to influence such decisions."
- *Redress of consumer grievances:* "Canadian protection laws may be ineffective in relation to data on Canadians stored outside the country."
- *Sources of supply of materials:* "TBDF might also conceivably affect the choices corporations make about the sourcing of materials. This could occur if production planning and control of inventories, including ordering of materials, were highly centralized with the help of TBDF."
- *Industrial organization:* "It is also argued that TBDF allows production and inventory levels to be rationalized on a worldwide basis, providing multinationals with cost advantages over national firms. . . . TBDF has been associated by some authors with a centralization of key management decisions at the headquarters of multinationals."[24]

Policy issues arise not so much from the actual transfer of data as from what happens before and what happens after: Who prepares the software? Who has access to the data? Who processes the information? How is it used? Since corporate decisions are made where access to information is easy, the political concern in a branch plant economy centres on the transfer of decision making. Multinationals stand to realize significant gains in efficiency from the more rapid transport of data that the new technology offers, while employment in their branch operations is further restricted. American air carriers can look after Canadian clients from their headquarters in the U.S. American computer companies can service and maintain Canadian computers by remote control. In both examples, jobs paid for by consumers in Canada are diverted outside the economy. Management functions, too, can be transferred to headquarters. The Canadian branch plant economy can become, as it were, a terminal economy in both the technical and the medical sense of the word.

> Information is power and economic information is economic power. Information has an economic value and the ability to store and process certain types of data may well give one country political and technological advantage over other countries. This in turn leads to a loss of national sovereignty through supranational data flows.[25]

The Clyne Report recommended that the government act to regulate trans-border data flows "to ensure that we do not lose control of information vital to the maintenance of national sovereignty."[26] It is not clear what is technically possible in the regulation of TBDF or even what is legally possible. Should Canadian data services be disrupted as a result of interruptions at the foreign data control centres caused by strikes, terrorism or actions taken by foreign courts or legislatures, it is doubtful that either Canadian governments or Canadian corporations could take any actions to restore the needed services. Nor could actions be taken to prevent the extra-territorial application of the laws of the country where data are stored to the Canadian data they contained. Once corporate data are exported, Canada would presumably lose jurisdiction over them. They might not be available to Canadian courts or agencies, thus diminishing the political authority of the Canadian government over its corporate citizens. As Allan Gotlieb et al. wrote, "Computers are seen as exacerbating the erosion of Canadian sovereignty and the already serious imbalance in the distribution of economic control in Canada."[27]

Once branch plants are connected to their head office control systems, it may not be possible for Canadian law to maintain its jurisdiction. On the contrary, U.S. law could well prevail over the Canadian branch. Because the commercial applications of these new technologies are rapidly being put into place and promising immediate benefits, there is great pressure, particularly from the American multinationals, to establish data communications by satellite between their branch plants and headquarters. It is uncertain whether host economies will be able to get a fair share of the benefits accruing to the multinationals.[28]

While these concerns have been expressed by government experts, they have not been shared by the telecommunications industry, whether Canadian- or foreign-controlled. The few Canadian success stories in telecommunications — Northern Telecom, Bell-Northern Research, Mitel — want access to the American market and so oppose proposals that government regulate TBDF lest congressional retaliation cramp their own style in the United States. Apart from its lead in digital technology, the Canadian industry is weak in the computer field. Canada cannot aspire to large-scale production of telecommunications equipment. Among all the industrialized nations, only Canada has failed to increase significantly the share of its gross national product attributable to electronics. By 1976 the Canadian imports of research-intensive manufactures were double its exports. Its rapidly growing trade deficit in electrical products had reached $900 million.

Part of the problem is related to foreign ownership. While only 20 per cent of the 700 Canadian electronics firms are foreign-owned, "these account for 55 per cent of the industry's sales. No other industrialized country in the free world has such a high degree of foreign ownership of its electronic industry."[29] One recent study suggests a close link between foreign ownership and the low level of research and development to which many observers connect Canada's poor performance in electronics manufacturing. Using the 1980 performance of all federally incorporated firms with Canadian computer-communications hardware sales above $13 million in 1980, R.W. Evans found that the foreign-owned firms spent 2 per cent of revenues on R & D, while the Canadian-owned firms spent an average of 7 per cent. If the foreign-owned firms had spent 6 per cent of sales on R & D — the average for their parent companies world-wide — this would have amounted to $181 million, producing some 2,400 more jobs. Canadian firms had net fixed assets in use that amounted to 24 per cent of 1980 revenues. The foreign-owned firms had net fixed assets in use averaging only 7 per cent of 1980 revenues. If they had spent as much on property, plant and equipment as the Canadian companies, they would have $724 million in net fixed assets in use, more than three times the $224 million actually spent. The giant IBM was a case in point. On a world-wide basis, it had net fixed assets amounting to 25 per cent of 1980 revenues. In Canada its net fixed assets were but 9 per cent of its Canadian sales.[30] Canadian branch plants do benefit from the so-called invisible inflow of U.S. technology estimated for 1976 to be worth $88 million in the electrical products field. However, the import of technology and invisible R & D does not often relate to exportable products, limits employment opportunities for highly qualified scientists, engineers and technicians, and perpetuates the truncation of Canada's research and development capability.

The American debate over the action that should be taken to reduce the negative economic and strategic effects for the U.S. of the transfer abroad of its technology has raised the spectre of Canada suffering seriously from its technological dependence.[31] In short, while the Canadian infrastructure in computer communications is strong, the inadequate size of the market, the low levels of research and development, and high tariffs prevent the industry from being fully competitive unless the government is willing to create a market through the regulation of trans-border data flow. By mid-1982 a clear government policy on these matters had still not been articulated, even though studies had been going on for over a decade.

Following the establishment of the Department of Communications in 1969 and the publication of some forty special reports on the many facets of telecommunications and computer technologies in 1971, the Canadian government lost its original sense of urgency. With the exception of fibre optics, all the technologies being commercially developed in 1982 were predicted a decade ago. As Alphonse Ouimet, the chairman of Telesat, has written, "without an overall plan, leadership has been difficult and regulatory decisions have had to be taken on an ad hoc basis which would not take into account their long-term implications for Canadian cultural and industrial sovereignty."[32] In 1977 the federal interdepartmental committee on computer communications was dissolved. In response to the warnings of the Clyne Report, another interdepartmental task force was set up to develop a close relationship with Canadian industry, facilitate more understanding of the TBDF issue, and develop a comprehensive approach to the questions involved.[33] The federal government has been adept at presenting position papers but hesitant to act.

As Peter Robinson points out, an effective policy would need to strike a balance between society's desire to benefit from the positive aspects of TBDF and its need to exercise a reasonable degree of control over its negative implications. "It is becoming clear that the issues are societal and require the development of appropriate balances among the competing political, economic, social and cultural goals of society."[34] But trans-border data flows are by nature international, so Canadian policy will need to consider the positions of other governments, particularly the concerns of the United States.

Negotiations, Continental and International
The United States views telecommunications aggressively as one of its most important trade thrusts for the foreseeable future. In contrast to Canada, the problem of telecommunications is seen in the U.S. not to

be a cultural but a technological and commercial question. The United States is already the leader and dominant economic figure in the knowledge-intensive industries. According to the communications expert, Oswald Ganley, in 1970, half of the United States' labour force was already employed in "communications and information-related activities," a sector that accounted for 30 per cent of U.S. GNP.[35] Communications and information goods and services are the number two export of the United States.[36] What the automobile was to the American economy of the Forties and Fifties, information will be to the economy of the Eighties and Nineties — the driving force that can rescue the troubled economy and sustain American global dominance.

Given the lead and the potential of the American information industries, the U.S. government has adopted a strong free trade approach to all matters affecting information and strongly resists foreign government attempts to place barriers in the way of the free flow of information. Barriers to trans-border data flow will affect the efficiency of American corporations and their ability to compete. Requirements that data be processed in host economies will reduce the productivity and earnings of American multinationals and jeopardize U.S. export markets.[37] Other countries' concerns for their technological and cultural sovereignty tend to be dismissed as a simple attempt to justify protectionist measures against the U.S. William Brock, the United States trade representative, wants the GATT agreements to be expanded to include services and so forestall other countries' increasing their protectionism via communications policies. Congress has already heard complaints about Canada's barriers that have imposed inefficiencies on U.S. corporations. The Vancouver Real Estate Board wanted to subscribe to Multi-List Inc.'s real estate listings service, but was denied permission unless the data were processed within Canada. Comshare Inc.'s request to invest in computer services in Canada was rejected by FIRA.[38]

Of particular concern to the American business community is paragraph 157(4) of the revised Bank Act. The amendment requires banks to "maintain and process in Canada any information or data relating to the preparation and maintenance of [their] records." American politicians and industry spokesmen have objected strongly to this provision, even though the amendment allows banks to maintain copies of or take extracts from these records and "further process information or data relating to such copies or extracts inside or outside Canada."[39] Although Americans have charged that the revision is protectionist and discriminatory, W.A. Kennett, the Canadian

234

inspector general of banks, has responded that the act does not constitute an interruption to the trans-border flow of data since duplicate records and information are allowed to flow freely as long as they are originally processed in Canada.[40]

Canadian officials detect a noticeable hardening of American attitudes towards Canada on these issues. In the context of the Reagan administration's self-conceived mandate to prove that it is helping the U.S. regain its dominance in the world economy, Canada has become a test case. If the U.S. cannot bring Canada to heel on the principle of the free flow of information, it is unlikely to win in Europe on the same issue. Americans fear that if Canada "gets away with" its amendment to the Bank Act, then similar actions will be taken in other countries. This explains why Canada, though a relatively small part of the international problem, is being taken by the United States as a proving ground for its strategy.

Under the Carter administration, section 301 of the U.S. Trade Act was amended, as we saw in chapter 5, to bring information services under its retaliatory provisions in order specifically to allow retaliation against the Canadian government's Bill C-58 of 1976. Bill C-58 was an amendment to the Income Tax Act which finally implemented what the O'Leary Royal Commission on Publications had recommended in 1961 and what Time-Life Inc. and the U.S. government had been fighting ever since — the withdrawal of the privileged tax status from the Canadian edition of *Time* magazine as a medium for Canadian advertising. In making Canadian ads in *Time* non-deductible for income tax purposes, Bill C-58 was attempting to secure the revenue base of authentically Canadian periodicals. In a parallel attempt to bolster the commercial base for Canadian television, the bill also made advertising on American television stations non-deductible.

While laying to rest the body of *Time*, Bill C-58 raised the genie of the American border broadcasters and gave Canadians a sense of what certainly lies in store should further efforts be made to support the economy of Canadian culture. Having lobbied to amend the U.S. Trade Act to include services, fifteen U.S. border television licensees laid a complaint before the Section 301 Committee of the Office of the Special Representative for Trade Negotiations in Washington, alleging that the Canadian legislation constituted "an unreasonable form of tax discrimination" which discriminated against United States commerce.[41] For a relatively minor issue from the American perspective — some $20 to $26 million are at stake in Canadian advertising on U.S. border stations, a mere 0.25 per cent of American TV advertising revenues, but 5 per cent of Canadian revenues — a disproportionate amount of political ill will has been generated in Washington. Congress retaliated by making the costs of attending conventions in Canada non-deductible from individuals' income tax, thereby striking a $100 million blow at the Canadian convention and tourism industry. This measure was eventually withdrawn, but the pressure of the border broadcasters did not fade. As a result of the section 301 complaint, President Carter announced in September 1980 that he would request Congress to pass mirror legislation forbidding the deduction from corporate tax of U.S. companies' advertising on Canadian media. This was seen to be a mild response to the border broadcasters' anger, but the precedent was important: the United States was implementing the principle of reciprocity in its dealings with its smaller neighbour. Although Carter's action bore no fruit, the Reagan administration has recommended that Congress enact legislation to authorize this retaliation. In February 1982, ten senators placed a proposed mirror bill in the *Congressional Quarterly* as a step towards further hearings on the subject.[42] Consideration by the U.S. Senate Finance Committee in June 1982 of a proposal to prevent U.S. companies from claiming a business-expense tax deduction on Telidon equipment imported from Canada — and so impose a 100 per cent tariff on the use of Canadian-made equipment[43] — is another indication of how a relatively moderate Canadian act of cultural self-defence has smouldered unresolved as a commercial grievance in Washington. This lingering dispute speaks volumes about the deadly earnest of American politicians' concern to beat back any threat to their information industry's well-being.

It would be wrong to consider Canada as the United States' only *bête noire*. France and Japan can launch their own satellites, and so pose a serious market threat to American dominance. The developing countries are challenging the legitimacy of the American principle of free information flows, the cornerstone of American information and cultural policies since the Second World War. When the issue becomes the sale of goods for which payments are made, not the free flow of ideas unrestricted by censorship, the notion of free flow becomes an obfuscation for that of free trade. And developing economies know well that free trade is the slogan of hegemonic, imperial economies. The Third World is demanding a New World Information Order in which it would have access to the technological knowhow that is still monopolized by the industrialized powers.[44] The United States has been resisting any efforts to restrict the trans-border flow of data on

236

grounds of national sovereignty, public order or national security. In effect, the American goal is to stop foreign governments from making policy on TBDF so that the American market's superior mass will attract data processing to it. Once an American-centred status quo has been created, international regulation can be expected to legitimize it.

Given the option of negotiating on a bilateral basis with the United States or in a multilateral forum like the OECD, Canada prefers the latter. In international negotiations it can generally find support for its position among other countries that have concerns about their sovereignty and their economies under the impact of American technology. International negotiations concerning telecommunications policy extend well beyond the relatively confined issue of trans-border data flow. Operating under the aegis of the International Telecommunication Union (ITU), administrative radio conferences provide an international mechanism through which countries can express their bargaining positions and negotiate mutually acceptable agreements. The rapid changes of technology since the 1959 World Administrative Radio Conference (WARC) and the expansion of the ITU's membership from 96 to 154 led to the 1979 WARC, where an attempt was made to develop an international framework for orderly growth of global communications for the rest of the century.[45] Since allocation decisions concerning the use of the electromagnetic spectrum and the scarce geostationary satellite orbital positions will be of crucial importance to Canadian domestic policy in such areas as the location of satellites, Canada resisted American proposals that would have allowed the U.S. unilaterally to operate stations on the frequency band reserved for Canadian television broadcasting.[46] The U.S. "open-skies" policy has led to plans for several American fixed satellite systems, creating an international concern that there will be a shortage of orbital positions remaining to satisfy other countries' needs. Canada opposed the United States on the grounds that it would restrict the future effectiveness of direct broadcast satellites. The electromagnetic spectrum is a scarce, finite resource. The United States' open-skies approach is an application of laissez-faire doctrine to telecommunications. The principle of "first come, first served" allows the technological leader to occupy the best frequencies and establish its hegemony, "consuming" the largest amount of the spectrum per capita. The United States' unwillingness to plan, its resistance to other countries' demand for equitable access, and its confidence that technology will open up enough possibilities to satisfy the demands of other countries are all positions that assume technological questions

237

can be decided on their merits in due course. But technology is not neutral and the principles, decided at further international conferences, that will be established throughout the Eighties on spectrum allocations, geostationary orbits and direct broadcasting satellites will affect relations between individuals, institutions and nation-states for many years.

The United States has two basic options when facing this international agenda. It can take a tough, America-first stance aimed at defending its present lead and maximizing its commercial advantages. If it follows this path and if it thinks American business interests are harmed, it could threaten to withdraw from future international negotiations in the same way the Reagan administration threatened to abort the United Nations Conference on the Law of the Sea. This is a highly unlikely scenario, because the U.S. has a vital interest in protecting its radio-frequency allocations. All American ships, aircraft and military communications depend on the security of the air waves. Were there no international order in telecommunications, any country could beam new stations into the U.S. and create chaos by such electronic interference. The need for global order forces the U.S. to seek accommodations with its international partners.

It if took a more benevolent view of its role in the international system, the U.S. might want to be more responsive to the Third World charge that it has taken up more than its fair share of the available natural resources of the electromagnetic spectrum. Oswald Ganley feels that the U.S. should openly acknowledge the threat that other countries see in its dominance. In this perspective, Canada could provide a safe starting point as a friendly power, giving the U.S. the chance to develop a workable international information policy.[47]

Although he recognizes the potential for conflict, Ganley considers the Canadian-American communications relationship is strong enough to be able to withstand the pressures for adjustment. Looking back over past accommodations between Canada and the United States, one can notice a record of successful resolution of conflicts over technical issues.

- The terrestrial telephone communications system of North America works as one integrated network whose revenues are shared on a 50:50 basis. The integration is complete, the operation successful. It may well serve as a model for the sharing of traffic and revenues on direct broadcast satellites.
- When the Carter administration proposed that spacing between

238

North American radio frequencies be narrowed from 10khz to 9khz, Canada strongly opposed this initiative. It lobbied very aggressively with Latin American countries to whom it supplied research studies quantifying the damage they too would suffer and among whom it generated support for its resistance to the change of frequency. The U.S. was aware of Canada's coalition and knew there were substantial objections from American industry. The issue was finally resolved when the Reagan administration shifted its support back to the 10khz status quo and effectively withdrew the issue from the bilateral agenda.

• Pressure from the U.S. to have land mobile radio services encroach on the UHF spectrum produced Canadian resistance. Canada argued that land mobile broadcasting would interfere with the frequencies it needed for television broadcasting. Slow progress was made at the technical level throughout the Seventies until a compromise agreement was made that appears to have satisfied both sides.[48]

The record of past conflict resolution does not mean that the solution of the major issues remaining on the agenda will be easy. The United States resists the notion of planning because it prefers to have its multinationals carve out their own share of the market. Canada prefers international planning so as to secure some guaranteed space within which its companies can operate on a secure basis. This is not to say that Canada maintains a consistently anti-American stand at world or regional negotiations. Canada supports the Third World in preferring a priori planning, in opposing the first-come-first-served principle, and in supporting the fair allocation of shares to all countries of positions in the spectrum and the geostationary orbit. On the use of high frequency bands, Canada sides with the United States because Canada also has international broadcasting interests, whereas the developing countries want to use the high frequencies for their domestic broadcasting.

What makes it still more difficult to anticipate how differences of national interest between Canada and the United States can be resolved are the internal conflicts within each country. In Canada, fierce federal-provincial disputes over jurisdiction put into question Ottawa's capacity to generate a comprehensive policy position on regulating the new technologies. The Canadian Radio-television and Telecommunications Commission faces major problems of its own in regulating the satellite monopoly of Telesat Canada, challenged as it is by CN-CP Telecommunications. For its part, the United States has both an iedological and an institutional problem to resolve. For an administration wedded to the doctrine of deregulation the radio waves are not seen as a scarce natural resource. In principle, no role for government is envisaged by Reagan supporters. At the same time, the multinational corporations want regulations in order to reduce the risks they face. Major political fights can be expected within the United States concerning the rewriting of the 1934 Communications Act now that technology has obliterated the distinction between longline telecommunications (which were established as a regulated monopoly) and data processing (which has not been regulated).[49]

While the political forces fight out their battles, the United States government suffers from an institutional weakness. It has no single structure with authority over information and communications policy that can represent U.S. interests abroad and develop a coordinated approach to policy making. Congress has developed a strong, bipartisan position which calls for a dramatic reorganization of government functions in this area where the U.S. has extremely high stakes. Congress has pressed the administration to take a leading role in filling the policy vacuum and developing a capacity to resist other countries' setting up barriers to trans-border data flow. The Department of State has managed to resist a takeover of international communications policy by the United States Trade Representative's Office.[50] As long as this institutional problem is unresolved, the United States government will not speak with as strong a voice as it could.

Even though Canadian policy is not yet articulated, Canada does enjoy some underlying strength as it faces the American pressures. It has a long tradition, going back to the 1930s, of an active government role in setting policy and regulations in broadcasting and telecommunications. Through this process it has developed strong institutions, both in the public and in the private sector, which are capable of holding their own in continental competition. As a result there is no need to make a massive effort to roll back the ownership pattern of the whole industry as is being attempted with the National Energy Program. Canada deals from a position of some strength, but with a much stronger power. Still, the U.S. has a long record of overreacting when what it deems its commercial interests have been impinged upon by actions taken by Canadian governments to create opportunities for the expression of Canadian creative energy and its communication to the Canadian public.

240

Continuity or Change in Cultural Threat

Americanization has long been seen as a threat to Canadian cultural, and therefore political, survival through the economics of the information industries. The American sociologist Samuel Moffett observed back in 1907 how Canadian newspapers patronized American press syndicates so that ''much of their matter in consequence is furnished by American writers from an American standpoint.'' The political consequence of Canada's tie-in through the economy of the wire service, through the means of transportation, and through other growing institutional linkages was the tendency of the two peoples to ignore the boundary between them and ''to merge the six million and the eighty-five million together.'' This early and enthusiastic apostle of American imperialism saw the result of the process to be a foregone conclusion: ''The English-speaking Canadians protest that they will never become Americans — they are already Americans without knowing it.''[51]

Moffett's identification of the basic problem was prescient, although his generalization was prematurely sweeping. Under the double pressure of the United States' powerful communications technologies and its aggressive politicians, Moffett's prediction of a virtual merging of the lesser into the greater English-speaking people no longer appears so fanciful. The difficulties preventing the federal and provincial governments in Canada from taking a few of the minimal steps considered necessary to support beleaguered cultural industries will make this point.

Broadcasting Resistance by the government of Canada to the distribution of American TV by U.S. domestic satellites will be seen in Washington as a move by Canada in restraint of American exports and could initiate a messy process modelled on the border broadcasting issue.

Some kind of retaliation is also being lobbied for by American cable companies, who are trying to protect themselves from the competitive threat of Canadian operators who are moving rapidly to wire up American cities. American firms cry foul because the Canadian Broadcasting Act restricts foreign direct investment in the broadcasting industry to 20 per cent ownership of companies, and so prevents the Americans from expanding into Canada. If they are successful in having a ''reciprocity'' clause inserted in the redrafted Communications Act, they could stop a Canadian penetration that has already reached over one-quarter of a billion dollars in U.S. cable systems. These Canadian cable companies, who came to maturity on the basis of the nationalist provisions of the Broadcasting Act and the protectionist decisions of the CRTC, can now be expected to lobby in Ottawa against nationalist communications policies so that they can continue to expand unimpeded in the vast American market.[52]

Magazines   The abandonment of *Time* magazine's Canadian edition has not resolved the problems of the Canadian magazine market. *Time* has reduced its advertising rates to compensate for the non-deductibility of its services and now makes more money despite its lower circulation than it did with the Canadian edition, by printing its standard edition with Canadian ads and mailing them at Canada's subsidized second-class postal rate. Though still American-controlled, *Reader's Digest* has been granted Canadian status as far as Bill C-58 is concerned. The newsstands continue to be loaded with American publications aimed at Canadian residents. Although Canadian customs regulations prevent the importation of "split runs" containing advertisements directed primarily to Canadians, administration and enforcement of this regulation are difficult.[53]

The periodical issue, which has been a source of irritation for over twenty years, remains unresolved because of the asymmetrical nature of Canada's cultural relationship with the U.S. As Isaiah Litvak and Christopher Maule note, Canada's problem "is compounded by the prominence of United States firms in Canada which are also major advertisers."[54] Likely government moves in this industry will not be dramatic. The Canadian Periodical Publishers Association as well as Maclean-Hunter have called for the withdrawal of preferential post office rates for foreign publications on the grounds that the postal subsidy should be granted only to Canadian periodicals, as provided for in the postal legislation. The subsidy should not be abused to enhance further the competitive position of American magazines whose overrun copies are simply "dumped in this country."[55] Reasonable though such a move would appear to Canadian eyes, any Canadian policy shift will doubtless be scrutinized carefully by American business whose interests are affected. Since the corporate interests in the publishing field are linked to those in the electronic media — Home Box Office is owned by Time Inc. — one can predict increasing, rather than decreasing, U.S. resistance to efforts to strengthen Canadian magazines.

Film   The distribution and exhibition systems for movies in Canada give a functional monopoly to Hollywood products in Canadian cinemas, a monopoly that makes it extremely difficult for Canadian-made movies to become commercially viable. By 1979 the Canadian box office of $276 million had become the United States' largest foreign market for movies. Nevertheless only 1 per cent of film revenue is reinvested in Canada, a figure that compares with 27 per cent of broadcasting revenues spent on Canadian production.[56] Consequently, the feature film production industry in Canada is starved of capital for financing the production and promoting the distribution of Canadian movies. As a result Canadian films hold a 3.5 per cent share of the country's theatre and TV screens.[57]

If the Canadian government is to go beyond the establishment of the Canadian Film Development Corporation (which has acted as a merchant banker for the feature film industry) and the capital cost allowance in order to establish an adequate financial base for the movie industry in Canada, it will have to adopt some variant of the levy and quota system that is used by all film-producing countries outside North America. The levy on box office receipts is a direct way to recycle money generated by consumers into the production of indigenous films. Quotas ensure that at least some specified portion of the films exhibited in any given year are Canadian. Even though the United States' other trading partners have some kind of film protection of this nature, Canada's entry into active defence of its film industry would be sure to elicit strong protest from the film conglomerates. Canada would be accused in the media of obstructing the free flow of information, of imposing censorship, but above all of reducing the exports of American products and the yield of American investments. Now that services have been brought under the purview of the U.S. Trade Act, Canadian efforts to affect the internal financial structure of the film market could bring the U.S. government into play with retaliatory action.

The long-standing dilemma of Canadian cultural survival has been intensified by the Reagan administration's move towards its trade doctrine of "reciprocity." The more effective Canadian legislation and regulation become in defending the Canadian principle of cultural sovereignty, the more likely they will be to restrict the Canadian market as an extension of the American communication system. And the more the Canadian market is restricted, the louder American business will complain that its commercial interests have been damaged. The louder American business fulminates, the greater is the likelihood of U.S. government retaliation under the various provisions of its protectionist legislation, which, in the name of defending U.S. commercial interests, holds a gun not just at Canada's economy but at its culture as well. The constraints continually pressuring Canadian governments to desist from acting to shore up their endangered culture and information industries get tighter as the need for action increases.

There is both a strong parallel and a striking contrast between the logic of Canada's position in its culture-cum-telecommunications environment and the logic of its military situation. In each policy sphere, rapid changes of technology have transformed the problems Canada confronts. While the new telecommunications techniques in the hands of American multinationals supported by the U.S. government directly threaten Canada's cultural integrity and economic well-being, the new generation of military means of surveillance and destruction offer Canada a possibility of shedding its postwar role of military satellite: a subject we turn to in chapter 11.

NATO, NORAD, and Canada's Military Options   11

A nation's capacity to establish its own military strategy, to deploy its own troops and to manufacture its own weaponry has often been taken as an indicator of the degree of its sovereignty. Sweden is seen to be sovereign in all three dimensions; Canada is not. Canada does not make its own strategy even though the Department of National Defence is capable of doing this. It has only partial control over how its troops will be deployed were war to break out. It cannot manufacture complete weapons systems without importing their key components. Canada is not alone in its military non-sovereignty. It is a founding member of a multilateral alliance, the North Atlantic Treaty Organization (NATO), but the military strategy for the alliance is determined in the final analysis by the policy of its dominant member, the United States of America. Unlike the other members of the alliance, Canada has a further bilateral dependency that is the product of a very advanced degree of integration in the continental part of the United States' military command and in the bulk of its military-industrial complex.

Although Canada's satellitic military status cannot be denied, there has been remarkably little public debate about the degree of dependence that is appropriate at this stage of the country's development. Despite the hearings that have been held and the reports that have been submitted by the House of Commons Standing Committee on External Affairs and National Defence and the Senate Subcommittee on National Defence, the media have brought little of the current debate among the experts to the attention of the Canadian public, which is probably less informed about military questions than the citizenry of any other NATO country. The renewal of the North American Air Defence Command (NORAD) during President Reagan's visit to Ottawa received considerably less attention in the media than the protesters demonstrating against acid rain. Neverthe-

245

less, the debate that arose in the United States over the defence budget and in Europe over nuclear weapons did spread to Canada over the issue of testing the Cruise missile in northeast Alberta. Canada's military role has potential to become once again a serious national issue — and bilateral irritant — particularly since the multilateral foundation to which the bilateral relationship is attached is being severely shaken by the tremors resulting from the advent of a U.S. administration that is more aggressive in its rhetoric, its policies and its strategy.

NATO: The Multilateral Military Context

In the atomic age, no nation is militarily independent in the sense of enjoying immunity to armed conflict. None is invulnerable to strategic nuclear weapons that can be delivered anywhere in the world. All would become victims of the radioactive fallout that would mortally poison those populations not directly annihilated in an exchange of mega-weapons that have been accumulated in such quantities that the destruction of human civilization has become a strong probability. Since the outbreak of the Cold War, the military dependence of the countries of Europe and North America has been institutionalized by the formation of two ideologically hostile camps, each grouped around its own superpower and each sustaining an alliance held together by military, political and economic considerations. The Warsaw Pact, the military expression of Soviet hegemony over eastern Europe, imposes a rigorous discipline on most of its members, who are controlled both by the physical presence of Soviet armed forces and their economic integration into the Soviet planning system. The North Atlantic Treaty Organization, whose formation preceded that of the Warsaw Pact, was built on both military and political considerations. It was the result of several countries' attempts in the late Forties to draw a somewhat reluctant United States into a peacetime collective-security pact that, by regarding a military attack on one member as an attack on all, was aimed at containing the process of communist expansion that had drawn, in Winston Churchill's phrase, an iron curtain across central Europe and threatened the stability of western Europe.

While the Europeans were seeking to ensure an American guarantee of their security and the United States was attempting to strengthen the European democracies, Canada was hoping to build a multilateral framework in which, in Gerald Wright's analysis, it could "more safely co-operate with its sometimes overpowering neighbour, the United States."[1] The cohesiveness of this alliance has always been in some doubt generally because of differing views among its members of the nature and gravity of the Soviet threat. In the first era of nuclear politics, when the U.S. possessed the capacity to destroy the Soviet Union's retaliatory forces and when the doctrine of massive retaliation associated with Secretary of State John Foster Dulles promised the Soviets total destruction in response to any aggression they might provoke, Europeans had few doubts about the American commitment to their defence. The U.S. appeared less reliable when Washington abruptly switched its strategic doctrine to one of flexible response, which implied that conventional weapons would be used against conventional military threats. The prospect of a less than automatic American nuclear response to a Soviet aggression encouraged both Britain and France to view the possession of their own strategic weapons as the only sure protection.[2] As a result, NATO was shaken in 1966 by General de Gaulle's withdrawal from the alliance in order to establish an independent French nuclear *force de frappe*. The symbolic value of controlling the strategy and deployment of their armed forces and the economic benefits that could spin off from the new military technology were considered by Gaullists to be worth the undoubted costs of producing a separate French line of atomic weapons and delivery systems.

With NATO's Harmel Report of 1968 came a new strategy in which détente, understood as a relaxation of tensions and an expansion of contacts between the West and the Soviet bloc, was seen to be compatible with military security based on nuclear deterrence. The seeds of the current crisis in NATO's strategic thinking were sown by the contradictions inherent in this doctrine of détente. The general perception that East-West tensions had relaxed led to some reduction of members' military contributions and some increase in apprehension about the Soviet military threat. One of the early results of Pierre Trudeau's promised new directions in foreign policy was the withdrawal of half of the troops that Canada kept stationed in Europe. During the Seventies, when the imbalance in conventional forces between the Warsaw Pact and NATO was growing, the U.S. lost its superiority over the USSR in strategic nuclear weapons. Once the Soviet Union achieved parity with the United States in its ability to deliver nuclear devastation via intercontinental ballistic missiles, the American strategy of flexible response lost its credibility. Détente had generated new apprehensions about the Soviet military threat. Faced by clearly expanding Soviet military power, NATO's European members pressed for something to be done. The deployment of the

247

new generation of Soviet "theatre" nuclear weapons, the SS-20, with a "hard target kill capacity," further undermined the credibility of American deterrence. These new "counterforce" missiles gave the Soviet Union the capacity to fight and win a nuclear war through a first strike. The old doctrine of mutual assured destruction by a second strike was in doubt. The nagging uncertainty in Europe concerning the integrity of the American commitment to guarantee the security of Europe against both conventional and nuclear attack surfaced again. Deep-seated European resentments about the United States' tendency to act unilaterally without consultation, and its somewhat simplistic views about Soviet military intentions, were also reactivated. These two responses were revived by what Europeans felt were President Carter's vacillations — for example, his perceived softness in response to the Soviet occupation of Afghanistan and then his hard line on the boycott of the Moscow Olympics.

The words and deeds of the Reagan administration have further exacerbated the existing strains within NATO. The reignition of a cold war looms as a growing possibility. Although even the voices of caution in the administration speak with strongly anti-Soviet tones, the Department of State under Alexander Haig embraced a NATO-centred perspective that would continue close negotiations between the United States and its European allies. But Alexander Haig was not able to impose the State Department view on the administration, as his resignation indicated. The stronger voice in American foreign policy has come from the Pentagon, where Caspar Weinberger has taken to new limits the American tendency to act unilaterally without consulting its NATO colleagues: selling arms to the enemies of Israel in order to court friends among the Arabs and attempting to build up American military superiority in every weapons system to the point that the United States can challenge the Soviet Union in any potential theatre of war.

The solidarity of the NATO alliance has loosened under the impact of what appears to Europeans to be dangerous and irresponsible naïvety. Exactly what are the administration's aspirations remains unclear. The Republican election platform of 1980 unambiguously promised military superiority. Weinberger has talked to Congress about redressing the vulnerability of the U.S. Without actually declaring a need for military supremacy in all weapons systems or in all types of military forces, he believes in the need to correct "a margin of superiority in many categories of Soviet strategic nuclear, tactical nuclear, and conventional forces."[3] European confidence in the drastic new American appraisal of the Soviet menace is not strengthened by the American tendency to see communism as the root of all evil in the Third World. Weinberger stretched European credulity when he claimed that the "Soviet attempt to expand its influence in the Caribbean Basin by lending direct and indirect support to totalitarian movements in Central America is another threat to our interests."[4] European governments believe in maintaining deterrence if not by withdrawing theatre nuclear weapons, then by matching the SS-20s with the Cruise and Pershing missiles to retain a relationship of nuclear equilibrium with the Soviet bloc. They do not believe that the balance of power should be changed by the United States' trying to become militarily superior. Such European concerns did not prevent President Reagan from announcing, on October 2, 1981, a defence build-up centred on the controversial MX missile. Since the MX would not be secure against an enemy first strike, the plan, in Senator Gary Hart's view "put a hairtrigger on nuclear war in which both sides could be tempted to use their missiles to avoid losing them."[5]

The cumulative trend of Pentagon thinking that Reagan has brought to a head is the abandonment of the doctrine of mutual deterrence in favour of a counterforce policy envisaging the option of limited nuclear war — a "potentially destabilizing and dangerously provocative thrust in American defence planning."[6] U.S. strategy has, in effect, shifted from defence to offence. European leaders continue to support détente as the correct strategic aim both as a long-term target for positive interdependence between East and West and as the precondition for a shorter-term normalization in Poland. Attempting to break Poland free from the Warsaw Pact, they fear, would only produce an explosive destabilization of the overall equilibrium, just as embarking on a program to build a neutron bomb would only serve to accelerate the arms race. While nuclear disarmament is the cry of the peace movement in the streets, European strategic thinking endorses a process of balanced arms reduction as part of a security policy, not its alternative. This is in sharp contrast with the Reagan view that negotiations can only succeed if the Americans have first built up their military capability beyond that of the Soviet Union.[7]

The more irritated its European partners become with the United States, the more anxious Canada becomes about its position. Apart from its prime military role of guaranteeing North American security by maintaining the peace in Europe, NATO's importance to Canada has always been political. Canadian participation in this multilateral defence organization was to give Canada a counterweight to its exclusive bilateral dependence on the United States, and so offer Ottawa the chance to find support for its generally less anti-communist positions among the European partners. The Trudeau government has learned that this strategy bears a price tag. When it decided to withdraw half its troops from Europe as part of its attempt to redefine Canadian foreign policy in more narrowly self-interested terms, the government did not understand the link between military and political influence. When it tried to establish a contractual link with the European Community in 1974 to implement the foreign policy diversification promised by the Third Option of Mitchell Sharp, Ottawa discovered that its paltry military contribution had been noticed. Canada was given to understand that establishing a contractual link required in return making a serious military contribution to European defence. Demonstrating a renewed commitment to NATO was an important factor in the decision to buy $200 million worth of German Leopard tanks and the decision to spend $1.5 billion on 18 Aurora long-range patrol aircraft with sophisticated anti-submarine warfare capability. Canada's acceptance in 1977 of the NATO Defence Planning Committee's target of a 3 per cent annual real rate of growth of its defence expenditures signalled beyond question the Trudeau government's conversion back to the cause of collective security as a counterbalance.

According to U.S. Defense Department figures, Canada ranks thirteenth out of the fourteen NATO countries that have military forces. It devotes 1.8 per cent of its gross domestic product to defence, compared with the NATO average of 3.8 per cent, and has 1 per cent of the total labour force engaged in the armed forces as against a NATO average of 2.8 per cent. Only Luxembourg and Iceland (which has no forces at all) come behind Canada. To come up to the NATO average, Canada would have to more than double its annual defence budget and almost triple the strength of its armed forces.[8] A political consensus has emerged in Ottawa on the need to bolster Canadian forces. In December 1980, the House of Commons Standing Committee on External Affairs and National Defence urged the government to strengthen its military commitment.[9] In February 1982, the Senate Subcommittee on National Defence recommended that the government spend $1.3 billion to increase the regular forces from 80,000 to 92,000, raising the contingent in Europe from 5,400 to 7,800.[10] Although these targets are higher than those envisaged by the government, Ottawa has notified NATO that it is moving seriously to bolster its NATO contribution by prepositioning military equipment in

Norway and raising its defence expenditures 35.2 per cent over the next two years despite the general restraint on increasing the budget.[11] By the spring of 1982, the *Financial Post* went as far as to say on its front page, "Canada plays the NATO hawk."[12]

There may be an irony in the timing of this new drive by Canada to pay its dues and regain full status in the European military club. John Holmes writes that NATO becomes "of greater importance to us as the most likely means of control over United States strategic policy and of differing with them, if need be, in company."[13] But as David Cox notes, the more divergence there is between American and European views on external issues like the Middle East, the more divided NATO becomes. And the more divisions there are within NATO between Europe and the U.S., the more Canada accepts its dominant partner's approach to strategic questions.[14] It is as if the multilateral defence circuit were an optional extra; Canada's bilateral defence relationship is the standard vehicle.

NORAD: The Bilateral Defence Dependency

When NORAD is described in official discourse, it is presented as the North American component of the NATO defence system. In reality, Canada's bilateral defence relationship with the United States would continue whatever happened to NATO. While imperial centres have waxed and waned and while technologies have changed dramatically, the constant fact of Canadian military history since the first white settlements is Canada's status as a defended country — the military corollary of its colonial position as a political and economic extension of an imperial power. The American imperium may be less authoritarian than the French and less paternalist than the British, but Canada remains as ever entirely dependent on its dominant partner for protection in case of war. The Monroe Doctrine asserted American hegemony in the western hemisphere, but President Franklin Delano Roosevelt's speech at Chautauqua in August 1936 constituted the first pledge of American defence assistance to Canada. By August 1940, as the Ogdensburg Declaration put it, the "defence of the two countries constituted a single problem": North America had become one area in military terms. "If you create a vacuum over what in fact remains the most vital air space in the world, because it happens to be situated between the Soviet Union and the United States," Brian Cuthbertson told SCEAND, the House of Commons Standing Committee on External Affairs and National Defence, "then the Americans as a superpower are bound to react."[15]

251

Put starkly, the conventional wisdom of the military and diplomatic bureaucracy considers that Canada has no autonomous defence option. Canada defends itself so that the United States won't do so in its place. The rationale for this strategy was articulated by Nils Ørvik as "defence against help":

> The greater the small state's strategic significance for the larger, the more it will have to invest in military capabilities both to deter and to assure the neighbouring state that its military presence is not required on the small state's territory for the purpose of denying it to others.[16]

If Canada were to opt out of North American air defence, the United States would continue to maintain a system for identifying and tracking missiles and aircraft over Canada and would operate some capability for intercepting manned bombers.[17] As the "glacis" or protective buffer outside the exposed border of the U.S. heartland, Canada has little choice but to cooperate in continental defence.[18] Canada cannot ignore American strategic requirements which are the chief determinant of its defence policy, a policy that has been mainly reactive to the politics of its superpower neighbour. The Canadian perception of the nature of the Soviet threat to itself becomes irrelevant. As David Cox pointed out in 1968, "the direct military threat from the Soviet Union or other external power is less salient for Canadian decision-makers than considerations of the need to co-operate in the general context of the Atlantic Alliance and in the specific context of its obligations to the United States."[19] Canada participates in NATO to spread its bilateral dependence; it participates in NORAD to maintain some national control over how the Americans defend it. In other words, membership in military alliances presents Canada with a sovereignty paradox, as Michael Tucker explains.

> [I]f Canada did not participate in the air defence of North America this role would be performed solely by American forces. To have opted out of these alliance relationships, or not to have entered into the latter, would have meant, in effect, a reduction of Canadian sovereignty; thus the perplexing paradox facing a lesser power neighbour to a superpower, that alliance commitments have been as much a source of as a derogation from its sovereignty.[20]

The North American Air Defence Command, which was created officially by an exchange of notes between Canada and the United States on May 12, 1958, can be seen as a means of formalizing Canada's contribution to the continental defence of the United States at a manageable cost and with some consideration for the symbolic value

252

of Canadian sovereignty. The Canadian government decided what commitment it would make to North American air defence. NORAD organized the command and control of the Canadian and American forces committed to defend North American air space in the event of an attack. In return for Canadian participation, the U.S. accepted some safeguards concerning overflights, aerial refuelling, the deployment of forces and the operation of U.S. facilities on Canadian territory. In the definition of the functions of NORAD and in the decisions concerning the levels and nature of each country's contribution, the United States has not "run roughshod over Canadian interests,"[21] according to Danford Middlemiss. These rules of the game, as Middlemiss told SCEAND, "effectively legitimize what would in any event prove to be an inescapable U.S. presence in Canada and thereby help to prevent the U.S. from simply acting unilaterally in Canadian air space on behalf of its own defence interests."[22]

When NORAD was renewed in 1968 the Soviet bomber threat was still considered to be of major significance. By 1975, anti-bomber defence had taken second place to NORAD's detection and surveillance functions,[23] but Canadian early warning systems were playing a smaller and smaller role as they became more and more obsolescent. The next generation of defence technology may prove to be either a political embarrassment, or a relief. Back in 1968, David Cox warned that, if radar stations were phased out and replaced by an airborne warning and control system (AWACS), "the dilemma, how to participate, if at all, and how to know what is happening to Canadian air space, may become more acute."[24] By 1982, the fact that an AWACS system was operational meant "that active air defense will not depend on Canadian participation."[25]

With the advent of the missile age, Canadian geography lost much of its strategic importance; by the Seventies the deterrence function had been taken over by intercontinental ballistic missiles (ICBMs) and submarine-launched ballistic missiles. The development of a Soviet air-launched cruise missile (ALCM) following the failure of SALT II (the second round of the Strategic Arms Limitations Talks) could result in a revived threat of long-range bombers carrying these missiles. In this unhappy situation, new NORAD defences would be required and, according to Franklyn Griffiths, "the political cooperation of the Canadian government would become even more important to the United States than it was in the 1950s before the ICBM reduced American interest in continental air defence to its present low level."[26] If Canada were to maintain its growing claims to sovereignty in the

Arctic and the circumpolar North, it would require greatly enhanced defence expenditures to pre-empt direct American action.

Until such time as an ALCM threat materializes, it appears that NORAD, though a central preoccupation of Canada's military establishment, has become peripheral to the Pentagon which has allowed the joint enterprise to be downgraded in recent years. John Holmes has pointed out that the pressure for sustaining NORAD comes less from the American than the Canadian military.

> Canadian territory is less important to the U.S. in the missile age and there are those in the Pentagon who see the advantage in managing continental air defence without having to worry about the sensitivities of foreigners.[27]

As American analyst John Hamre writes, "technology today provides an opportunity for long-distance detection without relying on Canadian participation."[28] Testimony before SCEAND in 1980 indicated very little, if any, evidence of public pressure from the U.S. government aimed at getting Canada to do anything as far as NORAD was concerned. To judge from the Atlantic Council report, some military thinking in the U.S. about Canada has large elements of banana-republic unconcern:

> The armed forces of Canada, which include significant and proportion-ate numbers of Canadians from all provinces, are a manifestation of Canadian unity. In view of the U.S. security interests in a united Canada, the United States should continue to nurture its Canadian military ties.[29]

In short, the military rationale for NORAD has shifted considerably, so much so that it could be considered now to be in doubt.

Strategic reasons are not the only cause for Canadian participation in military alliances. As for NATO, so for NORAD: Canada's political rationale for the agreement was to give Canada an institutional input into U.S. decision making on strategic matters. But the Atlantic Council doubts how significant this input presently is. Indeed in its opinion, a "chief psychological problem for Canadians" is the sense that "they are not in a position to have an effective input into global military and security decisions."[30] There is little question that Washington unilaterally defines the strategic objectives of NORAD. If Canadian participation in American strategy making cannot be credibly maintained as NORAD's political raison d'être, its rationale has to be considered at a lower common denominator. It is a gesture by Ottawa that symbolizes a will towards good Canadian-American relations.

Despite the strikingly reduced persuasiveness of either the military or the political rationale for continuing NORAD, the SCEAND review of the agreement showed a bipartisan consensus that the agreement should be renewed. Its position articulates the conventional wisdom: Canada benefits directly from making a contribution to the deterrence of an external military threat through its early warning capabilities against a surprise attack; it is guaranteed air defence in times of crisis; it gets useful information from the surveillance of space; its cost-sharing arrangements with the U.S. military permit Canada to obtain these services at prices far below those it would have to pay were it to embark on these operations on its own; furthermore, it receives indirect benefits such as its access to technically advanced military equipment, more complete knowledge of American intentions than would otherwise be available, and data gathered through U.S. intelligence networks.[31] For these benefits it has been prepared to pay some costs, not just the $322 million it spends annually on NORAD, but also some loss of sovereignty, the international perception that Canada's involvement in NORAD compromises its independence, the possibility that Canada will be drawn into a conflict it would wish to avoid at almost any cost, and the possible distortion of its defence policy and purchasing priorities.[32] Notwithstanding these disadvantages which, if plainly put, include the possibility of Canada's playing a role in instigating a nuclear holocaust, SCEAND concluded that "the benefits received far outweigh the costs incurred."[33]

Not all observers are convinced by SCEAND's reasoning. Douglas Ross has developed a powerful critique which pokes gaping holes in the NORAD logic. "The sole conceivable rationale for the system must be built upon the highly improbable scenario in which the Soviet authorities launch a precursor bomber assault."[34] While it is ineffective as a defensive mechanism, Ross believes it could be used to aid an American "counterforce" first-strike attack on the vulnerable elements of the Soviet arsenal.

> It is entirely possible that NORAD could become an important adjunct to a provocative style "nuclear diplomacy" by the United States government in the political crises of the decade to come. If one values mutual deterrence . . . NORAD's potentially complementary role in the articulation and execution of first-strike threats is not reassuring.[35]

If it is in Canada's interest to lessen the need for both sides to rely on hairtrigger launch-on-warning postures, Canada should be opposing the role of Strategic Air Command bombers as counterforce first-strike weapons with their air-launched cruise missiles. If the function of a modernized NORAD is to coordinate such destabilizing arsenals, Canada's participation in this new stage of the arms race would be against its best interests. The cost-sharing argument begs the question whether the tactical nuclear game is the right one to play. If it is the wrong one, then Canada's alleged bargain is still a waste of money that could better be spent on conventional forces in Europe or a strengthened capacity to defend the North. As for getting military intelligence, Canada could get whatever the Americans would be willing to release through its participation in NATO.

A decade ago Colin Gray noted that "sceptical, pragmatic analysis of the different dimensions of NORAD is notable for its absence," and went on to speculate that the strongest pressure for renewal would stem from the Canadian Forces' Air Defence Group and from some quarters in the Department of External Affairs whose boat would be rocked by a decision not to renew. Writing of the decision that had to be made in 1973, he predicted accurately that the boat would not be rocked.

> Since there are no overwhelming arguments for non-renewal, it is highly probable that the natural official inclination to keep things as they are will prevail. In the absence of telling arguments that counsel strongly against renewal, it is quite possible that the conservative instincts of officials in Ottawa will serve well the tenor, if not the content, of Canadian-United States relations. After all, renewal will upset nobody; non-renewal just might.[36]

Ten years later Colin Gray's prediction still stood. The NORAD agreement was renewed during President Reagan's visit to Ottawa in March 1981 with one potentially significant change: it had become the North American *Aerospace* Defence Command, recognizing Canada's potential participation in American space surveillance.

Although this fifth renewal could be taken to mean that Canada has no strategic choice to make for another five years, this is not the case. Decisions have to be made within this time frame that will either intensify, reduce or redirect Canada's bilateral defence role. These decisions centre on the acquisition of extremely expensive equipment. Just as the decision to keep Canada's interest rate higher than the American has closed down Canada's macroeconomic policy options, so the decision to buy into the next generation of American weapons systems would preclude Canada's responding to other, more nationally relevant defence priorities.

The history of Canadian military equipment decisions is replete with unhappy stories of ill-considered programs. HMCS *Bonaventure*, the obsolete aircraft carrier that was refitted only to be scrapped; the Avro Arrow, the last and best fighter of an impressive series of aircraft, that was aborted just when it was ready to go into production; the Bomarc missile, which the government refused to arm with the warheads for which it had been designed; the new Aurora ASW surveillance airplane designed to search out nuclear submarines which are, however, invulnerable except to other subs; the proposed new generation of naval warships which will not need their sophisticated weaponry to carry out the enforcement of Canada's proclaimed 200-mile coastal sovereignty: the Canadian military and the Canadian government have a long record of investing in military systems that cannot be effective, were acquired because someone else wanted to sell them, were designed only to fit in with NATO needs, or were inappropriate to Canadian defence requirements.[37] In the light of this performance over the decades, the Canadian public might well ask for a complete review of what options Canada faces in its military equipment expenditures till the year 2000. Some decisions clearly have to be made because of the obsolescence of existing weapons systems. Once taken, they will acquire in the analysts' eyes an aura of inevitability. Once implemented they will soon be irreversible.

Unless public debate sparks a major government reformulation of its entire military strategy together with its economic rationale, the most likely course that Canada will take is the pursuit of the present policy of buying extremely expensive items of specialized U.S. weaponry. The cost will be high and the payoff, some nominal increase in sovereignty. In the first decade of NORAD the United States paid a substantial portion of the cost involved in establishing SAGE, the Semiautomatic Ground Environment control system, in North Bay and sold Canada the partially obsolete Voodoos and dubious Bomarcs at substantially reduced costs.[38] Now Canada pays in full. It received no pricing favours when it contracted to buy McDonnell-Douglas F-18's. Canada now pays a higher percentage of the direct costs relating to NORAD installations in Canada as part of a policy, Brian Cuthbertson told SCEAND, to "take over control of those facilities which the United States had financed and manned in Canada in the 1950s and early 1960s."[39] The next step in increasing national control over the Canadian section of NORAD surveillance will be the Regional Operations Control Centres that will be commanded by Canadians, located within Canada and using mainly Canadian aircraft.[40] As

SCEAND was told, the question is essentially one of dollars.

> The Americans are quite prepared for us to control our own air space
> from Canadian control centres if we will go ahead and build those
> control centres . . . the decision rests with us if we are prepared to
> spend the money. . . . If we want independence, we have to pay for
> it. [41]

Another and costly factor will be the upgrading or replacement of the
existing radar systems in the north and south of the country which have
long been considered increasingly obsolescent. [42]

Beyond the incrementalist strategy of paying large amounts to
modernize the NORAD system of attack warning and assessment lies
the option of taking a giant step further in the direction of military
integration by participating in the research and development of a new
generation of military technology. The most obvious candidate
relevant to NORAD is the use of space-based surveillance technology.
While this system appears to offer the best technical prospects, there is
a feeling among the Canadian military that United States military
planners may prefer to develop these radar systems entirely under
national control — a possibility that is enhanced by the Reagan
administration's proclivity to reduce American dependence on its
allies' cooperation. [43] Those who do not want to miss the new
technological boat argue for an early commitment to such participation. Thus the chief of research and development at the Department of
National Defence:

> If we do not become involved now, we will risk the United States
> Department of Defense developing systems for North American air
> defence that do not necessarily account for Canadian interests and
> requirements. [44]

He did not hesitate to link the military argument with its economic
corollary: "In case of further delay, industrial opportunity will decline
progressively as United States contractors undertake work that
otherwise could have and perhaps should have been done in Canada."
Whether the Americans would want Canadians to participate is a
probability that Cuthbertson doubts.

> They do not need us in the satellite technology. If we want to go into it
> on a co-operative basis then we would have to pay whatever amount of
> money would seem to bring benefits. But there are no leverages
> available to us that I can see that would get us into the satellite
> business. . . I just do not see why they would want us in. [45]

Some Americans have seen the reluctance in the other camp. The Atlantic Council has rejoiced in the change of NORAD's "A" from Air to Aerospace, considering that this change reflects "a mellowing of former Canadian attitudes opposing any Canadian involvement in space defense while opening the door for greater Canadian contributions in this area."[46] According to press reports the United States has already suggested that Canada consider making a larger contribution towards sharing heavy research costs in space technology. A Canadian official was quoted as saying that the "U.S. defence department seems willing to develop more cooperative programs, but it wants to see us put a little more up front — either in funds or in people."[47]

In recommending that the government seriously consider active participation in the development of space-based surveillance, SCEAND had dollar signs dancing in its head. J.D. MacNaughton, vice-president of Spar Aerospace, had testified that this "could provide the Canadian space industry with a long-term, very high technology market base."[48] No argument is made about Canadian military equipment purchases without the economic implications coming rapidly to the fore. The hope for industrial benefits from space-based surveillance is but one example of the close relationship between NORAD's military rationale and its economic raison d'être, the Defence Production Sharing Arrangements.

The Defence Production Sharing Arrangements

If North America has been one area for defence purposes since the Ogdensburg Declaration in June 1940, it has been one area for military production for most of the time since the Hyde Park agreement of April 1941. The Defence Production Sharing Arrangements (DPSA) of 1959 followed the cancellation of the Avro Arrow program and the aborting of a long-term strategy of high technology development in the defence industry. With Canada's military industry facing economic disaster, the United States agreed to guarantee Canadian industrial access to the United States defence market as part of the price the U.S. was willing to pay for Canadian adherence to continental defence planning. Canada was exempted from the tariffs of the Buy America Act. Canadian firms became eligible for U.S. research and development grants and could get classified information through loosened security regulations. Strategic continentalism had produced economic integration in the defence industry. The economic benefits have been highly visible, the costs less so. According to the Standing Senate Committee on Foreign Affairs, 10-12,000 persons are directly employed in manufacturing items for prime contracts and subcontracts with the United States under the DPSA. These are jobs in high technology fields such as transportation, communications and navigation.[49] Since its establishment the program has generated some $10.5 billion of two-way trade of which the U.S. has taken a slightly larger share,[50] as Table 11-1 shows.

The costs to Canada of defence production sharing are the corollary of the integration of Canada's defence industry in the American. Canadian military industry prosperity depends very directly on the level of U.S. demand. Layoffs result when there are declines in American government defence spending. Since the major defence firms in Canada are branch plants — "more than 50 per cent of the prime and subcontracts placed in Canada are with Canadian corporations at least 70 per cent U.S. owned"[51] — heartening statistics concerning the extensive trade in high technology products have to be set against the drain on the current account caused by the repatriation of dividends and other service payments. More serious in the long term, the integration of the Canadian into the American military-industrial complex has resulted in a truncated Canadian industry incapable of surviving without American research, development, design, components and machine tools. And a military economy without a mind of its own necessarily spawns a military policy-making capacity with little capacity for independent thought. As Ernie Regehr, an independent researcher, put it, Canadian defence planners are "unable to approach Canadian security from a perspective other than that built into United States weapons technology."[52]

As for the attempt to get Canadian content in "offset procurement" when major purchases are made of American equipment such as the McDonnell-Douglas F-18, little contribution is made by these deals towards developing an autonomous technological capability. The Senate committee took a dim view of the practice.

> Production done continually under license, even of highly sophisticated components, does little or nothing to give this industry the necessary viability to get into U.S. or other markets with its own products. It creates an unfortunate dependence on imported technology. Once an offset contract is complete, the vast majority of the additional jobs it created are likely to disappear. In such a system there is nothing to stimulate the development of research-based innovative products.[53]

The possibility of rebuilding the radar lines or entering into space-based surveillance systems offers a prospect that government

TABLE 11-1

CANADA–U.S. DEFENCE PRODUCTION SHARING
PROCUREMENT, JANUARY 1959–DECEMBER 1980
($ millions)

Year	U.S. Procurement in Canada	Canadian Procurement in U.S.	Balance (in favour of the U.S.)
1959	96.3	108.2	(11.9)
1960	112.7	196.3	(83.6)
1961	142.6	94.3	48.3
1962	254.3	127.4	126.9
1963	142.0	152.0	(10.0)
1964	166.8	173.3	(6.5)
1965	259.5	130.1	129.4
1966	317.1	332.6	(15.5)
1967	307.7	293.9	13.8
1968	320.0	134.2	185.8
1969	299.8	171.5	128.3
1970	226.5	222.9	3.6
1971	216.3	180.6	35.7
1972	175.0	193.5	(18.5)
1973	198.8	232.0	(33.2)
1974	150.0	281.4	(131.4)
1975	188.5	232.7	(44.2)
1976	191.1	879.0	(687.9)
1977	314.1	299.5	14.6
1978	267.0	315.6	(48.6)
1979	367.7	294.6	73.1
1980	481.7	489.3	(7.6)
Total	5,195.5	5,534.9	(339.4)

Source: U.S. Division, Defence Programs Branch, Department of Industry, Trade and Commerce.

expenditures will increase and so industrial benefits will accrue. No discussion is evident that these major expenditures would be used to develop a long-term strategy aimed at using large military purchases to meet the goal of enhanced industrial competitiveness. What programs exist support further incremental integration. The Defence Industry

Productivity Program of the Department of Industry, Trade and Commerce encourages deeper penetration of the U.S. market by Canadian defence firms. The preoccupations of government officials in this field are with the short term: how to get a share of the massively increased defence budget that the Reagan administration is determined to spend, and how to beat back the new protectionist measures taken by Congress that have threatened the very basis of the balanced trade envisaged by the DPSA. Since 1973 special conditions have been introduced into the Defense Appropriations Act that restrict the freedom of the military departments to spend the funds that have been authorized. The Berry amendment prevents Canadian firms from supplying the United States military with uniforms, parachutes and life rafts. The Byrnes and Tollefson amendments prohibit American procurement of naval vessels or major components of hulls and superstructures from foreign sources. The Bayh amendment prohibits funding research and development from foreign sources unless there is no American source that is equally competent. Many other restrictions limit procurement to suppliers from small business, from depressed industries, from minority groups and so on. There is even an amendment, ASPR 1-315, requiring all government purchases of jewel bearings be made from the William Langer Jewel Bearing Plant in Rolla, North Dakota![54]

With Canada's new commitments to purchase American aircraft, U.S. military sales to Canada are expected to jump from an annual figure of $500 million to $750 million. Just when the U.S. deficit appeared to be getting out of hand, Congress passed an amendment to the defence appropriations bill for 1982 that will prevent the U.S. military from purchasing most goods or equipment containing foreign "specialty metals." This new protectionist twist could cost Canada an estimated $100 million in defence equipment sales each year.[55] The Atlantic Council has called attention to the "numerous specific measures in U.S. law and procurement regulations which adversely affect the operation of the Defence Production Sharing Program."[56] It is likely that these difficulties will be resolved because of the Pentagon's strong interest in Canadian industry as an integral part of its North American defence preparedness planning. During the crisis months of 1981 the Department of Defense made it clear to the White House that, where retaliatory measures were being considered in response to the NEP and FIRA, defence production sharing was off limits. The nervousness in Ottawa about the prospects of defence production sharing underlines the satellitic dependence of this component-producing industry. Since Congress has no qualms about acting in what it considers the United States' best interest, the continuation of defence production sharing will depend more on American political thinking than on Canadian policy. Thus it could be argued that economic considerations no longer need to determine its military policy. If the Americans consider that the decentralization of military industrial plants across North America will reduce their vulnerability to attack, the DPSA will remain in force. If that is so, Canada's shift to some other strategic approach to its military equipment requirements need not be restrained by its role in the continental military industry.

The Strategy/Weaponry Options
The kinds of choices Canada might make in its re-equipment programs would necessarily be linked to strategic decisions about a reoriented role for the Canadian armed forces. By way of illustration, but in no way as a complete list of possibilities, three different directions could be suggested as alternatives to the incrementalist-integration option now being tacitly pursued.

The Free Ride   Since a military establishment is not required because Canada has no conceivable reason to attack another country, since there is no threat of attack upon Canada against which its military establishment can make any effective preparation, since the United States will maintain its own defence preparedness against nuclear attack from the Soviet Union whatever Canada does, it can be argued — as James Eayrs has done — that Canada could drastically reduce its military establishment and so eliminate major portions of its defence budget.[57] There would, of course, be a price to pay for saving so much money. Even if Canada maintained its contribution to European defence, it would be seen to have partially opted out of the Atlantic club and would bear the full brunt of the ostracism from the European Community that it tasted once before in the early Seventies. There would be additional costs to be borne in reducing its symbolic sovereignty. Canada's opting out of its share of North American air defence might not noticeably affect the United States' ability to deter possible attacks, but it is very likely, especially given the jaundiced eye with which Washington now regards Ottawa, that such a step would be seen as an unfriendly act. If Canada's participation in NORAD is of greater diplomatic than military significance, then its opting for a free ride would be likely to have powerful symbolic repercussions throughout the American political system. Economic retaliation would not be unthinkable. "If we relieved ourselves of the burden of defence expenditures." writes John Holmes, "I feel also that the United States Congress would regard this as an artificial means of spurring our competitive position in trade and would insist on more non-tariff barriers to our exports."[58]

It is doubtful that the free-ride approach could be sold to the Canadian public, which would take it as an abandonment of Canada's military tradition of supporting its allies in war and peace. It is even more unlikely that the Canadian government would be able to persuade its military community to accept such a radical departure from four decades of continental praxis. After all, it was the Canadian military who created the NORAD system ten months *before* Parliament began to debate the merits of the agreement. It was the Canadian high command who put the Canadian forces on alert two days *before* the prime minister and cabinet approved this action in response to the Kennedy confrontation with Khrushchev over the installation of Soviet missiles in Cuba.[59] Even if it became politically acceptable, it is unlikely that the no-defence option would increase Canadian sovereignty. Canada would have no capacity to forbid the use of Canadian air space to the American military. Canadian terra firma might remain under Canadian control, but not its air space. If the no-equipment approach was designed to be the corollary of a neutral, nuclear-free strategy, it would be illusory because unenforceable. Neutralism is an expensive, not a cheap, military option.

Armed Neutralism   If Canada really wanted to establish a nuclear-free zone as a contribution to a reduction of East-West tensions and a world program of disarmament, it would, paradoxically, have to undertake a massive program of rearmament. For if Sweden rather than Austria is the model, Canada would not only need to be able to establish and maintain its neutralism vis-à-vis its superpower neighbours but would also have to become industrially self-reliant in producing its own armaments. The task is not impossible. Sweden, with a population about the size of Ontario's, has managed to develop a military-industrial strategy that has had extremely successful results both in its outstanding military products and in the technological excellence of its civilian economic spin-off. Twenty-five years ago Canada was on the verge of a similar future, with the development of significant airplane and electronic systems capabilities and the evolution of a manufacturing capacity central to a modern economy. It had developed the most powerful and advanced aircraft engine in the world. This strategic thrust in military equipment was based on a significant line of successful aircraft developed since the Second World War. To relaunch such a weapons development program would require the dedication of colossal amounts of capital and labour. It is hard to see Canada developing the political will for such an option unless the United States' political climate became so extreme that the American military, not the Soviets', had become the chief Canadian defence concern. Short of this barely conceivable turn of events, it is difficult to see either the Canadian military or the Canadian public wanting to assert true defence sovereignty along Gaullist or Swedish lines.

National Surveillance   In between the two extremes of complete disarmament and sovereign rearmament there is a middle position. The white paper of August 1971, *Defence in the 70s*, proposed a reordering of military priorities with the surveillance of Canadian territory and the protection of Canadian sovereignty in first place.[60] Through amendments to the Territorial Sea and Fishing Zones Act and the Arctic Waters Pollution Prevention Act, Canada had extended its claim to sovereignty from three to twelve miles and its claim to control over vessels in the Arctic to one hundred miles from shore. The voyage of the S.S. *Manhattan* through the Northwest Passage in 1969 had underlined the need for Canada to have a quasi-military surveillance and control capacity, a need that was further increased by the extension of Canada's claim to sovereign control over a zone 200 miles from the Atlantic and Pacific coasts. In reality Canada has little capability for enforcing these claims. The enormously expensive Auroras are too sophisticated for surveillance over fishing boats and the Maritime Command's destroyers are inappropriate for enforcement — even when they are seaworthy.[61] This suggests that Canada's practical needs for enforcing its claims to sovereignty over vast economic zones off its ocean coasts and in the Arctic require the necessary equipment.

The development of medium-technology military and naval equipment adequate to this task might provide a more practical, if less dramatic, focus for Canada's military-industrial strategy than either the improbable armed neutralism or the integrating incrementalism currently being considered. Canada still has the technical capacity to produce competitive medium-sized aircraft. It is conceivable that by developing this capacity into a new generation of technologically unsophisticated but reliable ships and aircraft, Canada could have an export niche that did not compete with the big-power weapons merchants or foster the dangerous arms race in mega-destruction. The adoption of a national-equipment thrust would not be incompatible with sustaining Canada's participation in NORAD and NATO, but it might offer a more acceptable option than entering space-based militarism as a junior participant. A northern surveillance capability could strengthen Canada's claims to the economic resources in the Beaufort Sea and the Arctic and could dovetail with the development of a northern NATO command that gave Canada a more distinct role than its present function in European defence. Such a northern strategy would withdraw Canada's northern sovereignty problem from the context of the United States' legal contestation of the Canadian claim and promote a diversification of Canada's relations with the Nordic countries in Europe.[62]

To suggest that Canada has to make equipment choices, and therefore strategic choices, implies that the Canadian military have a strategy-making capacity. The practice of the Department of National Defence has been to act as a junior member of the international alliance, initialling strategy documents produced by the Pentagon. While the Department of External Affairs may not accept the Reagan administration's simplistic cold-warrior view of the Soviet threat, it is not clear whether the Department of National Defence is able to counter the new American line with strategy thinking of its own. Does Canada have a response to the Reagan administration's program to modernize its strategic nuclear weapons and to upgrade its North American defence capacity as a factor in accelerating the arms race? Does Canada have a position on outerspace laser weapons systems whose development could further destabilize East-West relations? Does the Canadian government accept the U.S. view on ballistic missile defence? At the heart of the American debate are questions such as these which concern the proper definition of nuclear deterrence and the nature of strategic stability. Canada appears to have no view of its own other than to endorse whatever the current American administration is doing and agree with however this position may be rationalized. It seems Canada has to participate in American deterrence even if the Reagan administration's nuclear escalation is destabilizing the East-West equilibrium.

To read between the lines of the Macdonald Report on the Royal Canadian Mounted Police, it becomes clear that Canada has no independent intelligence capacity either. Instead it relies on a branch plant approach to spying. Although that section of the report dealing

266

with international intelligence is itself written in a kind of cryptic code, one can infer from its muted message that Canada's reliance on its allies for foreign intelligence about threats to the country's security has very serious military and foreign policy implications. Specifically it points out "the danger [in other words the actuality] of Canada's security intelligence agency adopting the outlook and opinions of a foreign agency, especially of an agency which has come to be depended upon heavily [such as the CIA]."[63] The report goes on to point out that the emergence of new issues and changes in the international climate have blurred "the once clear distinction between one's friends and those whose friendship is less manifest or reliable," suggesting there is a demonstrably greater need for Canada to have its own political, economic and intelligence capability.[64] It would appear just as valid to challenge the acceptance of being a small cog in the international intelligence machine as in the military scenario-building process. The development of an autonomous intelligence and strategy capacity and the shift to a more nationally useful generation of military equipment need not provoke a confrontation with the Pentagon or an abrogation of the Defence Production Sharing Arrangements. They might suggest that in the strategic and industrial dimensions, Canada has national interests of its own that need to underpin any commitments it makes to multilateral security and bilateral defence.

Continuity or Change: A Non-Nuclear Chance?

In 1977, Brian Cuthbertson wrote that "Canada today has more options available to it for defence than it has had since the late 1940s. This derives mainly from changes in the strategic environment that allow for a redefinition of continental defence requirements which favour a greater separation of Canadian national and continental defence requirements."[65] One component of the strategic environment was the change in military technology which invalidated the defence-against-help theory. Canada's geographical position as a buffer zone became far less crucial than it had been before the advent of missiles and surveillance satellites.

The arrival of the new Reagan administration did not alter the state of the technology or even the trend to increased defence spending which had been started under President Carter. The change that Reagan represented was the political commitment to build up fortress America and the anti-communist ideological conviction necessary to ensure a clear victory in the Pentagon for the school believing in counterforce nuclear strategy. Through its membership in NORAD Canada is actively, though not expressly, supporting a strategic change with which its political leaders explicitly disagree. While the prospects for world survival have been worsened by this dangerous change, the prospects for Canada's getting off the nuclear arms-race escalator have improved. There is ample room for Canada to contribute to the conventional defence of Europe and to provide more adequate surveillance in the coastal and Arctic regions to which it claims sovereignty, and thereby make a responsible contribution to collective security, without provoking Washington by appearing to be taking a free ride. By opting out of its junior-partner role in NORAD, Canada could not expect to deflect the United States of America from its perilous course. But by augmenting its contribution to NATO, it would be able to strengthen the European forces with which it agrees and which, together, have greater clout in Washington. The change that Reagan presents Ottawa in the military field is thus the opportunity to provide leadership on the most dangerous issue in the world by not following one of its most dangerous governments.

Part IV

The Canadian-American Relationship in the Eighties

The Canadian-American Relationship in the Eighties

It has been the thesis of this study that the National Energy Program's announcement in October 1980 and the Reagan election victory in November 1980 heralded a crisis in the relationship between Canada and the United States. Relations between the two countries had been in a state of *instability* at least since 1971 when Nixonomics shattered Canadian, if not American, illusions about the special relationship. The U.S. had secured largely unrestricted access to the Canadian economy and in return granted Canada exemptions from policies which it had designed to defend its interests against the rest of the world (chapter 1). The events of the four seasons following Reagan's inauguration demonstrated how the interactions between Washington and Ottawa were characterized by acute *stress* in which the chief protagonists on both sides reacted with hysteria, panic and other indications that they felt their values were threatened by what the other side was doing to them (chapter 2). Having established the situational prerequisites and the psychic conditions for crisis, the next nine chapters of our analysis investigated the main dossiers on the bilateral policy agenda so that we could establish to what extent the crisis marked a *turning point* in the relationship.

Recapitulating briefly, readers will recall:

- The National Energy Program represented a historically unprecedented intervention by the federal government to make major structural transformations in the ownership, power and rent-collecting configurations of an industry considered of strategic importance (chapter 3).

- In contrast to the NEP, where the Canadian government prevailed, it was the American government that won in the struggle over the extension of the powers of the Foreign Investment Review Agency. Not only did the Americans succeed in forcing Ottawa to back off

271

from its projected measures to strengthen FIRA, but they also forced Ottawa to renounce the application of the NEP model to other sectors of the economy and so abandon its commitments to elaborate an interventionist industrial strategy (chapter 4).

- In the troubled area of trade, the picture is less one of a particular victory or loss than of a permanent state if not of siege then of threat. The growing atmosphere of America-first protectionism in Congress found a new slogan in "reciprocity." The legislation incorporating this notion menaces Canada with retaliation for a wide range of export promotion policies of which it may be accused by any aggrieved American commercial interest (chapter 5).

- Actual conflict in the resource field is comparatively low, but the continued continental integration of its various renewable and non-renewable staple-extracting sectors leaves Canada with fairly bleak prospects owing to the depletion of its easily available resources, the GATT-sanctioned difficulties in raising the level of processing before exports, and the obstacles that high costs of energy and money place in the way of any salvation through megaprojects (chapter 6).

- Canadian political and economic leaders (along with their European counterparts) have expressed anger, frustration and helplessness in the face of the high interest rates and exchange rate pressures caused in large part by the huge government deficits and tight money policy which have been the product of Reaganomics (chapter 7).

- As a result of the politics of deregulation and getting the government off the backs of business, there is no question that the Reagan administration's actions have worsened Canadian-American "atmospherics" both literally and figuratively — increasing the volume of acid deposition exported into central Canada and raising the level of bitterness expressed by Canadians concerned about their natural environment (chapter 8).

- At the same time as Canadians failed to make progress on the acid rain problem by directly intervening in the American political process, they also made very few gains by negotiating formal treaties. President Reagan personally poured years of difficult bargaining down the drain by withdrawing the fisheries and maritime boundaries treaty from the Senate. After a year of reviewing and pressuring, the administration pressed for more concessions, then decided not to sign the United Nations Law of the

Sea convention, leaving up in the air the status of this major effort to bring to the jurisdiction of the seabed the rule of law, some equity for poor nations, and major gains for Canada (chapter 9).

- In matters of culture and communications, the changes represented by the Reagan administration's coming to power confirmed trends already apparent in the Seventies: a hostility to Canada's belated attempts to set up some cultural defences and a powerful pressure to impose free flows of information and open skies as the principles guiding international policies on telecommunications and transborder data flow (chapter 10).

- In the military field, Reagan's administration represented the defeat of the détente and deterrence school and the victory of the proponents of tactical nuclear warfare and an escalation of the arms race. Through NORAD directly and through NATO indirectly, Canada faces great pressure to participate in a strategic program that would destabilize East-West relations (chapter 11).

The Continuing Crisis

12

There is enough evidence in the nine principal policy issues we have examined to suggest that 1981 did indeed represent a turning point in the Canadian-American relationship. For these changes were not coincidental. They reflected basic shifts in the way each country had defined its national interest in responding to the internal and external problems it faced. For its part the United States had been trying to regain the primacy in world affairs it had lost in the process of taking on a losing struggle to impose its will over Asian nationalism in Indo-China: military primacy over the Soviet Union and economic primacy over Japan and the European Community. As rationalization for this double quest, the Reagan administration has revived two doctrines from America's ideological heritage. A Manichean anti-communism allows it to justify a program to remilitarize through massive government intervention in the defence industries while restricting its expenditures on aid to the Third World. A free-market doctrine provides theoretical grounds for capitalizing on its economic strengths by pushing its international partners to accept its investment, its trade and its services, while no acknowledgement is made of the manifest trade protectionism and restrictions on inward foreign investment which defend its own economic weaknesses from foreign competition.

At the same time as the Reagan administration continued its rearmament and girded its loins with an almost biblical sense of self-righteousness, Canada underwent a different transformation. After a decade of uncertainty, two events declared a new phase had begun. Quebeckers' refusal in a referendum to give their government a mandate to negotiate Sovereignty-Association let the air out of the separatist balloon; patriation of the constitution with an amending formula offered an end to years of federal-provincial bickering. The provisional resolution of these political problems of national unity

274

allowed greater energies to be devoted to dealing with Canada's economic and cultural problems. A growing awareness of how bleak were Canada's economic prospects — even before world recession aggravated them beyond foreseeable repair — made politicians realize that the country would have to try to extricate itself from some of its American-centred dependency if it was to improve its chances of survival as a viable state with a central government able to justify its existence in the face of the increasingly autonomist provinces. The National Energy Program declared the federal government's intention to regain some of the power that had been decentralized into provincial hands over the previous twenty years. In contrast with the previous coincidence of world views between Ottawa and Washington, Ottawa remained ideologically pragmatic, maintaining its internationalist beliefs in striving for world peace through international institutions, for détente between East and West, and for some economic levelling between North and South — views that now clashed with those of the Reagan government.

Meanwhile in Republican Washington the mood of magnanimity befitting a world power was gone. In its place had developed the quarrelsome pugnacity of the fighter who has passed his prime and who, in the words of Robert Osgood, was "talking loudly while carrying an inadequate stick."[1] "Reciprocity" might be an inadequate stick for the purposes of beating Japan or the European Community into submission, but it was not inadequate to the task of imposing its will on its weaker, more vulnerable neighbour to the north. Gone was the accommodating American attitude characteristic of what Peter Dobell recalled as "a close and trusting alliance relationship."[2] Gone too was the Americans' benign "ignorant friendliness and goodwill" which, in Willis Armstrong's phrase, characterized the taking-Canada-for-granted syndrome of the special-relationship days.[3] Gone even was the mood of the Seventies, when Canada tended to suffer the "unintended adverse effects" of Congress's unpredictable but not malevolent retaliatory policies.[4] In the place of benevolence and inadvertence the new doctrine of reciprocity had emerged. The congressional authorization of linkage — retaliation against targets different from the cause of complaint — confronted Canada with institutionalized and unpredictable vulnerability to U.S. administrative decisions. Reciprocity between the two unequal powers condemned the weaker partner to continued inferiority by repeated applications of quite ample administrative measures to hold back the competition of a Bombardier, a Rogers, a Stelco, a Nova or a Telidon. Uncertainty was aggravated by American indifference to Canada's special needs and different ways. The prospect that retaliation would be used to discipline Canada for trying to develop its own solutions to its own very real problems was enhanced by the aggressiveness that characterized official Washington's attitudes to Canada. William Brock, the United States trade representative, dismissed, in public, Ottawa's cultural policy as book burning and spoke, in private, of the need to punish Canada. Paul Robinson, American ambassador to Canada, lectured Ottawa for spending too much on social services and chided the government for worrying more about acid rain than Soviet armaments.[5]

While still ignored as a serious factor in international political affairs,[6] Canada was no longer taken for granted in economic matters. On the contrary, it was singled out as a test case for American international economic policies on investment, trade and services. Far from enjoying exemptions from American international economic policies, Canada was expected to be an exemplar to the world. As an American senior official admitted during one of the secret but stormy confrontations of 1981, "Yes, we judge Canada differently than Indonesia."[7] While not permitting Canada to act like a state capitalist developing country, Washington was equally concerned to prevent Canada from behaving like a protectionist industrialized economy on the model of Japan or the European Community. Any deviations from its historic role as a resource hinterland and a captive market were clearly to be resisted. Only the status quo was acceptable.

Canada might have been willing to accept the status quo of the Sixties, but its industrialized trading partners had forced down tariff barriers while erecting new non-tariff barriers to trade which had changed the rules of the international economic game. Canada had an open economy and so had to pay the price for not being strong enough to make its own decisions. Like a number of countries that are the minor partner in an unbalanced duopoly — Korea-Japan, Ireland-Britain, Poland-USSR — Canada's dependency is overwhelmingly centred in its dominant partner. In attempting to respond to the new global context within which it had to operate, Canada was trying to assess those areas where it might enjoy some comparative advantage and to devote its policy making to enhancing the few areas of superiority that compensated for the many disadvantages it suffered as a small, truncated market economy. In sum, Canada wanted to reduce the disadvantages it perceived in its dependence on the U.S., while the United States was quite naturally determined to retain them.

This divergence of interests explains why many observers agreed by 1981 that the relationship would remain strained. "One can forecast with confidence," said John Curtis of the Institute for Research on Public Policy, "that the standard list of Canadian-U.S. irritants will get longer and more complicated until a new stability, satisfying to both sides, is found. Elements of disharmonization . . . will characterize every issue."[8] A research group advising American multinationals on the level of risk they face abroad wrote that "relations will become far more strained in the near future," and foresaw a vicious circle developing in which "political tensions, confrontations, and stalemates further undermine a weakened economy which, in turn, make achieving a political compromise less and less likely, as the pie itself declines in size."[9]

Since American businessmen and American politicians have developed ideas as intractable as they are unreal about Canada's nationalism and the aggressive competitiveness of Canadian entrepreneurs, it seems predictable that conflicts will be triggered constantly by the individual activities of Canadian entrepreneurs seeking markets in the U.S. as they try to optimize their productivity. At the same time, different attitudes towards the proper role of the state as well as incompatible actions by the governments of the two countries will continue to supply justifications for each side's grievances against the other. Unlike the turning point of the classic crisis in medical cases, from which the patient either succumbs or recovers, the obstinate conflicts that characterized the turning point of 1981 appear to have set a pattern of continuing stress for the foreseeable future. In the face of this grave prospect, Canada will have to reassess its capacities for managing its most important foreign relationship.

Foreign Policy as a Proxy for Managing the Relationship

Since the period after the Second World War when the American relationship emerged as Canada's most important external connection, it has been managed on a tactical basis. Issues were addressed functionally and on their individual merits as they happened to come onto the agenda. Governments did not intervene with grand schemes to orchestrate the myriad separate interactions of the relationship into any overall pattern. Business looked after its own problems. There was virtually no provincial involvement in defining national positions. Bureaucrats in both capitals frowned on the practice of linkage, the tying of negotiations over bilateral issues in one policy area with outcomes in another area. The concept of retaliation was rejected as inappropriate for a relationship of such apparent intimacy and friendliness so that scenarios to deal with American retaliatory threats were not developed. The corollary of its studied lack of a policy towards the United States was Canada's almost compulsively energetic involvement in world affairs which was executed with Washington's reaction very much in mind.

Canada participated in international affairs partly to make good its claim to be an independent nation-state with its own foreign policy. It also reckoned that working actively in international organizations would provide a "counterweight" in negotiating with the United States, since it believed it had more chance of achieving certain goals in Washington if it acted as part of a larger group. Canada undertook certain international actions, such as U.N. peacekeeping, at the explicit or implicit behest of the United States, with the understanding that this would build up credits it could cash in during bilateral negotiations. Its unassuming and unprovocative "quiet diplomacy" was even thought to yield Canadian diplomats influence, in the corridors of Washington, over the shape of American foreign policies. However well these maxims for coping with Washington may have worked in the past, there is good reason to think that they are inadequate for the future.

Foreign Policy as a Displacement of Dependence
Potentially, Canada's foreign policy can act as a factor countering continental absorption by asserting to Canadians that Canada has a separate and different role to play on the world stage. Long since past are the heady days of Canada's diplomatic golden age when it participated, if somewhat sceptically, in launching the Colombo Plan for aid to the underdeveloped members of the Commonwealth, and when it played an active role in the establishment of the major international organizations which created the framework for the postwar world. The recognition for Canada's special internationalist role in a tense world came in the form of the Nobel Peace Prize awarded to Lester Pearson for his participation in creating the United Nations Emergency Force to keep the peace between Egypt and Israel after the Suez crisis. Much of Canada's postwar self-confidence was based on the sense that it had a useful international role to play as a middle power unsullied by imperialist ambitions. Whereas no claim could be made that Canada had a separate military personality or presence, it still can be argued that Canada is "foremost" enough to play a responsible part in a world fraught with critical issues.[10]

278

Whether Canadian foreign policy reaches its potential in this regard is a matter of debate among critics.

Participating in the North-South arena appears to be the area where Canada can affirm its objectives with the least danger of conflict with its neighbour. Even though the United States under Reagan is acting from the self-serving rationalization that free enterprise can better serve the destitute nations than aid from the wealthy ones, there are no grounds to blame Washington for Canada's relatively weak performance in the aid field. For a government whose prime minister has long singled out the North-South problem as a vital foreign policy concern, the gap between Canada's rhetoric and performance remains embarrassingly wide.[11] There is little question that Canada has the capacity to play in this sphere a major role of which it could be proud. "Canada is still one of the best-equipped, or least impaired, nations to undertake the bridge-building role," according to Bernard Wood of the North-South Institute.[12] Canada is an agricultural power accounting for one-fifth of international wheat grain exports. It is a major producer of primary products, which gives it many economic interests that could be explored in cooperation instead of in competition with Third World countries. Despite the fact that Canada itself has been involved in cartels in the marketing of grain and uranium, it has resisted the establishment of producer organizations for primary products such as copper that are of great importance to less developed countries. Although it has accepted special responsibilities in the discussions about a New International Economic Order, there is, according to the North-South Institute, "an inexplicable gap between Canada's proposed determination . . . to help developing countries develop their capacities to export goods and services, and Canada's extreme reluctance . . . to allow them to compete for the opportunity to supply under Canadian aid programs."[13] For Canada to meet its commitment to give official development assistance at the rate of 0.5 per cent of gross national product would require a doubling of its aid budget by 1985. Without being laggard, Canada is still not exemplary in this field where it can claim no external impediment to championing developing countries' interests. It has also opposed a reform of the financial system favoured by the South to establish a link between development assistance and special drawing rights with the International Monetary Fund. In effect, Canada has shown itself afraid of getting out of step with its industrialized partners, arguing unconvincingly that it would reduce its capacity to help the Third World if it lost influence with the more significant economic powers in the summit club.

On the major world issues that preoccupy the great powers, the claim is no longer made, as it was in the Sixties, that Canada's special relationship with the United States gave it influence over American foreign policy making in such crucial matters as Washington's Cold War policy.[14] John Holmes advised that Canadians not be tempted by the illusion "or the promise of what might be called an equitable share in the U.S. policy process." On the contrary, Ottawa cannot escape the constant calculation "of how to balance our own attitudes and interests with the deference we owe to those of our major ally."[15] Canada may not agree with the United States but cannot disregard its position — and the possible consequences of disagreeing with it — when making foreign policy. What this meant in practice was that, in those difficult cases for Canada when the United States and its European allies disagreed, Canada chose to line up with its imperial partner: for instance on the Middle East, on Afghanistan and on the Moscow Olympics.[16] Some take comfort in the view that it was the U.S. which moved towards Canadian positions during the Seventies on Vietnam, Cuba and détente. Canada's recognition of China may have eased President Nixon's move along the same path. But in general, it is hard to argue that the coincidence of positions between Canada and the United States results from the U.S. following Canada's lead rather than the opposite. Indeed Canadian diplomats concerned with the American relationship openly argue that Canada should give its support to the United States on multilateral issues that concern it as a superpower in order to develop some credit and goodwill at the State Department when it comes to issues that specifically affect Canada's national interests.[17] The advocacy of indirect means of influence for Canada in Washington bears a striking resemblance to the old quiet diplomacy approach and offers as little concrete evidence of its effectiveness.

International Institutional Participation as Counterweight

Canada used participation in the international organizations it helped construct after the Second World War to extract itself from an uncomfortable bilateral inferiority, by pulling its weight in multi-member institutions in which it enjoyed titular equality with the others, including the United States. John Holmes articulated the general consensus that they are essential to Canada: "They create the fabric of the world in which we could survive and prosper."[18] Since the Third World gained a majority in the United Nations General Assembly in the Sixties, the United States has become disillusioned with this organization that it was so instrumental in founding. For Canada, whose goals were not so threatened by this shift of power from the North to the South, the U.N. has remained an important forum in which it could find allies on issues bearing directly on Canadian interests such as the Law of the Sea.[19] Indeed, as the Reagan administration withdrew its support from the principle of dealing with major global issues through international organizations, they offered Canada some opportunity not to be seen "as a docile dependent of the North American superpower."[20] The potential should not be exaggerated.

In the European Economic Community, Canada has developed very little weight it can use as a counter to its American dependency. Though a potential commonality of interests exists in some areas (resisting the extra-territorial application of American law via the multinational corporations), there are other issues (GATT negotiations on trade and investment) where the major European countries share the United States' great-power hostility to any resource economy's attempts to improve the benefits it extracts from capital invested by industrialized economies. With Japan, Canada has even less weight to be used against the United States. Indeed, Washington's separate deal with Tokyo over the limitation of Japanese car exports showed how the U.S. could use Japan as a counterweight against Canadian interests.

NATO is generally cited as the classic example of Canada's using an international organization to offset its satellitic relationship, but subscribing to NATO strategy can force it back into further bilateral dependence. Canada's agreement to permit the United States to test its Cruise missile on the Primrose Range in northeastern Alberta was a case in point. It could be seen as an example of counterweight to the extent that the introduction of a new generation of American missiles was a collective NATO decision to respond to the Soviet Union's installation of the SS-20 counterforce missiles in eastern Europe. To the extent that it represented an adoption by Canada of the Reagan administration's extreme Cold War strategy — Prime Minister Trudeau justified the Cruise missile testing on the grounds that "we must also show the Soviet Union that we can meet them gun for gun if necessary"[21] — it showed a vicious circle to be in operation, counterweight diplomacy bringing Canada back to bilateral dependence.

Even where Canada does have concrete issues at stake, participation in international organizations can prove counterproductive. Canada has direct interests in Latin America and the Caribbean, for instance. Its banks and multinational resource companies have major investments there. Its tourists spend millions of dollars seeking the southern sun and it has received hundreds of thousands of immigrants from the area. But the weight of the United States' interests is far greater, both in the Caribbean and throughout Latin America. As a result, it has always been difficult for Canada to be active in the Western Hemisphere because, as John Harbron put it twenty years ago in connection with the Organization of American States (OAS), Canada would be pressed to bias its positions to the American line.[22] Unlike the consultative mechanisms of the Commonwealth which operate by consensus, the OAS makes decisions by votes in which the minority is bound by the majority. Canada has always felt it would be placed in an invidious position in this system, unable to resist or temper Washington's hegemony. The U.S. administration's Caribbean Basin Initiative seemed to reflect a more realistic understanding that economic aid would go further in the long run to help the countries of Central America than the export of arms and military advisers.[23] The House of Commons Subcommittee on Canada's Relations with Latin America and the Caribbean argued that, while Canada should continue to participate in discussions of the Caribbean basin plan, it should "strongly assert Canada's own distinct interest and role."[24] Given the dominance of the United States in the Inter-American Development Bank, such Canadian self-assertion would still have to be expressed on an independent basis without participating in multilateral initiatives.

Canada was an enthusiastic, if junior, participant in the establishment of the economic and financial institutions that shaped the postwar world economy. It took an active part in founding and operating the World Bank, the International Monetary Fund, the General Agreement on Tariffs and Trade, and later the Organization for Economic Cooperation and Development. In the Seventies it was promoted to membership in the economic summit and it has participated in less formal trilateral meetings of Japanese, European and American trade ministers. For all this diligent participation, it is increasingly doubtful whether these institutions are serving rather than subverting Canada's actual economic objectives. At the Tokyo Round of the Multilateral Trade Negotiations, Canada's attempts to gain greater processing before resource exportation were not heeded either by the U.S. or by Japan and Europe. Canada was left out in the cold. As the main Canadian negotiator, Rodney Grey, commented, "The MTN may come to be seen as marking the beginning of the end of the order in which Canada prospered."[25] GATT is being used by the U.S. to attack both FIRA and the NEP and to oppose Bombardier's bid to supply

New York City's new generation of subway cars. As a host economy for foreign direct investment, Canadian interests have come under tremendous pressure from the capital-exporting countries in the OECD's formulation of an investment code for multinational capital. Canada's entry into the economic summit club can be taken as a recognition by the international community of its significant international position. But when it is realized that Canada was admitted because the United States wanted a pro-American presence around the table to balance the admission of Italy to the previous club of five (France, Germany, Japan, United Kingdom, United States), it can be seen that Canada's international action may not so much be an escape from as a perpetuation of its American dependency.

The Trade-off of Multilateral Support for Bilateral Credit
When Lester Pearson sent peacekeeping troops to Cyprus in response to Lyndon Johnson's request, Johnson supported the Auto Pact in Congress as an exchange of favours. Trading good Canadian deeds internationally for American concessions bilaterally proved remarkably unsuccessful in the late Seventies and early Eighties. Canada's rescue of six American diplomats at the cost of closing its embassy in Tehran yielded forests' worth of good press in the United States in the spring of 1980, but the "Iranian caper" did nothing to dampen the hostilities of American businessmen and politicians who were denouncing FIRA and the NEP a year later. Ottawa's calculated support for Washington's sanctions against Iran in retaliation against the Iranian seizure of the American embassy and hostages did not produce the hoped-for Senate consent for the fisheries and maritime boundaries treaty.[26] Cooperation with the United States at the Tokyo Round of the Multilateral Trade Negotiations did not yield the expected reductions of the Buy America obstacles to Canadian exports of light rapid urban transit trains.

This dilemma was illustrated by the vacillations in Ottawa's stance during 1981-82 towards the civil war in El Salvador. The Canadian external affairs minister originally supported those who protested the atrocities perpetrated by the junta in suppressing the peasant revolt, and implicitly rejected Washington's thesis that the rebels were an arm of Soviet subversion. Mark MacGuigan then apparently responded to direct pressure from Alexander Haig and gave tacit support for the electoral process of the regime which Washington was determined to prop up.[27] There is little evidence that supporting the U.S. in El Salvador earned Canada diplomatic credits for application to bilateral questions. As the documents analyzed in chapter 2 showed, Haig was as deeply involved in exerting pressure on the NEP and FIRA as was William Brock or Donald Regan.

On balance it would appear that a decade's somewhat irresolute pursuit of the Third Option has not led to the hoped-for resolution of Canada's continental dilemma. The original doctrine published in 1972 over the signature of Mitchell Sharp, then secretary of state for external affairs, proposed to reduce Canada's American dependency by expanding its relations with other countries.[28] The status of the proposal was ambivalent. It represented the Department of External Affairs' thinking about how best to respond to President Nixon's termination of the "special relationship," but it did not represent a consensus of cabinet. The Department of Finance — and particularly its deputy minister, Simon Reisman — disagreed with the premise that Canada should reduce its economic dependence on the United States. Mitchell Sharp's statement was more like a white paper than a declaration of firm government strategy. While it implied that important structural changes would be needed in the economy for its proposed diversification to take place, the occasional pronouncements by ministers of industry, trade and commerce that the government would move in the direction of the requisite industrial strategy never bore fruit. No agreement had been achieved with the provinces. At best the Third Option was a declaration by the country's foreign office about how it would like to see Canada's international role develop. In the long term no significant trade diversification took place. Canada's foreign policy remained reactive, governed by no apparent strategy other than to retain the United States' goodwill.

Confirmation that a turning point in the Canadian-American relationship had been reached in the early Eighties can be found in the Department of External Affairs' own recognition that the Third Option had failed. In what was a very significant but little noticed announcement that Canada's approach to its foreign policy had been turned on its ear, Mark MacGuigan told the Empire Club in January 1981 that Canada would now be guided by a new and more hard-nosed realism grounded in considerations of economic self-interest. "It's not enough for us to be the world's leading internationalists," he declared. Instead of playing boy scout to the world, MacGuigan announced that Canada would henceforth be guided in its actions by a new doctrine he labelled "bilateralism," meaning it would "concentrate its resources to achieve the necessary political relationships with a limited number of key countries."[29]

The adoption of "bilateralism" as the theoretical basis for Canada's foreign policy had two fundamentally important implications for the Canadian-American relationship, as the articles and speeches given during the same period by the under-secretary of state for external affairs confirmed. Allan Gotlieb's first message was that prime attention had to be given to the Canadian-American relationship: "Above all this objective requires the successful management of the U.S. relationship to which it is intimately linked."[30] MacGuigan had said that the bilateral relationships to which priority had been given must be subject to "central policy management." Gotlieb explained that this meant a fundamental departure from Canada's previous approach to its American relationship. Affirming that "Canadian policy needs to adopt a strategic approach to succeed," he went on to maintain that the realization of Canadian economic development objectives required a long-term strategy: "It needs a coherent approach on the part of the government in pursuing Canadian interests vis-à-vis the United States."[31]

A Canadian Strategy Towards the United States

For Allan Gotlieb to call for a "strategic" and "coherent" approach to the Canadian-American relationship was to call for a minor revolution in the ways of Canadian government, because Canada cannot be said ever to have had an American strategy as such. While developing counterweights, offering the U.S. support on multilateral issues, and participating in international organizations may all have parts to play in an overall approach, these indirect instruments of policy must be regarded as secondary to the basic and direct problem of developing a satisfactory approach to Canada's American relationship.

From the Forties through to the Seventies, Canada's approach to dealing with the United States had been a running illustration of muddling through. The intellectual core of this incrementalism amounted to certain rules of thumb passed on from bureaucrat to politician to bureaucrat: get the best deal you can without getting too close; don't link issues; maintain good personal relationships between counterpart officials; expect preferential exemptions from damaging American legislation in return for conserving the United States' preferential access to the resources and markets of the Canadian economy; the relationship is special, a partnership unique in the world. That such nostrums took the place of serious thought about Canada's dominant external relationship was understandable if not justifiable. The continental economic pie was expanding, apparently perpetually.

Even if Canada's share of it was not as large as it might have been, it was ample. The Americans were Canada's best friends. And even if they were not, there was nothing to be done about it. There were no critical problems that could not be resolved by politicians or civil servants flying down to Washington for a heart-to-heart with their American counterparts.

The difficulties involved in defining an all-embracing American strategy were most graphically illustrated when Pierre Trudeau first came to power in 1968. He had defined his mandate as bringing reason to prevail over passion in politics through such means as careful and deliberate reviews of Canada's major policy needs, starting in particular with foreign policy. Nevertheless, the white paper that resulted from the external affairs review, *Foreign Policy for Canadians*, failed to come to grips with Canada's American policy.[32] It proposed strategies for Latin America, for Europe, for the Pacific Rim, but the American relationship defeated the diplomats: it was too all-encompassing, they felt, to be reduced to black and white. It took the shock of Nixonomics in August 1971 to push the government into print on the problem. Even then, as we have seen, the Third Option was more an essay than a strategy paper, a vague sketching of possible scenarios with neither economic implications nor institutional consequences spelled out in any detail. It was given more attention by scholars than by civil servants for whom its generalities were too vague or too contested by rival departments to form an authoritative guide for their action.[33]

During the brief Clark government in 1979 no cabinet document was prepared that came close to offering a strategy for the American relationship. Indeed not having a general policy was a conscious choice, since it was presumed to be too difficult an undertaking in so large and divided a country whose provincial components' regional strategies would differ from each other.[34] Members of the subsequent Trudeau government admit that cabinet has not thought through an overall strategy towards the United States. During 1981 the American relationship was discussed in cabinet far more frequently than normal, but on an ad hoc basis because specific issues had forced themselves to the top of the political agenda, not because Canada's individual policies towards the United States were being pursued within the framework of an overall *Sudpolitik*, as it were. The MacGuigan-Gotlieb position indicated that the rationale for not having a strategic approach had eroded: Canada could no longer afford the luxury of ad hoc improvisation for what is its single, most overpowering international relationship.

In mid-1982 the situation appears very grave. Canada's economy is so open that its governments have little macroeconomic control and only partial microeconomic policy-making capability. The economy faces historically high interest rates that will persist for as long as Reaganomics dictates. Having thrived on selling off its resources, Canada now confronts the problem of their depletion. New sources of energy and further extraction from existing deposits are becoming far more costly. If the pie is not actually shrinking, its ingredients are proving more expensive. National welfare in any case is not increasing. Deficits in manufacturing will continue to escalate. The desperate condition of the automobile industry may be the most graphic example etched on the public mind of the dilemma resulting from a branch plant economy, but the long-term prospect in the information industries is considerably worse. Even the hope of extracting industrial benefits regionally from the great megaprojects proposed in the energy field has been crushed by the fall of world energy prices and Washington's pressure to retain a privileged dominance for American companies in Canadian resource engineering.

The threats of and movements towards retaliation that have emanated from Washington since Ronald Reagan came to power may turn out to have provided a helpful shock jarring Canadians from their complacency. The American relationship has long provided the context within which Canadian existence is led, a context that has been mainly invisible to the naked eye of the average Canadian. This invisibility has allowed Canadians to tolerate degrees of interference in their affairs, a level of control from the south, and restrictions on their self-government that they would never have accepted from Great Britain. The Canadian government in the Seventies was mainly preoccupied with fighting the threat of "parallel power" that was identified with Quebec separatism. American intervention in Canadian politics to prevent Ottawa from keeping its election promises on the NEP and FIRA has made visible the extent to which the United States represents a parallel power even more threatening to the viability of the country. Inadvertent though it may have been, Canadians and their governments are now forced to take seriously what the American scholar Roger Swanson has called Canada's national security threat.

Thus, within this present era of continental insecurity, the United States has become a national security threat to Canada because of an

287

inadvertent United States hegemony. This hegemony results from a continental involvement of tremendous disproportionality coupled with an unusually low number of national-cultural barriers between the two nations.[35]

In pointing out the nebulous, unconventional nature of the American security threat to Canada, Swanson was explaining how the creation of military, economic and cultural barriers is essential to the maintenance of Canadian sovereignty. This assertion of Canadian self-defence is "necessary and legitimate to the extent that it encourages a distinctive culture and national identity: the issue is not whether Canada is anti-American," he argued, "it is whether the inadvertent power and the profound nationalism of the United States are really irresistible forces."[36]

Whether the forces are irresistible may well depend on the means available to resist them and the capacity to manage those means. The combination of a branch plant structure in Canada and a wall of tariff and non-tariff barriers in the United States threatens to maintain a process some have labelled deindustrialization. Though not deliberately aimed at Canada, the export of American industrial pollution is poisoning one of Canada's most precious assets, its recreational and wildlife areas. American entertainment and leisure industries relayed through powerful telecommunications conglomerates have a devastating effect on what is at best a marginal and fragmented cultural system. In short, Canada's interest can be seen as not coinciding with the unchecked satisfaction of American corporate objectives. If the Department of External Affairs has recognized that Canada's situation is critical, the time has surely come for the defining of an American strategy to be attempted.

Policy experts are already drawing attention to the impossibility of effectively making decisions on individual aspects of the bilateral relationship without relating them to a coherent overview. In reviewing Canada's dilemmas in the automotive trade, John Kirton suggests, for instance, that the Canadian approach "begin with a far more encompassing doctrine about the Canada-United States relationship in a global context."[37] Senior managers of the Canadian government confide that the need for a clarification of ideas is far more basic than concerns about appropriate structures. Nothing can be done, it is said by senior officials, without a political decision being made about the nation's goals. But there is no strategy in place which will give to new policies and new decisions the coherence and coordination that Mark

MacGuigan and Allan Gotlieb are recommending in the management of the Canadian-American relationship.

At the level of strategy, Canada has to make a choice between two basic stances. It can continue to take a complaisant and defensive position, relying on the pretence of bonhomie at the summit, squirting the brush fires that erupt under the smoke, and hoping that all will turn out for the best — even if the best has become very much a worst possible scenario of high interest rates, huge balance of payments deficits, unresolved structural crises in the economy, and continued undermining of the Canadian cultures. This would be what Abraham Rotstein has called to assume the role of eunuch in North America.[38] Alternatively, it can take the whole problem of the American relationship under consideration and attempt to define a strategy which states the country's objectives and faces the Americans' responses to them directly. Such a strategy, whose need could have been justified two decades ago for internal reasons, is required for external reasons now that the U.S. administration has authority to "link" issues by retaliating in one area for grievances originating in another.

The formulation of an American strategy for Canada will not be an easy task. A monumental effort will be needed to reconcile the divergent interests of the manufacturing heartland and the resource-producing hinterlands, to support the outward-looking, high technology industries that are hoping to penetrate the American market, to accommodate the inward-looking, labour-intensive industries that still call for quotas and tariffs, to satisfy farmers and trade unions that markets and jobs will expand and increase while at the same time assuring consumers that costs can be kept competitive. It might take a royal commission as the former minister of finance, John Crosbie, has suggested, or it might require a specially created institute not just to develop but also to maintain a strategy which would have to be constantly brought up to date in the light of changing circumstances and new crises in several dozen separate policy fields.

Canada's strategy towards the United States cannot be a policy document produced by the federal government in isolation. If Canada's American strategy is to guide Canadian relations with the United States over the next two decades, it will have to be developed through the participation of the main groups in society: the provincial governments; big, medium and small business; farmers' organizations and trade unions, voluntary associations, cultural organizations and the media, along with politicians, technical experts and bureaucrats. Their understanding and willing acceptance of the strategy's broad goals

289

would be a basic prerequisite for its successful implementation. The task is daunting.

Canadians cannot expect a panacea; any document that offered one would be suspect. Trade diversification, for instance, has proven a chimera under both Progressive Conservative and Liberal governments. Diefenbaker's promise to divert 15 per cent of Canadian trade to Britain proved to be a bluff which the British themselves called. The Third Option did not reduce Canada's overwhelming dependence on bilateral trade with the United States. This does not mean that the effort to expand Canadian trade beyond the confines of North America should not be a component of Canada's global strategy; it means that the strategy cannot lean on a single, insubstantial buttress. Nor can free trade any longer be seriously countenanced as a broad solution to Canada's problems. Tariffs have been reduced as a result of the Tokyo Round so that they remain a relatively small impediment to trade compared to the much more serious non-tariff barriers that keep growing in all jurisdictions. The sectors of Canadian industry that have experienced modified forms of free trade — automobiles, defence production, farm equipment — have not produced economic salvation. They have generated technologically dependent, managerially backward and economically weak industries that provide a cautionary rather than an exemplary experience. There is little evidence, as we saw in chapter 5, that the United States would want to establish a free trade zone with Canada on any basis other than as resource satellite.

Watchwords like "independence" or absolute goals like eliminating integration are equally useless as the cornerstone for a comprehensive American strategy for Canada. In some fields, such as controlling environmental pollution, further continental integration may prove unavoidable if Canada is to resolve its problems in conjunction with their chief source in the U.S. Nor will slogans like "quiet diplomacy" suffice to characterize the nature of intergovernmental relations which are more likely to be characterized by political bargaining between a multitude of government entities in negotiations that will be public rather than private. There is, in short, no single formula, no alchemist's magic to be sought.

This said, the strategy should have a general, overarching objective, such as to make the country by the year 2000 viable in the several basic dimensions necessary for the country's survival as a coherent state economically able to pay its own way and culturally able to communicate with its own peoples. What counts as being "viable" in each sector of society would have to be determined separately for each case. The National Energy Program's goal of self-sufficiency might be retained as appropriate for energy but rejected as unfeasibly autarchic for the defence industries. Attaining the objective of viability might require the reduction of the rate of exploitation of some resources, such as water, or the more careful husbanding of others, such as the forests. A comprehensive macroeconomic target would be to shift the current account from its large deficit into balance so as to stabilize the debt load that the country is carrying, and then to move from balance into surplus so as gradually to diminish that foreign debt burden.

Enough progress has been made in the evolution of the country's cultural industries for the parameters of cultural viability to be defined with some precision. If by cultural viability we mean the ability of the creative talent in each field to communicate with its public, it might be said that policies in the fields of theatre, radio broadcasting and music had already achieved a national market sufficient for Canadian theatre, radio and music to be viable nationally if only it was adequately protected from foreign dumping. Book publishing and film making along with television broadcasting might be candidates for a key-sector approach to turn them from being vulnerable to the new telecommunications revolution to being vigorous media through which Canadians learn to experience the nature of their own society.

The achievement of such goals would require difficult social choices that would have to be spelled out. Levels of consumption might have to be reduced through increases of taxation to allow more investment to be financed from within the economy's savings mechanisms rather than calling on the limited resources of the international capital markets. The excessive importation by American branch plants would have to be addressed by negotiating more vigorously sector by sector with the multinationals operating in Canada — as suggested by the 1981 budget — in order to harness their potential to make a positive contribution to the economy. Mirror legislation might be required to counteract the disincentives provided by such American programs as the Domestic International Sales Corporation and the batteries of protectionist measures contained in the U.S. Trade Act and individual states' Buy America laws. Countervailing legislation might also be required to prevent the extra-territorial extension by American courts of their jurisdiction into Canada so as to permit the rationalization of inefficient, branch plant sectors, where mergers or joint public-private Canadian-American corporations would enable uncompetitive firms to become competitive on the world scene. It stands to reason that considerable results would flow from concerted efforts to obtain viability. Once the target of capturing economic rents from energy was articulated by Eric Kierans in the early Seventies, it did not take long for provincial and federal governments to adjust their policies in order to extract for the public greater benefits from the energy sector. Once the demand for a viable economy is coherently expressed in a form that is meaningful for each sector of society and industry and in a way that the public also can clearly understand, it is likely that the economy will begin to move in the desired direction. For this reason as well, participation by the major societal forces in developing a strategy towards the U.S. is essential.

Some transitions would be hard to effect. Correcting the imbalance in the structure of Canadian exports and imports would be especially difficult. Canada's partners in the OECD think of it as their Pandora's box of resources. The European Community, no less than Japan, is unresponsive to Canadian objectives and concerns. Canada's isolation at the Tokyo Round and in the negotiations concerning the "national treatment" of investment capital at the OECD has consistently indicated this. The international facet of Canada's American strategy might well concentrate as a result on generating support among other middle-sized powers that are both exporters of raw materials and interested in broadening their industrial bases. This implies a shift of focus, not a change of principle, for Canada vis-à-vis international organizations. Canada has long supported their maintenance as the necessary legal and institutional framework for international trade. Instead of pretending to be an industrialized economy and adopting the same positions as the other members of the summit club, Canada might find it could serve its own objective of viability as well as contribute to a more equitable distribution of wealth in the world by developing a middle-power consensus that could be expressed not just at the economic summits but at the OECD, the IMF and GATT.[39] International negotiations are constantly taking place. Although Canada plays a relatively minor role in great-power diplomacy, it might find it had real influence if it acknowledged how much it held in common with developing countries in its need for a GATT-type code to govern the behaviour of multinational corporations or in its interest in rational marketing schemes for raw materials which ensured an adequate return to producing countries. Rather than resisting the American desire for a GATT for investment and a GATT for services, Canada might make a more positive contribution to the international economic order by taking a lear as a host economy experienced with branch plant performance and conscious of the need for a fair regime that stems the drain of resources caused by foreign direct investment from the poor countries towards the rich. The fact that Canada is not a pure case, since it has its own multinationals operating abroad, could be an advantage if it inspired Canadian positions that were sensitive both to the needs of the dominant and of the dominated. Creating a formal coalition of middle powers would probably be unrealistic; becoming an exponent of their interests and representing their concerns about the impact of the major economies on the minor might well be within Canada's capability.

There is little question that such a major policy exercise is feasible. Royal commissions, parliamentary committees, task forces, academic studies, consultants reports and government documents have looked at these problems individually industry by industry, sector by sector and in many cases several times each. The intellectual problem would be to achieve coherence in the synthesis; the political problem would be to gain consensus for the conclusions. Assuming a long-term strategy could be worked out, three major problems would remain. Would the federal government have the institutional capacity to implement such a strategy? Would the other key players — business, the media, the trade unions, the political parties and, most important, the provinces — be willing and able to coordinate their efforts? Would the United States accept such an effort by Canada to take its destiny more firmly in its own hands? These are the issues to be addressed in chapter 13.

Implementing a Strategy

13

If the new American doctrine of "reciprocity" envisages the practice of retaliation across different issue areas as we saw in chapter 5, Canada will no longer be able to deal with its American relationship on an issue by issue basis. On the contrary, it will be forced to develop a capacity for linking issues between different departments within the federal government, between the federal and provincial levels of government, and between different industries in the private and/or public sectors. If, in addition, the divergence of interests between the two countries implies, as we suggested in chapter 12, that their relationship will remain in a state of continuing crisis for the foreseeable future, then Canada will need to develop a strategic capability so as better to utilize its assets and minimize the damage caused by American actions. When Mark MacGuigan told the Empire Club that the relationship required central policy management, and when Allan Gotlieb remarked that Canada needed "a strategic approach to succeed," the directors of Canada's foreign policy were calling for an institutional revolution. Despite the best efforts made in the late Seventies to turn the Department of External Affairs into a central agency with enough power to develop strategy and to direct its implementation by the other federal departments, the government still lacked the strategic capacity for the task.

External Affairs as Strategic Agency
Compared to the incoherence which the division-of-powers system inflicts on the American government's capacity to formulate and implement foreign strategies, Canada's federal government enjoys many advantages. The cabinet-led, parliamentary system under the leadership of the dominant party with a permanent and expert civil service at its command has the potential for producing policies of great

coherence. The cabinet-committee system, masterminded in the late Sixties and fine-tuned in the Seventies by Michael Pitfield first as deputy secretary to the cabinet, then as clerk of the Privy Council, has the capacity, in theory, to bring the unwieldy structures of the federal bureaucracy under the direction of the elected politicians who periodically try to formulate the priorities for their time in office and give coherence to the choices their government must make.

In practice, during the Seventies these institutions did not manage either to generate or to implement a broad external strategy. In the main they provided a passably reactive system. The Privy Council Office (PCO), which is meant to provide both prime minister and cabinet with a policy assessment capability, demonstrated virtually no capacity for strategic analysis in foreign policy matters in general or the Canadian-American relationship in particular. The Prime Minister's Office (PMO) no longer offered what Ivan Head provided for ten years: continuing non-bureaucratic advice to the prime minister on the international and American issues that had reached the public agenda. Since his departure from the PMO in 1978, Head's policy advisory role has been transformed into a bureaucratic function performed by the secretary to the cabinet committee on foreign and defence policy. Since this committee's major budget decisions have not been controversial and since the prime minister is the one who has in practice made the important decisions on foreign policy issues, this is the one cabinet committee that is poorly attended and considered to be of little political significance. The most important cabinet committee, Priorities and Planning (P & P), does deal with critical decisions, including the response to crises that have arisen, but neither P & P nor its "mirror committee" of deputy ministers has a long-term strategic capability of its own. Potentially more promising is the committee of deputy ministers that mirrors the cabinet committee on foreign and defence policy. This is a cumbersome body that monitors all issues and, in attempting to coordinate everything, appears to be little more than a forum for the senior bureaucrats to communicate regularly with each other. Its ineffectiveness as a management body was signalled in the summer of 1981 when, in response to the American crisis, a separate group of those senior government officials with a direct involvement in the American relationship met for breakfast on Tuesdays at the Department of External Affairs as an ad hoc crisis-management team. In short, the cabinet-committee system, for all its much-vaunted rationalism as a policy-planning institution, did not prove capable of either devising or orchestrating the implementation of the kind of far-reaching strategy being proposed by MacGuigan and Gotlieb.

As for the Department of External Affairs, however hard it tried to claim for itself the status of a central agency, it did not achieve that position during the Seventies when it proved unable to dominate the traditional line departments. Finance; Agriculture; Energy, Mines and Resources; Industry, Trade and Commerce: these major line departments have long sustained their own direct connections with their counterpart institutions in the United States, as have the Bank of Canada, the National Energy Board, the Canadian Radio-television and Telecommunications Commission and others. These directly managed Canadian-American functional relationships seriously affect the capacity of Canada's foreign affairs department to play the coordination role that it wants to have.

We have already seen that External Affairs was unable to impose its proposed Third Option strategy on the line departments despite the fact that the secretary of state for external affairs was Mitchell Sharp, a former senior civil servant, former minister of finance, and a senior member of the cabinet, enjoying the confidence of the prime minister and the respect of his colleagues. If Mitchell Sharp could not establish the authority of External Affairs over the line departments, even in the period of Canadian-American tension following August 1971, it was clear that what was essentially a foreign service could only become an institution capable of central policy management if its authority was enhanced and its policy responsibilities were broadened.[1]

An effort was made in the late Seventies to do just that: transform External Affairs into a central agency. The critical transition came with the appointment in 1977 as under-secretary of state of Allan Gotlieb, who was a friend of the prime minister and who had extensive experience as a deputy minister of other departments in working closely with Michael Pitfield. With Pitfield's sanction, he was granted the right to review all cabinet memoranda having international implications, given access to all ministers, and became the principal adviser on foreign policy for the whole government. External Affairs was to acquire as its prime institutional mission the role of a modern central policy agency with responsibility for identifying priorities and formulating strategy. In addition, it was to oversee and coordinate the whole range of government activities as far as they affected Canada's international relationships.[2] The department was reorganized at the top to give it a greater capacity to make policy and it was enhanced abroad by the absorption of the immigration department's foreign service officers and the assignment of more authority to the heads of mission over officers from other departments. Notwithstanding these changes, the department's ability to exercise control over all government policy in its external dimension remained more theoretical than real, particularly with regard to the United States, since it had no actual power to require line departments to seek its blessing before they elaborated positions in energy, agricultural or monetary policy that affected their American relationship.

Despite Gotlieb's best efforts, the reputation of External Affairs elsewhere in the government continued to decline. The department's traditional responsibility, representing Canada to nations outside North America, had developed an ethos among its officers giving prime value to the literate, generalist diplomat on the model of an Escott Reid or a Charles Ritchie able to write brilliant political reports about the evolving situation in different lands. When operating in the Canadian-American context in tandem with senior civil servants from the line departments, the External Affairs generalist tended to appear officious and redundant — a fifth wheel present at discussions for the sake of form, not by virtue of the expertise that he or she brought to the topic. Since economic factors predominated in Canadian-American issues, External's loss of many of its economists to other departments had further weakened its authority. This did not mean the department was considered incompetent in its own bailiwick. On the contrary, its relationship with such younger departments as Communications and Environment, for whom the Canadian embassy in Washington had provided strong and capable diplomatic support, was close and satisfactory.

Nevertheless External's reputation is one of being supine vis-à-vis the Americans. It was seen to be willing to give up too much ground during the pipeline negotiations of 1977. Having taken over from the Department of Transport responsibility for negotiating air routes with the United States, it negotiated deals without expertise and without strength, giving up concessions to the Americans for which it gained little in return except the satisfaction of reporting that agreements had been made. To the extent that External Affairs was perceived to be an institution seeking peace at any price, it was hard for it to gain acceptance as the commanding institution masterminding Canada's America strategy. The exclusion of External Affairs from the group of officials who formulated the National Energy Program dramatically reflected the feeling in Ottawa that External represented the U.S. to Canada, not the other way around — a sentiment that did some injustice to the nationalism of the department's leadership and of its U.S. bureau. But, as William Dobell pointed out, External's lack of institutional power was the main impediment preventing it from acquiring central-agency status.

> If External Affairs obtains leadership control of, say, international commercial policy, and maintains its sway over international legal policy, its authority will have been sufficiently consolidated for it to move into the central-agency category.[3]

As if following Dobell's injunction, the government moved in 1981 to strengthen External Affairs further. In response to the crisis over FIRA and the NEP, a cabinet memorandum was circulated instructing line departments to inform External Affairs of their policies that might have some impact on the tense Canadian-American relationship. In addition to boosting External's authority as policy coordinator, a major reorganization of the government in January 1982 moved the trade division from Industry, Trade and Commerce to External Affairs. On paper this reorganization answered Dobell's criterion: it gave External mastery of the major foreign policy functions of the government by integrating the trade with the representational and policy mandates. It was as if the policy-formulating brainpower developed by Gotlieb would now have the necessary heft that came from directly commanding the commercial muscle power.

In reality, there is reason to doubt that the new super-ministry will actually develop a strategic capacity. For one thing, it will take many months, even years, for one department to absorb the other. For another, it is not clear whether External Affairs, with its current penchant to make grand strategy, will end up by dominating Trade or vice versa. It is quite possible that the trade section, with its continentalist propensity to prefer accommodation to confrontation, will become the tail wagging the External dog — a possibility made more likely by the appointment as under-secretary of state of Gordon Osbaldeston, who, as the progenitor of the government's 1981 anti-interventionist economic development policy, adheres to the prevailing view in the bureaucracy that making accommodations with American positions is preferable to articulating strategies that give priority to Canadian interests. What further obscures the outcome of the reorganization is the likelihood of conflict within the new tricephalous institution. Possibly its three ministers — the secretary of state for external affairs, the minister of international trade and the minister of state for external relations — will learn to work in harmony, but it is more likely that they will find that the bureaucratic imperatives of protecting their separate turfs will push them into conflict. There is also considerable potential for adverse consequences on the morale of those working in this super-ministry.

As it was, the changes of the late Seventies had already created a crisis of morale described by the McDougall royal commission as "mistrust, confusion, uncertainty, and real questions as to whether the objectives of the exercise — more effective use of human resources — will be achieved."[4] Diplomats had been given no clear explanation of the impact of the new senior policy-making groups on their career prospects. Senior officers had become increasingly reluctant to accept head-of-mission assignments abroad since they knew their policy input from abroad would be negligible. "This attitude percolates down through the ranks and is devastating to morale." Despite all the efforts to generate a policy-making capacity in the department, the royal commission reported that "management is failing to provide employees with any sense that the system is being run with regard to plan or logic or that it is doing any more than simply reacting to current crises instead of planning for the longer-term needs of the organization."[5] These problems of morale have largely derived from the promotion to senior positions at the assistant deputy minister level of civil servants from other departments, not of diplomats from within the ranks. The concern that, in order to rise to the top, it is better to get out at the middle may well be increased by the effort to absorb hundreds of trade officials. Noteworthy in the royal commission's extensive report on conditions of foreign service was the almost complete absence of any mention of service in the United States, apart from comments reported from certain "clients of the foreign service" who questioned "whether sufficient resources were allocated to the really important issues such as new elements in Canada-U.S. relations."[6]

Devoting adequate resources to Canada's American relationship has always been an institutional problem for the Department of External Affairs. It created a U.S. Bureau in 1977 so as better to coordinate the department's American relationship, but its importance has varied over time, declining during Don Jamieson's incumbency as minister but reviving after 1979.[7] The U.S. Bureau's coordinating goal is organizationally impeded by the functional structure of the department, which scatters the many officials who deal with the United States in specialized policy divisions. The United States may dominate 70 per cent of Canada's trade, but, in the logic of Canada's foreign service, it is but one country to be dealt with as just part of the whole international system with which External Affairs interrelates. The U.S. Bureau has but a dozen officers, fewer than the Bureau of Asian and Pacific Affairs or the Bureau of African and Middle Eastern Affairs.

The prevailing view in Ottawa is that existing institutions should be made to do the jobs they are supposed to do. There is no alternative, in the opinion of the Standing Senate Committee on Foreign Affairs, to leaving the handling of the American relationship to External Affairs.[8] It is true that the creation of new institutions necessarily produces overlaps, wrangles and a considerable period of transition difficulties. But if Canada needs to transform the way it conceives and administers its American relationship, it may still be better to risk these problems — problems that are in any case going to be experienced under the new super-ministry as it copes with its growing pains. If one of the reasons for Canada's difficulty in paying sufficient attention to its American relationship has been the priority given by the Department of External Affairs to overseas relations, one way to signal that a genuine change is being made would be to create a new institution of government solely concerned with coordinating the implementation of the country's American strategy. This could be an organization similar to the White House's Office of the United States Trade Representative or National Security Council and staffed by civil servants specializing in American affairs. These "Americanists" would pursue their normal careers by staying in this area, not switching to a posting abroad as soon as they had acquired some expertise in, for example, trans-boundary pollution, as now happens in External. This American office could take over the expanded functions of the embassy and consulates throughout the United States. Its staff would be recruited less for traditional diplomatic talents than for their more commercial, political and economic abilities to relate to businessmen, deal with interest groups and keep a vigil over economic developments. Above all it would monitor the American political process in order to develop a detailed knowledge of the complex workings of the entire United States' polity as well as a capacity to exert influence within it.

It is said by the current managers of the American relationship that the U.S. impact on Canada is so pervasive that no system is fully capable of dealing with it. Some affirm that, though the present machinery is not adequate, conceptual, not institutional, problems are the central shortcoming.[9] While one can concede that the articulation of Canada's goals and the definition of a strategy to deal with the United States remain the most basic need, enhancing the federal government's capacity to manage the future relationship in a

300

coordinated way would rapidly become of prime importance. So too would be the still more difficult problem of developing a provincial consensus supporting an American strategy.

The Provinces and American Representation

To posit an American strategy that has the agreement and support of the provinces may appear utopian to students of Canadian federalism. For many years it has been well known that some provinces have been more likely to agree with the positions of Washington than with those of Ottawa. As Kal Holsti and Thomas Levy wrote, "a number of provincial administrations seemed to be allied with those private and governmental interests in the United States that are concerned about an emerging consensus in Ottawa for at least minimal controls on continued American investment."[10] Apart from the regulation of foreign investment, there have been serious differences between individual provinces and the federal government on cable-TV, commercial deletions or the petroleum export tax, when their stand "more closely reflected U.S. positions than that of the Canadian federal government."[11] The highly antagonistic style and the bad feelings that have long typified the relations between the prime minister and the provincial premiers make it difficult to discern the potential for a federal-provincial consensus on an appropriate American strategy for Canada.

Rationalists who would prefer to see a coherent Canadian policy expressed by the federal government may well lament "the increasing proclivity of provincial administrations to deal directly with leading American firms and with the federal and state levels of government [which] does compromise the ability of the government of Canada to present a unified, rational, and domestically supported bargaining stance to the United States."[12] But Canada is a federal state with powerful provinces which have a direct interest in the conduct of Canada's foreign policy, particularly of its international economic relations. As provincial powers have expanded, the premiers have increasingly challenged the role of the federal government in articulating the collective national interest. Realizing how crucial would be the impact on their economies of the tariff decisions made during the Tokyo Round of the Multilateral Trade Negotiations, the premiers pressed for more participation in the formulation of the federal government's negotiating position. As a result of what turned out to be a positive experience in provincial-federal cooperation, Ottawa has accepted an increased involvement by the provinces in its

301

decision-making process. In 1980, in response to provincial pressure, it agreed to establish regular federal-provincial consultations on trade policy.[13]

In the decade of the Seventies provincial activity in the international sphere increased dramatically. The larger provinces opened their own quasi-diplomatic offices abroad. At home they established new bureaucratic institutions to handle their burgeoning international relationships. Outside Quebec, which allocates the lion's share of its resources for external activities to relations with France and *la francophonie*, the bulk of the provinces' international relations has been very largely centred on their neighbouring states, with whom they have undertaken informal arrangements and understandings and even signed formal agreements in specific areas of mutual interest. Provinces make agreements with their neighbours on the regulation of trans-border traffic flow and truck load limits. They deal with U.S. federal agencies and American multinational corporations, the money markets in New York, and the Securities and Exchange Commission. With Ottawa's concurrence, many have opened offices in American cities similar to consulates or trade commissions. Some want to establish political delegations in Washington, a desire that Ottawa has vigorously resisted in the name of its prerogative to present a single, national position to the United States government. The positions of Quebec, Alberta and Ontario on the question of a Washington office and Ottawa's responses to them shed some light on the potential for a federal-provincial strategic consensus towards the United States.

Quebec
Because of the Trudeau government's long campaign to deny Quebec separatists their goal of independence, Ottawa has had more conflict with Quebec than with any other province on foreign policy questions in general. When it comes specifically to American relations, resistance by Ottawa to Quebec's desire for provincial representation in Washington makes it extremely difficult to resolve the same problem for the other provinces. The original thrust of the Parti Québécois government's international efforts continued the long-term strategy of the Quebec Liberal government to affirm its cultural reality abroad by emphasizing its relations with France, the mother country, even though the economic return from a very considerable investment of resources was minimal. Premier Lévesque's own personal affinity with the Americans only had a gradual impact on Quebec's basic stance towards its foreign relations. Unlike Lévesque, the generation of civil servants and politicians in positions of authority had had little

connection with the United States, having earlier left for Europe as students who consciously rejected American cultural models in favour of rediscovering their French roots. The lack of early concern for the United States even among separatists could be seen in the absence from the Parti Québécois' original program of a policy on the United States. Only the planks that called for the withdrawal by an independent Quebec from NATO and NORAD raised, though indirectly, the question of Quebec's American relationship. Once in power, René Lévesque took the province's American policy in his own hands, going to New York to make what turned out to be a disastrous speech to the Economic Club in February 1977. Although the Ministry of Intergovernmental Affairs regained its authority over Quebec's American relations after this debacle, there is strong evidence that, because of its greater preoccupation with the francophone world, it did not develop a coherent American strategy of its own. Lise Bissonnette argues convincingly that the 1979 fiasco of Quebec's aborted attempt to establish a lobbying office in Washington demonstrated the absence of any coherent policy planning towards the United States during the late Seventies.[14]

Even if Quebec's overt objectives in the U.S. seem similar to those of the other major provinces — to foster commercial relations, encourage American investment in the economy, attract tourism and maintain a good image for the province in the capital markets — the government is understandably assumed by Ottawa to have a covert strategy complementing its goal of achieving independence. Prime in this regard is the move to win gradual acceptance in the United States for Quebec as a distinct political entity so that diplomatic recognition would be granted more quickly after the achievement of separation from Canada. The promotion of Quebec's image as an entity that governs itself without Ottawa's help and the establishment of political links with the American government take on a significance that similar efforts by another province would not have. Thus actions by Quebec in the United States that seem quite normal by provincial standards take on a sinister hue when perceived as proto-separatist activities. Quebec has dramatically increased its efforts there. For instance, its Ministry of Intergovernmental Affairs has established a U.S. Bureau as a separate department and managed to quintuple the budget for its public relations efforts in the United States from $200,000 to $1 million. By 1980, Quebec was spending $3 million on its American offices (three times what Ontario spent) and their public relations efforts. In 1981, when the more pragmatic Jacques-Yvan Morin replaced the more francophile Claude Morin as minister of intergovernmental affairs, a further shift towards emphasizing the American relationship was made.

Quebec has had some success in being taken seriously by the United States government. Because of the strategic implications of a radical and independent Quebec straddling the St. Lawrence River, the United States expanded its Quebec consulate into a quasi-embassy, appointing a senior political diplomat to the post in the same way that it had strengthened its political links with the Basque independence movement in Spain. The American consul established connections with the highest levels in the Quebec government and was instrumental in persuading the P.Q. leadership to induce the party to withdraw the offensive positions about NATO and NORAD from its policy program. All the while that President Carter and his cabinet made officially neutral but clearly pro-Canada statements, the State Department was building a sound base for its relationship with Quebec should the province become independent.

Although the American consul dissuaded the Quebec government from pursuing its idea of establishing a delegation in Washington, the issue of the province's political representation in the United States has not been settled. There is no question in the minds of senior Quebec civil servants that Ottawa fails to represent Quebec's political views in the United States. They talk of a symbiosis between Ontario and Ottawa, both in the Department of External Affairs and in Industry, Trade and Commerce. They take seriously the expressions of American hostility over the NEP and FIRA, fearing that punitive American retaliation would target Quebec as much as Ontario since Quebec is the Liberal party's federal stronghold. They are very sensitive about their inability to respond effectively to such American misapprehensions as the alarms expressed when the government announced its intention to nationalize part of the asbestos industry. Were it to have its own office in Washington, they feel, Quebec would get information much faster and would be able to respond more quickly. As it is, the political information relayed to them by Ottawa is considered close to useless. Quebec has to make do with an officer from its New York delegation travelling every week to Washington to collect intelligence and develop contacts within the American government. For Ottawa, the trick is to satisfy Quebec's legitimate needs as a province without at the same time giving ground on points of real principle that would favour eventual independence.

The province's economic interests in the United States are focused on its neighbouring regions: the states of New England, New York and Pennsylvania, where it has developed its second-largest market outside the Canadian provinces. In contrast to its elaborate industrial strategy, *Bâtir le Québec*, which boldly called for an interventionist economic program to shift Quebec industry from the soft, labour-intensive sectors to those of high technology, economic recession has forced Quebec's policies to support (with Ottawa's tariff and subsidy cooperation) whatever industries could offer jobs and to encourage whatever companies could hope to penetrate the export market.[15] Since most francophone companies are small, they are encouraged to learn the ropes of exporting first in the anglophone provinces before tackling the American market. Quebec's goals in the American economy lie principally in three areas: to encourage multinational resource firms to increase their transformation of resources (particularly asbestos and aluminum) within Quebec; to gain access for the urban transit vehicles of Bombardier in the re-equipment of American municipal transportation systems despite the Buy America barriers that have been erected in their path; and to expand the export of hydroelectricity in order to increase the cash flow of Hydro-Québec and the economic rents that the government can extract from its largest enterprise. In none of these policy thrusts is there a significant divergence between Quebec's and Ottawa's perception of the national interest. Quebec's rhetoric under both Liberal and Péquiste governments has been hostile to FIRA, but Bernard Bonin observes that "there seems to have been little disagreement in practice between Quebec and Ottawa with regard to specific applications, in spite of philosophies of policies that one painstakingly tries to show to be at odds."[16] In sum while political contradictions remain high, and unresolvable, economic commonalities characterize the Quebec-Ottawa dimension of the Canadian-American relationship.

Alberta
The province producing 85 per cent of Canada's oil and gas, one-half of its coal and one-fifth of its agricultural produce has been in conflict with Ottawa over economic and industrial policies for over a decade. It has successfully resisted Ottawa's attempt to impose export taxes on oil and gas. It has fought less successfully, but no less bitterly, against the federal government's attempt to increase its control over the energy industry. Alberta does not share the central-Canada view that foreign investment should be regulated by a review process. It believes the Americans to be its best friends and disapproves of such institutions as

FIRA which anger the country to which it sells 85 per cent of its exported products and on which it is entirely dependent for its prosperity. This said, it is surprising how congruent are the objectives of Edmonton and Ottawa. Alberta's Conservative politicians inveigh against FIRA, but they are more nationalist than Ottawa in the demands they place on foreign investors by requiring high levels of Alberta content in the projects for which foreign investors request provincial permits — so much so that the National Planning Association of Washington warns that the Canadian content requirements laid down by Alberta for projects needing permits for industrial development, oil sands, power plants and coal development will have significant consequences for U.S. construction and equipment firms.[17] Ottawa favours the further processing of raw materials within Canada as a general principle; Alberta has taken vigorous steps towards the development of a downstream petrochemical capability within the province. If it has a grievance against Ottawa in this regard it is for not managing to extract concessions from the American petrochemical industry during the Tokyo Round for a reduction of its tariff protection. During the first ten months of the National Energy Program, the conflict between Edmonton and Ottawa was so intense as to pre-empt Washington's effort to wage its own fight against the NEP. Since the Alberta-Ottawa agreement of September 1, 1981 the basic convergence of the two governments' positions has been obscured by their continued political hostility.

On the question of Alberta having its own political office in Washington, a serious confrontation does not appear to be brewing, if only because bureaucratic and political opinions in Edmonton vary on this question. The satisfaction expressed at the senior political level about a Washington office is not shared within the bureaucracy of the Alberta government. The problem seen from the cabinet table is not in the quality of Canada's representation in Washington; it is a disagreement over federal policies. A full-time office is not considered necessary. The premier gets good support from the Canadian embassy when he travels to the United States where, for his part, he is careful not to raise issues of federal-provincial conflict. For individual requirements, Alberta will send a team of experts to have meetings, for instance, with the Federal Energy Regulatory Commission.

Officers in FIGA, the Federal and Intergovernmental Affairs Department, consider they should have their own office in the American capital. They have five international offices — in London, Tokyo, Hong Kong, Los Angeles and Houston — which send back reports to Edmonton relevant to Alberta's concerns, but of all foreign cities, Washington makes the most decisions that directly affect Alberta's well-being. We need someone on the spot to tell us what is happening, FIGA officers say. They maintain it is inadequate to have the Canadian ambassador brief the cabinet once or twice a year, and it is simply unrealistic for the embassy to offer blithely to find out whatever the provinces want to know. For one thing, the embassy is too understaffed to be able to satisfy the provinces' needs. For another, the process of formulating questions and sending them to Washington cannot take the place of having Albertan officials on the spot whose job is to interpret and respond to American events with the interests of their province constantly at heart.

Like provincial officials in all provinces, Albertans complain that the information flow External Affairs provides is terrible. As an example, the author was doing his research in FIGA on September 29. On the previous day it had received from the Department of External Affairs a package of communications the most recent of which was dated August 28. It included a report on a congressional committee meeting of July 16 on which FIGA had been fully informed through independent channels on July 19, ten weeks earlier. Apart from the delays, the information provided to the provincial governments is inadequate because it is uneven: most of the communication between Ottawa and the embassy takes place over the telephone, and External Affairs officers do not feel it their business to write summaries of the phone traffic for their provincial confrères. As a result, the provinces hear about meetings and events that have occurred, but seldom get advance notice of what is going to happen — which they might like to do something about. Even the distribution of telegrams is inadequate: messages received in Ottawa from Washington are circulated more often than the ones that Ottawa sends Washington. The provinces tend to get reports on Canadian-American meetings held in Washington, but not of similar meetings of officials held in Ottawa. Even crucial Canadian-American documents are not communicated as a matter of course. (Queen's Park learned about the Gotlieb letter to William Brock of December 16, 1981 by reading a report on it in the *Financial Post*.) With so many more contacts than Edmonton has to watch over, Toronto is even more concerned about its problem of inadequate representation in Washington.

Ontario
Although Ontario is seen to have the most cooperative relationship with External Affairs, the province has gone further along the road to

307

separate representation in the U.S. than any other. Canada's industrial heartland, which nurtures over 50 per cent of the country's manufacturing capacity, is seriously threatened by the international process of trade liberalization which exposes its high-cost industries to competition from the newly industrialized countries, by the growth of American non-tariff barriers which keeps its high technology pioneers out of the large American market, by the escalation of energy costs, by the erosion of the Canadian common market, and by the problem of wage increases outpacing productivity gains. Although it has embarked on its own protectionist policies, its own industrial incentive programs, and its own export-promotion schemes, it is frustrated by what it sees as Ottawa's insufficient defence of Canadian interests in the United States. It feels that the federal government has not pressed vigorously enough to forestall the disastrous decline of the automotive industry and has not been able to gain adequate offsets through the Defence Production Sharing Arrangements for the new generation of American military equipment that the Canadian armed forces are purchasing. The embassy is not felt to grasp the complexities of American politics; the ambassador's occasional briefings of the Ontario cabinet have been considered condescending rather than adequate. In short, Ontario feels badly represented in the United States by External Affairs.

Its dissatisfaction is related to the complex agenda it has for its American relations. Ontario wants to maintain a competitive fiscal and regulatory environment, while offsetting the American states' aid to the automobile and other industries that compete with Ontario's manufacturing. At the same time, it fears the pressures that are pushing its branch plant economy towards a still more vulnerable warehouse economy, so it is urging subsidiaries of foreign-controlled multinationals to take on world product mandates and become internationally competitive. It is mindful of the balance that needs to be kept so that pressing the Americans on industrial issues will not jeopardize the positive relationship that exists in tourism. At the same time, it wants Ottawa to act strongly against the protectionism of the Surface Transportation Assistance Act and the state-level Buy America legislation which threatens the export of Canadian steel. The province maintains extensive contacts with its neighbouring states with whose governors Premier Davis has established generally warm personal relations.

However good its relations may be at the state level, there is continual pressure from Queen's Park to have a direct presence in

308

Washington. It was in 1971 that Premier Davis first announced that Ontario would open its own office in Washington. This elicited a quick protest from Mitchell Sharp, then secretary of state for external affairs. Ontario would be setting a precedent with dangerous implications for Quebec separatism. External offered a compromise: space in its embassy for an Ontario official, an offer that was later withdrawn. Finally it was agreed that the ambassador would brief the Ontario cabinet periodically, that the embassy would establish a provincial liaison officer in Washington, and that material would be circulated from External Affairs to the province. Unsatisfactory though this compromise turned out to be, no change occurred in this situation until the autumn of 1981 when External Affairs agreed to take on loan an officer, David Trick, from the Ministry of Intergovernmental Affairs to work in the Canadian embassy for a six-week period. It is significant that this step was taken in a field in which there was close cooperation, if not actual integration, between the positions of the Ontario and the federal government: environmental policy. The experience was so successful that it was repeated again early in 1982 and was followed by the loan of a staff lawyer from Manitoba's attorney-general department to help monitor the politics of the Garrison Diversion Unit. The experiment does indicate that the extension of provincial representation in Washington may result more from a convergence than a conflict of interests between Ottawa and the provinces.

There is some apprehension in Queen's Park that, were it to open its own office, the results might be counterproductive. The embassy would protect its own sources and resist the province's access to them. Washington officials might resent being canvassed over lunch or drinks for information from several sets of Canadian officials rather than one. Where the federal and provincial governments disagreed, the provincial presence in Washington would give the American government a direct opportunity to play off one against the other, to the detriment of both. The pursuit of a program of loaning provincial officials to the embassy offers the hope that, at least where provincial and federal policies coincide, a more fruitful collaboration and learning would transcend the alienation that has marked so much of the federal-provincial relationship concerning the United States. This would strengthen the lines of communication between the embassy and the provinces and avoid the expense and duplication of opening provincial offices in Washington. Were this cooperation to prove fruitful in the long term, it might help develop the confidence — first among bureaucrats and thena mong politicians — that is the necessary prerequisite for the emergency of a federal-provincial consensus on an American strategy for Canada. This consensus could include Quebec oince Ottawa had overcome its suspicions of Quebec's real goals and once Quebec was willing to accept officially its participation in confederation for the foreseeable future. Certainly the idea of an American strategy would not be anathema to provincial thinking. At their annual conference in 1977, the provincial premiers stated their view that, given "the large volume of Canadian trade with the United States . . . it is entirely appropriate for the provinces to assume a more prominent role in Canada-United States relations."[18] In 1981 they "called on the federal government to work with the provinces to develop an economic strategy for Canada and to resolve the crisis in confidence which has beset the country."[19] The federal-provincial relationship is a bargaining process. While it would be extremely difficult to achieve eleven-party agreement to a particular document, federal-provincial collaboration and consensus on separate, sectoral issues is entirely within the realm of the possible.

Qualms in the Private Sector

The problems involved in formulating and implementing a concerted American strategy are not confined to achieving horizontal coherence between departments in the federal government or vertical coordination between the federal and provincial levels. What is also required for a national consensus is an even more demanding prerequisite, the participation of business, the media, labour and the political parties.

The prospect is improbable in Canada. In Japan a close coordination between business and government lies at the heart of that country's dazzling economic performance. Even in the United States, the heartland of free enterprise, business expects strong support for its interests from the political system and gives strong support in return. By contrast, the business community in Canada has been hostile towards the federal government for a quarter of a century, ever since its champion, C. D. Howe, left politics. If confidence is the touchstone of business performance, then the basic requirement for business support of a provincially-accepted and federally-led strategy is missing. This is not just because of the power of the American branch plants in the Canadian economy. While it is true that Canadian business generally echoes the American business critique of Canadian government intervention (even though American business does not oppose U.S.-style government intervention in the economy in such forms as massive space research programs and colossal defence expenditures), it is also true that the small and medium business sectors are extremely hostile to the federal government because of its policies, including nationalist ones like the NEP. This hostility is frightening according to members of business research organizations who consider that, in a confrontation between Ottawa and Washington, business would not support the federal government but would tend to endorse the American position.

The responses of business to national issues in Canada illustrate how Canada's American relationship is not wholly external in character. The American view becomes internalized in Canada through the multinational corporations and the companies whose continental interests parallel those of the multinationals, and by intellectuals, particularly economists, trained in the free-market paradigms whose policy applications further the interests of multinational enterprise. The interlocking elites of the Canadian and American corporate worlds develop complex networks that mobilize the bias of their organizations so rapidly and effectively that it becomes impossible to tell whether a particular business person's view is American or Canadian. At the October 13, 1981 meeting of top-level officials held in the American ambassador's residence in Ottawa one of the proposals made by Secretary of the Treasury Donald Regan to counter the back-in of the NEP had actually come from the Canadian businessman Jack Gallagher, chairman of Dome Petroleum. According to the minutes of the meeting, "Regan raised issue of 'slide-in' rather than back-in as suggested by Gallagher of Dome in July and passed out copies of Gallagher letter."[20]

Professional observers of the business community in Canada like to distinguish between the alarmist pack thinking of business people who mouth a completely unreal view about the virtues of unhampered free enterprise and the more balanced view of the better informed executives who recognize the reality of Canada's mixed economy and see how it can be made to work for them. Cabinet ministers who deal with business talk of the ignorance of even chief executive officers of important companies and maintain that they have no intelligent understanding of government in Canada. Business lawyers talk of the bad mood throughout the community — the worry, the anger, the discouragement, the visceral hatred directed at the prime minister who is scapegoated for their problems of mounting debt or falling cash flow. Major Canadian corporations are concerned lest their prospects for penetrating the American market be blocked by Washington's "reciprocity" measures that retaliate against their U.S. operations because of some Canadian legislation. Branch plant managers wonder whether they will be excluded from government procurement contracts under a more nationally conscious energy dispensation. Small and medium businesses struggle to stay afloat in an economic environment whose high interest rates they blame on Ottawa rather than on Washington. They also accuse Ottawa, not Washington, of causing the bad atmosphere of the Canadian-American relationship which damages business confidence and discourages them from taking risks in the Canadian economy. It would, in other words, be an enormous task to bridge the two solitudes of business and government with a level of understanding and a way of communication that could renationalize the consciousness of the nation's largely denationalized elite — the managers, the bankers, the lawyers, the underwriters whose interests are biased towards the source of their income, the continental market, and who have in past decades shown little recognition of the value for them of a viable Canadian economy. The challenge would be to show them how their interests would be served by establishing a more self-sustaining Canadian economy in which branch plant and medium business, Canadian multinational and small business could find a valid place.

In June 1982, Premier Peter Lougheed said "Perhaps we have reached a stage in Canada where it is possible to . . . develop a new spirit of cooperation and mutual trust — and I emphasize the word TRUST — between business and government."[21] The prospect of building trust may be less unlikely than it first appears because a generational change is occurring within the ranks of Canadian big businessmen, some of whom, like Conrad Black and Bob Blair, while continental in the scope of their corporate activities, are nationalist in their approach. As opinion leaders within their own elite, their views may gradually have a multiplier effect throughout the corporate world. Many of the big corporations in banking, in steel, in transportation, in petrochemicals, in high technology are becoming stronger — the recession notwithstanding — and their executives are expressing a commensurately increased self-confidence. Many branch plant managers know that their future depends on developing a mandated Canadian specialization, without which their functions risk being taken over by computer-directed staff at their multinationals' head offices. Small and medium business, which is the locus for the development of new technology and the major source of new employment, is being educated by such lobby organizations as the Canadian Federation of Independent Business to see the value of a closer relationship with

312

government. The step from dropping the hallowed scapegoat of government-as-source-of-all-evil to envisaging a concerted stance towards economic development in general and the American market in particular is not large.

To be taken, this step would need to be supported by the institutions that form and communicate both mass and elite opinion. There is no assurance that the media would respond any more positively to the notion of an American strategy for Canada than would business. Although Canadian publishers and media corporations have been major beneficiaries of a variety of policies to protect them against American competition and provide sheltered markets to assure their prosperity, an important change has taken place in their business operations which makes it less likely that they would support a national strategy in the future. Over the past decade or two a process of expansion abroad — particularly into the American market — has turned formerly national (and nationalist) companies into multinational corporations with a strong interest in not ruffling the feathers of the American eagle. Maclean Hunter, the diversified publishing and broadcasting company that once strongly supported the preservation of the Canadian periodical industry against the inflows of American magazines, now has more net assets employed in its foreign business operations, largely in the United States, than it has in Canada. Torstar Corporation, the owner of the editorially nationalist *Toronto Star*, has now acquired significant American holdings through its takeover of Harlequin Enterprises. In 1980, Torstar's non-Canadian operations accounted for 51 per cent of total operating revenue, 73 per cent of operating profit and 48 per cent of identifiable assets. The newspaper chain that owns the *Globe and Mail*, Thomson Newspapers Ltd., had American operations in 1980 that accounted for 61 per cent of its operating income and 57 per cent of its total assets.[22] As these continental interests grow, it is reasonable to expect that corporate pressure on the editorial bias of the private media will be decreasingly supportive of a strategy for national regeneration.

The public broadcasting system would not experience the same pressures to oppose a new national strategy. On the contrary, its programmers and reporters would be likely to support an approach which had its roots in the thinking of the Aird Report. In any case, private sector editorial hostility does not doom a cause, as numerous election campaigns have proven. Furthermore, editorial bias is not generally consistent across all issues. The *Globe and Mail*, which Canadians on the political left consider anti-nationalist because of its hostility to FIRA, is seen in the State Department to be dangerously nationalist because of its attacks on the United States for not waging the war on trans-boundary pollution with greater vigour.

While the role of the media in forming opinion cannot be ignored, the development of a consensus to support an American strategy would be affected by other institutions as well. The great antipathy felt by organized labour towards both business and government would offer a formidable obstacle to the process. It is not just the American-controlled industrial unions which would find it hard to accept a strategy that might include their evolution towards complete autonomy from their U.S. parent bodies. The Canadian unions, which tend to be the more radical in their approach towards management, would be suspicious of any strategy whose economic component would probably comprise a rescue operation premised on the mobilization of national savings for investment at the cost of consumption and perhaps lowered welfare in the short term.

Set against this institutional psychosis of distrust is a complicating factor — the declining popularity of big labour which the opinion analyst, Michael Adams, considers to be at a postwar low. There are two implications of the unions' loss of public support. On the one hand, the potential hostility of union leadership to a proposed American strategy that had government and business support would carry less weight than ever. On the other hand, union executives wanting to revive their popularity might consider that their support of a new national strategy would be good politics, given the greater nationalism reported in public opinion polling.[23]

The extent to which public opinion could be mobilized for an American strategy would depend more on the actions of leading federal and provincial politicians than on either organized labour or other organized groups of citizens. In a parliamentary system with highly disciplined parties, there are minimal opportunities for effective citizen participation. The political outcome would hang less on the views of the grass roots than on the decisions of the major party leaders. At the provincial level of politics it would appear that an American strategy which recognized the provinces' regional development needs would be acceptable. After all, the pattern in the Seventies has been for provincial governments of all ideological hues to be more nationalist than the federal government. In federal politics the NDP's left-nationalist support would likely be qualified only by the need of the opposition party to criticize whatever the government proposes. While the Liberal cabinet has strong anti-nationalist spokesmen within its

314

present ranks, its future direction could just as easily become more nationalist if it takes its advice from Jim Coutts,[24] as it could be more continentalist under the leadership of John Turner.

A Progressive Conservative government would not necessarily reject a strategic approach to its American relations. It is true that Joe Clark, John Crosbie and Flora MacDonald went out of their way to denounce the Liberals' handling of the American relationship, blaming the 1981 crisis on Trudeau's personal actions, Liberal economic mismanagement and the NEP.[25] Still it is unlikely that the Progressive Conservatives would be able to dismantle the National Energy Program any more easily than they were able to privatize Petro-Canada in 1979. By 1984 the petroleum industry will have adjusted to the NEP's whole system of grants and permits and will have little taste for a further round of policy confusion and uncertainty. In the face of a catastrophically worsening economic scene, the necessity for a more careful exploitation of the country's limited assets through more comprehensive planning and coordination will force both bureaucrats and politicians of whatever party is in power to move towards the definition of a strategic approach to government policy. How the American system would react to Canada's adoption of a strategic approach to its American relationship would be another unknown in the equation.

American Responses to a Canadian Strategy

Canadian commentators have observed with understandable apprehension that, since Nixonomics in 1971, the United States has dealt with Canada not as a special relation but as one of its normal foreign relationships. Rather than letting its Canadian relationship fall between the stools of domestic and foreign policy, the United States has been developing demanding codes of global investment and trade policy which it applies to all its international partners. If there is any lingering "special" attitude in its treatment of Canada, it is to expect its northern neighbour not to be exempted but to be more exemplary in adhering to these norms. It is as if the United States has discovered over the past decade how important Canada actually is in the achievement of its global objectives. Because Canadian behaviour, it is thought, will significantly affect the success of the U.S. strategy for trade liberalization, for a GATT for services, for an international investment code, Canada's policies matter increasingly to Washington. One can view this development with legitimate apprehension because its consequence could very well be Washington's embarkation on a course of constantly threatening retaliation if Ottawa continues to diverge from American preferences.

This study has documented the Reagan administration's ideological response to the single initiative of the National Energy Program, the self-righteousness that felt justified in punishing Canada for violating the precepts of free-market economics, and the double standard that disregarded the trade-distorting protectionism of its own investment, trade and foreign policies. Owing to Canada's geographical proximity, its linguistic accessibility, its cultural similarity, the temptation is very great for the United States to continue to demand higher standards of "national treatment" from Canada than the United States accepts in Mexico, Japan and the European Community, or practises itself. The possibility cannot be denied that any corporate interests even potentially injured by the prospect of Canada's American strategy might try to stir up another but more hysterical alarm about the "Cuba to the North," based on this moral absolutism. It should, indeed, be assumed that any effective policies designed to implement a strategy to make Canada viable by the end of the century would impinge on certain American interests that would be bound to protest on the grounds of discrimination, retroactivity or interference with the tenets of free enterprise. Resistance to these policies by American lobbyists both inside Canada and in Washington should be expected. Multinational corporations are among the staunchest defenders of the status quo in all areas of policy, so the most dogged resistance to any change is likely to come from American interests in Canada. If they followed the precedent of their reaction to the NEP, they would flex their political muscle in Washington so as to maximize their impact on Canada. And they would do this by turning up the volume of their free-market moralism in order to arouse the retaliatory responses of the American political system.

It is not chiselled in stone that the United States must necessarily respond in such a narrowly self-interested way. Indeed, a diametrically opposite response to Canada can be justified by the very same circumstances. In an era of American military and economic decline, the United States is sufficiently weakened that it is now forced to listen to its allies, since it can no longer impose on them its preferred solutions to world problems, whether these be in Namibia or the Caribbean, NATO or the Middle East. A realistic American appraisal of its international requirements would recognize that the U.S. needs Canada's survival as a viable state and an active collaborator in redefining the international order that it can no longer effectively control alone. There is a value to the U.S. in Canada's being able to pull its weight in the world at economic summits or in the North-South dialogue. For symbolic reasons too, Washington needs good relations with Canada as an indication that it can get on with its allies. In this sense, America cannot afford not to get on well with its continental partner. The Americans do not benefit from gratuitous trouble with Canada. They are continually beleaguered in the world, accused of exploitation in the Third World, of provocation in Central America, of brinkmanship in Europe. In the light of the pressures that Washington faces in relating to its international partners on such issues as sharing the telecommunications spectrum and working out codes for the performance of multinational corporations, it is quite possible for the Canadian-American relationship to be presented to American leaders as a chance, in the words of the Canadian-American Committee, "to pioneer on a bilateral basis some of the processes that must soon be used multilaterally to deal effectively with the new problems already arising as other countries respond to their economic challenges."[26] This does not mean that Canada should let itself be used for American purposes rather than its own, but if Canada were perceived as the United States' distant early warning system, it could become a country to be lived with, not made an example of or bullied. Finding a modus operandi with an ally that was articulating interests somewhat different from those of the United States could become an act not of magnanimity but of the broad self-interest of a superpower that has to learn to deal with states in both the industrialized and the developing worlds that are considerably more nationalist than Canada.

For the United States to take the broad rather than the narrow view of its best interest in Canada would require a change in awareness among the influential leaders in the American business, political and intellectual elites among whom Canada is largely ignored. This influential public needs to be educated about Canada's right to exist as a different country with values that are not necessarily those of the United States, its right to make its own rules and create its own solutions to its own problems, its right to intervene in its own affairs without Washington's prior consent being sought or given, its right to have access to its own markets. Informed Americans need to have an awareness of how Canada suffers the environmental devastation resulting from policies it has no share in making. They need to be impressed with the service that Canada has given the United States in the past by its prior engagement in both world wars. These opinion leaders also need to be informed of the excesses of official American

317

representations in demanding standards of Canada that the U.S. does not abide by itself. They need to know how asymmetrical is the American-Canadian relationship as far as its economic and cultural costs and benefits are concerned. A full picture of what true reciprocity would look like if there were really equitable balances between the two countries in such items as their share of skilled jobs generated by resource extraction or the amount of governmental subsidization of R & D, would help correct notions that Canada somehow is getting a free ride in the continental economy.

The re-education of American elites is not going to happen spontaneously. A component of a thorough American strategy would have to include a truly massive effort at public relations, since the onus would be on Canada to get its position across to its neighbour. The American media need the soberly documented evidence that Canadian institutional controls on foreign investment are not so different in result from American judicial restraints on foreign corporate activities, that the interference by Canada with the market differs little in effect from American protectionism of the Buy America variety.

It would be important for Canadians to convince American opinion that, as landlords, they have the right to change the conditions of the lease. Canada would have to make it clear in the United States that its aims were not to cut back the volume of economic intercourse between the countries but to alter its components, not to discriminate vengefully against U.S. capital but to alter its form, not to hurt American interests but to respond to Canada's own urgent needs. Presuming the existence of basic goodwill on both sides, American counterparts would be more likely to react in a conciliatory way if the program for Canadian viability was seen as a comprehensive and realistic strategy without "socialistic" or anti-American overtones. Canada's position would be received, if not with joy, at least with respect, particularly if Americans knew that its strategy had achieved broad support from both the Canadian public and Canadian elites.

The effective communication to Americans of a serious Canadian strategy towards the United States would probably require an effort some hundred times greater than what is now expended by the Department of External Affairs in the United States. Figures produced for the Standing Senate Committee on Foreign Affairs indicate that Canada spends $.10 per capita on information programs in the United States, or one dollar for every $18,000 of bilateral trade. This compares with the European expenditure of $.63 per capita or one dollar for every $200 of bilateral trade — differences in the magnitude

318

of six times and ninety times. The committee observed, "there is widespread unawareness, disinterest and misunderstanding of Canadian viewpoints and policies in the United States. *Much* more needs to be done by Canada to combat this."[27] It may be indicative of the priorities attached to public relations by the U.S. Bureau of External Affairs that it is unable to provide an update on the Senate's figures, which were published in 1974. As one senior mandarin put it, Canada needs to make a massive effort on U.S. public opinion, doing a professional job to sensitize Americans to the validity of Canada's positions.

A professional job might mean having government offices in one hundred and fifty American cities, not fifteen, with officers able to impinge on the political process at the level of interest groups and opinion leaders throughout American society. Perhaps this would mean splitting the budget of External Affairs into two more equal portions, one devoted to the United States, the other to the rest of the world. Perhaps it would require that the government find new funds for this purpose. However it is done, the gaping imbalance between the resources devoted to Canada's most important foreign relationship and the resources devoted to all Canada's other foreign relations cries out for correction. Perhaps the prime minister and the cabinet should more frequently visit Washington and New York to convey the essence of Canadian policy directly to the American public. What is certain is that in the last major crisis the NEP flew completely out of hand as an issue in the United States. The hysterical distortions were not scotched in time and led to a largely unnecessary worsening of the bilateral relationship.

It is Canada's obligation to inform its neighbour about actions or policies that affect American interests. Were Canada to adopt a more comprehensive strategy towards the United States, the role of communicating its aims and programs would be crucial to the strategy's success. If it were met with the same misinformed, anti-Canadian editorial opinion as greeted the NEP, it would trigger the same pressure for retaliation which gives Canadian mandarins nightmares. Such an irrational response would be a signal that Canada had failed to mobilize its potential support throughout the American political system and to communicate its point of view. Canada is the United States' biggest foreign customer. It follows that there are significant interests from California to Florida, from Oregon to Maine whose profit margins and prosperity depend on the Canadian market. These are latent allies whose support for good relations with Canada

319

could be activated were Canada's diplomatic machinery operating effectively in the United States. They could be the most receptive audience to the message of Canada's America strategy: it is in the best interests of the United States for Canada to survive as an independent nation. This view was expressed to the Canadian parliament by no less a personage than President Nixon in the form of three principles:

- each nation must define the nature of its own interests;
- each nation must decide the requirements of its own security;
- each nation must determine the path of its own progress.[28]

The Nixon Doctrine was not wildly utopian. As the American Canada-watcher, John Sloan Dickey, observed, it is highly unlikely that Canada could hold together as a nation, if it became merely a client-state of the U.S. This would have serious consequences for the United States. On the other hand,

> A confident, independent Canada may not be the dominant, certainly it is not the only United States interest, but it assuredly is the keystone of all other United States national interests in the Canada-U.S. relationship.[29]

This is a message which a more self-confident business community could also transmit to its continental colleagues. The informal network provided by the continental corporate interlocks could be used in reverse to transmit Canada's strategic message to American boardrooms. Even the branch plants could be brought into service to send back to head office the word from Canada about its national intentions.

A successful effort to reframe the vision of Canada held by the relevant American elites would not prevent conflict. It would only help improve the atmosphere for the resolution of conflicts and the choice of American courses of action. What would still be needed would be adequate mechanisms for dealing with disputes arising from the collision of specific diverging interests.

Dealing with the United States
The ways and means through which Canadians and Americans have negotiated and resolved problems are striking both for their variety and their impermanence. Summit meetings between the president and the prime minister are a highly visible and important institution whose utility can be deceptive. When personal relations were good, as they were between President Carter and Prime Ministers Trudeau and Clark, the Canadian-American relationship was mistakenly thought to be in good health, even though Congress was becoming intransigently

320

protectionist. Canada is low on any American president's agenda. Little should be expected from these largely ceremonial meetings except the cultivation of goodwill in the Oval Office. If there is a desire at the top for accommodation, this can help other negotiations. Lesser officials in the administration get the signal to cooperate rather than obstruct their Canadian counterparts.

Another largely formal exchange takes place through the interparliamentary meetings of congressmen and members of parliament. While no decisions are made and no commitments given, considerable learning can take place on either side about each neighbour's different objectives and constraints. Regular, formal meetings of both countries' cabinet ministers have been attempted, but proved too unwieldy to be of value. Joint ministerial meetings have not taken place since 1970. Continuing committees of officials have also been established and, in the case of the Permanent Joint Board of Defence, have survived for decades, providing useful forums for exchanging views, if not for making actual decisions. Most attractive to observers has been the one supranational institution, the International Joint Commission, which has managed to regulate the highly contentious issues in water management generated by the common boundary throughout the twentieth century. The IJC model has not proven to be contagious. Neither the Canadian nor the American government has been willing to give up further amounts of sovereignty to a joint organization that can make decisions removed from the political arena.[30] Direct, though non-institutionalized, bureaucratic relations between regulatory bodies or line departments account for the bulk of the bilateral intergovernmental relationships, especially when these are untroubled by crises or political incident. If a new American department or the old External Affairs became a true central agency in charge of the American relationship, the regulatory agencies and line departments would necessarily continue to look after the nuts and bolts relations between the two countries within their own spheres of responsibility.

Some emerging issues of sufficient importance may best be handled by setting up ad hoc teams devoted to the one problem. The role of Mitchell Sharp as Northern Pipeline Commissioner, acting as the single interlocutor representing Canada to the United States on the Alaska Natural Gas Transportation System, appears to have been a successful precedent for other single issues that require special monitoring and management, but the debacle over the fisheries and maritime boundaries negotiations will make both governments hesitate before appointing special representatives to handle thorny issues without adequate political support.

Those commentators on the Canadian-American relationship who agree that the level of conflict between the two countries will remain high suggest further mechanisms will be required to keep these tensions under manageable control. The Canadian-American Committee has recommended that a small but permanent early-warning system be established in each capital, which could alert the other government to the potential ill effects that could result for the other from unilateral actions being planned. It would provide a focal point to mobilize the necessary personnel who could provide a consulting process to conciliate the opposing views and develop alternative proposals that could meet the objectives of the one side while causing less injury to the other.[31] In effect, this notion is an institutional proposal to revive the prior consultation that was commonplace in earlier, less antagonistic times. It does not come to grips with the reality that when a major program such as Nixonomics or the NEP is being prepared in secret, advance consultation is, by the nature of the process, not possible. Harald Malmgren and Marie-Josée Drouin have proposed that the process of dealing with bilateral economic problems be formalized in a joint trade commission that would have as its task the management of the differences between the two countries. The formal framework, they maintain, would force a desirable degree of specialization in the two capitals and "help educate a new generation of political and economic experts to replace the old hands who managed the relationship successfully from the 1940s to the 1960s."[32] Attractive though such a formal institutionalization of the relationship may seem, it would appear to fly in the face of the evolving reality — the increasing politicization of economic issues between the two countries as Congress, the American states, and interest groups become directly involved on the American side of the border. The political mood favours Congress's appropriating more policy-making, investigating and adjudicating power, not devolving its power to a supra-national, supra-political institution.

If the trend is towards greater politicization of the relationship, a more effective, if less conventional, innovation could be a transformation of the nature of Canada's ambassador to the United States. Tradition and the career imperatives of a professional foreign office have made the ambassador of Canada in Washington a senior diplomat. There is a good case to be made to have that post filled by a senior politician holding cabinet rank in the Canadian government. As a general rule, Washington holds foreign ambassadors in low regard, knowing that they are but communications links between one government and the other and understanding that their propensity is to downplay elements of conflict in order to preserve the appearance of good relations. As a result, when the White House has serious, rather than routine, business to conduct with a foreign government, it sends a representative to its capital to deal directly. The frequent meetings between American and Canadian cabinet ministers during 1981 over the NEP and FIRA demonstrated how readily the embassy and the ambassador were bypassed when problems become important in Washington. One exception to this rule in Washington is the Soviet ambassador whose formal role on the Central Committee of the Communist Party of the Soviet Union gives him credibility as a plenipotentiary of the USSR. When dealing with the Soviet ambassador the Americans know they are dealing not with an intermediary but a decision maker. A strong member of the cabinet or a recently retired minister with the appropriate political personality — an outgoing manner, an authoritative demeanour, an ability to relate "one on one" with American politicians — would give the Canadian voice in Washington an authority it cannot have from a career diplomat. A Flora MacDonald or a Donald Macdonald, a John Turner or a John Crosbie would be able to carry out Canada's American strategy presenting Ottawa's position loud and clear to the White House, to Congress and to the American media. Participating in the weekly cabinet meeting in Ottawa, she or he would bring to the Priorities and Planning Committee an immediate connection with the Washington scene that no External Affairs memorandum could equal. On returning to Washington, he or she would be able to bring the views of the Canadian government directly to whatever trouble spot had to be confronted, short-circuiting the diplomatic channels whose delays and hesitations can account for a good deal of the misunderstandings of Canadian actions that spread so quickly around the corridors of the Capitol.

One unexpressed premise of these proposals for further mechanisms to manage the Canadian-American relationship is that the pretence that issues should not be linked will have to be abandoned. While it will always remain preferable to deal with each issue directly and on its own merits, observers and practitioners alike clearly feel that Canada's management of its American relationship needs to be more coherent and comprehensive. Given the many different and independent institutions involved on the American side, it is often difficult to link issues even when linkage is desirable. It will, for instance, be difficult for Quebec to use its proposed long-term sale of hydroelectricity to the eastern United States in order to gain exemptions from the Surface Transportation Assistance Act so that Bombardier can export its light rapid transit vehicles to American municipalities without first having to export its jobs by setting up U.S. branch plants. The quid would be a reasonable exchange for the quo, but the public-utility corporations have no direct connection with Congress which passed the damaging legislation.

The reluctance to link issues on the Canadian side is more prudential than institutional: the fear is constantly expressed that, in a straight power struggle with the United States on a particular issue, Canada will lose. The academic literature provides ample justification for this fear. Hugh Aitken argued twenty years ago that, when it comes to bargaining, Canada has only been successful when it has had a physical advantage in its superior supply of lumber or energy. Because Canada has few means of retaliating effectively against the United States, it must always prove that a policy it wants is actually in the interests of the United States.[33] In a confrontation, the United States enjoys considerable invulnerability: a rich and diversified economy with a lot to lose can afford to lose a little.

The fear of retaliation lurks below the surface of Ottawa's political discourse. A less frantic view of the relative strengths of the two governments in dealing with each other would not yield as fearful a view as the conventional wisdom would have it. While it is true that the United States is a far more powerful country, it is also true that the United States government has to pay attention to myriad world concerns and devote its best people and its major resources to those problems. Conversely, while it is true that Canada is much weaker than its neighbour, it is also true that it can concentrate its major attention on the American relationship, recruit its best people to handle these issues, and develop an expertise which their American counterparts can rarely equal. So while it may be prudent for both sides to resist linking issues in order to simplify the resolution of individual differences, it should be an integral part of Canada's American strategy that issues would be linked at the higher levels of political interaction even though the political costs within the country would be high: Alberta would be loath to lose, say, a gas export opportunity because Ottawa and Quebec were insisting that Bombardier be exempted from the Surface Transportation Assistance Act. In any case, it is now necessary to be prepared for the retaliation promised by "reciprocity," so as to inform American politicians and administrators of the costs that Canada would impose on American interests in response to U.S.

retaliation against Canada. For Canadian support of American foreign policy on Iran, on Africa, on the Middle East, Canada has exacted very little in political returns. A more powerful American-centred department, implementing a more comprehensive strategy with more effective representation throughout the U.S. political system should be able to deal centrally with issues, making trade-offs between one area and another in exploring settlements. If access to Quebec's hydro power cannot be traded for changes in the Surface Transportation Assistance Act, then perhaps it can be used to gain a reduction in the American tariff on petrochemicals. To raise the question of making deals with the American government involving changes in legislation is to open the dossier of dealing with Congress, a particularly weak Canadian suit.

The Department of External Affairs has traditionally dealt with the American government only through the formal channels offered by the Department of State on the convenient if untenable assumption that the United States had a unitary form of government. It is even dangerous to assume that the State Department can negotiate on behalf of a unitary form of executive. In fact the U.S. administration is divided into many quasi-autonomous departments with separate, and often overlapping and competing, responsibilities. Just in basic economic matters of interest to Canada, the Department of Defense controls the working of the Defence Production Sharing Arrangements, the Commerce Department administers claims about countervailing duties and unfair trade practices, the Treasury Department is in charge of inward foreign investment, the Office of the U.S. Trade Representative controls relations with GATT, while the State Department has jurisdiction over matters at the OECD. An effective embassy must be skilled at dealing separately and together not just with these departments but also with the many regulatory commissions dependent both on the executive and on Congress.

Dealing with Congress raises problems of far greater complexity with which Canada has only had experience in recent years. Following pressures from the Prime Minister's Office during the Seventies, after the reprimand from the Senate that it had neglected Congress too long,[34] and under the advice of Peter Dobell,[35] the Canadian embassy in Washington has responded to the new reality in American politics — the shift in foreign policy-making power from the administration to the economic committees of Congress. Given its limited resources of personnel and funds, the embassy is probably doing all it can in coping with a virtually impossible assignment: monitoring the enormously complex legislative process and trying to divert damaging legislative initiatives before they become entrenched as law. It is argued that there are limits to the embassy's effectiveness in lobbying Congress: sleeping dogs should be left to lie; too much activity can remind the Americans of other differences and engender retaliation that might not otherwise have taken place; lobbying for support on an issue opposed by the administration can be resented by the White House as intervention in American political affairs or providing ammunition for its political enemies. Calculations clearly have to be made in each case about the value of gaining some friends as against the danger of aggravating some enemies, but arguments that emphasize the adequacy of present Canadian effectiveness need to be treated with scepticism. If Canada's lobbying power is sufficient, why did the National Energy Program generate so much misunderstanding on the part of its opponents whose arguments were not countered before they became the accepted truth on Capitol Hill?

While it may be granted that there are limits to the amount of energy that should be spent directly on Congress, it does not follow that Canada's present lobbying capacities are adequate to its needs. After Israel's air strike at Iraq's nuclear plant, the Israeli lobby mobilized and turned around American opinion within a matter of hours. Japan hires professionals who are able to bring to bear on Washington the full weight of the many interests such as car dealers or electronics retailers who benefit from good American-Japanese relations. With many new issues appearing unexpectedly each day in the United States, Canada needs first-class, front-line representation by officials who are able to deal with a whole array of different institutions. On each issue, such as the Bombardier/Budd case, the relevant set of players has to be singled out, a strategy has to be designed and then coordinated, negotiations have to be undertaken to establish what trade-offs are possible and desirable. Much of the success or failure of a grand American strategy would hang in the end on the vigour, the persistence, the effectiveness of Canadian officials working at the grass roots of the American political and commercial system.

● ● ● ●

It is too early to tell how the Canadian-American relationship will emerge from the crisis it suffered in 1981. Much depends on the responses of both countries. If Canada can deal with the coming period of continuing high levels of stress and conflict by becoming an assertive state capable of identifying its interests and attempting to achieve them, it will be doing a great service to itself and its lingering identity problems. If the United States keeps to the low road of retaliatory protectionism, then it may be Canada's lot to have to stand up to the retaliation of its neighbour. Times would remain very difficult, but Canada could count on some support from its European allies who are also suffering from the application to their companies of American extra-territoriality in the Soviet gas pipeline affair. If the United States can regain the high road of a broad understanding of its best interests, there will remain many problems to resolve. Canada's adoption of an American strategy would represent the choice for change, a change within Canada and a change in the Canadian-American relationship. At the end of the long road of transition there would be a hope for a new era of stability, as the two countries established an equilibrium based on a more equitable sharing of the continent's physical and human resources and a more creative exploitation of each nation's own capacities.

Canada and the
Mulroney Challenge   14

By June 1984 when the Trudeau era ended, many of the important issues involved in the 1981 crisis had come close enough to resolution for a new political equilibrium to be established between Canada and the United States. Since the troubled months of 1981, the Canadian-American relationship had been functioning on the basis of more mutuality of interest, greater equality in negotiations, and considerable respect on both sides. Dedicated anti-nationalist though Pierre Trudeau may have been,[1] in its final year or two in office, his government had moved to affirm the autonomy of the Canadian state in North America to a degree few would have been able to predict on the basis of its formal statements. But no sooner had the prime minister put the finishing touches on the peace initiative which he used as his valedictory on the international stage than his successors made it clear that they would rewrite the script for Canada's role in North America and the world. John Turner, the winner of the Liberal party's leadership contest, was a figure long identified as an opponent of the Trudeau opus, most particularly as a corporate spokesman critical of those manifestations of state interventionism, such as FIRA and the NEP, that troubled the business community. During his brief weeks as prime minister, Turner found himself forced by U.S. economic nationalism to temper his continentalist leanings with assertive stances of his own in order to defend the interests of those Canadian businesses that were still falling victim to protectionist attacks from Congress. When, on September 4, 1984, a majority Progressive Conservative government was elected in a landslide, Canada was given a further push in the continentalist direction. While it is true that, as leader of the opposition, Brian Mulroney had claimed he would carry on the mission begun by Trudeau's peace initiative, which had challenged American East-West policy in its basic assumptions, Canada's new prime minister promised to revive the long-dead special relationship by

328

propitiating the United States. Mulroney's prime ministership seemed destined to wipe out Trudeau's legacy of affirming Canada's distinctiveness in North American relations. By the spring of 1985, the stabilization period of 1982-84 appeared in perspective to be like a punctuation mark closing one historical epoch — before a radically different period began.

1982: Adjusting to a New Equilibrium

The geopolitical context for the Canadian-American relationship during the last Trudeau years featured a dogmatic American administration defying a frustrated, even angry, consensus of its OECD and Third World trading partners. The most serious source of tension was the Reagan cabinet's macroeconomic policies, which produced a dangerously escalating U.S. deficit. The United States' attendant high interest rates aggravated Third World problems in repaying debt, drained loan capital from the rest of the world to the U.S., and forced other countries in self-defence to raise their interest rates even higher, to levels that curbed their economic growth. While the United States' economy boomed from its dose of covert Keynesianism, its allies pleaded for it to cool the recovery through fiscal restraint. In international conference after international conference, a dialogue of the deaf was repeated. The U.S. administration denied that any connection linked its deficit with its interest rates, boasted of its economic success and told the Third World to open up its markets to foreign investment and imports.

While its trading partners were unable to get the United States to accept their positions, the Americans found that they were equally incapable of imposing their will internationally. This impasse was most dramatically illustrated when the U.S. tried to abort the construction of the Soviet natural gas pipeline to western Europe in 1982. While the Reagan administration failed to grasp that the U.S. was unable to dictate international economic policy, the U.S. economy's global lead continued to shrink. The American share of world trade in high-technology products had dropped during the decade 1971-81 from 30 to 22 per cent, while Japan's share had increased from 4 to 12 per cent.[2] High American rates of interest were sucking up loanable funds from around the world, driving the U.S. dollar even higher and further worsening the American trade deficit. The rate of inflow of foreign capital was so high that the United States, it was predicted, would become a net debtor by 1986.[3]

On the military front, the United States' decline was not just in the field — most graphically in its failed intervention in Lebanon — but in formal policy. Defense Secretary Caspar Weinberger's military doctrine explicitly acknowledged the limits of U.S. power. Advising that U.S. forces should only be deployed in situations "deemed vital to our national interests,"[4] he recognized that "recent history has proven that we cannot assume unilaterally the role of the world's defender. So while we may and should offer substantial amounts of economic and military assistance to our allies in their time of need . . . we cannot substitute our troops or our will for theirs."[5]

When in 1982-83 the U.S. was unwilling to put more money into the International Monetary Fund so that members' withdrawal limits could be increased, it appeared that the United States was withdrawing from the world order it had helped create.[6] On the one hand, it was retreating from its global responsibilities: American official development assistance fell to 0.25 per cent of its gross national product. On the other hand, it was less able to exercise its power in international economic institutions. At the GATT ministerial meeting of 1982, the U.S. could not force the European Community to back down from subsidizing its agricultural exports. It took till December 1984 for the U.S. to get trade in services even put on GATT's agenda.[7] At the same time, in the OECD it was unable to impose its will on the question of limiting mixed credit financing by its European competitors, who had made inroads in the Third World by mixing economic aid with commercial deals.[8] As Zbigniew Brzezinski lamented, "Global change is certainly not susceptible to solitary American control."[9]

While Canada sided with Japan and the European Community at summit debates on these issues and even proposed under the aegis of its finance minister, Marc Lalonde, that the OECD form a common front to pressure the United States to lower its interest rates,[10] it also supported the United States on a number of questions. It agreed that the problems of Third World debtor nations should be dealt with case by case rather than by attempting to achieve a single general solution. On GATT questions, Ottawa favoured, as did Washington, another round of multilateral trade negotiations.[11] At the GATT ministerial meeting of November 1982, Secretary of State Allan MacEachen played an important and appreciated role as chairman in keeping a very divisive meeting from falling apart. More important still as a signal of its good intentions on international investment policy, Canada signed the OECD investment code in May 1984. Now a significant player at the international summit, Canada had become an important ally for the United States on the world stage.

330

The Reagan administration had gradually come to appreciate the value of Canadian support on a number — if not all — of those issues on the international agenda that were seen to be crucial in Washington. As it approached its mid-term elections in 1982, President Reagan's team backed away from its initial hard-line stances on Canadian internal policies and moved to take more seriously the management of its relationship with its northern neighbour. After a year and a half in office, the Reagan team had accepted some of the realities of its situation. Though some Canadian policies did not conform entirely to American interests, they turned out to be far closer to American standards than were the protectionisms of Japan or the European Community. Trudeau's non-conformism could be annoying. After two weeks of private criticism of the U.S. administration's economic and monetary policies before the 1982 economic summit conference at Versailles, he went public with his questioning of the premises of American policy towards the Soviet Union and its strategy for arms reduction negotiations.[12] Trudeau's "Ask Al" comment, a sarcastic innuendo about the president's intelligence, was never forgotten by the presidential entourage. Still, Canada's value to the United States in a broader world perspective was now accepted.

A key to the behavioural change in Washington's relationship with Canada was the replacement of Alexander Haig by George Shultz as secretary of state in the summer of 1982. Shultz knew Canada well from his earlier careers in business, as a director of Bechtel on whose board he had served with the Liberal dauphin John Turner, and in politics under President Nixon, for whom he had written a report on American strategic resources that included Canada's energy potential as a crucial factor. Once installed in the Reagan cabinet, he acted to get the Canadian-American relationship back on the rails, suggesting to his new Canadian counterpart at their first exploratory encounter that this top-level meeting of the secretaries of state be regularized at a rhythm of four times per year in order to keep the dozens of issues on the bilateral agenda under control.[13] The personal dynamic for this operational summitry was good: Shultz and MacEachen had known each other as young men at the Massachusetts Institute of Technology. Now they were powerful members of their respective governments — Shultz having the confidence of the president and considerable seniority in the administration; MacEachen, now basking in the title of deputy prime minister, having free rein to preside over a Department of External Affairs that had come close to being a central agency.

Having institutionalized a ministerial summit with Canada, Shultz

331

proceeded to strengthen the capacity of the Department of State to implement decisions made at these quarterly meetings. James Medas, a skilled political operative at the White House, where he had been responsible for the president's relations with the state governors, was brought to the State Department as deputy assistant secretary of state to coordinate and monitor the implementation of decisions made by Shultz and MacEachen. By giving Canada more high-level bureaucratic attention than any other American ally received, Shultz was recognizing the "intervulnerability" of the two countries' systems and the importance of preventing problems on either side of the border from turning into major conflicts that could damage American interests.[14]

The process of adjustment was mutual. The Trudeau government's energies had been taken up in the first two years after its 1980 mandate with repatriating the Constitution and implementing an ambitious energy program. These battles were still being fought when the government suffered two unexpected blows. World oil prices peaked and began to fall, invalidating the basic premise of the 1980 NEP and dooming the 1981 industrial strategy whose assumption was that a series of megaprojects in the energy field would act as a high-cost new engine to drive Canadian economic growth. Instead the country was hit by the worst recession it had experienced since the 1930s, a depression that was accentuated by the outflow of capital engendered by the massive Canadianization that had taken place in the energy industry in 1981. With its spending capacity decimated, there was little for the government to do but renounce its interventionist dreams and try to revive its somewhat shattered faith in the magic of the free market.

Stopped dead in its economic tracks, the government was also battered in its political path, largely by policies of its own making. Its worst error was the surprise tax reform measures contained in the 1981 budget, which managed to offend almost every constituent of the Liberal party's middle-class coalition of support. Constrained by provincial hostility on almost every front, criticized constantly by an anti-nationalist press that scapegoated FIRA and the NEP as the cause of Canada's woes, the Trudeau government was in a parlous state halfway through its mandate. Having been shocked by the violence of the Reagan administration's reaction to its energy program and investment policies, Ottawa resolved to temper these policies in order to buy peace in its external relations.

For immediate impact, clear signals were given by personnel changes at the top that Canada was mending its ways. A cabinet shuffle in September 1982 replaced the nationalist Herb Gray, minister for regional industrial expansion and minister responsible for FIRA, with Ed Lumley, an energetic politician with a pro-business stance and a friendly rapport with his counterparts in the Reagan cabinet. At FIRA itself, the incumbent commissioner, Gorse Howarth, was replaced by Robert Richardson, also known for his anti-interventionist beliefs and his good relations with the business community. The redoubtable Marc Lalonde moved from the Department of Energy, Mines and Resources, and his place was taken by the accommodating Jean Chrétien, who could more easily smooth those rough edges of the NEP that were still causing anger in the energy industry. At External Affairs, the somewhat brittle Mark MacGuigan was replaced by the experienced and unflappable Allan MacEachen. Once the high-profile ministers who had been the target of American complaints had been shunted aside, a chorus of soothing noises could be heard from Ottawa. With Trudeau playing choir master in a conciliatory interview with James Reston in the *New York Times,* [15] with top U.S. executives being flown in by the dozen for a red carpet treatment in Ottawa, there was good reason for *Maclean's* to celebrate this cosmetic campaign to cover up the wrinkles in the Canadian-American relationship with a cover story in October 1982 titled "Friends Again." [16]

Of longer-term significance was the move in the Department of External Affairs to work out what had been previously considered inappropriate, a general strategy towards the United States. By early 1983, the department submitted a report to cabinet that painted a sombre picture of increasing conflict with its southern neighbour, which was now entering "a period of political uncertainty and internal pre-occupation." [17] With threats to Canadian interests breaking out in a protectionist Congress every week, cabinet approved this document, which proposed to bury quiet diplomacy and to increase Ottawa's ability to do battle in the American political system with a $650,000 increase in its budget for lobbying. In September 1983 a reorganization at External Affairs merged the department's political and trade wings, which had been created by disruptive changes the previous year when the government's trade and diplomatic services had been brought under the same roof. In the case of External's United States branch, this rationalization produced a strong unit with greater bureaucratic heft that could more effectively manage the increasingly demanding bilateral agenda under the energetic direction of Assistant Deputy Minister Derek Burney. In effect, both governments had adjusted their players and their practices in order to take a far more strategic approach to the management of this, the world's most complex and intense bilateral relationship. For all the improvements in process, the Canadian-American agenda remained laden with economic issues and problems of sovereignty.

Continental Economic Issues

On the American agenda the two main items — the National Energy Program and the Foreign Investment Review Agency — remained the same, but their capacity to cause irritation had largely subsided.

Energy

The NEP of October 1980 and the subsequent Ottawa-Alberta agreement of September 1981 had been based on the assumptions that the world price of oil would rise steadily for the foreseeable future and that governments could take proportionately larger shares of the economic rents. When oil prices failed to rise in accordance with the planners' projections but fell in response to the realities of the world market, pressure from the industry forced the Canadian and Albertan governments to improve conditions for corporate cash flow by reducing their tax take and letting controlled prices rise. Alberta cut its royalties in April 1982. Ottawa followed suit in May with an *NEP Update* that lowered some taxes and raised some regulated prices.[18] As a result, operations became more profitable for all firms, national and foreign. In slowly retreating from government intervention and moving towards market discipline in response to the energy industry's pleas, Ottawa was also removing the NEP as a major bone of contention with the United States. With the average price of oil at 92 per cent of the world level by early 1984, the Americans' national interest argument had lost most of its force: the market had won out and the government had given up its hidden subsidy for Canadian manufacturing. With oil exploration at record levels in Alberta, 1983 saw the first net addition to Canadian oil reserves since 1969 and the American corporate interest in highly profitable balance sheets for its multinationals was satisfied.[19] Only the 25 per cent Crown interest in frontier developments remained as a major issue, the "back-in" being brought up regularly by Secretary of State Shultz at his quarterly summit meetings.[20] As Mobil Corporation dragged its feet in the development of the Hibernia field, hoping that political change would bring it back the billions in equity it had lost to the NEP, Shultz maintained his pressure with a formal letter on June 17, 1983, to his Canadian counterpart, calling the Crown interest "unfair and unreasonable."[21]

Gas

Just as the world market dictated Canadian policy responses in oil, it was the American market that forced Ottawa off its policy course in gas exports. Canadian exports of natural gas represented only 4 per cent of the U.S. market, but accounted for one-third of Canadian production and two-thirds of Canadian profits in natural gas. By the Duncan-Lalonde formula worked out at the request of the U.S. in 1980, gas was sold at a uniform price linked to the energy equivalent cost of oil that Canada had to import. Long-term contracts were signed on a "take or pay" basis, which insured that the heavy costs of constructing pipelines could be amortized. In the United States an incomplete process of deregulation amidst falling demand caused chaotic market conditions and a temporary gas bubble that finally combined to lower prices in the American market. American consumers of Canadian gas became unhappy with having to pay the higher prices stipulated in contracts signed before the market eased. Canada came under intense U.S. pressure via Congress, where at one point 40 separate proposals were being considered to authorize retroactively breaking gas import contracts with Canada and to force a reduction of Canadian gas export prices. The White House joined in the campaign to pressure Ottawa to renegotiate its gas contracts, describing its efforts in a letter sent to 75 congressmen. After brave words by Energy Minister Jean Chrétien that he would not bow to such pressure, since Canada was not to blame for the problems of the U.S. gas market, Ottawa did give in, lowering its price 11 per cent in the spring of 1983 and, in the summer, offering a further incentive discount of 25 per cent on purchases over one-half of the contracted volumes.[22]

Investment Policy

With the failure of the Alsands and Cold Lake tar sands projects, with the indefinite postponement of the Alaska Natural Gas Transportation System and the blocking of the Arctic Pilot Project for shipping liquified natural gas to southern markets, Ottawa's search for a dynamic of economic growth returned to secondary industry. Since more capital had been flowing out of the country than had been coming in since 1977, it was felt that something had to be done to change FIRA's reputation as an obstacle to new foreign investment in the economy, however ineffectual its regulatory behaviour had been in practice. Under the aegis of Herb Gray, the June 1982 federal budget had already announced a set of measures to streamline the agency's handling of applications. The ceiling for the faster, 21-day handling of "short form" applications was raised from projects worth $2 million involving 100 jobs to applications of $5 million involving 200 employees. The ceiling for FIRA involvement in indirect takeovers was raised to $15 million and 600 jobs.[23] By December 1982 a series of interpretation notes was published to give prospective investors clearer guidelines about the agency's criteria for judgment. For 1983 FIRA's approval rate rose to 94 per cent from 86 per cent in 1982. In the phrase of the outspoken American ambassador, Paul Heron Robinson, Jr., FIRA was now a "lap dog."[24]

Besides taking its own initiatives to streamline the screening process, Ottawa had also encouraged the United States to take its complaints about FIRA to arbitration by the General Agreement on Tariffs and Trade. In July 1983 the GATT tribunal rendered a Solomon-like judgment. While Canada's right to screen foreign direct investment was not questioned in principle and while its right to get foreign investors to make commitments to produce for export was confirmed, FIRA's practice of extracting undertakings from prospective investors to restrict imports in favour of buying Canadian products was judged a violation of GATT's article 3 on "national treatment." Having agreed in advance to abide by the ruling, Canada promptly indicated it would reword the legislation, asking foreign firms merely to grant Canadian companies a "full and equal opportunity to compete."[25] FIRA was off the agenda as an issue.

In pulling FIRA's teeth, Ottawa had been responding to pressure from the provinces and the private sector and to the Reagan administration's strong doctrinal concern to beat down barriers to free flows of investment in the international economy. In 1984 Canada went the extra mile to accommodate the interests of a prominent multinational economic sector. After a year's intensive lobbying by the foreign banks in Canada, Ottawa announced in April 1984 an amendment to the Bank Act that would double their asset ceiling from 8 per cent to 16 per cent of the Canadian market.[26]

Less and less was Canada acting as a host economy anxiously monitoring capital inflows; more and more it was acting as a capital-exporting country. The data indicated why this was so. Foreign control in the Canadian economy had fallen from 36 per cent in 1970 to 26 per cent in 1981.[27] In the five years from 1978 to 1983, Canadians invested $30 billion of long-term capital in businesses abroad, while foreigners invested $22 billion in Canada.[28] The Ottawa government's behaviour changed as well. From an exclusive concern with screening incoming foreign investment, it started to concern itself with how Canadian investment abroad was treated, joining Britain in pressing American state governments to abandon their application of unitary tax laws to subsidiaries of Canadian multinational corporations. Responding to American measures that damaged Canadian interests produced a far longer list of grievances on the Canadian side of the bilateral agenda.

The Canadian Agenda

While it was the administration more than Congress that was pressing Canada on the main American economic grievances of energy and investment policy, it was the legislature more than the executive that created most of Canada's economic grievances against the United States. Reacting to the massive American trade deficit the way it had to the recession — strengthening its protectionist defences in answer to pleas for help from ailing businesses — Congress continued its well-established custom of seriously threatening Canadian exports, sometimes directly, often inadvertently.

Steel is the most salient example of an inadvertent congressional threat to Canadian exports, since the various measures proposed and implemented to reduce steel imports into the American market were aimed at European or Third World producers, measures that sideswiped Canada in the bargain. Steel also furnishes the best example of Canada's more assertive stance in dealing with American threats to its interests. When on July 5, 1983, the Reagan administration announced that the tariff on imports of specialty flat-rolled steel would be doubled to 20 per cent and quotas introduced on imports of bar, rod and alloy tool steel, Canada decried the restrictions as unfair because it did not subsidize the export of specialty steel to the U.S. as did the offending European Community. Besides, the U.S. had a favourable trade balance with Canada in this metal. Accordingly, in January of the following year, Canada broke new ground in its relations with the United States by retaliating with increased duties on selected U.S. steel imports, as permitted by GATT.[29]

Retaliation, or the threat of retaliation, in response to direct attacks by Congress on Canadian interests confirmed that Canada was acting more like an equal partner as it dealt with continental conflict. A freeze on the issuing of licences to Canadian truckers had been won in February 1982 by American trucking interests, who alleged that Canadian regulations discriminated against them. The Interstate

337

Commerce Commission's chairman later admitted that there was no justifiable reason for this moratorium: "No intentional discrimination is being practiced by Canadian authorities against American motor carrier applicants."[30] Nevertheless, it took till the end of November, after the ICC had concluded an investigation confirming that no discrimination by the Canadian provinces against U.S. motor carriers had existed, for this unilateral restriction on Canadian trucking in the U.S. to be lifted. While retaliatory moves against American trucking by Manitoba and talk that Ontario might follow suit may have played some role in the final outcome, direct representations by the Canadian government to explain the rationale for Canadian policy were the more important factor.

Lobbying is a common denominator of almost all Canada's responses to U.S. protectionist threats.[31] In the case of softwood lumber, a petition from an American lobby group of forest companies for massive duties against allegedly subsidized Canadian softwood lumber imports, provoked an unprecedented counterlobby. In cooperation with the Canadian and provincial governments, the trade unions and the companies involved, an industrial organization, the Canadian Softwood Lumber Committee, launched a massive, $4 million effort to provide information to the U.S. quasi-judicial bodies that dealt with the issue. Political support was generated among American consumer and retail groups to help fight off the proposed 65 per cent duty that threatened to devastate the British Columbia lumber industry.[32]

Canada's lobbying efforts have been remarkably successful. The U.S. Commerce Department ruled against the Budd Company in its petition for a countervailing import surcharge against the Bombardier subway cars that New York City's transit authority contracted to buy. In December 1982 a bill to abrogate the Auto Pact and put quotas on the import of Canadian cars was amended in Canada's favour.[33] The softwood lumber export issue was resolved satisfactorily on May 24, 1983, when the U.S. Commerce Department announced that countervailing duties would not be imposed on Canadian imports.[34] After $500,000 had been spent in lobbying by both sides, the U.S. International Trade Commission threw out a countervail petition against the import of potatoes from the Maritimes.[35] Hogs, fish, blended sugar, raspberries, cement — Canada did well warding off threats both large and small during this period, though it could not tell how long its luck would hold. American companies and their congressional organizations were becoming more adept at raising the

338

issue of unfair subsidies in challenging foreign competition. The tendency was to argue that if a foreign practice did not fit the American way, it should be considered a subsidy. With protectionist pressure rising in tandem with the escalating U.S. trade deficit, individual successes in Canadian lobbying could not dispel a growing atmosphere of uncertainty on the trade front.

The spectre of continuing unpredictable threats limiting Canadian access to the crucial American market contributed to a dramatic reversal in Canadian strategic thinking. In September 1981, at the peak of the Canadian-American crisis, the Priorities and Planning Committee of cabinet commissioned an interdepartmental task force to do a study on Canada's trading options. The consensus that developed in the bureaucratic team after consultations with the private sector and the provinces was to bury the "third option" approach of diversifying Canadian trade away from American markets. While accepting the multilateral system as the context for Canada's trade prospects, the paper that was ultimately published by the minister for international trade favoured making a bilateral deal with the United States, possibly with a formal exemption from the GATT. While the task force officials wanted to urge as broad a free trade pact with the U.S. as they could get away with, concern among MPs about their constituents' jobs caused the proposal to be limited to a number of sectoral free trade deals with Washington. The cabinet had been impressed both by the growing dependence of the Canadian economy on trade with the United States and by the increasing vulnerability to unpredictable trade-restricting actions that congressional protectionism threatened. It endorsed the sectoral free trade idea that the minister of international trade, Gerald Regan, put forth in a white paper in late August 1983.[36]

The U.S. administration's response to the Canadian proposal was positive. Ronald Reagan's 1980 campaign notion of a North American accord had not been forgotten, even if it had stalled in 1981. U.S. efforts to stimulate another round of multilateral trade liberalization had been no more successful. If Canada was taking the initiative, the U.S. could not be accused of imperialist motives that might provoke an outburst of economic nationalism north of the border. By early 1984 sectoral negotiations with Canada, together with a free trade proposal with Israel, had become a high-priority item at the Office of the United States Trade Representative. On February 17 Trade Representative William Brock and International Trade Minister Gerald Regan met to discuss trade liberalization and agreed to study the free trade potential of a short list of four sectors: urban mass transit equipment, the steel industry, agricultural equipment and computer services.[37] On June 6 Brock and Regan met again, though no decision was made about commencing formal negotiations, since electoral uncertainty hung over both political systems.

Uncertainty also shrouded both sides' ulterior motives. Was the Canadian government doing much more than putting something constructive on the bilateral agenda in order to divert political attention from the bad feelings that acid rain, the back-in and several dozen lesser issues evoked? Was the U.S. administration as interested in making a deal with Canada as it was in using the bilateral talks as a bargaining lever for putting pressure on its other trading partners to agree to a new "Reagan" round of trade negotiations?[38] It was as difficult to be sure about the possible benefits as it was to be able to predict the costs of a deal. While most mainstream economists believed the benefits would be dramatic, some cautioned against exaggerating the putative productivity gains. Certainly free trade would provide no solutions for such major problems in the Canadian economy as the loss of comparative advantage in its resource industries, the high cost and overcapacity in the fisheries, the deficiencies in agriculture caused by insufficient research, inadequate reforestation policies or the country's perennial labour problems. As for the probable closing down of branch plants, such economic costs had to be considered alongside the even less quantifiable prospect of losses in Canada's sovereign policy-making capacity.[39] Until such time as a free trade pact exempting some or all Canadian exports from American non-tariff barriers had been negotiated with the administration and passed by Congress, Canadian businesses and Canadian governments were faced with having to defend their interests issue by issue in a never-ending game of American roulette.

Issues of Sovereignty

Problems involving Canada's political integrity as a nation state and its cultural survival as a coherent community are as permanent features on the bilateral agenda as issues of investment and trade. In this broad group of sovereignty problems, Canada displayed two quite different behaviour patterns in the final stage of the Trudeau era. On those sovereignty issues such as extra-territoriality, maritime boundaries and East-West relations for which Canada could generate multilateral support, it exhibited considerable strength in its dealings with the United States. But in regard to military, cultural and environmental policies whose scope was kept within continental limits and for which significant international support could not be mobilized, Canada proved less able to hold its ground in the bilateral relationship.

Continental Issues

The Military   The great debate of 1982 and 1983 on whether Canada should allow the United States to test the Air-Launched Cruise Missile (ALCM) over the Canadian north left the impression that the Canadian government had more freedom of manoeuvre than it actually enjoyed. Discussions of an umbrella agreement by Canada to permit the testing of a series of American weapons had been initiated during the Carter presidency by the Permanent Joint Board of Defence. On his first visit to Ottawa in April 1981, Defense Secretary Caspar Weinberger had formally raised the question of testing the Cruise missile. The decision to authorize the negotiation of a framework understanding for the U.S. to test its weapons in Canada was made by the Priorities and Planning Committee of cabinet in October 1981, though the negotiations were only finalized in the form of an agreement signed in February 1983. The actual debate on testing the Cruise missile appears to have been both a diversion and a formality. The prime minister diverted debate from the major strategic issue — the introduction of the ALCM represented a major change in North American weapons technology that would, as the scientist John Polanyi argued, probably induce a Soviet response in kind[40] — by misleadingly linking this NORAD issue to Canada's NATO commitments.[41] Close observers of the debate did not believe that cabinet had a real decision to make. In a period when Ottawa was making a deliberate effort to try to maintain good relations with Reagan's Washington, the refusal to permit the testing of the Cruise, it was thought in government circles, would have provoked a major rupture in the Canadian-American relationship.

Cultural Industries   While the military could no longer be considered an authentic criterion of sovereignty in Canada, the vitality of Canadian culture remained a crucial indicator of national well-being. Nevertheless, during the final Trudeau years, three factors conspired to force a rethinking of federal cultural strategy for the major mass media and to undermine the possibility of healthy Canadian cultural development. Continuing rapid technological change in the production and delivery of electronic programming made it increasingly difficult to rely on the country's existing cultural institutions as defences against swamping by new forms of American cultural

341

penetration. The growing economic importance of the cultural industries as significant generators of both jobs and revenue made the quantity of cultural activity more politically important than its substance. The government's policy not to offend the American government by impinging on U.S. corporate interests made it difficult to envisage almost any cultural development policy that would not be unacceptable, because it could be denounced by some American corporate interest as protectionism. Although policy makers were aware of the threat to a viable national culture — and therefore to Canada's ultimate political sovereignty — posed by the impending multiplication of American programming, the need to resist cultural assimilation became subordinated to more tangible economic and technical considerations. On the assumption that consumers demanded the distribution of more U.S. programming services, the key decision in Ottawa was to choose cable as the prime delivery system. Cable, it was felt, was at least susceptible to some degree of regulation.

With more continental corporations moving in to exploit the new technology, a theoretical debate on the virtues and vices of the free market versus state intervention in cultural policy took place. The Federal Cultural Policy Review Committee, under the strong influence of neo-classical economist Albert Breton, came down on the side of the free market: the sovereign consumer was the proper arbiter of cultural objectives; the market was the most efficient mechanism for the production of cultural goods; bureaucratic control is excessive in Canada, where public intervention is only justified to ensure that minorities receive their cultural preferences.[42] Since the message had passed through the bureaucratic system that anything perceived as even being somewhat detrimental to American business interests could not be contemplated as an element of Canadian policy,[43] the Department of Communications was faced with the task of defining policies for the various sectors of Canada's cultural industries that would do little more than rationalize the further Americanization of Canada's cultural consumption. The common denominators of the new Liberal policies were to give preference to expanding viewer choice rather than increasing Canadian content; to developing jobs in the private sector rather than maintaining a state-led broadcasting system; to marketing Canadian products internationally rather than developing delivery systems for Canadian productions.

The policy paper *Towards a New National Broadcasting Strategy* [44] dropped the notion of protecting Canadian programming as the central preoccupation. As Communications Minister Francis Fox expressed his sense of impotence, he could not build "walls above the stratosphere."[45] The reception of satellite transmissions by individual dishes was liberalized, but the cable system was chosen as the prime means for delivering programs in a way that could increase choice of all kinds, in both languages and in all parts of the country. While strong Canadian programming and the maintenance of a broadcasting system as a vehicle of social and cultural policy were declared as goals, it was not clear how these two objectives could be achieved without a massive increase of the government's broadcasting budget. True, a Canadian Broadcast Program Development Fund was established to be administered by the Canadian Film Development Corporation, now rechristened Telefilm Canada, but the conditions — the private sector had to provide two dollars for every public sector dollar that was contributed — indicated that the independent Canadian producers for whom the money was destined would be forced to make deals with Hollywood studios to supply products for the American market. And if programs had to be pre-sold for the American market before they could be financed, the old patterns of "licence plate" productions would be reinforced with Canadian crews providing the back-up for American stars working in Hollywood North. When in the summer of 1982 Canada signed an agreement with the United States to establish direct broadcasting from satellites that would give 95 per cent of Canadians access to U.S. programming from Canadian satellites, a leaked federal broadcasting strategy document commented that "liberalization of the system, in the absence of any other measures to strengthen the capacity of Canadian broadcasters and program producers to improve and increase production, means the end of a Canadian broadcasting system."[46] To this the president of the CBC, Pierre Juneau, added a note of resigned acceptance: "We should be careful not to panic. In drama, we've already lost our audience to American programming, and the new signals won't make the situation much worse than it already is."[47] By 1984 merely 3 per cent of drama programming in English Canada was Canadian. In explaining why Canadians tend to misunderstand the nature of their social problems, CBC Vice-President Bill Armstrong pointed out that "what is called the Canadian media system is not very Canadian at all," since the levers of power are "not even in Canada at all. For the most part they are in New York and Hollywood."[48]

That the chief executives of the Canadian Broadcasting Corporation could be so glum might appear paradoxical, since the government's policy paper on the subject, *Building for the Future: Towards a*

343

Distinctive CBC, agreed that the CBC should be a broadcasting alternative to the private sector and a vehicle for expressing and producing Canadian culture.[49] The paper proposed that the CBC would have 80 per cent Canadian content in prime time and would accomplish this difficult objective by buying 50 per cent of its programming from independent producers. Since the corporation was not given enough budget to achieve either objective, the policy paper could be dismissed by the *Globe and Mail* as a formula indicating "that the only way to save Canadian television broadcasting is to throw open the doors to foreign programming."[50]

The Canadian Radio-Television and Telecommunications Commission was brought under closer government control. The unworkable pay television decision of 1982, which had been forced on the CRTC by a government unable to withstand the pressure of the cable and American movie industry, was revised in 1984 to produce a commercially viable private-sector dual monopoly, the Canadian market being split along the Manitoba-Ontario border. The same year, licences for a variety of specialty channels were granted for "tiering" through the cable system. Two of the channels, CNN News and Nashville Network, would show exclusively American programming. The Arts and Entertainment Network, the Sports Network and the Learning Channel would have high concentrations of American programming. The only Canadian-owned service, MuchMusic, offering continuous rock videos, not surprisingly would draw most of its programs from the United States and the United Kingdom. Predictably, expanded choice meant expanded U.S. programming. As the president of Rogers Cable argued to the CRTC, "We have to move more towards the American model in Canada."[51]

The same branch-plant thrust underlay the government's new approach to film as expressed in *The National Film and Video Policy*.[52] This document, accepting the assumption that Canada was the legitimate domestic market of U.S. film distributors, talked neither of a quota for Canadian productions nor a box office levy that could generate funds for Canadian film production. With the aim to build a competitive private production sector, Telefilm Canada was given the mandate to administer a number of funding policies that would, in effect, help link the private sector still more closely to the American majors. A public sector thrust was maintained in the perpetuation of the National Film Board, but the NFB's film production activities were to come to an end. This move would terminate the major source of subsidization for French-language films and in effect put out of business the only consistent producer of internationally acclaimed Canadian material. This whole set of cultural policies was an eloquent testament to the covert decision-making power in Canada of the American entertainment industry. No formal issues needed to be brought up at the quarterly Shultz-MacEachen meetings, since the American national interest was being so well served by the federal government's policy process.

If the government's approach to broadcasting and to the new technologies of communication was to achieve a controlled Americanization through the cable delivery system, its approach to transborder data flow (TBDF) was to throw up its hands in despair. After two years of work, an interdepartmental task force on TBDF was dissolved without reaching a position after consulting a dozen interest groups and involving 20 government departments. With the United States pressing at every possible international forum (but against considerable Third World and OECD resistance) for the adoption of free trade in information and services, Canada's failure to develop an alternative to dependence on commercial developments within the American industry indicated that it would allow continental market forces to determine ultimate policy decisions.

Pollution   Environmental interdependence was brought to the awareness of Europeans during this period when in a single year the area of forests in West Germany damaged by the long-range transport of airborne pollutants escalated from 8 per cent in 1982 to 34 per cent in 1983. Canadian government estimates placed damage resulting from unchecked acid rain as costing 8 per cent of the gross national product, $1.1 billion in tourism and $15 billion in salmon, agriculture, forest industries and buildings.

Although bilateral negotiations towards an agreement on reducing emissions causing acid rain had broken down in June 1982 over the U.S. refusal to accept the establishment of any target for acid deposition consistent with the survival of lake and forest life, the scientific work groups still had their last set of reports to complete. Not even the work of scientists was immune to the Reagan administration's refusal to countenance emission controls. Raymond Robinson, head of Canada's Federal Environmental Assessment and Review Office, went so far as to accuse President Reagan of destroying 70 years of bilateral cooperation on pollution. In a speech to the National Academy of Sciences approved by the Department of External Affairs and by Environment Minister John Roberts, he accused the U.S. government of manipulating and suppressing scientific information about acid rain and cutting off money for pollution cleanups agreed to by the two countries. Despite the substantial agreement among scientists about the ways to control acid rain, non-experts had intervened to rewrite the scientists recommendations.[53] Former Progressive Conservative environment minister John Fraser confirmed the all-party consensus of anger and despair. In a speech in New York, he bemoaned the U.S. government's "constant interference," avoidance and postponing of research. The administration was "perpetrating hokum" in its efforts to avoid taking action on "the worst environment hazard ever to face my country."[54]

Hopes were raised in 1983 by the appointment of William Ruckelshaus to head the Environmental Protection Agency. The proposal for an experimental plan to reduce emissions from the Ohio River Valley states which Ruckelshaus brought to the Reagan cabinet would have reduced transborder pollution by some 25 to 30 per cent. It made no difference that the federal and provincial governments agreed early in 1982 to proceed unilaterally to reduce their own emission levels 25 per cent by 1990. Even though American opinion polls confirmed that strong majorities of the public continued to support cleanup programs and even though the primary campaigns of the Democratic candidates for the presidency were producing commitments to support clean-air legislation, the administration dug in its heels. Canadians learned from President Reagan's 1984 State of the Union Address that Ruckelshaus had been defeated: the president said no action would be taken. Still more research was needed. The utilities and mining interests of the Ohio River Valley were as delighted as the Canadian government was appalled. On February 22, 1984, the Department of External Affairs delivered one of its strongest protest notes, registering its "deep disappointment" with this "unacceptable breach of U.S.A. commitment."[55] It showed, in the words of Environment Minister Charles Caccia, "an avoidance of responsibility, a paucity of political will."[56]

Caccia did not lack political will himself. Having failed on the bilateral front, he turned for support first to the provinces, then to the international community. In March 1984 Caccia prevailed on his provincial colleagues to agree, again without corresponding American action, to increase their reductions of emissions by a further 25 per cent by 1994 at an estimated cost of $10 to $20 billion over the next 20 years.[57] A few days later, in what the *Globe and Mail* called an

346

"international coup," he hosted in Ottawa a conference of the nine European nations who had committed themselves to cutting acid rain emissions by 30 per cent. Twenty-five thousand dollars was spent to publicize the conference's message in the United States — that the U.S. was out of step with the other responsible industrialized countries of the "30 per cent club" — but Caccia's message fell on deaf ears.

The Reagan administration's refusal to respond was as adamant on airborne pollutants as it was on the threatened poisoning of Lake Ontario by the Hooker Chemicals and Plastics Corporation's chemical dumps that were leaking into the Niagara River. There is no question who was villain and who victim in this asymmetrical environmental dependency. The United States was responsible for 99 per cent of the contamination, while Canadians made up 80 per cent of those drinking the water endangered by a host of toxins.[58] Hooker's Hyde Park dump alone was estimated to contain 2.5 tonnes of TCDD dioxins, the deadliest synthetic chemical yet produced.[59]

Where entrenched American corporate interests had less at stake than the chemical companies with dumps along the Niagara gorge, Canada fared better along the border. In the continuing struggle against the Garrison Diversion Unit, where North Dakota's economic development plans came up against vocal and effective lobbying in U.S. politics by the Audubon Society, the continuing representations by Ottawa and Winnipeg met with far greater success. On December 14, 1984, a 12-member commission set up by Interior Secretary William Clark voted to scrap the Lonetree Reservoir, which would have shifted dangerously polluting waters from the Mississippi to the Hudson Bay watershed. The secretary of the interior had agreed in advance to accept the commission's ruling. If, as expected, Congress went along with this recommendation, then a long-standing war that had been apparently won then lost again on several occasions would indeed have been won for good.[60]

Multilateral Issues

Extra-territoriality   Weak though it was on its own, in those sovereignty issues where Canada acted in conjunction with a multilateral consensus, it took firmer positions, often with much greater success. Extra-territoriality is a constant issue in an interdependent world where multinational corporations are tempting vehicles for national policy makers. When the Reagan administration tried in 1982 to prevent Europe from completing its contracted natural gas pipeline from the Soviet Union by depriving participating European sub-sidiaries of U.S. firms of their home-based technology, it found it had bitten off more than it could chew. The retaliation of France, Italy and Great Britain forced the United States to retreat, having lost more than $2 billion worth of business in the process.[61] When in August 1983 a Florida branch of the Bank of Nova Scotia was subpoenaed by a Florida grand jury in a drug traffic case and fined $50,000 a day for not revealing data sought by the U.S. from an account in a Bank of Nova Scotia branch in the Cayman Islands — an action that would have forced it to violate Cayman Island law — Canada was joined by Great Britain and the Caymans in pressing the United States to desist from this violation of an international legal principle.[62]

The European Community has itself mounted a campaign against the Reagan administration's attempt to increase its extra-territorial controls through a new Export Administration Act. For the first time, it would give the president authority to declare export bans for foreign policy reasons and impose import sanctions against defiant companies, even retroactively on contracts already signed.[63] The European countries protested against American proposals to limit the export of U.S. technology and give the American government authority to demand constant supplies or information even from foreign companies. While international pressure was applied to the United States to desist from extending its extra-territorial reach, the U.S. was also under strong pressure in the OECD, where it remained the odd man out again, to accept a consensus that defended the sovereignty of governments in cases of overlapping jurisdictional claims.

Canada has drawn some strength from this developing multilateral consensus. It introduced legislation, the Foreign Extraterritorial Measures Bill modelled on British, French, New Zealand and Australian laws, to give the federal attorney general power to prohibit compliance of Canadian companies with extra-territorial measures and to prevent the removal from Canada of documents demanded by a foreign court.[64] In its bilateral diplomacy, Canada has also been willing to take a stand on issues that impinge on its sovereignty. In another case involving the Florida courts, Canada strongly objected to the violation of its sovereignty through the kidnapping in Canada of a businessman wanted for trial in Florida. Canada's representations were strong enough ultimately to induce both the U.S. secretary of state and attorney general to intervene and ask Florida to parole the kidnapped person. As George Shultz put it, "It is simply in the [U.S.] national interest that this case no longer be permitted to intrude upon our relations with one of our most important and highly valued neighbors, allies and trading partners."[65]

Boundaries at Sea   That Canada has considerably more international heft than most Canadians will concede was confirmed in 1984 at the International Court of Justice, where both the United States and Canada had taken their Atlantic maritime boundary for resolution. Whatever the ruling turned out to be, the agreement in advance by both sides to accept the court's judgment indicated the United States' acceptance of an international and institutional process of conflict resolution. It bode well for the resolution of the several other maritime boundary disputes created by the two countries' extension of their jurisdiction to the 200-mile limit. Both sides had complaints about the final outcome, which divided the area disputed between the countries in half. At stake for Nova Scotia was 30 per cent of its fishery and 3,600 jobs. The allocation to Canada of the northern part of Georges Bank assured Nova Scotian fishermen of approximately the same 50 per cent share of the scallop catch and 25 per cent of the ground fish that they had harvested in 1983.[66]

To be sure, for every problem resolved, several more sprouted on the agenda. The American response to the International Court's decision was to call for a year's moratorium in the implementation of the ruling. The main Canadian concern was to resume negotiations to create a joint management scheme or mutual restraint arrangement to conserve fish stocks from depletion along the lines of the aborted fishery treaty of 1979. While British Columbia's Skagit Valley was saved by a treaty approved by the U.S. Senate on June 28, 1984, on the basis of an agreement made through the International Joint Commission,[67] the salmon treaty that had been under negotiation for 13 years and allegedly finalized in 1983 eluded ratification when Alaska objected to the size of its quota of Chinook salmon. In April 1984 deliberate U.S. challenges to Canadian sovereignty in the Beaufort Sea and at Prince Rupert and the Dixon Entrance off the British Columbia coast through the calling for petroleum exploration leasing rights were new issues requiring settlement.[68] Canada's firm assertions of its positions augured well for an ultimately satisfactory balance sheet of dispute settlement in this dossier.

Foreign Policy   In the final months of Pierre Trudeau's last term in office, Canada's foreign policy took on an unusually clear colouring that transcended the normal pale hues imposed by the American

349

relationship. The most noteworthy diplomatic actions were taken not to build up diplomatic credits with Washington but directly to influence American foreign policy, even at the cost of hindering Canada's success rate in bilateral issues.

In Central America, where Canada's role was negligible but Canadian apprehension considerable lest the United States attempt to achieve a military solution, the government took public positions it could easily have avoided. It attempted to influence American policy by direct criticism. In March 1983 Canada co-sponsored a United Nations resolution condemning human rights violations in Guatemala, a client state of the U.S. At a regular quarterly meeting of the secretaries of state that spring, Allan MacEachen urged George Shultz to eschew a military approach to resolving the problems of Central America. On April 22, 1983, Pierre Trudeau expressed direct criticism of American policy at a news conference where he spoke of "major divergences" between the two countries' views of the situation. A year later MacEachen resisted American pressure to visit its protégé state El Salvador, as part of his official tour in Central America even though the same trip included a stop in Nicaragua, the mining of whose territorial waters by the United States MacEachen had publicly criticized as a violation of international law.

Although Canadian comments were peripheral to American concerns in Central America, Canada's angry reaction to the invasion of Grenada by U.S. forces in October 1983 indicated with dramatic clarity that, within the bounds of diplomatic niceties, Canada was not afraid to speak straight at the risk of displeasing Washington. Also, the Reagan team's refusal to consult either the British or the Canadian government before launching its invasion of this Commonwealth country showed that the alliance leader was willing to act without regard for the concerns of its partners.

The diplomatic rebuff to Canada in Grenada found a counterpoint in Prime Minister Trudeau's valedictory on the diplomatic stage. The virtues and failings, the motivations and consequences of Trudeau's peace initiative have been analyzed elsewhere in greater detail.[69] What was relevant to the Canadian-American relationship was the fact that Trudeau's call for an end to "megaphone diplomacy" was an obvious criticism of the United States' handling of the East-West relationship. Both the five measures that Trudeau proposed and the general idea of a militarily weak alliance member claiming to have advice to give the superpowers, caused audible resentment at senior levels of the U.S. administration. Although it is true that the State Department was vexed with Canada for breaking ranks and calling attention to the emperor's state of undress in strategic doctrine, it is also evident that the Trudeau initiative did have a real impact, moderating the rhetoric of President Reagan and contributing to a renewal of the East-West dialogue on arms control.[70] Canada may have been shut out from White House deliberations concerning Grenada, but Trudeau successfully invited himself into the Oval Office and the Kremlin to help change the tone and the agenda of East-West negotiations.[71]

On many other international issues, Canada was no more successful in affecting the United States' policy than were its other allies. On the refinancing of the International Monetary Fund and the International Development Agency, Canada joined its OECD partners in vain, trying to convince the U.S. that an increase in its capital contribution was needed for international economic stability. On the Law of the Sea, Canada was at the forefront of those pushing the United States to adopt the United Nations treaty.[72] When Washington attempted to outflank the Law of the Sea with a reciprocal states agreement among the major seabed mining powers, Canada worked actively to derail this mini-treaty and deny the United States the benefits that it felt should accrue only to valid signators of the U.N. treaty.

In showing signs of being a "principal power" and exercising its autonomy, Canada indicated that a considerable process of maturing had taken place.[73] No longer was it afraid to confront the United States when it felt American foreign policy was seriously misguided or when its own interests were at stake. It then had to suffer the consequences of its independence. When Finance Minister Marc Lalonde presented his candidacy for the presidency of the OECD, the United States punished the author of the NEP by working hard behind the scenes for the candidate put forward by the French government, socialist though it was. Still, Canada's national persona seemed to have come of age on the international stage. Then in the summer of 1984 a political transformation took place. At the very moment that Canada seemed able to consider accepting its own political maturity, its political leadership changed and it reverted under new management to the historically more familiar patterns of continental dependence.

Turner, Mulroney and the Conversion to Continentalism

However much Canada's autonomy may have been affirmed during the first half of 1984, the second half of that portentous year demonstrated a return to an old pattern of Canadian conciliation with the United States. After Pierre Trudeau decided to retire and the Liberal leadership campaign had narrowed the possible successors to John Turner and Jean Chrétien by the spring, U.S. Ambassador Paul Heron Robinson, Jr., observed that the United States was in a no-lose position: whether immediately, after the Liberals' convention in June 1984, or in the near future, after an election campaign that might see the new leader of the opposition, Brian Mulroney, brought to power, "the future of our relationship cannot help but improve." Citing the Canadian government's increased military spending in recent years, he went on to predict: "If Turner comes in, it will improve even more, and if Mulroney comes in, it will improve more than that."[74]

In his campaign for the Liberal leadership, Jean Chrétien made it clear that he was a friend of business and a politician who could get on with Uncle Sam even while standing up for Canadian interests. On foreign direct investment he held to the qualified position that "it is important that foreign capital come into Canada. We need it. But we need a screening process to improve the investment."[75] After he had beaten Jean Chrétien, John Turner, the new Liberal prime minister, lost no time in proving Ambassador Robinson's point. Canadian foreign policy, he told the *Toronto Star*'s Richard Gwyn in June, is going to be business with the United States as it used to be and it's going to be all about business.[76] On foreign investment Turner's answer hung on the need for jobs:

> It is important when we need jobs so badly, and thereby investment, that we make it clear as a government that we welcome investment from all over the world subject to conditions imposed on that investment for the benefit of Canada.[77]

Turner, as a corporate lawyer in a major Toronto firm, a member of the boards of several blue-chip continental corporations, and a closet critic of the NEP and FIRA, spoke for the interests of the Canadian corporate elite, for whom good relations with the United States had far higher priority than concerns about international politics or national identity.

During his few weeks in office, Prime Minister Turner showed how he wished to change the way of handling the Canadian-American relationship. He also revealed how much he was constrained by the new character of the relationship. On July 4 the new prime minister dramatized his new style in bilateral relations by his much-publicized attendance at Ambassador Robinson's Independence Day reception, a party that Pierre Trudeau had never deigned to attend. On the National Energy Program, Turner indicated he would favour moving to world prices for all oil even though the foreign multinationals would gain the

352

most from this windfall. His energy minister, Gerald Regan, publicly asserted that no part of the NEP was sacred.[78] Showing he was as good as his word, Regan further eased the natural gas export pricing rules by freeing Canadian sellers to negotiate prices with American buyers as of November 1, provided that the price did not fall below the Toronto level and that new deals received the approval of the National Energy Board.

Where the demands of western Canadian business conflicted with the interests of the central Canadian consumer but coincided with American needs, the Turner government was willing to satisfy the first and the third at the expense of the second, but where Canadian business interests came into conflict with American interests, Turner's government proved as willing to stand firm as had been his predecessor's. When the U.S. International Trade Commission recommended global quotas and higher tariffs against all steel imports under section 201 of the Trade Act, the Canadian government took a strong stance. Secretary of State for External Affairs Jean Chrétien told his American counterpart, George Shultz, at their first quarterly meeting in July 1984 that Canada strongly objected to this measure, for which there was no justification as far as Canadian steel exports were concerned. International Trade Minister Francis Fox made two visits to Washington, threatening strong responses. Canada would exercise its right under the GATT to demand compensation for U.S. moves to restrict Canadian steel exports either by exacting easier access for other goods or by retaliating against American exports to Canada. To underline the threat, he gave Washington a potential hit list for retaliation should the U.S. curbs on Canadian steel exports be implemented.[79] Turner may have wanted to challenge the Trudeau legacy in style, but he found himself compelled by the realities of American economic nationalism to exercise the government's new-found capacity to do what would previously have been unthinkable: try to impose its will on the United States by threatening retaliatory responses.

If John Turner's brief stay at 24 Sussex Drive itself represented a considerable shift in the tone of the Canadian-American relationship, his displacement by Brian Mulroney on September 4, 1984, confirmed that a change of direction had indeed occurred. Canadians that day elected in a landslide the most avowedly pro-American prime minister in Canadian history. That some of his most fervent statements contained inherent contradictions did not seem to trouble either Mulroney or his party. In the course of his year and a half in federal politics, Brian Mulroney had promised all things to all voters. He had repeatedly affirmed he would give his American allies "the benefit of the doubt," specifically in such military operations as the invasion of Grenada.[80] Yet he had also frequently assured Canadians that he would continue the thrust of Pierre Trudeau's commitment to peace and disarmament. He had constantly affirmed his support for the Atlantic alliance by saying his government would increase its contribution to NATO, and he had spoken favourably about the need for generosity towards the Third World, without explaining how he would achieve these financially demanding commitments when he was also attacking the size of the federal government's deficit. To make sense of these contradictory positions one has first to understand the new prime minister's political persona and the team of players around him, in order then to weigh the Conservatives' prospects for transforming the Canadian-American relationship.

Mulroney: His Persona and His Team
Mulroney was born and brought up in a town on Quebec's north shore that would not have existed, as he is fond of repeating, without American direct investment capital. Baie Comeau was founded by the Chicago *Tribune* in 1938 as a resource town set up literally to hew wood as an export staple to feed the paper's presses. As his biographers put it, Baie Comeau was a "perfect little microcosm of Brian Mulroney's best of all possible worlds":

> The important decisions were made elsewhere and most of them were made outside the country. The town owed its very existence to the vision of an entrepreneur from Chicago, and its growth was fuelled by the decisions made in Minneapolis, London and elsewhere. There is no evidence that Mulroney ever saw anything wrong with this scheme of things.[81]

There was very little possibility that Mulroney's early socialization would have fostered in him a sense of a Canadian national interest that was different from jobs linked to the prosperity of the staple-consuming American head office.

Later, after he set up in practice as a lawyer in Montreal, Mulroney's early career experience was in labour-management negotiations and Quebec politics. His Irish charm, his colloquial French and his populist touch brought him a considerable degree of success based not on intellectual breadth or policy depth but on personality and drive. With his blue-collar background, his middle-class education, his flair for self-dramatization and, as time went on, his strong network of

354

connections through the Quebec political and business elites, he was well qualified to take on, at mid-career, the role of chief Canadian spokesman for another American resource-exploiting conglomerate when he became president of the Iron Ore Company of Canada in 1977.

At the time, IOC was part-owned by the Hollinger Consolidated Gold Mines and five U.S. steel companies but controlled by Hanna Mining of Cleveland. Following the exhaustion of the Mesabi range in Minnesota, Hanna had moved into Ungava and the North Shore, a region whose prosperity quickly became inextricably linked to the American iron and steel economy. Charged with public relations and labour-management negotiations rather than with executive decision making, Mulroney's qualities suited admirably the role of manager of a firm that was a creature of its foreign shareholders. Without any clash of personal values, he could easily identify with the interests of the American head office, whose goals he could enthusiastically embrace. If it was to the advantage of the parent company to close down an iron ore mine and turn Schefferville into a ghost town, he had the considerable talent — underestimated to its cost by the Liberal party — to carry out this hatchet work by engaging government support and trade union cooperation, so that he received plaudits from the press for turning a corporate failure into a personal success. These responsibilities further developed his vaunted charm, the essentially manipulative style that had helped him get his way more by pleasing, stroking and persuading than by wielding actual power. Brian Mulroney was, in short, a model comprador*: a man who succeeded not from self-generated objectives but as an agent doing a job dictated by those who employed him and those who could fire him.

As preparation for a third career in political leadership, Brian Mulroney's background was quite inappropriate for conventional notions of the political leader as an autonomous and primary player on the political scene, actively injecting his or her program into the political system. After all, he was inexperienced in the workings of government and ignorant of the complexities of public policy. But if the political leader is expected to be an intermediary rather than an initiator, an instrument of the various interests who backed, supported,

---

*Originally the native manager for a foreign establishment in China who served the interests of the company by acting as factotum and intermediary with the local population. In Canadian sociology, compradors are the senior executives of branch plants who follow the directives of their foreign headquarters.

voted for him or her, then it was quite possible that Brian Mulroney would meet the needs and expectations of political leadership in a country fed up with the initiatives — constitutional, economic and diplomatic — taken by the Liberal party under Pierre Trudeau. As a politician, Mulroney had shown a remarkable flexibility in his positions. In the campaign for the leadership of the Progressive Conservative party in 1983, he was a hard-liner on Quebec, implying that Joe Clark was soft on separatism; in the 1984 election campaign, he made capital in denouncing John Turner's anti-separatist comments and presenting an image of reconciliation with Quebec nationalism. In 1983 he was clearly in tune with the Conservative convention delegates, of whom a clear majority supported a Reaganite, bipolar view of the world, preferred increased defence expenditures to more foreign aid, and advocated a foreign policy more closely aligned with that of the Reagan administration.[82] By 1984, following the evident success of Pierre Trudeau's peace initiative among the Canadian public, Mulroney supported the notions of peace and disarmament.

If the prime minister is a weather vane politically speaking, it is essential to know the views of those he has placed in key positions of power, since the stands he takes may be largely determined by the force and direction of the political winds that blow through his support system. (During his brief tenure in government, John Turner's continentalist values were turned into autonomist actions because the political subordinates he inherited were largely loyal to the Trudeau legacy of assertiveness towards the United States.) In Brian Mulroney's case, it is the internationalist breeze that is deflected and the continentalist winds that blow strong. Joe Clark may hold the prestigious portfolio of External Affairs, but the influence of his internationalist voice has been blocked by subtle but important structural changes in the cabinet system. The Department of External Affairs has lost its central agency role as dominant manager of the government's relations with the outside world. The secretary of state for external affairs (SSEA) has also lost his cabinet committee on foreign and defence policy in which the SSEA was chair and the minister of national defence a mere member. The envelope for external affairs, development assistance and national defence, once under the SSEA's control, has been taken over by the Priorities and Planning Committee chaired by the prime minister. These moves suggest that the politics of peace will be primarily played for local consumption rather than for international effectiveness. Already in the first months of the Mulroney mandate this pattern had been established with the politically brilliant appointments of former Ontario NDP leader Stephen Lewis and former red Tory MP Douglas Roche as Canadian ambassadors to the United Nations and the disarmament negotiations respectively.

The first policy tests of the new government's positions showed that the Progressive Conservatives' definition of peace bore a distinctly American accent.

- Joe Clark declared in his first speech to the United Nations as external affairs minister that Canada would join the Organization of American States.[83] If joining the OAS would bind Canada more closely to American positions south of the Rio Grande at a time when the U.S. government was claiming the right to intervene by force in Central America,[84] this would make an independent peacekeeping role for Canada in restraining a U.S.-sponsored invasion of Nicaragua highly problematic.
- Canada joined the United States and ten other nations at the U.N. General Assembly to vote against a resolution calling for a nuclear arms freeze between the two superpowers.[85] Even though Norway, Denmark, Iceland and Greece had refused to vote against the freeze resolution, solidarity with NATO (i.e., agreeing with the United States) was to take priority over disarmament initiatives.
- After External Affairs Minister Clark had admitted, at a NATO foreign ministers meeting in December, that cabinet was split over whether to oppose or endorse President Reagan's Strategic Defence Initiative,[86] Prime Minister Mulroney unqualifiedly backed the "Star Wars" concept in February. Using language as hawkish as that of Margaret Thatcher and showing no apparent concern for the destabilizing consequences of the militarization of space for East-West relations,[87] Mulroney executed an about-turn from Trudeau's peace initiative, which he had endorsed during the 1984 election campaign.

These policy positions indicated that it was the continentalists in Mulroney's cabinet who had been given more substantial power. The Department of National Defence was bestowed on Robert Coates, a long-standing political enemy of Joe Clark's and strong proponent of rearmament within the framework of the U.S. military economy. Coates's stature was enhanced by membership on the Central Priorities and Planning Committee, from which the minister of national defence had previously been excluded. A further weakening of the power of External Affairs and its moderate secretary of state was the allocation of international trade, whose officials had been integrated in the Department of External Affairs, to the Cabinet Committee on Economic and Regional Development chaired by Sinclair Stevens, the most ideologically right-wing of Mulroney's senior cabinet ministers. The most powerful portfolio of all, Finance, was given to Michael Wilson, a consistent advocate of the multinational corporation as the best hope for Canadian economic recovery.

With External Affairs downgraded, it would seem that policies having to do with Canada's relations with other countries would be secondary to those having to do with United States. The wild card in this cabinet constellation was the role to be played by the prime minister himself. Immediately after his election, Mulroney had made it clear that Canadian-American relations were his primary concern: "Good relations, super relations with the United States will be the cornerstone of our foreign policy."[88] He also indicated that the Conservatives' whole economic strategy was predicated on hitching the Canadian economy more closely to the American. The prime minister's first major action was to visit Washington just eight days after taking office, even before holding a press conference in Ottawa. His first major public speech was to the Economic Club in New York, where he confirmed not just that FIRA was dead but that the NEP's back-in was next on the Tory "hit list." Canada, he said, "is open for business — again."[89] These actions suggest that Mulroney intended to act as if he were his own minister of United States relations. He wisely retained Allan Gotlieb, the most effective ambassador Canada has ever had in Washington, as his emissary to the Reagan court.

Mulroney's whole career and character made it quite understandable that he should want to play the prime role in dealing with the United States; yet his ability to carry this off successfully was questionable. For one thing, he had inadequate bureaucratic resources to bear such an increased burden, whether in the Prime Minister's Office, where his press officer was the only person with Washington experience, or in the Privy Council Office, where he inherited a small staff of international relations generalists who were in no way equivalent to the U.S. president's National Security Council. For another, he was himself unusually inexperienced in international affairs, the multilateral context for his bilateral dealings with the United States. In a televised interview in December 1984, he acknowledged how he had hitherto underestimated Canada's actual importance on the world stage. Referring to a dinner with some ambassadors from Third World countries, he admitted he was "both pleased and somewhat surprised at the Third World, at their enthusiasm for Canada, and Canada's role in the world."[90] That he should have little feel for the complexities of Canada's considerable presence in international affairs was understandable, since he had read on the subject and travelled abroad so little and had shown so few signs of interest in the great global issues of his age during his previous careers.[91] Entering the prime minister's office with such light intellectual baggage, he would have to do a lot of on-the-job learning — something very difficult to accomplish at the apex of power, where the incumbent is under constant pressure on a myriad of other issues. Early signs indicated that Mulroney did not feel comfortable with playing an active role in international summitry. Notable by its absence was the prime minister's acceptance of invitations to pay formal visits to Canada's major historical partners in Europe, Asia or the Third World.

More serious as herald of Brian Mulroney's handling of Canada's direct relations with the United States were the seriously distorted notions he expressed in December 1984 even after settling in as prime minister.

• On the previous management of the relationship:

> People who criticize from the bleachers are the same people who for twenty years were in charge of Canadian-American relations, our largest trading partner, friend and ally, treated them like enemies, barraged them with insults, never gave them the benefit of the doubt, and then wondered why we never got along.

• On summitry and the general tenor of the relationship in past years:

> If the atmosphere [between the two countries] is polluted and spoiled by bickering and nastiness and vindictive remarks then it's unlikely that anything good will emerge from two heads of state getting together. . . . I don't think we can afford vexatious and pernicious economic attitudes that drive opportunities away.

• On his own approach to handling the relationship:

> All I am saying is we will defend Canadian autonomy and integrity at all times and in all circumstances but that doesn't mean that we have to harass and heap vitriol on them. . . .
> Nor would I acquiesce with anything that is not in Canada's national interest. The fact that I try and conduct myself in a friendly and civil manner doesn't suggest, I don't believe anyway, any lack of sovereignty on our part. . . . I don't feel it diminishes our national strength . . . to be cordial with our friends and neighbours.[92]

What he understood as "Canada's national interest" became the issue, as did the substance of his "friendly and civil manner." Already in June 1984 as leader of the opposition, Mulroney had carried out his "Operation Charm," a trip to Washington where he had promised he would abolish FIRA and rescind the back-in along with the other surviving provisions of the NEP. For a politician whose reputation was based largely on his skill as a negotiator, it seemed that the Progressive Conservative leader had developed a novel continental bargaining style of giving to the Americans the positions they wanted without obtaining any understanding that they would deliver some *quid* that Canada wanted for the *quo* it was offering.

Given the prime minister's comprador experience, his right-wing governing team, and his unquestioningly pro-American stances, the prospects were more than bright for the new Progressive Conservative government to elicit an excellent reception from the Reagan administration. The United States response to the departure of Trudeau and the arrival of Mulroney has indeed been one of clear delight. As Jeffrey Simpson reported the mood in Washington, "the Reaganites could scarcely conceal their satisfaction."[93] The president's senior foreign policy adviser spoke glowingly of the new Reagan-Mulroney rapport and suggested significantly "we are on the way to recreating the 'special relationship.' "[94]

If the special relationship meant that the interests of the two countries were now seen to be complementary rather than competitive, that the style of their interaction was to be quiet rather than confrontational, and that the role Canada played vis-à-vis the United States was to be deferential rather than independent, the prospect of achieving a return to the old special relationship of the 1960s seemed promising.

The Prospects

National Interests
In its first speech from the throne, the Mulroney government described the "wellsprings of trust" between Canada and the United States:

> My government has taken the initiative to restore a spirit of goodwill and true partnership between Canada and the United States. My government is pleased by the positive response it has received in both the government and private sectors of the United States.
>
> There are many areas where the national interests or the national policies of the two countries diverge or compete. There are, as well, numerous and as yet untapped possibilities for fruitful cooperation

between our two countries. Restoring a climate of goodwill between our governments was an essential step towards the resolution of our conflicts and the realization of all of our opportunities.[95]

The language was not strikingly different from Liberal rhetoric, but the definition of the national interest in investment policy was dramatically changed. Already in the first weeks of its mandate, the cabinet approved FIRA's recommendation to allow the sale of a large Canadian-owned oil company, Voyager Petroleums, to U.S. interests.[96] By December the Tories were ready with their *coup de grâce*. Industry Minister Sinclair Stevens announced the formal dismantling of the Foreign Investment Review Agency and its replacement by an institution called Investment Canada whose mandate it was to encourage foreign investment.[97] Apart from takeovers in the cultural industries, only the very largest foreign takeovers would be screened. The criterion of acceptability was weakened from the proposals having to demonstrate "significant benefit" to merely showing a "net benefit" to the Canadian economy. In the words of the finance minister's economic statement, *A New Direction for Canada*:

> Canada must adopt a more positive stance towards foreign investment if we want to attract the capital to create the job opportunities, attract new technology and introduce new production processes and management systems, all of which will make our industries more competitive.[98]

These early signals suggested that the Conservative government's notion of national interest was approaching the position that what was good for the continental economy was good for Canada. Certainly in the energy field, concerns about self-reliance in petroleum seemed to have been quietly abandoned. The incentives given by the government in response to industry's demands favoured the export of as much oil as possible, as in the pre-1973 regime. With transportation costs to the mid-west market less than to central Canada, Alberta interests, now strongly represented in the government caucus, supported the strengthening of north-south linkages again, under conditions of deregulation.

Style
Even in those areas where the Canadian government did identify interests that were divergent from American positions, it seemed likely that they would be dealt with according to the norms of quiet diplomacy as defined in the 1960s: not making a row in public but letting matters be handled quietly by technocrats and diplomats behind

361

the scenes.[99] Following Joe Clark's failure to gain accommodation on the acid rain question from George Shultz at their first quarterly ministerial meeting in October 1984, the new Conservative Environment Minister Suzanne Blais-Grenier indicated a major strategy shift had been decided by Ottawa on the style of environmental relations. Canada was no longer to be a world leader in pushing other nations for acid rain controls. At an international meeting in London she said she was not going to press Britain or the United States to join the "30 per cent club" of countries that had agreed to reduce their sulphur dioxide emissions by that amount in a decade. As for the previous government's highly public diplomacy, she was categorical: "I don't see myself going to the U.S. border and shaking my fist."[100] The previous bipartisan stance of exerting maximum pressure on the U.S. administration had been terminated.

The shift to a style of accommodation on Canada's most bitterly contentious issue was confirmed by the prime minister a month before his first formal summit meeting with the U.S. president. Reversing the conventional Canadian complaint that the United States produces far more pollution than Canada — 26 million tonnes of sulphur dioxide emissions, compared to 5 million tonnes — Mulroney turned the finger of blame on Canada. He asserted that Canada is "behind the Americans in emission control in many significant areas" and took the position that Canada would have to clean up its own act before expecting concessions from the United States. Blaming previous Liberal governments' inaction for Washington's indifference to past Canadian proposals on acid rain, he put the case for environmental boy scoutism. Canada would bargain with the U.S. "with clean hands and say, 'Yes we have done or we have begun the process of doing our share of the job. Now here is what we want you to do.' "[101]

There could be no doubt that Prime Minister Mulroney's generous applications of political charm and the abandonment of a confrontational stance on acid rain would have a major payoff in his summitry. The excellent personal rapport between the prime minister and the president was certain to yield invaluable PR on St. Patrick's Day, 1985, when Prime Minister Mulroney hosted a presidential visit from Ronald Reagan in Quebec City. Good summitry could also be counted on to oil the wheels of personal diplomacy at lower levels of the governmental machinery.

Role

In the special relationship associated with Pearsonian diplomacy, both governments eschewed articulated strategies in dealing with each other. There was simply an understanding that both would act with each other's interests at heart. When the U.S. government, in applying its international economic policy, had inadvertently acted in a way that damaged Canada, Ottawa had merely to send a mission to Washington to work out an exemption. With the new Canadian government defining its interests in a discourse largely similar to that of the Reagan administration, it was quite likely that Canada's role vis-à-vis the United States could quickly be adjusted to fit the old model as far as the United States' interests were concerned. The prime minister's repeated affirmations that he would give American foreign policy the benefit of the doubt, even in such a grave matter as a Caribbean invasion, indicated that diplomatic sailing should be fairly smooth. Within its first months in office, the government had distanced itself from its predecessor's opposition to the U.S. venture into Star Wars military technology. The prime minister justified his support for the Star Wars project on the grounds of sovereignty: "And it is with a decision to assert our sovereignty and to protect Canada and to make sure that Canada is listened to with a modest degree of respect and understanding, that we have decided to assume our own responsibilities. Canada will shoulder its fair share of the load."[102] Yet the government was agreeing to the Pentagon's long-expected modernization program for North American air defence in which Canada would pay barely 10 per cent of the total $6 billion bill. While bearing 40 per cent for a new radar network, the North Warning System, it would not be making any contribution to the Advanced Warning and Control Systems, the airborne surveillance systems that are expected to fly more missions over the Arctic, where Canada claims sovereignty, than Canada's own rare surveillance flights.[103]

The evidence of the prime minister's words and actions bears out the analysis of his biographers:

> In international affairs, to the degree he has ever considered them, Mulroney sees Canada in a firm lockstep with the United States. It is not making light of the simplicity of his position to suggest that he accepts the Yalta theory of spheres of influence as it applies to Canada.[104]

All that stands in the way of a continuing special military relationship is an incipient credibility gap between the Conservatives' political promise and their economic performance. Defence Minister

Robert Coates promised Defense Secretary Caspar Weinberger that Canada would "take its full share of the burden" and undertake to play a bigger role in NATO, but the new Conservative government moved in fact to cut by $154 million the military budget, which the Liberals, for their part, had been increasing at the rate of 3 per cent per annum since 1979. The military policy question became even more uncertain with Coates's hasty resignation from the cabinet in February 1985.

As far as the United States' role vis-à-vis Canada was concerned, however, it was not obvious that Canada could benefit from the exemptionalism that it had enjoyed two decades previously. American economic nationalism does not give much credit to personal chemistry. On October 9, Congress passed the Trade and Tariff Act of 1984 that further strengthened the U.S. battery of contingency protection measures. While Canadian officials expressed relief that the final act was not as bad as had been feared, this omnibus bill nevertheless did:

- ease the task of a complaining U.S. industry in proving it had been injured by foreign dumping or subsidies;
- clarify how a dumping or countervail investigation could be initiated even before imports had entered the American market;
- give the president new powers to retaliate against countries that require export performance from foreign-controlled subsidiaries — a long-standing American complaint against Canada;
- grant the president authority to press foreign governments to ease their restrictions on trade in services and high-technology products;
- retaliate on the border broadcasting issue with mirror legislation; and
- create a new non-tariff barrier in the form of the requirement that all imported steel pipe and tube made of steel be stamped with permanent markings to show their country of origin.[105]

Observers predicted that, with the U.S. trade deficit at $123 billion in 1984, the 99th Congress would bring back onto the agenda most of the tougher measures of protection that had failed to pass in 1984.[106]

In the winter of 1984-85, protectionist threats were directly targeting imports of Canadian hogs, fish, potatoes, softwood lumber and steel. The best will in the world from the White House would cut little ice on specific congressional measures to retaliate against Canadian exports deemed to be hurting some American business or other.

As for the prospects of the Mulroney government negotiating a free trade agreement with the Reagan administration, the climate in 1985 was very different from what it had been when the last such deal had been struck in the form of the Auto Pact in 1965. Gary Hufbauer and Andrew Samet reported that the deep concern in Congress about the U.S. trade deficit meant reciprocity must govern all trade agreements: any concessions on foreign access to the U.S. market would have to be paid in full by American access to the foreign market.[107] Unless hard calculations showed benefits would balance from a move towards trade liberalization, American political interest would quickly fade. Beyond this general reluctance to do Canada any favours, careful research also showed that the prospects of coming to an agreement either on sectoral or general free trade were narrow. There were few sectors other than agricultural equipment that presented the prospect of a balanced package for each side. The power of special interest lobbies in the U.S. system virtually insured that any attempt to barter a sector where the U.S. gained in the Canadian market for a sector where the U.S. lost to Canadian competition would be blocked. Nor did the chances for a general exemption for Canada from U.S. non-tariff barriers seem much better, there being little inclination in Congress to tamper with countervailing and anti-dumping laws by giving Canada special treatment. It is no more conceivable politically that the administration would be willing to challenge the states' Buy America laws than that the provinces would give up their own local procurement regulations. After all, as Fred Bergsten, director of Washington's Institute for International Economics, observed, "Regardless of its free trade rhetoric, the Reagan administration has allowed more restrictive measures in the past two years than any administration since the 1930s."[108]

On the Canadian side, the free trade project appeared almost as problematic. Even though Donald S. Macdonald was throwing his weight as chairman of the Royal Commission on the Economic Union and Development Prospects for Canada on the side of the free traders, even though the Business Council on National Issues was preaching its version of a trade enhancement agreement, and even though the finance minister had expressed interest in free trade along with the minister of international trade, the government remained undecided. Charles McMillan, the prime minister's chief policy adviser, had publicly cast doubts on the free trade notion, worrying about closing off access to major external markets like Japan. Frank Miller, the new premier of Ontario, the second most powerful government figure in Canada and, necessarily, a powerful player within the Progressive Conservative party, had also gone on the record with his misgivings.

Each government kept its options open. In Washington the Office of the United States Trade Representative and the International Trade Commission held hearings in January 1985 about the probable economic effects of Canadian-American free trade. Later that month the minister of international trade in Ottawa produced yet another discussion paper on the question that leaned heavily in the direction of a "comprehensive bilateral trade agreement."[109] The process of exploration continued almost as gingerly as it had under the Trudeau government.

The unarticulated assumption justifying Canada's deferential role in its old special relationship was that, by supporting the United States on multilateral issues and by giving the U.S. access to its markets and raw materials, Canada would benefit from special treatment that would meet its own needs. Though it is quite easy to see how Canada in the late 1980s could respond to American desires, it is more difficult to envisage why the United States would be likely to comply with Canadian needs. If, after years of adamant insistence on research rather than action, the Reagan administration finally decided to reverse its position and spend the billions that are necessary to reduce emissions causing acid rain and to clean up the toxic wastes polluting the waters of Lake Ontario, then the Mulroney strategy would have been proven a resounding success. But if the prime minister turned out to have given away his cards — abolishing FIRA and putting the NEP on his hit list — without getting any return for his concessions, then years of gradual development of a more autonomous and self-directed approach by Canada towards its American relationship would have been thrown overboard for no return.

One litmus test of the Mulroney-Reagan special relationship would be the unemployment level. If foreign investment did not come flooding into the economy, creating hundreds of thousands of jobs as Mulroney has promised, but merely trickled in to take over and close down Canadian enterprises; if unchecked pollution wreaked major damage on the tourist, forestry and fishing industries of central and eastern Canada; if Canada's exports to the U.S. market kept being targeted for retaliation by still more effective non-tariff measures: then the brand new Canadian-American relationship would have paid off far more for the United States than for Canada.

Another litmus test would be Canadians' sense of satisfaction about their country's role in the world. If the senior levels of Ottawa's civil service could adapt to the notion that Canada would not oppose the United States' withdrawal from the complex network of international institutions that it had helped to create and that served Canada's international interests; if the Canadian public could accept its government's support for the United States' militarization of space and for American military solutions to civil wars in Central America: then the government would be secure in its approach. But if the Canadian consciousness were not fully Americanized by its consumption of American programming and if it rejected the notion that the appropriate stance for Canada was to give the United States the benefit of the doubt, even in a military approach to Central America, then, too, the Mulroney approach would have failed.

The last time a Progressive Conservative government held power in Ottawa when a Republican administration was in office at the White House was from 1957 to 1960. During those three years Ottawa brought about a permanent integration of Canada's military forces in the American military system by finalizing the North American Air Defence Command. It also achieved a permanent integration of Canada's military economy in the U.S. military-industrial complex by aborting Canada's independent fighter interceptor, the Avro Arrow, and accepting a branch-plant role through the Defence Production Sharing Arrangements. Whether as dramatic an integration as the Diefenbaker-Eisenhower team accomplished can be realized by the Mulroney-Reagan duo depends on the "window of opportunity" the governments have until 1988 when the next presidential campaign gets under way and the Canadian government enters an election phase.

The loss of sovereignty resulting from the expansion of economic transnationalism, argues Seyom Brown, constitutes a basic disenfranchisement of national populations. As the preservation of cultural diversity has been a major contribution of the nation-state system,

> the increasingly inadequate reach of national governments into the functioning of the transnational economy . . . is depriving world society of perhaps its only existing effective means of husbanding the pluralism that has hitherto stimulated mankind's proudest accomplishments in the realms of philosophy, literature, fine arts, science, and even technological-economic development.[110]

The Mulroney challenge to Canada lies in its explicit and implicit "transnationalism." If the new government maintains its original commitment to continentalism, with mere gestures made in the direction of autonomy, the political struggle in Canada is likely to focus on defining the nature of the national interest.

The severe cuts to the budget of the Canadian Broadcasting Corporation and other crucial cultural institutions in November 1984 gave a triple message as a blow against public television, a rebuff to the liberal media establishment and a declaration of faith in the free, necessarily continental market for culture. The cuts to the environmental budget for the research on toxic chemicals that discovered dioxin in Lake Ontario mirrored the Reagan regime's disregard for ecological issues[111] — and pulled the rug from under the previous Canadian position that urged the Reagan administration to reinstate its research on Great Lakes pollution. It is quite conceivable that the Progressive Conservative government could impose a comprador expression of the national interest and become an active agent in the undermining of the Canadian state's capacity to protect its polity, its economy and its culture. It is equally possible that Canadians' awareness of their need for a viable economy, a safe world, a healthy environment and a self-sustaining culture will prevent the Mulroney government from achieving more dramatic moves towards economic, military or cultural integration. Having adjusted under Trudeau from crisis through stabilization towards autonomy, Canada's relationship with the U.S. under Mulroney in 1985 seemed poised for a sea change that only future analysts would be able to assess.

Appendix

People Interviewed for This Study*

David Adam, Consul for Investment and Finance, Canadian Consulate in New York

Michael J. Adams, President, Environics Research Group Ltd., Toronto

Veronica M. Ahern, Associate Administrator for International Policy, U.S. National Telecommunications and Information Administration

Lina G. Allard, Chef de Cabinet, Cabinet du Chef de l'Opposition officielle, Assemblée nationale du Québec

John F. Anderson, Assistant Deputy Minister (Policy), Department of National Defence

John W. Anderson, Editorial Writer, *The Washington Post*

Michel Andrieu, Director, Economic Policy Division, Department of Communications

Paul Asselin, Directeur, Direction Amérique du Nord, Ministère de l'Industrie, du Commerce et du Tourisme, Gouvernement du Québec

Michel Audet, Sous-ministre associé, Ministère de l'Industrie, du Commerce et du Tourisme, Gouvernement du Québec

Paul Audley, Consultant on Communications and Cultural Policy, Toronto

Tom Axworthy, Principal Secretary to the Prime Minister (1, 2)

Antoine Ayoub, Directeur, Groupe de recherche en l'économie de l'énergie, Université Laval

Charles A. Barrett, Director, Economic Research Group, The Conference Board of Canada

Carl Beigie, President, C.D. Howe Research Institute, Montreal

Roger J. Beland, Senior Representative, Quebec Government, Dallas, Texas (2)

Joel I. Bell, Executive Vice-President, Petro-Canada, Calgary

---

*The bulk of the interviews lasted one hour. For the first edition of this book, most were conducted during September and October 1981; for the second, mainly in May and July 1984. Interviewees for both editions are marked (1,2); for the second only, (2). Titles are those held at the time of the first interview. Positions are in the government of Canada unless otherwise indicated.

369

Hon. E.J. Benson, President, Canadian Transport Commission

Marcel Bergeron, Sous-ministre adjoint, Ministère de l'Industrie, du Commerce et du Tourisme, Gouvernement du Québec

Lise Bissonnette, Rédactrice en chef, *Le Devoir*

Conrad Black, Chairman of the Board, Argus Corporation Limited, Toronto

Dennis Blair, Staff Member for Western Europe, National Security Council

Robert Blair, Chairman and CEO, Nova, an Alberta Corporation

Stephen Blank, Partner, Multinational Strategies Inc., New York

Bernard Bonin, Départment d'Économique, École nationale d'Administration publique, Montréal

Peter Borré, Principal Deputy Assistant Secretary for International Affairs, U.S. Department of Energy

Gerald K. Bouey, Governor, Bank of Canada (1,2)

John Brady, Senior Policy Adviser, International Relations Branch, Ministry of Intergovernmental Affairs, Government of Ontario

François Bregha, Canadian Arctic Resources Committee, Ottawa (1,2)

J.P. Bruce, Assistant Deputy Minister, Environment Canada (2)

Robert Bryce, former Deputy Minister, Department of Finance

Alan Buckley, Program Administrator, International Political and Social Analysis, The Conference Board, New York

Derek H. Burney, Assistant Deputy Minister, United States Branch, Department of External Affairs (2)

Jacques A. Bussières, Adviser (International), Bank of Canada

John Carson, Director, International Relations Branch, Ministry of Intergovernmental Affairs, Government of Ontario

Alf Chaiton, Policy Adviser to the Minister of Industry, Trade and Commerce (1, 2)

Hon. Jean Chrétien, Minister of Justice

W. Edmund Clark, Senior Assistant Deputy Minister, Department of Energy, Mines and Resources (1,2)

Max Clarkson, former Dean, Faculty of Management Studies, University of Toronto

Wayne V. Clifford, Executive Director, International Division, Department of Federal and Intergovernmental Affairs, Government of Alberta

Kevin J. Clinton, Research Adviser, International Department, Bank of Canada

M.A. (Mickey) Cohen, Deputy Minister, Department of Energy, Mines and Resources (1,2)

Arthur E. Collins, Ph.D., Associate Deputy Minister, Department of Energy, Mines and Resources (2)

Terry Colli, Staff Economist, Canadian Embassy in the United States

John Conder, Chief, International Department, Bank of Canada

Stanton Cook, Publisher, Chicago *Tribune*

Jim Coutts, former Principal Secretary to the Prime Minister (1,2)

John G. Crean, Robert Crean & Co. Limited, Toronto (2)

Hon. John C. Crosbie, former Minister of Finance

Marshall A. Crowe, President, M.A. Crowe Consultants Inc., Ottawa (1,2)

Richard L. Dalon, Provincial Pipeline Coordinator, Alaska Highway Gas Pipeline Project, Department of Federal and Intergovernmental Affairs, Government of Alberta

Douglas V. Davis, Attorney for the Chairman, U.S. Federal Communications Commission

N. Della Valle, Chief, U.S. Division, Defence Programs Branch, Department of Industry, Trade and Commerce

Louis A. Delvoie, Director General, International Security and Arms Control Bureau, Department of External Affairs (2)

G.H. Dewhirst, Director General, Policy, Research and Communications Branch, Foreign Investment Review Agency (1,2)

William Diebold, Jr., Senior Research Fellow, Council on Foreign Relations

Douglas Ditto, Deputy Head, Commercial Division, Canadian Embassy in the United States

Peter C. Dobell, Director, Parliamentary Centre for Foreign Affairs and Foreign Trade (1,2)

Arthur W. Donner, Economic Consultant, Toronto

James Donovan, Directeur, Direction/États-Unis, Ministère des Affaires intergouvernementales, Gouvernement du Québec

Charles Doran, Director, Center of Canadian Studies, School of Advanced International Studies, Johns Hopkins University

Bernard J. Drabble, Associate Deputy Minister, Department of Finance (2)

David Duinker, Canadian Consulate, Chicago (2)

Peter Dunn, Counsellor, Québec Government House in New York

P.T. Eastham, Director General, Office of U.S. Relations, Department of Industry, Trade and Commerce (1,2)

C.G. Edge, Chairman, National Energy Board (1,2)

David C. Elder, Director, Coordination Division, Department of External Affairs (2)

George Elliott, Minister (Public Affairs), Canadian Embassy in the United States

Philippe Eloy, Conseiller économique, Ministère du Développement économique, Gouvernement du Québec

Hershell Ezrin, former Consul, Canadian Consulate in New York

William L. Farrell, Vice-President, Salomon Brothers, New York

Elliot Feldman, Director, University Consortium for Research on North America, Harvard University

Max Field, President, Marathon Realties, Chicago (2)

Gordon Floyd, President, ICC/Public Affairs Management Inc. (2)

Robert R. Foulkes, Manager, Public Affairs, Petro-Canada, Calgary

Robert Fowler, Assistant Secretary to the Cabinet (Foreign and Defence

Policy), Privy Council Office (1,2)

Ross Francis, Director, Defence Relations, Department of External Affairs (2)

Paul Fraser, Canadian Consulate in New York

Charles Freedman, Chief, Department of Monetary and Financial Analysis, Bank of Canada

George E. Freeman, Deputy Governor, Bank of Canada

Hon. Richard Funkhouser, Director, Office of International Activities, U.S. Environmental Protection Agency

J.P. Gallagher, Chairman and CEO, Dome Petroleum Limited, Calgary

Oswald H. Ganley, Executive Director, Program on Information Resources Policy, Harvard University

Robert Gayner, Consul General, Canadian Consulate, Chicago (2)

Jacques Gérin, Deputy Minister, Environment Canada (2)

Claude Germain, Direction de la Coordination économique, Ministère des Affaires intergouvernementales, Gouvernement du Québec

Claud Gingrich, International Trade Counsel, Committee on Finance, United States Senate

Edward Goldenberg, Executive Assistant to Hon. Jean Chrétien (2)

Allan Gotlieb, Under-Secretary of State for External Affairs

Alain Gourd, Senior Assistant Deputy Minister, Department of Communications (2)

John Grant, Director and Chief Economist, Wood Gundy Limited, Toronto

Sylvie Gravel, International Relations Branch, Department of Communications

Hon. Herb Gray, Minister of Industry, Trade and Commerce

Roberto Gualtieri, Deputy Secretary, Ministry of State for Science and Technology (2)

Tony Halliday, Senior Adviser and Coordinator of Sectoral Studies, Department of External Affairs (2)

James Harlick, Second Secretary, Canadian Embassy in the United States (1,2)

Bernard Harvey, Sous-ministre adjoint aux Opérations centrales, Ministère de l'Environnement, Gouvernement du Québec

Ross Harvey, Executive Assistant to NDP Leader, Legislative Assembly, Government of Alberta

Ivan L. Head, President, International Development Research Centre (1,2)

Paul Heinbecker, Director, United States General Relations Division, Department of External Affairs (1,2)

Alfred O. Hero, Jr., Director, World Peace Foundation, Boston

Peter Herrndorf, Vice-President and General Manager, Canadian Broadcasting Corporation

John Honderich, *Toronto Star* (2)

W.H. (Bill) Hopper, Chairman and CEO, Petro-Canada, Calgary

Gorse Howarth, Commissioner, Foreign Investment Review Agency
James F. Hudson, General Manager, U.S.A. Division, Toronto-Dominion Bank
Douglas J.R. Humphreys, Deputy Governor, Bank of Canada
Adele Hurley, Executive Coordinator, Canadian Coalition on Acid Rain
Suzanne L. Hurtubise, Attaché politique, Cabinet du Chef de l'Opposition officielle, Assemblée nationale du Québec
Hon. Lou Hyndman, Provincial Treasurer, Government of Alberta
George Jaeger, Minister, U.S. Embassy (2)
Ted Johnson, Executive Assistant to the Prime Minister (1,2)
Hon. Donald J. Johnston, President of the Treasury Board
Patricia Johnston, Vice-President, Canadian Federation of Independent Business
Robert Johnstone, Deputy Minister, Department of Industry, Trade and Commerce
Pierre Juneau, Deputy Minister, Department of Communications (1,2)
James F. Keeley, Department of Political Science, University of Calgary
Michael G. Kelly, Director, International Finance Division, Department of Finance (2)
Eric Kierans, Department of Economics, McGill University
John Kirton, Department of Political Economy, University of Toronto
Arthur Kroeger, Secretary, Ministry of State for Economic and Regional Development (2)
Huguette Labelle, Deputy Minister, Secretary of State (2)
Hon. Marc Lalonde, Minister of Energy, Mines and Resources
Steve Lande, Assistant U.S. Trade Representative, Office of the United States Trade Representative
Jeffrey M. Lang, Professional Staff Member, Committee on Finance, United States Senate
R.E. Latimer, Assistant Deputy Minister, International Trade, Department of Industry, Trade and Commerce
Nate Laurie, Ministry of State for Social Development (2)
Claude Laverdure, Deputy Director, Federal-Provincial Coordination Division, Department of External Affairs
François Lebrun, Président et Directeur général, Société de Développement industriel du Québec
Edward G. Lee, Assistant Under-Secretary for United States Affairs, Department of External Affairs
Ernest S. Lee, Director, Department of International Affairs, AFL/CIO
Hon. Merv Leitch, Minister of Energy and Natural Resources, Government of Alberta
Bruce Lister, Chief, Intergovernmental and Regional Unit, Fiscal Policy and Economic Analysis Branch, Department of Finance (1, 2)
Wingate Lloyd, Director, Office of Canadian Affairs, Department of State

James Lorimer, Publisher, James Lorimer & Company, Toronto
Patricia A. Lortie, First Secretary (Energy), Canadian Embassy in the United States
Hon. Edward C. Lumley, Minister of State for Trade
Hon. Donald S. Macdonald, Senior Partner, McCarthy and McCarthy
Hon. Flora MacDonald, former Secretary of State for External Affairs
Hon. Allan J. MacEachen, Secretary of State for External Affairs (2)
Hon. Mark R. MacGuigan, Secretary of State for External Affairs
Helmut Mach, Department of Federal and Intergovernmental Affairs, Government of Alberta
Hon. Roy MacLaren, Minister of State for Finance (2)
Harald B. Malmgren, President, Malmgren Inc., Washington
de Montigny Marchand, Associate Under-Secretary of State, Department of External Affairs
Robert J. Martin, International Economic Relations Division, Department of Finance (2)
Thomas Maxwell, Chief Economist, The Conference Board of Canada (1,2)
Albert G. McDonald, Deputy Minister, Department of Tourism and Small Business, Government of Alberta
Ian McDougall, Osgoode Hall Law School, York University
J. Peter Meekison, Deputy Minister, Department of Federal and Intergovernmental Affairs, Government of Alberta
John Meisel, Chairman, Canadian Radio-Television and Telecommunications Commission (1,2)
George Melloan, Deputy Editor of the Editorial Page, *The Wall Street Journal*
William S. Merkin, Director for Canadian Affairs, Office of the United States Trade Representative
Karl E. Meyer, Editorial Board, *The New York Times*
D. Wayne Minion, Chairman, Alberta Petroleum Marketing Commission
Gordon F. Mintenko, Minister-Counsellor (Commercial), Canadian Embassy in the United States
Robert J. Montgomery, Counselor of Embassy for Political Affairs, U.S. Embassy (2)
Reid Morden, Director-General, Government Policy and Operations Bureau, Department of External Affairs (2)
Frank J. Morgan, Executive Vice President, The Quaker Oats Company, Chicago (2)
Hon. Jacques-Yvan Morin, Ministre des Affaires intergouvernementales, Gouvernement du Québec
William D. Mulholland, President and CEO, Bank of Montreal
Don Munton, Research Director, Canadian Institute for International Affairs
Michel Nadeau, *Le Devoir*
Edward Nef, Senior Legislative Counsel to U.S. Senator Max Baucus (1,2)
James R. Nininger, President, The Conference Board of Canada, Ottawa

Robert Normand, Sous-ministre, Ministère des Affaires intergouvernementales, Gouvernement du Québec
Bruce Nussbaum, Associate Editor, *Business Week*
Hon. Martin O'Connell, former Minister of Labour
Richard O'Hagan, Vice-President, Public Affairs, Bank of Montreal
Hon. H.A. (Bud) Olson, Minister of State for Economic Development
Sylvia Ostry, Director, Department of Economics and Statistics, Organization for Economic Cooperation and Development (1,2)
James E. Page, Director of Canadian Studies, Secretary of State (2)
R.J. (Randy) Palivoda, Department of Federal and Intergovernmental Affairs, Government of Alberta
Anne Park, Deputy Director, U.S. Transboundary Relations Division, Department of External Affairs
Geoffrey Pearson, Visiting Fellow, Institute for Research on Public Policy (2)
Ross Perry, Consultant, Singer Associates, Toronto
Douglas D. Peters, Vice-President and Chief Economist, Toronto-Dominion Bank
Hon. J.W. Pickersgill, former Minister of Transport
Michael Pitfield, Clerk of the Privy Council and Secretary to the Cabinet
M. Yvon Pomerleau, Directeur des Études en Relations économiques internationales, Ministère de l'Industrie, du Commerce et du Tourisme, Gouvernement du Québec
J.D. Porter, Managing Director, Independent Petroleum Association of Canada
Robin Porter, Environmental Officer, Office of Canadian Affairs, Department of State
Richard Pouliot, Sous-ministre associé, Ministère de l'Énergie et des Ressources, Gouvernement du Québec
Larry Pratt, Department of Political Science, University of Alberta
R. Cranford Pratt, Department of Political Economy, University of Toronto
Robert Rabinovitch, Assistant Secretary to the Cabinet (Priorities and Planning)
George Rejhon, Counsellor (Environment), Canada Embassy in the United States
Grant Reuber, former Deputy Minister, Department of Finance
R.L. Richardson, Commissioner, Foreign Investment Review Agency (2)
Sean Riley, Adviser to the Minister of Finance (1, 2)
Hon. John Roberts, Minister of the Environment
Colin Robertson, Federal-Provincial Co-ordination Division, Department of External Affairs
Hon. Paul Heron Robinson, Jr., Ambassador of the United States of America to Canada
Peter Robinson, International Aspects of Informatics, Department of Communications (1,2)

David B. Rohr, Staff Director, Subcommittee on Trade, Committee on Ways and Means, U.S. House of Representatives

Claude Roquet, Sous-ministre associé pour les Affaires internationales, Ministère des Affaires intergouvernementales, Gouvernement du Québec

Peter Russell, Department of Political Economy, University of Toronto

A.E. Safarian, Department of Political Economy, University of Toronto

Sol. W. Sanders, Senior Writer, *Business Week*

Marc Santucci, Adviser to Assistant U.S. Trade Representative for Investment Policy

Kalmann Schaefer, Assistant to the Chairman for International Communications, U.S. Federal Communications Commission

J. Blair Seaborn, Deputy Minister, Department of the Environment (1,2)

Richard G. Seaborn, Deputy Director, Academic Relations Division, Department of External Affairs

Brian Segal, President, Ryerson Polytechnical Institute, Toronto

Hugh Segal, Secretary of the Policy and Priorities Board of Cabinet, Government of Ontario

Michael R. Sesit, International Money Management Editor, *Business Week*

Gerald E. Shannon, Minister, Canadian Embassy in the United States (1,2)

Hon. Mitchell Sharp, Commissioner, Northern Pipeline Agency (1,2)

John J. Shepherd, Partner, Nordicity Group (2)

David W. Slater, Chairman, Economic Council of Canada

Robert W. Slater, Assistant Deputy Minister, Environment Canada (2)

Don Smith, Managing Director, Shearson Loeb American Express, Washington

Richard J. Smith, Minister, United States Embassy to Canada

Stuart L. Smith, M.D., President, Science Council of Canada (2)

Gary Soroka, Second Secretary, Canadian Embassy in the United States

Donald W. Stevenson, Deputy Minister, Ministry of Intergovernmental Affairs, Government of Ontario

Ian A. Stewart, Deputy Minister, Department of Finance (1,2)

Campbell Stuart, Director General, Surface Transportation, Department of Industry, Trade and Commerce

Max Stucker, Partner, Arthur Andersen & Co., Chicago (2)

Barbara Sulzenko, Policy Adviser to the Minister, Department of Industry, Trade and Commerce (1,2)

Ken Taylor, Consul General, Canadian Consulate in New York

Nicholas W. Taylor, President, Lochiel Exploration Ltd., Calgary

Dale Thomson, Department of Political Science, McGill University

Alexander C. Tomlinson, Senior Advisor, The First Boston Corporation, New York

George Tough, Assistant Deputy Minister, Department of Energy, Mines and Resources (1, 2)

Peter Towe, Ambassador, Canadian Embassy in the United States

John Trent, Executive Director, Social Science Federation of Canada (1,2)

David Trick, Intergovernmental Affairs Officer, International Relations Branch, Ministry of Intergovernmental Affairs, Government of Ontario (1,2)

Hon. John N. Turner, Partner, McMillan, Binch

Sandy Vogelgesang, Economic Minister-Counselor, United States Embassy (2)

Manfred Von Nostitz, Director, United States General Relations Division, Department of External Affairs (2)

Raymond J. Waldmann, Assistant Secretary for International Economic Policy, U.S. Department of Commerce

David J. Walker, Director, Development Priorities and Evaluation, Department of Economic Development, Government of Alberta

Gabriel L. Warren, Director General, International Telecommunications, Department of Communications

Stephen H. Weiss, Managing Partner, Weiss, Peck & Greer Investments, New York

Bruce Wilkinson, Department of Economics, University of Alberta

Marvin S. Wodinsky, Economics and Trade Section, Bureau of United States Affairs, Department of External Affairs

Bernard Wood, Director, North-South Institute (2)

Stephen Woollcombe, Counsellor (Economic), Canadian Embassy in the United States (1, 2)

Clayton Yeutter, President, Chicago Mercantile Exchange (2)

Notes

Part I: Conditions for Crisis

[1] *Nickle's Daily Oil Bulletin*, September 15, 1981. The survey was sponsored by the Canadian Petroleum Association.

[2] "Poll Finds Reagan's Economic Plan Raises Hopes," *New York Times*, January 19, 1982.

[3] James A. Robinson, "Crisis," in *International Encyclopedia of the Social Sciences*, vol. III (New York: Crowell, Collier and Macmillan, 1968), pp. 510-11.

Chapter 1: The Shaking of the Special Relationship

[1] John Kirton, "Canada and the United States: A More Distinct Relationship," *Current History*, vol. 79 (November 1980), p. 117.

[2] Livingston T. Merchant and A.D.P. Heeney, "Canada and the United States — Principles for Partnership," *Department of State Bulletin*, August 2, 1965, p. 9. "In consultations with the United States, Canadian authorities must have confidence that the practice of quiet diplomacy is not only neighborly and convenient to the United States but that it is in fact more effective than the alternative of raising a row and being unpleasant in public."

[3] Gerald Wright, "Anxious Days are Here Again," *International Journal,* vol. XXXVI, no. 1 (Winter 1980-81), p. 233.

[4] Peter C. Dobell, "Negotiating with the United States," *International Journal*, vol. XXXVI, no. 1 (Winter 1980-81), p. 21.

[5] Mitchell Sharp, "Canada-U.S. Relations: Options for the Future," *International Perspectives*, special issue (Autumn 1972), pp. 1-24.

[6] Roger Frank Swanson, "The Ford Interlude and the U.S.-Canadian Relationship," *American Review of Canadian Studies*, vol. 7, no. 8 (Spring 1978), pp. 3-17.

[7] Peter C. Dobell, "The Influence of the United States Congress on Canadian-American Relations," *International Organization*, vol. 28 (Autumn 1974), pp. 903-29.

[8] Garth Stevenson, "Continental Integration and Canadian Unity," in W. Andrew Axline et al., eds., *Continental Community? Independence and Integration in North America* (Toronto: McClelland and Stewart, 1974), pp. 194-217.

[9] For the best political economy description of this process in Alberta and Saskatchewan see Larry Pratt and John Richards, *Prairie Capitalism: Power and Influence in the New West* (Toronto: McClelland and Stewart, 1979). For a general discussion of the bureaucratic expansion of provincial governments see Alan C. Cairns, "The Governments and Societies of Canadian Federalism," *Canadian Journal of Political Science*, vol. X, no. 4 (December 1977), pp. 695-725.

[10] *Foreign Ownership and the Structure of Canadian Industry: Report of the Task Force on the Structure of Canadian Industry* (Watkins Report) (Ottawa: Queen's Printer, 1968).

[11] *Eleventh Report of the Standing Committee on External Affairs and National Defence Respecting Canada-U.S. Relations*, Second Session, 28th Parliament (Wahn Report) (Ottawa: Queen's Printer, 1970).

[12] Government of Canada, *Foreign Direct Investment in Canada* (Gray Report) (Ottawa: Information Canada, 1972).

[13] Royal Commission on Book Publishing, *Canadian Publishers & Canadian Publishing* (Toronto: The Queen's Printer for Ontario, 1972).

[14] Richard D. French, *How Ottawa Decides: Planning and Industrial Policy-Making 1968-1980* (Toronto: Canadian Institute for Economic Policy/James Lorimer & Co., 1980), chapters 5 and 6.

[15] James Laxer, *Canada's Economic Strategy* (Toronto: McClelland and Stewart, 1981), p. 13.

[16] "MacGuigan Rakes U.S. 'Interference'," *Toronto Star*, October 19, 1980.

[17] Albert Breton, "The Economics of Nationalism," *Journal of Political Economy*, vol. 27, no. 4 (1964), p. 377; and Harry G. Johnson, "A Theoretical Model of Economic Nationalism in New and Developing States," *Political Science Quarterly*, vol. 80, no. 2 (1965), pp. 176, 183.

[18] *Major Canadian Projects, Major Canadian Opportunities: A Report by the Consultative Task Force on Industrial and Regional Benefits from Major Canadian Projects* (Blair-Carr Report) (Ottawa: Industry, Trade and Commerce Canada, June 1981).

[19] John J. Shepherd, "An Economic Strategy for Canada: Our Political Economy Regained," in The Walter L. Gordon Lecture Series, vol. 3, *An Economic Strategy for Canada* (Toronto: Canada Studies Foundation, 1979), pp. 9-27.

[20] Speech by Robert Blair, president and chief executive officer of NOVA, an Alberta corporation, delivered to the Empire Club, Toronto, Ontario, November 19, 1981.

[21] Hedrick Smith, "Reagan: What Kind of World Leader?" *New York Times Magazine*, November 16, 1980, p. 172.

[22] Charles F. Doran, "Canada and the Reagan Administration: Left Hand, Right Hand," *International Journal*, vol. XXXVI, no. 1 (Winter 1980-81), pp. 236-40.

Chapter 2: Crisis in the Capitals

[1] Anon., "Notes for a Recap of our Dialogue on the National Energy Program," confidential American document dated December 17, 1981.

[2] Gary Clyde Hufbauer and Andrew James Samet, "Investment Relations between Canada and the United States," in The Atlantic Council Working Group on the United States and Canada, *Canada and the United States: Dependence and Divergence* (Cambridge, Mass.: Ballinger, 1982), p. 141.

[3] Letter to the Honorable James G. Watt, secretary of the interior, March 26, 1981 from the lawyers of St. Joe Minerals, pp. 2, 5.

[4] This chronology is based mainly on "Notes for a Recap."

[5] U.S.A. Note from Secretary of State, March 5, 1981.

[6] David Crane, *Controlling Interest: The Canadian Gas and Oil Stakes* (Toronto: McClelland and Stewart, 1982), p. 25.

[7] "Notes for a Recap."

[8] "Brock Outlines Trade Policy for Congress; Opposes Trade Distorting Government Intervention," Information Release, United States International Communication Agency, 81-47 EC.

[9] Editorial, "Welcoming Mr. Trudeau," *Wall Street Journal,* July 9, 1981.

[10] Robert Stephens, "Trade Trouble: Protectionist Policies Fuel U.S. Resentment," *Globe and Mail,* July 15, 1981.

[11] Harald B. Malmgren, "Storm Flags Up For Canadian Business," *World Trade Outlook,* vol. 3, no. 7 (1981), pp. 4, 5.

[12] Art Pine and Frederick Rose, "Neighborly Feud," *Wall Street Journal,* August 6, 1981.

[13] Hyman Solomon, "U.S. Steps Up Its Drive To 'Punish' Us," *Financial Post,* August 22, 1981.

[14] Similar thinking was reported by John Honderich, "How Reagan Might Lower Boom On Us: Energy Policy and FIRA Have Americans in a Rage," *Toronto Star,* August 29, 1981.

[15] Ibid.

[16] John Carson-Parker, "Stop Worrying About the Canadian Invasion," *Fortune,* October 19, 1981, p. 200.

[17] "September 8 Meeting in Washington," Memo from D.R. Whelan, chief, multilateral and bilateral energy relations, Department of Energy, Mines and Resources, September 22, 1981.

[18] Jane Seaberry, "Administration Eyes Sanctions Against Canada," *Washington Post,* September 10, 1981.

[19] "Canada's Policies Attacked by U.S.," *Globe and Mail,* September 23, 1981; Myer Rashish, "North American Economic Relations" (Speech to the Center for Inter-American Relations, New York, September 22, 1981), mimeo.

[20] Letter from Alexander Haig to Mark MacGuigan conveyed by Ambassador Robinson from the U.S. embassy.

[21] Anon., "Summary Record of Discussion at US Ambassador's, October 13th," October 13, 1981. Memo marked Confidential.

[22] Ibid.

[23] David R. Macdonald, deputy United States trade representive, Opening Statement before a joint hearing of the Subcommittee on International Economic Policy and Trade and the Subcommittee on Inter-American Affairs of the House Committee on Foreign Affairs, October 21, 1981.

[24] "Notes for a Recap."

[25] Letter from the Secretary of State for External Affairs to Alexander Haig, November 5, 1981.

[26] *Economic Development for Canada in the 1980s* (Ottawa: Government of Canada, November 1981), p. 12.

[27] Ibid., p. 13.

[28] Confidential telegram dated December 2, 1981 and delivered December 4, 1981. Emphasis added in excerpts quoted.

[29] External Affairs draft dated December 15, 1981.

[30] "Dinner Meeting on Back-In," Memo from Richard Smith, U.S. notetaker, December 16, 1981.

[31] The Canadian memorandum on the same meeting made the same point: "The U.S. side could not understand why we considered the Brock letter to be offensive. . . . In the U.S. view, the Canadian reply was offensive, and not helpful. . . . We

replied we had no choice but to reply to the Brock letter since it was explosive and would have been embarrassing if it became public and had been left unanswered. Our rule of thumb in drafting the reply was to match the tone of the Brock letter, no more, no less." "Canada-U.S. Contact Group Meeting, December 16, 1981," December 17, 1981, Confidential.

[32] Peter Cook, "U.S. Files Challenge to FIRA with GATT," *Globe and Mail*, April 1, 1982.

[33] James A. Robinson, "Crisis," in *International Encyclopedia of the Social Sciences*, vol. III (New York: Crowell, Collier and Macmillan, 1968), pp. 510-11.

[34] Ibid.

Part II: Continental Economic Issues

[1] See, for example, Michael B. Dolan, Brian W. Tomlin and Harald von Riekhoff, "Integration and Autonomy in Canada-United States Relations, 1963-1972," *Canadian Journal of Political Science*, vol. XV, no. 2 (June 1982), pp. 331-37; Charles Pentland, "Political Integration: A Multidimensional Perspective," in Andrew Axline et al., eds., *Continental Community? Independence and Integration in North America* (Toronto: McClelland and Stewart, 1974), pp. 42-66; Daniel Drache, "Rediscovering Canadian Political Economy," in Wallace Clement and Daniel Drache, eds., *A Practical Guide to Canadian Political Economy* (Toronto: James Lorimer & Co., 1978), pp. 1-53; and John H. Redekop, "A Reinterpretation of Canadian-American Relations," *Canadian Journal of Political Science*, vol. IX, no. 2 (June 1976), pp. 227-43.

Chapter 3: The National Energy Program and Canadianization

[1] Edward F. Wonder, "The U.S. Government Response to the Canadian National Energy Program," mimeo (Washington, January 1982), p. 19.

[2] Larry Pratt and John Richards, *Prairie Capitalism: Power and Influence in the New West* (Toronto: McClelland and Stewart, 1979), p. 80.

[3] American companies could deduct from their U.S. income the cost of drilling in Canada — an advantage aimed to help increase U.S. energy supplies. See David Crane, *Controlling Interest: The Canadian Gas and Oil Stakes* (Toronto: McClelland and Stewart, 1982), pp. 176-98.

[4] Glyn R. Berry, "The Oil Lobby and the Energy Crisis," reprinted in Richard Schultz et al., *The Canadian Political Process*, 3rd ed. (Toronto: Holt, Rinehart and Winston, 1979), p. 255.

[5] *The Oil Import Question: A Report on the Relationship of Oil Imports to the National Security* (Shultz Report), April 1970, p. 94.

[6] Quoted in James Laxer, *The Energy Poker Game: The Politics of the Continental Resources Deal* (Toronto: New Press, 1970), p. 8.

[7] A.W. Cockerill, "Canada — Economic Colony," *The Guardian*, December 4, 1971, p. 4.

[8] Canada, Department of Energy, Mines and Resources, *An Energy Policy for Canada — Phase I*, vol. 1, *Analysis* (Ottawa: Information Canada, 1973).

[9] Canada, Department of Energy, Mines and Resources, *An Energy Strategy for Canada: Policies for Self-Reliance* (Ottawa: Supply and Services Canada, 1976), pp. 152-53.

[10] Michael Tucker, *Canadian Foreign Policy: Contemporary Issues and Themes* (Toronto, McGraw-Hill, 1980), pp. 88-90.

[11] Department of Energy, Mines and Resources, *An Energy Strategy for Canada.*

[12] *The Oil Import Question*, Appendix H, p. 297.

[13] *The State of Competition in the Canadian Petroleum Industry* (Bertrand Commission), vol. III, *International Linkages* (Ottawa: Department of Supply and Services, 1981), pp. 45-50.

[14] Ibid., pp. 34, 41.

[15] *The National Energy Program* (Ottawa: Energy, Mines and Resources Canada, 1980), p. 17.

[16] Glen Toner and François Bregha, "The Political Economy of Energy," in Michael S. Whittington and Glen Williams, eds., *Canadian Politics in the 1980s* (Toronto: Methuen, 1981), p. 20.

[17] Joel I. Bell, "Notes for an Address to Canadian-American Committee: Views on Canada. Canada's National Energy Programme," Chicago, Ritz-Carlton Hotel, March 20, 1981, p. 4.

[18] L.R. Pratt, "The Roots of Energy Policy: Canada's National Energy Program and the Multinational Corporation" (Paper presented to University Consortium for Research on North America, Harvard University, December 8, 1981), pp. 14-16.

[19] Quoted in Mel Watkins, "In Defence of the National Energy Program," *Canadian Forum*, June-July 1981, p. 7.

[20] Notes for Remarks By The Right Honourable P.E. Trudeau, Halifax Board of Trade, Halifax, N.S., January 25, 1980, p. 5: "The Liberal plan seeks to achieve energy security at a fair price for all Canadians. Our energy program for the 1980s consists of 7 major commitments. We would start at once to: (1) Set a Made in Canada pricing policy to secure adequate supplies of energy at reasonable prices. (2) Achieve energy security through the accelerated development of Canada's domestic potential and the ensuring of Canada's off-shore supply. (3) Develop a more balanced energy program through the replacement of oil by natural gas and other energy forms. (4) Strengthen and expand Petro-Canada as an instrument of national policy. (5) Place a new emphasis on conservation and the promotion of energy alternatives. (6) Ensure that Canada's energy sector becomes more Canadian-owned and controlled. (7) See that energy becomes part of the larger economic strategy, forming the core of any industrial or regional development approach."

[21] House of Commons, April 14, 1980, pp. 5-6.

[22] Anthony McCallum, "50% Canadian Share in Oil and Gas Industry Aim of Ottawa Policy," *Globe and Mail*, September 17, 1980.

[23] Edward F. Wonder, "U.S.-Canada Energy Relations," in The Atlantic Council Working Group on the United States and Canada, *Canada and the United States: Dependence and Divergence* (Cambridge, Mass.: Ballinger, 1982), p. 80.

[24] Peter Morici, Arthur J.R. Smith and Sperry Lea, *Canadian Industrial Policy* (Washington: National Planning Association, February 1981), p. 98.

[25] Christopher K. Leman, "Comparing Canadian and U.S. Regional Energy Conflicts: Beyond Greed and Envy," in Christopher K. Leman, ed., *Regional Issues in Energy Development: A Dialogue of East and West* (Cambridge, Mass.: Harvard Centre for International Affairs, September 1981), p. 20.

[26] James G. Watt, secretary of the interior, "Statement before the House Energy Subcommittee on Oversight and Investigations," August 6, 1981, p. 6.

382

27 G. Campbell Watkins, "Mr. Lalonde and the Price Mechanism: Or Never the Twain Shall Meet," in G.C. Watkins and M.A. Walker, eds., *Reaction: The National Energy Program* (Vancouver: The Fraser Institute, 1981), pp. 55-73.

28 Morici et al., *Canadian Industrial Policy*, p. 97.

29 Government of Canada, *The National Energy Program: Update 1982* (Ottawa: Minister of Supply and Services Canada, 1982), p. 14.

30 Pratt, "The Roots of Energy Policy," p. 26.

31 B. Wilkinson and B. Scarfe, "The Recycling Problem" (Paper prepared for the Ontario Economic Council Energy Conference, Toronto, September 27-28, 1979), cited in B.W. Wilkinson, *Canada in the Changing World Economy* (Montreal: C.D. Howe Research Institute, 1980), p. 93.

32 Richard Smith, minister, U.S. embassy, Ottawa, to Stephen Clarkson, November 30, 1981. Cited with permission.

33 *National Energy Program*, p. 47.

34 Confidential letter from J.P. Gallagher to an American politician, May 26, 1981, given the author by the writer.

35 Smith to Clarkson, November 30, 1981.

36 Peter M. Towe, "Canada's National Energy Program" (Speech to the American Gas Association, New York City, October 13, 1981), p. 8.

37 Wendy Dobson, *Canada's Energy Policy Debate* (Montreal: C.D. Howe Institute, 1981), p. 29.

38 Royal Commission on Canada's Economic Prospects, *Final Report* (Ottawa, November, 1957), Appendix H, p. 494.

39 *National Energy Program*, p. 39.

40 Marc Lalonde, "Notes for an Address to the Financial Post Conference: 'Year One: What's Ahead After 12 Months of the NEP?' " Calgary, October 27, 1981, p. 8.

41 *National Energy Program*, p. 47.

42 Towe, "Canada's National Energy Program," p. 10.

43 Morici et al., *Canadian Industrial Policy*, p. 102.

44 Lee Smith, "The Making of the Megamerger," *Fortune*, September 7, 1981, p. 58.

45 The Fifth Amendment to the U.S. Constitution, adopted in 1791, provided that private property could not be taken for public use without just compensation. Garth Stevenson, "Property Rights are not Imperiled," *Financial Post*, May 8, 1982.

46 Bob Hepburn, "64% Back Ottawa in Canadianizing Oil Industry: Poll," *Toronto Star*, January 23, 1982.

47 Jennifer Lewington, "Canadian Firms Get Break in Energy Bill," *Globe and Mail*, February 27, 1982; and Paul Taylor, "New Speculation about Incentives Spurs Oil Shares," *Globe and Mail*, April 9, 1982.

48 Report of Petroleum Monitoring Agency cited in Jennifer Lewington, "Energy Projects Hurt by Disputes," *Globe and Mail*, December 28, 1981.

49 Anthony McCallum, "Oil Companies Shifting Funds to Frontier," *Globe and Mail*, January 4, 1982.

50 Jennifer Lewington, "Imperial Puts Aside Ownership Question by Going to Farm-outs, Joint Ventures," *Globe and Mail*, February 17, 1982.

51 *NEP Update 1982*, pp. 73-77.

52 Donald Daly, "Canadianization is Good for Civil Servants," *Policy Options*, vol. 2 (September/October 1981), p. 52; and Ronald Anderson, "Canadianization Cost May Exceed Benefits," *Globe and Mail*, April 7, 1982.

[53] Barry Critchley, "Business Points Finger at Ottawa's Spending," *Financial Post*, May 1, 1982.
[54] *NEP Update 1982*, p. 46.
[55] Paul Taylor, "Shell Will Shed Non-Petroleum Businesses," *Globe and Mail*, February 25, 1982.

Chapter 4: FIRA and Ottawa's Industrial Strategy Options

[1] Government of Canada, *Royal Commission on Canada's Economic Prospects, Final Report* (Gordon Report) (Ottawa: Queen's Printer, 1957), p. 389.
[2] *Foreign Ownership and the Structure of Canadian Industry: Report of the Task Force on the Structure of Canadian Industry* (Watkins Report) (Ottawa: Privy Council Office, January 1968).
[3] *Eleventh Report of the Standing Committee on External Affairs and National Defence Respecting Canada-U.S. Relations*, Second Session, 28th Parliament (Wahn Report) (Ottawa: Queen's Printer, 1970).
[4] Government of Canada, *Foreign Direct Investment in Canada* (Gray Report) (Ottawa: Information Canada, 1972).
[5] Richard Schultz, "Canadian Regulation of Foreign Investment" (Preliminary notes for Seminar on Canadian-U.S. Relations, Harvard University, November 17, 1981), p. 3.
[6] Harald von Riekhoff, John H. Sigler and Brian W. Tomlin, *Canadian-U.S. Relations: Policy Environment, Issues, and Prospects* (Montreal: C.D. Howe Research Institute, 1979), p. 87.
[7] Richard Vine, deputy assistant secretary of state, Testimony before the Joint Economic Subcommittee on Inter-American Economic Relations, January 27, 1976.
[8] Julius Katz, assistant secretary of state, Interview with Michel Nadeau, *Le Devoir*, March 25, 1978.
[9] Thomas Enders, American ambassador to Canada, Speech at Stanford University, May 3, 1979.
[10] Jacob Kaplan, "U.S. Resource Policy: Canadian Connections," in Carl E. Beigie and Alfred O. Hero, Jr., eds., *Natural Resources in U.S.-Canadian Relations*, vol. 1 (Boulder, Colorado: Westview Press, 1980), pp. 120-21.
[11] "Trudeau Industry Plan: Play our Energy Card," *Toronto Star*, February 13, 1980.
[12] House of Commons, April 14, 1980, p. 6.
[13] Herb Gray, "Notes for a Speech," The Canadian Advanced Technology Association, April 9, 1980, p. 10.
[14] Herb Gray, "Notes for a Speech," The Empire Club of Canada, Toronto, April 24, 1980, p. 10.
[15] Herb Gray, "Economic Nationalism and Industrial Strategy," annual symposium, École des Hautes Études Commerciales, June 3, 1980, p. 4.
[16] Herb Gray, "Notes for a Speech," Association of Canadian Financial Corporations, June 20, 1980, p. 5. Emphasis in text.
[17] Herb Gray, Speech to Canada/Japan Businessmen's Conference, Tokyo, August 8, 1980, p. 4.
[18] Herb Gray, "Industrial Strategy Revisited," Niagara Institute, May 6, 1981, p. 20.
[19] FIRA deals with 20 per cent of the expansion of foreign direct investment. Mark

Lukasiewicz, "FIRA: Damned Often, Praised Seldom," *Globe and Mail*, August 11, 1979.

[20] C. Fred Bergsten, "International Investment: The Need For A New U.S. Policy" (Statement before the Subcommittee on International Economic Policy, Committee on Foreign Relations, United States Senate, July 30, 1981), p. 3.

[21] Ibid., p. 6.

[22] Ibid., p. 7.

[23] Gary Clyde Hufbauer, "The U.S. Response to Foreign Performance Requirements" (Statement before the Subcommittee on International Economic Policy of the Senate Foreign Relations Committee, Oversight Hearings on Trade Related Performance Requirements, September 28, 1981), p. 5.

[24] Raymond J. Waldmann, assistant secretary for international economic policy, U.S. Department of Commerce, Statement before the Subcommittee on Inter-American Affairs and Subcommittee on International Economic Policy and Trade, Committee on Foreign Affairs, U.S. House of Representatives, October 21, 1981, p. 2.

[25] Robert Hormats, assistant secretary of state for economic and business affairs, Statement before the Subcommittee on International Economic Policy of the Senate Committee on Foreign Relations, October 28, 1981, p. 2.

[26] Gary Clyde Hufbauer and Andrew James Samet, "Investment Relations Between Canada and the United States," in The Atlantic Council Working Group on the United States and Canada, *Canada and the United States: Dependence and Divergence* (Cambridge, Mass.: Ballinger, 1982), p. 105.

[27] Quoted in Nicholas J. Patterson, "U.S. Stringent on Foreign Investment," *Financial Post*, March 13, 1982.

[28] Foreign Investment Review Agency, "Regulation of Foreign Investment in the United States," mimeo (Ottawa: FIRA, 1982), pp. 4-51.

[29] Foreign Investment Review Agency, "Foreign Investment in the United States: Controls, Restrictions, Prohibitions and Policies," mimeo (Ottawa: FIRA, 1981), p. 16.

[30] Hufbauer and Samet, "Investment Relations," pp. 124-25.

[31] Hormats, Statement, p. 2.

[32] U.S. Department of Commerce computer tape #IQ246.

[33] Statistics Canada, *Canadian Imports by Domestic and Foreign Controlled Enterprises* (Ottawa: Minister of Supply and Services Canada, 1981), p. vii.

[34] Foreign Investment Review Agency, "U.S. Complaints about the Foreign Investment Review Act," mimeo (Ottawa: FIRA, 29 September 1981), p. 5.

[35] Hufbauer and Samet, "Investment Relations," p. 123.

[36] Organization for Economic Cooperation and Development, *Declaration on International Investment and Multinational Enterprises*, 21st June 1976, Part II, para. 1.

[37] Ibid., Part II, para. 4. Emphasis added.

[38] "Investment Issues and Guidelines for Multinational Enterprises," Notes for a statement made by the secretary of state for external affairs at the OECD ministerial meeting, Paris, June 21, 1976, pp. 1-2.

[39] Statement by the Honourable Flora MacDonald at the OECD ministerial meeting, Paris, June 13, 1979.

[40] P.E. Heinbecker to Stephen Clarkson, February 11, 1982.

[41] Hufbauer and Samet, "Investment Relations," p. 110.

[42] Malcolm Baldrige, secretary of commerce, and William Brock, United States trade

representative, to Herb Gray, minister of energy, trade and commerce, April 9, 1981, pp. 1-2.

43 Richard Smith, minister, U.S. embassy in Ottawa, to Stephen Clarkson, November 30, 1981.

44 Foreign Investment Review Agency, *Quarterly Report*, April-June 1980, pp. 3-4.

45 Herb Gray to William Brock, July 8, 1981, p. 3.

46 Gray Report, pp. 253-90.

47 Livingston T. Merchant and A.D.P. Heeney, "Canada and the United States — Principles for Partnership," *Department of State Bulletin*, August 2, 1965.

48 David Leyton-Brown, "Extraterritoriality in Canadian-American Relations," *International Journal*, vol. XXXVI, no. 1 (Winter 1980-81), p. 193.

49 Smith to Clarkson, p. 2.

50 Gary Clyde Hufbauer and Andrew James Samet, "Canadian-American Investment Relations" (Paper given at a seminar on Canadian-U.S. relations, Harvard University, November 1981), pp. 19-20.

51 Ibid., pp. 21-22.

52 Ibid., pp. 25-26.

53 David R. Macdonald, deputy United States trade representative, Opening Statement before a joint hearing of the Subcommittee on International Economic Policy and Trade and the Subcommittee on Inter-American Affairs of the House Committee on Foreign Affairs, October 21, 1981, p. 4.

54 *Economic Development for Canada in the 1980s* (Ottawa: Government of Canada, November 1981), p. 13.

55 Ibid., p. 12.

56 Hufbauer and Samet, "Investment Relations," p. 106.

57 Richard D. French, *How Ottawa Decides: Planning and Industrial Policy-Making 1968-1980* (Toronto: Canadian Institute for Economic Policy/James Lorimer & Co., 1980), pp. 101-2, 113-22.

58 Smith to Clarkson.

59 Barry Beale, *Energy and Industry: The Potential of Energy Development Projects for Canadian Industry in the Eighties* (Toronto: Canadian Institute for Economic Policy/James Lorimer & Co., 1980), pp. 41-42.

60 Herb Gray, "Notes for the Keynote Address," Sixth Canadian National Energy Forum, Ottawa, November 9, 1981.

61 Gray Report, p. 324.

62 Beale, *Energy and Industry*, pp. 41-42.

63 Ibid., p. xi.

64 House of Commons, April 14, 1980, p. 6.

65 *Major Canadian Projects, Major Canadian Opportunities: A Report by the Consultative Task Force on Industrial and Regional Benefits from Major Canadian Projects* (Blair-Carr Report) (Ottawa: Industry, Trade, and Commerce Canada, June 1981), p. 54.

66 Section 10 (3) and 76 3.2 (2), emphasis added.

67 Peter Morici, Arthur J.R. Smith and Sperry Lea, *Canadian Industrial Policy* (Washington: National Planning Association, February 1981), p. 102, emphasis added.

68 Smith to Clarkson.

386

Chapter 5: U.S. Trade Policy and Canadian Economic Prospects

[1] Charlotte Montgomery, "NDP Fears Auto Job Losses," *Toronto Star*, February 15, 1980.

[2] Mary Trueman, "Better Auto Trade Deal Pledged by Trudeau," *Globe and Mail*, February 15, 1980.

[3] Harold A. Innis, "Address to the Conference on Educational Problems in Canadian-American Relations, June, 1938," in *Essays in Canadian Economic History* (Toronto: University of Toronto Press, 1956), pp. 239-40.

[4] A.R. Moroz and K.J. Back, "Prospects for a Canada-United States Bilateral Free Trade Agreement: The Other Side of the Fence," *International Journal*, vol. XXXVI, no. 4 (Autumn 1981), p. 833.

[5] Standing Senate Committee on Foreign Affairs, *Canada-United States Relations*, vol. III, *Canada's Trade Relations with the United States* (Ottawa: Supply and Services Canada, 1982), p. 9.

[6] Quoted from S.D. Metzger, "The Anti-Dumping System and the Trade Agreement Act of 1979," mimeo (1980), in Fred Lazar, *The New Protectionism: Non-Tariff Barriers and Their Effects on Canada* (Toronto: Canadian Institute for Economic Policy/James Lorimer & Co., 1981), p. 32.

[7] Lazar, *The New Protectionism*, p. 31.

[8] Metzger, "The Anti-Dumping System," p. 2.

[9] Lazar, *The New Protectionism*, p. 35.

[10] Ibid., p. 39.

[11] Ibid., pp. 40-44.

[12] Ibid., p. 28.

[13] Rodney Grey, "Some Issues in Canada-U.S. Trade Relations," MS for *Canadian Public Policy*, vol. 8, supplement (1982), p. 5.

[14] Lazar, *The New Protectionism*, p. 31.

[15] Ibid., p. 44.

[16] Peter Morici, Arthur J.R. Smith and Sperry Lea, *Canadian Industrial Policy* (Washington: National Planning Association, February 1981), p. 183.

[17] Rodney de C. Grey, *Trade Policy in the 1980s: An Agenda for Canadian-U.S. Relations* (Montreal: C.D. Howe Research Institute, 1981), pp. 46, 55.

[18] Morici et al., *Canadian Industrial Policy*, p. 180.

[19] Ed Lumley, "Notes for a Speech to the Annual Meeting of the American Public Transit Association," Chicago, October 9, 1981, p. 3.

[20] Grey, "Some Issues," p. 3.

[21] Special Committee on a National Trading Corporation, Fourth Report, *Canada's Trade Challenge* (Ottawa: Supply and Services Canada, June 1981), summary page.

[22] Standing Senate Committee on Foreign Affairs, *Canada-United States Relations*, vol. II, *Canada's Trade Relations with the United States* (Ottawa: Queen's Printer, 1978), p. 35.

[23] Grey, "Some Issues," p. 7.

[24] Grey, *Trade Policy in the 1980s*, p. 66.

[25] Standing Senate Committee, *Canada-United States Relations*, vol. II, p. 42.

[26] Special Committee, *Canada's Trade Challenge*, p. 35.

[27] B.W. Wilkinson, *Canada in the Changing World Economy* (Montreal: C.D. Howe Research Institute, 1980), pp. 61, 65, 67, 70, 78-79.

28 Department of Finance, *Economic Review, 1980.*
29 Standing Senate Committee, *Canada-United States Relations*, vol. III, p. 18.
30 Ibid., p. 26.
31 Carl E. Beigie, *The Canada-U.S. Automotive Agreement: An Evaluation* (Montreal: Canadian-American Committee of the National Planning Association [U.S.A.] and Private Planning Association of Canada, 1970), pp. 74, 135.
32 *The Canadian Automotive Industry: Performance and Proposals for Progress*, Inquiry into the Automotive Industry, Simon Reisman, Commissioner (Ottawa: Minister of Supply and Services Canada, 1978), pp. 235-36.
33 Standing Senate Committee, *Canada-United States Relations*, vol. II, p. 106.
34 Government of Ontario, *Canada's Share of the North American Automotive Industry: An Ontario Perspective* (Toronto: Ministry of Treasury, Economics and Intergovernmental Affairs, May 1978), p. 22.
35 Ibid., p. 14.
36 Gilbert R. Winham, *The Automobile Trade Crisis of 1980* (Halifax: Centre for Foreign Policy Studies, Dalhousie University, June 1981), p. 89.
37 I am indebted to James Keeley and his Ph.D. thesis, "Constraints on Canadian International Economic Policy" (Stanford University, 1980) for much of the information concerning the chronicle of these negotiations. See also John Kirton, "The Politics of Bilateral Management: The Case of the Automotive Trade," *International Journal*, vol. XXXVI, no. 1 (Winter 1980-81), pp. 39-69.
38 Gary Clyde Hufbauer and Andrew James Samet, "Investment Relations Between Canada and the United States," in The Atlantic Council Working Group on the United States and Canada, *Canada and the United States: Dependence and Divergence* (Cambridge, Mass.: Ballinger, 1982), pp. 55, 46.
39 Standing Senate Committee, *Canada-United States Relations*, vol. II, p. 103.
40 Rodney de C. Grey, "Canada in the North American Trading Economy," in *Developments Abroad and the Domestic Economy*, vol. I (Toronto: Ontario Economic Council, 1980), pp. 18-19.
41 Winham, *Automobile Trade Crisis*, p. 99.
42 Ross Perry, *The Future of Canada's Auto Industry* (Toronto: Canadian Institute for Economic Policy/James Lorimer & Co., 1982).
43 *The Canadian Automotive Industry*, p. 236.
44 Wilkinson, *Canada in the Changing World Economy*, pp. 160-67; and Standing Senate Committee, *Canada-United States Relations*, vol. II, p. 66.
45 Clifford L. Mort, chairman, Dow Chemical of Canada, Testimony before the Standing Senate Committee on Foreign Affairs, July 8, 1980, 9:9.
46 Robert Gibbens, "Potential Seen for Petrochemical Growth," *Globe and Mail*, October 9, 1981.
47 B.G.S. Withers, vice-president, Petrosar, Testimony before the Standing Senate Committee on Foreign Affairs, July 8, 1980, 9:15.
48 Jack S. Dewar, president, Union Carbide Canada Ltd., Testimony before the Standing Senate Committee on Foreign Affairs, July 8, 1980, 9:24.
49 The Hon. Hugh Planche, minister of economic development, Alberta, Testimony before the Standing Senate Committee on Foreign Affairs, March 26, 1981, 21:15.
50 Grey, *Trade Policy in the 1980s*, p. 31.
51 Mort, Testimony before SSCFA, 9:10.
52 Withers, Testimony before SSCFA, 9:13-14.
53 Planche, Testimony before SSCFA, 21:11.

388

[54] Julius Katz, senior vice-president, ACLI International Inc., White Plains, N.Y., Testimony before the Standing Senate Committee on Foreign Affairs, June 25, 1980, 7:26-27.

[55] Lawrence Krause, senior fellow, Brookings Institute, Washington, Testimony before the Standing Senate Committee on Foreign Affairs, June 25, 1980, 7:26.

[56] Fred Lazar, Testimony before the Standing Senate Committee on Foreign Affairs, July 10, 1980, 10:35.

[57] Grey, *Trade Policy in the 1980s*, p. 37.

[58] Senate Standing Committee, *Canada-United States Relations*, vol. III, p. 57.

[59] For a comprehensive statement of this position see Economic Council of Canada, *Looking Outward: A New Trade Strategy for Canada* (Ottawa: Information Canada, 1975).

[60] Paul Wonnacott and Ronald J. Wonnacott, "Free Trade between the United States and Canada: Fifteen Years Later" (London, Ont.: Centre for the Study of International Economic Relations, Working Paper 8011, March 1980).

[61] Wilkinson, *Canada in the Changing World Economy*, Appendix D, pp. 158-70.

[62] R. Schwindt, "Economic Integration and the Economics of Industry: North American Expectations vs. European Realities," mimeo (Simon Fraser University, 1982), p. 28.

[63] Grey, *Trade Policy in the 1980s*, p. 4.

[64] Senate Standing Committee, *Canada-United States Relations*, vol. III, p. 43.

[65] Ibid., p. 41.

[66] A.R. Moroz, "The Canada-United States Free Trade Option: And What of the United States," *Choices*, March 1982, p. 1.

[67] Senate Standing Committee, *Canada-United States Relations*, vol. III, p. 46.

[68] William E. Brock, "Priority Trade Issues of the 1980s," *Economic Impact*, no. 38 (1982), p. 33.

[69] Gary Hufbauer, "Introduction and Summary," in Gary C. Hufbauer, ed., *U.S. International Economic Policy, 1981: A Draft Report* (Washington, D.C.: International Law Institute, April 1982), pp. 1/30-37.

[70] Emilio Collado, "Reciprocity Legislation," in ibid., p. 5/11.

[71] Brock, "Priority Trade Issues," p. 30, emphasis added.

[72] Collado, "Reciprocity Legislation," p. 5/20, emphasis added.

[73] Ibid., p. 5/21.

[74] Ibid., p. 5/24.

[75] Andrew Samet and Gary Hufbauer, "North America," in Hufbauer, ed., *U.S. International Economic Policy, 1981*, p. 12/16.

Chapter 6: The Alaska Pipeline and Continental Resource Integration

[1] This chronicle is based on the following sources: John H. Ashworth, "Continuity and Change in the U.S. Decision-Making Process in Raw Materials," in Carl E. Beigie and Alfred O. Hero, Jr., eds., *Natural Resources in U.S.-Canadian Relations*, vol. I (Boulder, Colorado: Westview Press, 1980), p. 67 ff.; François Bregha, *Bob Blair's Pipeline* (Toronto: James Lorimer & Co., 1979); John N. McDougall, "Prebuild Phase or Latest Phase? The United States Fuel Market and Canadian Energy Policy," *International Journal*, vol. XXXVI, no. 1 (Winter 1980-81), pp. 117-38; Harald von Riekhoff, John H. Sigler and Brian W. Tomlin, *Canadian-U.S. Relations: Policy Environments, Issues and Prospects* (Montreal:

C.D. Howe Research Institute, 1979), pp. 70-74; Michael Tucker, *Canadian Foreign Policy: Contemporary Issues and Themes* (Toronto: McGraw-Hill Ryerson, 1980), pp. 87-90.

2 Bregha, *Bob Blair's Pipeline*, p. 37.

3 von Riekhoff et al., *Canadian-U.S. Relations*, p. 72.

4 I am indebted to John Donner for drawing to my attention this basic distinction between petroleum as energy and petroleum as resource and its profound implications for policy making.

5 Statement by Mitchell Sharp in Elliot J. Feldman, ed., *Canada and Mexico: The Comparative and Joint Politics of Energy* (Cambridge, Mass.: Harvard Center for International Affairs, Policy Paper No. 3, September 1981), p. 34.

6 Whether deliberately or not, some facets of Alberta government policy produced an artificial surplus crisis in natural gas.

  • Not pro-rating the gas market among the producers, as is done with oil, forces companies without sales contracts to wait for the market to expand or sell at reduced prices to petrochemical plants.

  • Government incentives encourage the drilling of gas wells which, if not brought under production for one year, get 100 per cent deduction from income tax as a dry hole.

  • The government refuses to leave its share of the gas in the ground, thereby taking some 35 per cent of the market; if government gas were left in the ground, producers with "surpluses" would be able to sell their gas.

The federal government agreed to increase the wellhead price for gas and gave other incentives for exploration.

7 Arlon R. Tussing and Connie C. Barlow, *Financing the Alaska Highway Gas Pipeline: What Is To Be Done?* (Institute of Social and Economic Research, University of Alaska, April 1979), p. 1, quoted in Arthur W. Donner, *Financing the Future: Canada's Capital Markets in the Eighties* (Toronto: Canadian Institute for Economic Policy/James Lorimer & Co., 1982), p. 56.

8 "U.S. will not Guarantee Alaska Pipeline Funding." *Globe and Mail*, October 28, 1981.

9 Eric Kierans in an address to the Canadian Economics Association, June 2, 1973.

10 B.W. Wilkinson, *Canada in the Changing World Economy* (Montreal: C.D. Howe Research Institute, 1980), p. 82.

11 Government of Canada, *Foreign Direct Investment in Canada* (Gray Report) (Ottawa: Information Canada, 1972), p. 21.

12 Wilkinson, *Canada in the Changing World Economy*, p. 85.

13 William T. Hogan, S.J., "Iron Ore," in Carl E. Beigie and Alfred O. Hero, Jr., eds., *Natural Resources in U.S.-Canadian Relations*, vol. II (Boulder, Colorado: Westview Press, 1980), p. 16 ff.

14 John I. Cameron, "Nickel," in Beigie and Hero, eds., *Natural Resources in U.S.-Canadian Relations*, vol. II, p. 45 ff.

15 John W. Whitney, "Copper," in Beigie and Hero, eds., *Natural Resources in U.S.-Canadian Relations*, vol. II, pp. 300-302.

16 Jeanne Kirk Laux and Maureen Appel Molot, "Potash," in Beigie and Hero, eds., *Natural Resources in U.S.-Canadian Relations*, vol. II, p. 143 ff.

17 Roma Dauphin, with the collaboration of Renaud Bernardin, "Asbestos," in Beigie and Hero, eds., *Natural Resources in U.S.-Canadian Relations*, vol. II, p. 248 ff.

18 Canadian Forestry Service, Environment Canada, "A Forest Sector Strategy for Canada," mimeo (Ottawa, 1981), pp. 2-3.

[19] Peter H. Pearse, "Forest Products," in Beigie and Hero, eds., *Natural Resources in U.S.-Canadian Relations*, vol. II, p. 426.

[20] Ibid., p. 455.

[21] Pearse, "Forest Products," p. 445; and Canadian Forestry Service, "A Forest Sector Strategy," p. 22.

[22] Harold D. Foster and W.R. Derrick Sewell, *Water: The Emerging Crisis in Canada* (Toronto: Canadian Institute for Economic Policy/James Lorimer & Co., 1981), pp. 30-31.

[23] Arthur F. Pillsbury, "The Salinity of Rivers," *Scientific American*, July 1981, pp. 54-65.

[24] Robert James McGavin, "Water, Water Everywhere — But Shortages are Coming," *International Perspectives,* July-August 1978, p. 30.

[25] Foster and Sewell, *Water: The Emerging Crisis*, p. 90.

[26] Denis l'Homme in Feldman, *Canada and Mexico*, p. 30; also Robert Bourassa "urged an increase in exports of hydro power to New England and New York," reported in Christopher K. Leman, ed., *Regional Issues in Energy Development: A Dialogue of East and West* (Cambridge, Mass.: Harvard Center for International Affairs, Policy Paper No. 2, September 1981), p. 56.

[27] Denis l'Homme in Feldman, *Canada and Mexico*, p. 32.

[28] Alfred O. Hero, Jr. "Overview and Conclusions," in Beigie and Hero, eds., *Natural Resources in U.S.-Canadian Relations*, vol. II, pp. 591, 576, 590.

[29] Jacob Kaplan, "U.S. Resource Policy: Canadian Connections," in Beigie and Hero, eds., *Natural Resources in U.S.-Canadian Relations*, vol. I, p. 114.

[30] Ted Greenwood with Alvin Streeter, Jr., "Uranium," in Beigie and Hero, eds., *Natural Resources in U.S.-Canadian Relations*, vol. II, p. 383; and Donald S. Macdonald, "Statement," in Canadian-American Committee, *Improving Bilateral Consultation and Economic Issues* (Washington, 1981), p. 15.

[31] Kaplan, "U.S. Resource Policy," p. 111.

[32] Energy, Mines and Resources Canada, *Mineral Policy: A Discussion Paper* (Ottawa: Supply and Services Canada, 1981), p. 151.

[33] Ibid., p. 147.

[34] Donald J. Patton, "The Evolution of Canadian Federal Mineral Policies," in Beigie and Hero, eds., *Natural Resources in U.S.-Canadian Relations*, vol. I, pp. 220-23.

[35] Hero, "Overview and Conclusions," p. 605.

[36] Garth Stevenson, "The Process of Making Mineral Resource Policy in Canada," in Beigie and Hero, eds., *Natural Resources in U.S.-Canadian Relations*, vol. I, p. 177.

[37] "From the days of the Physiocrats and David Ricardo, economists have been concerned with economic rent, a return for no functional role." Eric Kierans, "Report on Natural Resources Policy in Manitoba" (Prepared for the Secretariat for the Planning and Priorities Committee of Cabinet, Government of Manitoba, 1973), p. 47.

[38] Wilkinson, *Canada in the Changing World Economy*, p. 93.

[39] Ibid.

[40] Energy, Mines and Resources Canada, *Mineral Policy: A Discussion Paper*, pp. 59-66.

Chapter 7: The Macroeconomic Policy Context

[1] "Sharp Signals of Concern Cross Atlantic to Reagan," *Globe and Mail*, February 22, 1982.

[2] "PM Growing Impatient over High U.S. Rates," *Globe and Mail*, February 26, 1982.

[3] Richard Cleroux, "U.S. Economic Policies under Fire by Pawley at Close of NDP Session," *Globe and Mail*, February 15, 1982.

[4] R.B. Bryce, "Can We Have 'Made in Canada' Interest Rates?" *Choices*, February 1982, p. 1.

[5] Harold A. Innis, "Address to the Conference on Educational Problems in Canadian-American Relations, June, 1938," in *Essays in Canadian Economic History* (Toronto: University of Toronto Press, 1956), pp. 238-39.

[6] A.F.W. Plumptre, *Three Decades of Decision: Canada and the World Monetary System, 1944-75* (Toronto: McClelland and Stewart, 1977).

[7] Robert M. Dunn, Jr., *The Canada-U.S. Capital Market: Intermediation, Integration, and Policy Independence* (Montreal: C.D. Howe Research Institute, 1978), p. 105.

[8] Ibid., p. 107.

[9] Arthur W. Donner, *Financing the Future: Canada's Capital Markets in the Eighties* (Toronto: Canadian Institute for Economic Policy/James Lorimer & Co., 1982), p. 63.

[10] Ibid., p. 34.

[11] Data quoted from David Herskowitz in "Flaws Seen in Reaganomics," *Globe and Mail*, February 23, 1982.

[12] Thomas Courchene, *Money, Inflation, and the Bank of Canada*, vol. 2, *An Analysis of Monetary Gradualism, 1975-1980* (Montreal: C.D. Howe Research Institute, 1982), pp. 239-55.

[13] Arthur Donner, "Freeing the Dollar May Be the Best Bet," *Globe and Mail*, December 7, 1981.

[14] William Watson, "Short-term Pain May Cause Long-term Pain," *Financial Post*, February 27, 1982.

[15] Reuben Bellan, "Mad Money: The Case Against High Interest Rates," *Today*, August 8, 1981, pp. 14-15.

[16] Robert M. Dunn, Jr., "The Changing Pattern of Canada-U.S. Financial Flows," *Foreign Investment Review*, vol. 5, no. 1 (Autumn 1981), p. 8.

[17] John McCallum, "Controls May Help Bring Rates Down," *Globe and Mail*, February 22, 1982; and Clarence L. Barber and John C.P. McCallum, *Controlling Inflation: Learning from Experience in Canada, Europe and Japan* (Toronto: Canadian Institute for Economic Policy/James Lorimer & Co., 1982), chapter 5.

[18] B.W. Wilkinson, *A Statement on Current Economic Issues* (Ottawa: Canadian Institute for Economic Policy, October 1981), p. 7.

[19] Nicholas Hunter, "Mulholland Foresees Danger in Monetarism," *Globe and Mail*, April 30, 1982.

[20] Quoted by Ronald Anderson, "Inflation Fight Lost if MacEachen Goes," *Globe and Mail*, February 12, 1982.

[21] B.W. Wilkinson, "Long Term Capital Inflows and Balance of Payments Policy," in The Walter L. Gordon Lecture Series, vol. 3, *An Economic Strategy for Canada* (Toronto: Canadian Studies Foundation, 1979), p. 32.

[22] B.W. Wilkinson, *Canada in the Changing World Economy* (Montreal, C.D. Howe Research Institute, 1980), p. 118.

[23] Dunn, *The Canada-U.S. Capital Market*, pp. 54-55.

[24] Bank of Canada, *Annual Report*, 1981, p. 22.

[25] Wilkinson, *Canada in the Changing World Economy*, pp. 64, 122.
[26] Donner, *Financing the Future*, p. 73.
[27] Andrew G. Kniewasser, "Canada's Investment Program, 1981-2000," *Foreign Investment Review*, vol. 5, no. 1 (Autumn 1981), p. 16.

Chapter 8: Acid Rain and Environmental Dependence

[1] "Exchange of remarks between the President and Prime Minister Trudeau," Office of the Press Secretary, U.S. embassy, Ottawa, March 10, 1981, p. 3.
[2] Subcommittee on Acid Rain of Standing Committee on Fisheries and Forestry, House of Commons, *Still Waters. The Chilling Reality of Acid Rain* (Irwin Report) (Ottawa: Ministry of Supply and Services Canada, 1981), p. 19.
[3] Ibid., p. 91.
[4] Harold D. Foster and W.R. Derrick Sewell, *Water: The Emerging Crisis in Canada* (Toronto: Canadian Institute for Economic Policy/James Lorimer & Co., 1981), p. 55. The wide variety of cost estimates that have been made reflects the different assumptions and methodologies that have been used. The Congressional Office of Technology Assessment estimates the cost of a 10-million ton SO_2 reduction program at $3.4 billion per year. The U.S. National Commission on Air Quality estimates a 7.6-million ton program would cost $2.2 billion per year. The House of Commons (Irwin) report estimates it would cost $269-319 million per year to reduce Canadian emissions from power plants and smelters by 50 per cent.
[5] Don Munton, "Acid Rain — Silver Clouds can have Black Linings," *International Perspectives*, January/February 1981, p. 8.
[6] Don Munton, "Dependence and Interdependence in Transboundary Environmental Relations," *International Journal*, vol. XXXVI, no. 1 (Winter 1980-81), p. 181.
[7] *Joint Statement on Transboundary Air Quality by the Government of Canada and the Government of the United States of America*, n.d.
[8] Foster and Sewell, *Water: The Emerging Crisis*, p. 52.
[9] *Joint Statement on Transboundary Air Quality*.
[10] For a detailed account of the politics of these negotiations see Munton, "Dependence and Interdependence," pp. 167-77.
[11] *Memorandum of Intent between the Government of Canada and the Government of the United States of America Concerning Transboundary Air Pollution*, Ottawa, n.d.
[12] George Rejhon, "The Transnational Implications of Acid Rain: United States-Canadian Diplomatic Initiatives" (Paper presented to Case Western University, Cleveland, Ohio, March 28, 1981), p. 4.
[13] Philip Shabecoff, "Democrats Accuse Reagan of Trying to Kill Environmental Agency," *New York Times*, February 5, 1982.
[14] Philip Shabecoff, "U.S. Environmental Agency Making Deep Staffing Cuts," *New York Times*, January 3, 1982.
[15] Don Munton, "Reagan, Canada, and the Common Environment," *International Perspectives*, May/June 1982, pp. 3-4.
[16] Joanne Omang, "EPA Revision of Clean Air Act Leaves a 'Shell' Waxman Says," *Washington Post*, June 20, 1981.
[17] Philip Shabecoff, "Congress Divided on Clean Air Bill," *New York Times*, February 11, 1982.
[18] Philip Shabecoff, "Reagan Proposal on Clean Air Act Delayed by Split Among Advisers," *New York Times*, July 28, 1981.

[19] Munton, "Dependence and Interdependence," pp. 165-68.

[20] The Hon. John Roberts, "The Urgency of Controlling Acid Rain" (Speech to the Air Pollution Control Association, June 23, 1980), quoted in Munton, "Dependence and Interdependence," p. 176.

[21] Michael Keating, "U.S. 'Unfriendly' on Acid Rain," *Globe and Mail*, October 14, 1981.

[22] James M. Friedman, "Canadian Economic and Energy Policy Factors Affecting the Acid Rain Issue" (Speech given to a Congressional delegation, Washington, July 28, 1981).

[23] National Academy of Sciences, *Atmosphere-Biosphere Interactions: Toward a Better Understanding of the Ecological Consequences of Fossil Fuel Combustion* (Washington: National Academy Press, 1981), pp. 3, 7, 18.

[24] Subcommittee on Acid Rain, *Still Waters*, p. 100.

[25] Michael Keating, "Canada Takes Acid-Rain Woes to U.S. Public," *Globe and Mail*, September 30, 1981.

[26] John King, "Canadians Confront Congressmen over Acid Rain," *Globe and Mail*, October 7, 1981.

[27] Subcommittee on Acid Rain, *Still Waters*, p. 94.

[28] Ibid., p. 26.

[29] The member organizations of the Canadian Coalition on Acid Rain as of summer 1981 were: Algonquin Wildlands League, Allied Boating Association of Canada, The Unit on Public Social Responsibility (Anglican Church of Canada), Canadian Environmental Law Association, Canadian Nature Federation, Canadian Fishing Tackle Industry, Canadian Sport Fishing Institute, Canadian Sporting Goods Association, Canadian Wildlife Federation, Conservation Council of Ontario, Federation of Ontario Cottagers' Associations, Federation of Ontario Naturalists, International Atlantic Salmon Foundation, Inuit Tapirisat of Canada, National Survival Institute, Natural History Society of PEI, Northern Ontario Tourist Outfitters' Association, Ontario Federation of Anglers & Hunters, Ontario Lung Association, Pollution Probe, Sierra Club of Ontario, Société pour Vaincre la Pollution (SVP), STOP (Montreal), Temiskaming Environmental Action Committee, Tourism Industry Association of Canada, Tourism Ontario, Union of Ontario Indians, World Wildlife Fund (Canada).

[30] Testimony by the CCAR cited in Subcommittee on Acid Rain, *Still Waters*, p. 94.

[31] Keating, "Canada Takes Acid-Rain Woes to U.S. Public."

[32] The Province of Ontario, *A Submission to the United States Environmental Protection Agency Opposing Relaxation of SO_2 Emission Limits in State Implementation Plans and Urging Enforcement* (Ontario, Ministry of the Environment, March 12, 1981), Table 7.1, p. 102.

[33] James Rusk, "U.S. Blamed as Talks on Acid Rain Stalled," *Globe and Mail*, June 16, 1982.

[34] Subcommittee on Acid Rain, *Still Waters*, p. 92.

[35] Michael Tucker, *Canadian Foreign Policy: Contemporary Issues and Themes* (Toronto: McGraw-Hill, 1980), p. 93.

[36] O.P. Dwivedi and John E. Carroll, "Issues in Canadian-American Environmental Relations," in O.P. Dwivedi, ed., *Resources and the Environment: Policy Perspectives for Canada* (Toronto: McClelland and Stewart, 1980), p. 323.

[37] Tucker, *Canadian Foreign Policy*, p. 95.

[38] Ibid., p. 99.

[39] Kim Richard Nossal, "The Unmaking of Garrison: United States Politics and the Management of Canadian-American Boundary Waters," *Behind the Headlines*, vol. XXXVII, no. 1 (1978), pp. 25-26. See also John E. Carroll and Roderick M. Logan, *The Garrison Diversion Unit: A Case Study in Canadian-U.S. Environmental Relations* (Montreal: C.D. Howe Research Institute, 1980).

[40] Don Munton, "Great Lakes Water Quality: A Study in Environmental Politics and Diplomacy," in O.P. Dwivedi, ed., *Resources and the Environment: Policy Perspectives for Canada* (Toronto; McClelland and Stewart, 1980), p. 159.

[41] Ibid., p. 166.

[42] Foster and Sewell, *Water: The Emerging Crisis*, p. 62.

[43] Michael Keating, "U.S. Must Hasten Cleanup: Roberts," *Globe and Mail*, October 15, 1981, indicates that "Canada took the unprecedented step of doing tests in a U.S. plant because no U.S. agency was willing to do them." Rae Tyson, "EPA to Release Repair Funds for Sewage Treatment Plant," *Globe and Mail*, October 15, 1981: "Pressed by a torrent of criticism from both sides of the border, the U.S. Environmental Protection Agency will release funds to repair a sewage treatment plant that has polluted the Niagara River for more than three years."

[44] Munton, "Reagan, Canada, and the Common Environment," p. 4.

Chapter 9: Fisheries, Boundaries, and Sovereignty at Sea

[1] Geoffrey Stevens, "Political Fish," *Globe and Mail*, March 19, 1981.

[2] Erik B. Wang, "Canada-United States Fisheries and Maritime Boundary Negotiations: Diplomacy in Deep Water," *Behind the Headlines*, vols. XXXVIII-XXXIX (April 1981), p. 4.

[3] Ibid., p. 8.

[4] Ibid., p. 10.

[5] Ibid., pp. 12-13.

[6] *Globe and Mail*, September 10, 1979.

[7] Ibid.

[8] Stevens, "Political Fish."

[9] Ibid.

[10] Wang, "Diplomacy in Deep Water," p. 17.

[11] Ibid., p. 22.

[12] Ibid., p. 26.

[13] Ibid., p. 30.

[14] *Globe and Mail*, April 16, 1980.

[15] "A Note on Fisheries" in The Atlantic Council Working Group on the United States and Canada, *Canada and the United States: Dependence and Divergence* (Cambridge, Mass.: Ballinger, 1982), pp. 314-15.

[16] Ibid., p. 315.

[17] *Globe and Mail*, September 10, 1979.

[18] *Oversight Report on the U.S.-Canada East Coast Fishery Agreement and Boundary Treaty*, Subcommittee on Fisheries and Wildlife Conservation and the Environment, March 25, 1980 (Washington, 1980).

[19] Wang, "Diplomacy in Deep Water," p. 33.

[20] *Toronto Star*, October 22, 1980.

[21] Wang, "Diplomacy in Deep Water," pp. 33-34.

[22] *Toronto Star*, April 30, 1981.

[23] "A Note on Fisheries," pp. 317-18.

24 Brian Job, "Going for Broke: The Risks of COD Diplomacy with the United States" (Lecture to the Canadian Institute of International Affairs, Toronto, June 3, 1982).

25 Nicholas Burnett, "Why U.S. Torpedoed Sea-Law Talks," reprinted in *Winnipeg Free Press*, April 22, 1981.

26 John Temple Swing, "Law of the Sea: Fanfare and an Uncertain Future," *Christian Science Monitor*, March 9, 1981.

27 *New York Times*, August 2, 1981.

28 Michael Cope, "American Impreciseness Causing Crisis and Chaos," *Calgary Herald*, August 20, 1981.

29 Swing, "Law of the Sea: Fanfare and an Uncertain Future."

30 Burnett, "Why U.S. Torpedoed Sea-Law Talks."

31 Maks Westerman, "Mining the Seabed," *New York Times*, December 7, 1981.

32 Swing, "Law of the Sea: Fanfare and an Uncertain Future."

33 Melvyn Westlake, "Will Reagan Take the Law of the Sea into his Own Hands?", *The Times*, April 16, 1982.

34 Westerman, "Mining the Seabed."

35 Ibid.

36 Ian McGregor, "U.S. Snag in Law of the Sea Talks," *The Times*, August 17, 1981.

37 Westerman, "Mining the Seabed."

38 David MacDonald, "Seabed Mining Worries Reagan," *Winnipeg Free Press*, September 9, 1981.

39 Ibid. See also Bernard D. Nossiter, "U.S. Likely to Ask Sea-Law Revision," *New York Times*, December 10, 1981.

40 Bernard Nossiter, "UN Adopts Sea Law; U.S. Votes No," *New York Times*, May 1, 1982.

41 *Winnipeg Free Press*, September 8, 1981.

42 Louis Wiznitzer, "U.S. Blocks Law of the Sea Treaty," *Christian Science Monitor*, March 9, 1981.

43 *Globe and Mail*, May 18, 1981.

44 Donald Slimman, "The Parting of the Waves: Canada-United States Differences on the Law of the Sea," *Behind the Headlines*, vol. XXXIII (April 1975), pp. 17-18.

45 Michael Tucker, *Canadian Foreign Policy: Contemporary Issues and Themes* (Toronto: McGraw-Hill Ryerson, 1980), p. 177.

46 Slimman, "The Parting of the Waves," p. 20.

47 Tucker, *Canadian Foreign Policy*, p. 176.

48 Ibid., p. 177.

49 Ibid., p. 176.

50 *Calgary Herald*, September 5, 1980.

51 Slimman, "The Parting of the Waves," p. 18.

52 David G. LeMarquand and Anthony Scott, "Canada's International Environmental Relations," in O.P. Dwivedi, ed., *Resources and the Environment: Policy Perspectives for Canada* (Toronto: McClelland and Stewart, 1980), p. 90.

53 *Calgary Herald*, August 25, 1981.

54 Lincoln P. Bloomfield, "Riches of the Sea: Compromise or Conflict?" *Christian Science Monitor*, March 26, 1981.

55 Swing, "Law of the Sea: Fanfare and an Uncertain Future."

56 Westerman, "Mining the Seabed."

57 Wiznitzer, "U.S. Blocks Law of the Sea Treaty."

[58] *New York Times*, March 15, 1981.
[59] Nossiter, "U.S. Likely to Ask Sea-Law Revision." See also MacDonald, "Seabed Mining Worries Reagan."
[60] "U.S. Challenges Treaty on Seabed Resources," *The Times*, March 8, 1982.
[61] Louis Wiznitzer, "U.S. Refuses to Come Aboard for Law of the Sea Treaty," *Christian Science Monitor*, March 8, 1982.
[62] John King, "Sea Pact in Danger as U.S. Vacillates," *Globe and Mail*, February 19, 1982; and Bernard Nossiter, "Third World Group Plans to Complete Treaty on Seas," *New York Times*, March 9, 1982.
[63] Nossiter, "UN Adopts Sea Law; U.S. Votes No."
[64] Westlake, "Will Reagan Take the Law of the Sea into his Own Hands?"

Chapter 10: Cultural Survival and Telecommunications

[1] Speech by the Honourable R.B. Bennett in the House of Commons quoted in Frank W. Peers, *The Politics of Canadian Broadcasting, 1920-1951* (Toronto: University of Toronto Press, 1969), p. 441.
[2] Peers, *The Politics of Canadian Broadcasting*, p. 440.
[3] *Report of the Royal Commission on National Development in the Arts, Letters and Sciences, 1949-1951* (Massey-Lévesque Report) (Ottawa: Printer to the King's Most Excellent Majesty, 1951), pp. 274-71, 4.
[4] Alphonse Ouimet, "Canada versus U.S.A.," *Intermedia*, vol. 7, no. 6 (November 1979), n.p.
[5] Federal Cultural Policy Review Committee (Applebert), *Summary of Briefs and Hearings* (Ottawa: Minister of Supply and Services Canada, 1982), pp. 4-5.
[6] Ibid., p. 217.
[7] Frank W. Peers, *The Public Eye: Television and the Politics of Canadian Broadcasting, 1952-1968* (Toronto: University of Toronto Press, 1979), pp. 438-39.
[8] Isaiah A. Litvak and Christopher J. Maule, "Canadian Multinational Media Firms and Canada-United States Relations," *Behind the Headlines*, vol. XXXIX, no. 5 (1982), p. 5.
[9] Federal Cultural Policy Review Committee, *Summary of Briefs and Hearings*, pp. 4-5.
[10] Ibid., p. 222.
[11] Allan Gotlieb, Charles Dalfen and Kenneth Katz, "The Transborder Transfer of Information by Communications and Computer Systems: Issues and Approaches to Guiding Principles," *American Journal of International Law*, vol. 68 (April 1974), pp. 237-38.
[12] *Memorandum Opinion, Order and Authorization Before the Federal Communications Commission*, FCC 81-492, Washington, D.C. (released October 30, 1981), p. 5.
[13] Ibid., p. 26. The FCC approval violated the 1972 UNESCO agreement calling for prior consent from the receiving country and indicated that the United States was playing a tougher game than ever.
[14] Patrick Watson, "The Odds on Canadian Pay-TV," *Globe and Mail*, May 13, 1982; and Robert Fulford, "Paying the Price," *Saturday Night*, August 1982, pp. 3-6.
[15] John Meisel, A paper presented at the York University Conference on Mass Communications and Canadian Nationhood, Toronto, April 10, 1981.

[16] Committee on Government Operations, Thirty-Second Report, *International Information Flow: Forging a New Framework* (Washington: U.S. Government Printing Office, 1980), p. 23.

[17] Gotlieb et al., "The Transborder Transfer of Information," p. 229.

[18] Oswald H. Ganley, *The United States-Canadian Communications and Information Resources Relationship and its Possible Significance for Worldwide Diplomacy* (Cambridge, Mass.: Centre for Information Policy Research, Harvard University, 1980), p. 4.

[19] Gotlieb et al., "The Transborder Transfer of Information," p. 229.

[20] Consultative Committee on the Implications of Telecommunications for Canadian Sovereignty, *Telecommunications and Canada* (Clyne Report) (Ottawa: Supply and Services Canada, 1979), p. 2.

[21] Interdepartmental Task Force on Transborder Data Flow, Working Group on Sovereignty Aspects, *Mandate and Work Program*, October 9, 1981, p. 2.

[22] Peter Robinson, "Transborder Dataflow — A Canadian Perspective," *Information Privacy*, vol. II (March 1980), p. 57.

[23] Robert Sheppard, "Ride Computer Wave or Flounder in Backwater, Canada Warned," *Globe and Mail*, May 18, 1982.

[24] Price Waterhouse Associates, *A Review of the Economic Implications of Canadian Transborder Data Flows* (Toronto, February 1981), pp. 13-20.

[25] G. Russell Pipe, "National Policies, International Debates," *Journal of Communication*, vol. XXIX (Summer 1979), p. 118.

[26] Consultative Committee on the Implications of Telecommunications, *Telecommunications and Canada*, p. 64.

[27] Gotlieb et al., "The Transborder Transfer of Information," p. 247.

[28] W.E. Cundiff, "Issues in Canadian/U.S. Transborder Computer Data Flows," in W.E. Cundiff and Mado Reid, eds., *Issues in Canadian/U.S. Transborder Computer Data Flows* (Montreal: Institute for Research on Public Policy, 1979), p. 27.

[29] Oswald H. Ganley, *The Role of Communications and Information Resources in Canada*, Harvard University Publication P-79-1 (Cambridge, Mass., June 1979), p. 35.

[30] R.W. Evans Research Corporation," The Extent to Which Foreign Multi-Nationals Are Good Corporate Citizens in Canada," mimeo (Etobicoke, 1981), pp. 2-5.

[31] Ganley, *The Role of Communications and Information Resources in Canada*, pp. 38-41.

[32] Alphonse Ouimet, "Canada versus U.S.A." *Intermedia*, vol. 7, no. 6 (November 1979), p. 1.

[33] Elisabeth C. Kriegler, "Notes for an Address," Council on Foreign Relations, New York, May 12, 1981, p. 1.

[34] Robinson, "Transborder Dataflow — A Canadian Perspective," p. 55.

[35] Oswald H. Ganley, *International Communications and Information: The Need to Take it Seriously*, Incidental Paper 1-81-8 (Cambridge, Mass.: Center for Information Policy Research, Harvard University, August 1981), p. 13.

[36] Ibid., p. 17.

[37] Oswald H. Ganley, Testimony before the Subcommittee on Telecommunications, Consumer Protection and Finance of the House Committee on Energy and Commerce, April 29, 1981, pp. 6-7.

[38] Committee on Government Operations, *International Information Flow: Forging a New Framework*, pp. 17-18.

398

[39] *Banks and Banking Law Revision*, 1980, section 157, (4), (5).

[40] Ganley, Testimony before the Subcommittee on Telecommunications, Consumer Protection and Finance, p. 6.

[41] Isaiah A. Litvak and Christoper J. Maule, "Bill C-58 and the Regulation of Periodicals in Canada," *International Journal*, vol. XXXVI, no. 1 (Winter 1980-81), p. 71.

[42] Jim Bawden, "Electric Border Feud Turning Into Real War," *Toronto Star*, February 15, 1982.

[43] John King, "Canada-U.S. TV Dispute Lingers," *Globe and Mail*, May 15, 1982; and Jonathan Chevreau, "Ottawa Seeks to Counter U.S. Anti-Telidon Move," *Globe and Mail*, June 17, 1982.

[44] Ganley, *International Communications and Information: The Need to Take it Seriously*, pp. 13-15.

[45] Brian Segal, *The 1979 World Administrative Radio Conference: International Negotiations and Canadian Telecommunications Policy* (Ottawa: Supply and Services Canada, 1980), p. 9.

[46] Ibid., p. 28.

[47] Ganley, *The United States-Canadian Communications and Information Resources Relationship and its Possible Significance for Worldwide Diplomacy*, p. 81.

[48] Ibid., pp. 49-51.

[49] Stephen Breyer, *Regulation and its Reform* (Cambridge, Mass.: Harvard University Press, 1982), chapter 15.

[50] Ganley, *International Communications and Information: The Need to Take it Seriously*, pp. 7-10.

[51] Samuel E. Moffett, *The Americanization of Canada* (1907; reprint ed., Toronto: University of Toronto Press, 1972), pp. 96, 8, 114.

[52] Litvak and Maule, "Canadian Multinational Media Firms," p. 18.

[53] Litvak and Maule, "Bill C-58 and the Regulation of Periodicals," pp. 85-86.

[54] Ibid., p. 87.

[55] Federal Cultural Policy Review Committee, *Summary of Briefs and Hearings*, p. 165.

[56] Canadian Association of Motion Picture Producers, "The Forest and the Trees: Towards a National Film Policy," mimeo (Toronto, May 1982), p. 32.

[57] Ibid., p. 9.

Chapter 11: NATO, NORAD, and Canada's Military Options

[1] Gerald Wright, "NATO in the New International Order," *Behind the Headlines*, vol. XXXVI (April 1978), p. 4.

[2] Ibid., pp. 7-8.

[3] Leslie H. Gelb, "Weinberger Sees Flexibility on Military Spending," *New York Times*, April 21, 1982.

[4] Ibid.

[5] Douglas A. Ross, "American Nuclear Revisionism, Canadian Strategic Interests and the Renewal of NORAD," *Behind the Headlines*, vol. XXXIX (April 1982), p. 5.

[6] Ibid.

[7] For four perspectives on the tremors that are shaking NATO, see Zbigniew Brzezinski, "NATO, the Polish Crisis and the Legacy of Yalta," *Globe and Mail*,

March 2, 1982; Willy Brandt, "The 'Phantom Battle' Over NATO's Existence," *Globe and Mail*, March 3, 1982; Maurice Couve de Murville, "The Alliance's Future is Not in Question," *Globe and Mail*, March 4, 1982; and James Callaghan, "Growing Internal Divisions Could Immobilize Alliance," *Globe and Mail*, March 5, 1982.

[8] John Gellner, "Canada's Defence Load Too Light to Some Eyes," *Globe and Mail*, August 14, 1981.

[9] *Third Report of the Standing Committee on External Affairs and National Defence Respecting Canadian Policy on Future Defence Co-operation with the United States in the North American Region, with Particular Reference to NORAD*, First Session, 32nd Parliament, Ottawa, no. 29, 1980.

[10] "Canada's Forces Aren't Prepared for War: Senate," *Toronto Star*, February 11, 1982.

[11] James Bagnall, "Canada Hardens its NATO Line," *Financial Post*, December 19, 1981.

[12] James Bagnall, "Canada Plays the Nato Hawk," *Financial Post*, May 1, 1982.

[13] John W. Holmes, *Life with Uncle* (Toronto: University of Toronto Press, 1981), p. 92.

[14] David Cox, "Canadian-American Military Relations: Some Present Trends and Future Possibilities," *International Journal*, vol. XXXVI, no. 1 (Winter 1980-81), pp. 99-101.

[15] Brian Cuthbertson, Testimony before the Standing Committee on External Affairs and National Defence, First Session, 32nd Parliament, November 18, 1980, 23:19-20.

[16] Nils Ørvik, "Defence Against Help — A Strategy for Small States?" *Survival*, vol. XV, no. 5 (September-October 1973), p. 228.

[17] *Third Report of SCEAND*, 29:18.

[18] Cuthbertson, Testimony before SCEAND, 23:5.

[19] David Cox, "Canadian Defence Policy: The Dilemmas of a Middle Power," *Behind the Headlines*, vol. XXVII (November 1968), p. 8.

[20] Michael Tucker, *Canadian Foreign Policy: Contemporary Issues and Themes* (Toronto: McGraw-Hill Ryerson, 1980), pp. 149-50.

[21] Danford Middlemiss, Testimony before SCEAND, First Session, 32nd Parliament, November 18, 1980, 23:7.

[22] Ibid., 23:7-8.

[23] Tom Axworthy, "Soldiers Without Enemies: A Political Analysis of Canadian Defence Policy, 1945-1975" (Ph.D. thesis, Queen's University, 1978), p. 580.

[24] Cox, "Canadian Defence Policy," p. 9.

[25] John Hamre, "United States-Canada Defense Relations: A U.S. Perspective" (Paper prepared for the Annual Meeting of the Western Social Sciences Association, April 22-24, 1982), p. 13.

[26] Franklyn Griffiths, *A Northern Foreign Policy* (Toronto: Canadian Institute of International Affairs, 1979), p. 58.

[27] Holmes, *Life with Uncle*, p. 52.

[28] Hamre, "United States-Canada Defense Relations," p. 12.

[29] Atlantic Council, *U.S. Policy Towards Canada: The Neighbor We Cannot Take for Granted* (Washington, 1981) pp. 25-26.

[30] Ibid., p. 24.

[31] *Third Report of SCEAND*, p. 20.

32 Ibid., p. 21.

33 Ibid.

34 Ross, "American Nuclear Revisionism," p. 15.

35 Ibid., p. 16.

36 Colin S. Gray, "Canada and NORAD: A Study in Strategy," *Behind the Headlines*, vol. XXXI (June 1972), p. 19.

37 R.B. Byers, "The Canadian Military and the Use of Force: End of an Era?" *International Journal*, vol. XXX (Spring 1975), p. 295.

38 *Third Report of SCEAND*, p. 22.

39 Cuthbertson, Testimony before SCEAND, 23:18.

40 *Third Report of SCEAND*, p. 22.

41 Cuthbertson, Testimony before SCEAND, 23:19, 23:25.

42 *Third Report of SCEAND*, p. 17.

43 Cuthbertson, Testimony before SCEAND, 23:12.

44 M.E.J. Bobyn, Testimony before SCEAND, First Session, 32nd Parliament, November 25, 1980, 25:7.

45 Cuthbertson, Testimony before SCEAND, 23:28.

46 Atlantic Council, *U.S. Policy Towards Canada: The Neighbor We Cannot Take for Granted*, p. 24.

47 Hyman Solomon, "Defence Firms Eye U.S. Moves," *Financial Post*, January 10, 1981.

48 J.D. MacNaughton, Testimony before SCEAND, First Session, 32nd Parliament, November 25, 1980, 25:52.

49 Standing Senate Committee on Foreign Affairs, *Canada-United States Relations*, vol. II, *Canada's Trade Relations with the United States* (Ottawa: Queen's Printer, 1978), p. 90.

50 Solomon, "Defence Firms Eye U.S. Moves."

51 Douglas J. Murray, "U.S.-Canadian Defense Relations: An Assessment for the 1980s," in The Atlantic Council Working Group on the United States and Canada, *Canada and the United States: Dependence and Divergence* (Cambridge, Mass.: Ballinger, 1982), p. 250.

52 Ernie Regehr, Submission to the House of Commons Standing Committee on External Affairs and National Defence, November 13, 1980, p. 2.

53 Standing Senate Committee, *Canada-United States Relations*, vol. II, p. 91.

54 Murray, "U.S.-Canadian Defense Relations," pp. 243-44.

55 *Financial Post*, December 26, 1981.

56 Atlantic Council, *U.S. Policy Towards Canada: The Neighbor We Cannot Take for Granted*, p. 25.

57 James Eayrs, "Future Roles for the Armed Forces of Canada," *Behind the Headlines*, vol. XXVIII (April 1969), p. 7.

58 Holmes, *Life with Uncle*, p. 92.

59 Murray, "U.S.-Canadian Defense Relations," p. 233.

60 Department of National Defence, *Defence in the 70s* (Ottawa: Information Canada, 1971), p. 16.

61 R.B. Byers, "Defence and Foreign Policy in the 1970s: The Demise of the Trudeau Doctrine," *International Journal*, vol. XXXIII, no. 2 (Spring 1978), p. 327.

62 Griffiths, *A Northern Foreign Policy*, p. 37.

63 *Freedom and Security under the Law: Commission of Inquiry Concerning certain Activities of the Royal Canadian Mounted Police* (McDonald Commission), Second

Report, vol. I (Ottawa: Canadian Government Publishing Centre, 1981), p. 632.
[64] Ibid., p. 643.
[65] Brian Cuthbertson, *Canadian Military Independence in the Age of the Superpowers* (Toronto: Fitzhenry and Whiteside, 1977), pp. 270-71.

Chapter 12: The Continuing Crisis

[1] Robert E. Osgood, "The Revitalization of Containment," *Foreign Affairs*, vol. 60, no. 3 (1982), special issue on "America and the World," p. 500.
[2] Peter C. Dobell, "Negotiating with the United States," *International Journal*, vol. XXXVI, no. 1 (Winter 1980-81), p. 20.
[3] Willis C. Armstrong, "The American Perspective," in H. Edward English, ed., *Canada-United States Relations* (New York: Praeger, 1976), p. 3.
[4] Donald K. Alper and Robert L. Monahan, "Bill C-58 and the American Congress: The Politics of Retaliation," *Canadian Public Policy*, vol. IV, no. 2 (Spring 1978), p. 191.
[5] John Honderich, "Canadians No Longer Mr. Nice Guy to U.S.," *Toronto Star*, May 23, 1982.
[6] Year after year Canada is barely mentioned in *Foreign Affairs'* annual review of U.S. international relations, "America and the World."
[7] Remark attributed to Robert A. Cornell, deputy assistant secretary of the treasury in Richard Smith, U.S. notetaker, "Canada-U.S. Contact Group Meeting of December 16, 1981," mimeo (Ottawa 1981).
[8] John Curtis, "Reflections on Canada-U.S. Economic Relations in the Eighties" (Paper presented to the Fifth Lester B. Pearson Conference on the Canada-United States Relationship, Niagara-on-the-Lake, October 14-17, 1981), p. 6.
[9] Multinational Strategies, Inc., "Canada 1981-1985. The Longer-Term Environment for Business," mimeo (New York, 1981), pp. 117, 21.
[10] Norman Hillmer and Garth Stevenson, eds., *A Foremost Nation: Canadian Foreign Policy Making and a Changing World* (Toronto: McClelland and Stewart, 1977), pp. 1-2.
[11] Peyton V. Lyon and Brian W. Tomlin, *Canada as an International Actor* (Toronto: Macmillan, 1979), p. 32.
[12] Sandra Gwyn, "To Have and Have Not," *Saturday Night*, June 1981, p. 12.
[13] Lyon and Tomlin, *Canada as an International Actor*, p. 145.
[14] Peyton Lyon, "Quiet Diplomacy Revisited," in Stephen Clarkson, ed., *An Independent Foreign Policy for Canada?* (Toronto: McClelland and Stewart, 1968), p. 30.
[15] John W. Holmes, *Life with Uncle: The Canadian-American Relationship* (Toronto, University of Toronto Press, 1981), pp. 87, 102.
[16] There is reason to doubt that the Liberal government's support for the Olympic boycott was wholehearted: as leader of the opposition, Pierre Trudeau's spontaneous response to the boycott proposal was strongly negative.
[17] Confidential interviews.
[18] Holmes, *Life with Uncle*, p. 66.
[19] Michael Tucker, *Canadian Foreign Policy: Contemporary Issues and Themes* (Toronto: McGraw-Hill Ryerson, 1980), p. 119.
[20] Lyon and Tomlin, *Canada as an International Actor*, p. 32.
[21] Richard Cleroux, "Trudeau Wants to Show USSR West Can Meet It Gun for Gun," *Globe and Mail*, March 20, 1982.

22 John Harbon, *Canada and the Organization of American States* (Washington: Canada-American Committee, 1963), p. 22.

23 Michael Posner, "Trade Winds from Washington," *Maclean's*, March 8, 1982.

24 *Second Report of the House of Commons Subcommittee on Canada's Relations with Latin America and the Caribbean*, First Session, 32nd Parliament, December 8, 1981, 48:8.

25 Mark Lukasiewicz, "GATT Frays as Nations Breach, Ignore the Rules," *Globe and Mail*, June 7, 1982.

26 Victor Levant, "Eyeless in Persia: External Affairs in Iran," *This Magazine*, July-August 1980, p. 10.

27 Heather Robertson, "Al's Pal," *Today Magazine*, July 18, 1981, p. 8.

28 Mitchell Sharp, "Canada-U.S. Relations: Options for the Future," *International Perspectives*, special issue (Autumn 1972), pp. 17-24.

29 Mark MacGuigan, Text as Delivered of an Address by the Secretary of State for External Affairs, Dr. Mark MacGuigan, to the Empire Club of Canada, Toronto, Jan. 22, 1981, pp. 6-7. I am indebted to John Kirton for pointing out the significance of this speech.

30 Allan Gotlieb and Jeremy Kinsman, "Reviving the Third Option," *International Perspectives*, January-February 1981, p. 4.

31 Ibid., pp. 2, 3.

32 Government of Canada, *Foreign Policy for Canadians* (Ottawa, 1970).

33 See Garth Stevenson, "The Third Option," *International Journal*, vol. XXXIII, no. 2 (Spring 1978), pp. 424-31; and Harald von Riekhoff, "The Third Option in Canadian Foreign Policy," in Brian W. Tomlin, ed., *Canada's Foreign Policy: Analysis and Trends* (Toronto: Methuen, 1978), pp. 87-109.

34 Confidential interview.

35 Roger F. Swanson, "The United States as a National Security Threat to Canada," *Behind the Headlines*, vol. XXIX, nos. 5-6 (1970), p. 9.

36 Ibid., p. 14.

37 John Kirton, "The Politics of Bilateral Management: The Case of the Automotive Trade," *International Journal*, vol. XXXVI, no. 1 (Winter 1980-81), pp. 68-69.

38 Abraham Rotstein, "Independence Where the Nights are Long" (Paper prepared for the Canadian-United States Relations Seminar, Harvard University, April 27, 1982).

39 The notion of Canada's middle-power role at the economic summit was put forward by John Curtis, research director of the Institute for Research on Public Policy, at a seminar to the Centre for International Studies, University of Toronto, March 5, 1982.

Chapter 13: Implementing a Strategy

1 W.M. Dobell, "Is External Affairs a Central Agency? A Question of Leadership Controls," *International Perspectives*, May-June, July-August 1979, pp. 9-10.

2 John Kirton, "Les contraintes du milieu et la gestion de la politique étrangère canadienne de 1976 à 1978," *Études Internationales*, vol. X, no. 2 (juin 1979), pp. 322, 329.

3 Dobell, "Is External Affairs a Central Agency?" p. 12.

4 Government of Canada, *Report of the Royal Commission on Conditions of Foreign Service* (Ottawa: Supply and Services Canada, October 21, 1981), p. 15.

5 Ibid., pp. 20, 247.

[6] Ibid., p. 79.

[7] Kirton, "Les contraintes du milieu," p. 346. "Au sein du ministère, le groupe traditionnel des questions bilatérales canado-américaines occupait une place moins centrale dans les préoccupations des principaux gestionnaires et constituait un foyer moins déterminant des initiatives de coordination des Affaires extérieures."

[8] Standing Senate Committee on Foreign Affairs, *Canada-United States Relations*, vol. 1, *The Institutional Framework for the Relationship* (Ottawa: Queen's Printer, 1975), p. 27.

[9] Confidential interviews.

[10] Kal J. Holsti and Thomas Allen Levy, "Bilateral Institutions and Transgovernmental Relations between Canada and the United States," *International Organization*, vol. 28 (Autumn 1974), p. 893.

[11] Harald von Riekhoff, John H. Sigler and Brian W. Tomlin, *Canadian-U.S. Relations: Policy Environments, Issues, and Prospects* (Montreal: C.D. Howe Research Institute, 1979), p. 50.

[12] Holsti and Levy, "Bilateral Institutions and Transgovernmental Relations," p. 894.

[13] Wayne Clifford, "The Western Provinces of Canada: The Importance and Orientation of their International Relations" (Paper presented in Quebec City, October 1981), p. 10.

[14] Lise Bissonnette, "Quebec-Ottawa-Washington, the Pre-Referendum Triangle," *American Review of Canadian Studies*, vol. 11 (Spring 1981), pp. 64-74.

[15] Québec, *Bâtir le Québec: Énoncé de politique économique: synthèse, orientations et actions* (Québec, Développement économique, 1979).

[16] Bernard Bonin, "American Investments in Quebec" (Paper presented to Carnegie Endowment for International Peace conference, New York, June 5, 1981), pp. 10-11.

[17] Peter Morici, Arthur J.R. Smith and Sperry Lea, *Canadian Industrial Policy* (Washington: National Planning Association, February 1981), p. 139.

[18] Clifford, "The Western Provinces of Canada," p. 17.

[19] Final Communiqué, The Twenty-Second Annual Premiers' Conference, Victoria, B.C., August 11-15, 1981, p. 1.

[20] Anon., "Summary Record of Discussion at US Ambassador's, October 13th," October 13, 1981. Memo marked "Confidential."

[21] "Excerpts of Premier Lougheed's Address to the Investment Dealers' Association of Canada," Jasper, Alberta, June 21, 1982, p. 16.

[22] Isaiah A. Litvak and Christopher J. Maule, "Canadian Multinational Media Firms and Canada-United States Relations," *Behind the Headlines*, vol. XXXIX, no. 5 (1982), pp. 7-9.

[23] Terence A. Keenleyside, Lawrence LeDuc and J. Alex Murray, "Public Opinion and Canada-United States Economic Relations," *Behind the Headlines*, vol. XXXV, no. 4 (1976), p. 9.

[24] James Coutts, "Notes for an Address to the Policy Convention of the Liberal Party of Canada (Ontario)," November 27, 1981, mimeo.

[25] See "Notes for an Address by Rt. Hon. Joe Clark to the Canadian Society of New York," October 7, 1981, p. 6: "I deeply regret that the present government has chosen to give policy expression to our nationalist aspirations in a way that is so essentially negative."

[26] Canadian-American Committee, *Improving Bilateral Consultation on Economic*

404

Issues (Montreal: C.D. Howe Research Institute; Washington: National Planning Association, 1981), p. 14.

27 Senate Standing Committee, *Canada-United States Relations*, vol. 1, p. 73.

28 Richard Nixon, "Address to a Joint Meeting of the Canadian Parliament," April 14, 1972, *Public Papers of the Presidents*, p. 537.

29 John Sloan Dickey, *Canada and the American Presence: The United States Interest in an Independent Canada* (New York: New York University Press, 1975), p. 145.

30 Don Munton, "Paradoxes and Prospects," in Robert Spencer, John Kirton and Kim Richard Nossal, eds., *The International Joint Commission Seventy Years On* (Toronto: Centre for International Studies, University of Toronto, 1981), pp. 76, 81.

31 Canadian-American Committee, *Improving Bilateral Consultation on Economic Issues*, pp. 12-13.

32 Marie-Josée Drouin and Harald B. Malmgren, "Canada, the United States and the World Economy," *Foreign Affairs*, vol. 60 (Winter 1981-82), p. 413.

33 Hugh G.J. Aitken, *American Capital and Canadian Resources* (Cambridge, Mass.: Harvard University Press, 1961), p. 155.

34 Senate Standing Committee, *Canada-United States Relations*, vol. 1, pp. 47-49.

35 Peter C. Dobell, "The Influence of the United States Congress on Canadian-American Relations," *International Organization*, vol. 28 (Autumn 1974), pp. 903-29; and "Negotiating with the United States," *International Journal*, vol. XXXVI, no. 1 (Winter 1980-81), pp. 17-38.

Chapter 14: Canada and the Mulroney Challenge

1James Rusk, "FIRA to Be Revised, U.S. Executives Told," *Globe and Mail*, October 21, 1982: "Mr. Trudeau, who went out of his way to make them feel at home, emphasized to the group that he personally is not an economic nationalist and that economic nationalism was a policy pushed on the Liberals by the Ontario caucus."

2Peter Morici, *The Global Competitive Struggle: Challenges to the United States and Canada* (Washington: Canadian-American Committee, 1984), as cited by Ronald Anderson, "New Wave of NICs Will Keep World Economy Off Balance," *Globe and Mail*, November 15, 1984.

3Tim Congdon, "How U.S. Could Join the Debtor Nations," *The Times*, August 22, 1984.

4"Weinberger Outlines Role for Military Forces Abroad," *Globe and Mail*, November 29, 1984.

5Tom Wicker, "Mr. Weinberger's Tests," *New York Times*, December 2, 1984.

6John Kirton, "Canadian Foreign Policy in the 1980s," *Current History*, vol. 83, no. 493 (May 1984), pp. 193-96, 226-27.

7Brian Milner, "U.S. Wins a Point on Services Trade," *Globe and Mail*, December 17, 1984.

8Jennifer Lewington, "Washington Talks Loudly and Carries No Stick," *Globe and Mail*, December 17, 1984.

9Zbigniew Brzezinski, "From Loss of Nerve to Loss of Control: A Retrospective on the 1980s" (Address to Center for International Affairs, Harvard University, June 9, 1983), p. 12.

10John Gray, "Lalonde Suggests International War against U.S. Rates," *Globe and Mail*, May 9, 1984.

[11]Fred Harrison, "New Ways to Trade with U.S.," *International Perspectives*, March/April 1984, p. 8.

[12]Jeffrey Simpson, "Trudeau Assails U.S. over Soviet Policy; Lashes out at NATO," *Globe and Mail*, June 11, 1982.

[13]"Regular Talks Planned to Soothe Sore Spots," *Globe and Mail*, October 26, 1982.

[14]Charles Doran, *Forgotten Partnership: U.S.-Canada Relations Today* (Baltimore: Johns Hopkins University Press, 1983), pp. 54-57.

[15]James Reston, "A Talk with Trudeau," *New York Times Magazine*, October 3, 1982, pp. 40-41, 54-56, 70-71.

[16]"Friends Again," *Maclean's*, October 25, 1982.

[17]David Stewart-Patterson, "Top-Level Visits Part of New Federal Strategy on U.S." and "Crisis Atmosphere Fading in Canadian-U.S. Affairs," *Globe and Mail*, January 4, 1983.

[18]G. Bruce Doern and Glen Toner, *The Politics of Energy: The Development and Implementation of the NEP* (Toronto: Methuen, 1985), pp. 114-15.

[19]Nicholas Hunter, "Oil Profits Recover Sharply: 4 Majors Make $1.42 Billion," *Globe and Mail*, February 1, 1985.

[20]Douglas Martin, "Economically, Things Look That Much Worse in Canada," *New York Times*, November 14, 1982, and confidential interview.

[21]Confidential interview.

[22]Jennifer Lewington, "Edge Cites Dangers in Escape Clauses," *Globe and Mail*, August 6, 1983.

[23]Hyman Solomon, "More FIRA Moves to Come," *Financial Post*, July 10, 1982.

[24]Paul Heron Robinson, Jr., Speech to the Canadian Club of Chicago, January 27, 1983. Author's notes.

[25]John King, "Canada Broke Agreement on World Trade, Panel Says," *Globe and Mail*, July 13, 1983, and "Canada to Reword FIRA Act before Final GATT Decision," *Globe and Mail*, January 20, 1984.

[26]Martin Mittelstaedt, "Bill Allows Foreign Banks 16% of Market," *Globe and Mail*, April 12, 1984.

[27]"We've Reduced Foreign Control of Our Economy Trudeau Boasts," *Toronto Star*, May 31, 1984.

[28]Dianne Maley, "Investment Outflow Exceeds Inflow," *Globe and Mail*, January 1, 1985.

[29]Dan Westell, "Canada and U.S. Apply Duty Weapons in Steel Trade," *Globe and Mail*, January 5, 1984.

[30]"ICC Chief Feels Moratorium Was Imposed without Reason," *Globe and Mail*, February 7, 1983.

[31]Charles F. Doran and Joel J. Sokolsky, *Canada and Congress: Lobbying in Washington* (Washington: School of Advanced International Studies, Johns Hopkins University, 1984).

[32]David Stewart-Patterson, "Lumber Case Shows Value of Making a Unified Effort," *Globe and Mail*, September 4, 1984.

[33]John King and Jennifer Hunter, "U.S. House Vote Removes Threat to the Auto Pact," *Globe and Mail*, December 16, 1982.

[34]"Commerce Ruling Ends Lumber Import Probe," *Globe and Mail*, May 25, 1984.

[35]"U.S. Rejects Penalties on Canadian Potatoes," *Globe and Mail*, December 13, 1983.

[36]James Rusk, "Ottawa to Expand Trade Links with U.S. 'Partner,' " *Globe and Mail*, September 1, 1983; Department of External Affairs, *Canadian Trade Policy*

for the 1980s: A Discussion Paper (Ottawa: Minister of Supply and Services, 1983).

[37]Bruce W. Wilkinson, "Commercial Policy and Free Trade with the United States," in Maureen Molot and Brian Tomlin, eds., *Canada in International Affairs, 1984* (Toronto: James Lorimer, forthcoming), p. 11.

[38]Gary Clyde Hufbauer and Andrew James Samet, *U.S. Receptivity to Bilateralism in Canadian-American Economic Relations,* Report prepared for the Royal Commission on the Economic Union and Development Prospects for Canada, mimeo (Washington, 1984), p. 39.

[39]Wilkinson, "Free Trade with the United States."

[40]John C. Polanyi, "History Will Judge Cruise Decision," *Globe and Mail,* February 11, 1983.

[41]Thomas Walkom, "PM Cites NATO Partnership in Decision on Cruise Testing," *Globe and Mail,* March 24, 1983.

[42]*Report of the Federal Cultural Policy Review Committee* (Ottawa: Minister of Supply and Services, 1982).

[43]Confidential interviews.

[44]*Towards a New National Broadcasting Strategy* (Ottawa: Minister of Supply and Services, February 1983); and *Globe and Mail,* March 2, 1983.

[45]Francis Fox, Speech to the annual meeting of the Canadian Association of Broadcasters, October 26, 1983, p. 2.

[46]Jonathan Chevreau, "Broadcasters Keep Wary Eye on Satellites," *Globe and Mail,* October 30, 1982.

[47]"Protect Own TV Shows, Ottawa Tells Groups," *Globe and Mail,* March 3, 1983.

[48]Ben Fiber, "Social Issues Seen Distorted," *Globe and Mail,* May 2, 1984.

[49]*Building for the Future: Towards a Distinctive CBC* (Ottawa: Minister of Supply and Services, October 1983).

[50]John Gray, "New Broadcast Policy Opens Door to U.S. Shows," *Globe and Mail,* March 2, 1983.

[51]Dan Westell, "Pay-TV Fate Linked to U.S. Packages," *Globe and Mail,* March 1, 1984.

[52]*The National Film and Video Policy* (Ottawa: Minister of Supply and Services, May 1984).

[53]Michael Keating, "U.S. Suppressing Acid Rain Data," *Globe and Mail,* October 6, 1982.

[54]"U.S. Accused of Talking Hokum on Acid Rain," *Globe and Mail,* October 16, 1982.

[55]Text of note from the Embassy of Canada to the Department of State.

[56]Michael Keating, "Unresolved Issues Cloud Pollution Talks," *Globe and Mail,* April 2, 1984.

[57]Michael Keating, "Canada Decides to Go It Alone in Acid Rain Fight," and "Canada is Committed to Spending Billions on Acid Rain Cleanup," *Globe and Mail,* March 7 and 8, 1984.

[58]"U.S. Sources Key to Pollution Woes," *Globe and Mail,* June 8, 1983.

[59]Michael Keating, "Occidental Cleanup Proposal Inadequate Caccia Tells U.S.," *Globe and Mail,* August 2, 1984.

[60]"U.S. Commission Votes for Garrison to Be Scaled Down," *Globe and Mail,* December 17, 1984.

[61]Bernard Gwertzman, "Reagan Lifts the Sanctions on Sales for Soviet Pipeline; Reports Accord with Allies," *New York Times,* November 14, 1982.

407

[62]Fred Harrison, "U.S. Treads Softly over Foreign Subpoenas," *Financial Post*, December 3, 1983.

[63]Mark Lukasiewicz, "Reagan May Not Bow to Pressure to Ease Export Bill," *Globe and Mail*, June 6, 1983.

[64]Peter Robinson, "Transborder Data Flow: A Focus on Trade," Presentation to the conference on "The Management of Transborder Data Flows: U.S.-Canada and Beyond" (Columbia University, April 2, 1984), p. 6.

[65]Michael Tenszen, "Top U.S. Officials Urge Florida to Parole Jaffe," *Globe and Mail*, July 27, 1983.

[66]Bruce Little, "Ottawa Digesting Fisheries Ruling," *Globe and Mail*, October 17, 1984; and Giles Gherson, "Fishery Management Now the Issue," *Financial Post*, October 27, 1984.

[67]"Skagit, Tax Treaties Approved by Senate," *Globe and Mail*, June 29, 1984.

[68]William Johnson, "Canada Protests U.S. Sale of Leases," *Globe and Mail*, May 15, 1984.

[69]Harald von Riekhoff and John Sigler, "The Peace Initiative," in Maureen Molot and Brian Tomlin, eds., *Canada in International Affairs, 1984* (Toronto: James Lorimer, 1985).

[70]Richard and Sandra Gwyn, "Trudeau's Last Hurrah: Behind the Peace Initiative," *Saturday Night*, May 1984.

[71]John Kirton, "Trudeau and the Diplomacy of Peace," *International Perspectives*, July-August 1984, pp. 3-5.

[72]William Wertenbaker, "A Reporter at Large: The Law of the Sea," *New Yorker*, August 1 and 8, 1983.

[73]David Dewitt and John Kirton, *Canada as a Principal Power* (Toronto: John Wiley and Sons, 1983).

[74]Sherri Barron, "U.S. Envoy Sees Closer Ties with New PM," *Ottawa Citizen*, May 28, 1984.

[75]"Majority Favor Investment from Abroad: Gallup," *Toronto Star*, June 14, 1984.

[76]Richard Gwyn, "Better U.S. Ties a Priority for Tories, Liberals," *Toronto Star*, June 23, 1984.

[77]"Majority Favor Investment from Abroad: Gallup," *Toronto Star*, June 14, 1984.

[78]Jane Becker, "Regan Ready to Make NEP Changes," *Globe and Mail*, July 10, 1984.

[79]John Partridge, "Steel Firms Accuse Ottawa of Failure to Support Fight against U.S. Quotas," and David Stewart-Patterson, "Fox Vows to Retaliate on U.S. Steel Curbs," *Globe and Mail*, July 18, 1984.

[80]John Urquhart, "An Outspoken U.S. Friend in Ottawa," *Wall Street Journal*, September 24, 1984.

[81]Rae Murphy, Robert Chodos and Nick Auf der Maur, *Brian Mulroney: The Boy from Baie-Comeau* (Toronto: James Lorimer, 1984), p. 214.

[82]Patrick Martin, "Reading Foreign Policy Teacups," *Globe and Mail*, December 26, 1984.

[83]Jennifer Lewington, "Peace, Disarmament, Priority for Canada, Clark Declares at UN," *Globe and Mail*, September 26, 1984.

[84]William Johnson, "Armed Intervention in Central America Declared U.S. Right," *Globe and Mail*, February 1, 1985.

[85]Margaret Polanyi, "Canada Opposes Nuclear Freeze Call," *Globe and Mail*, December 13, 1984.

[86]Paul Koring, "Canada Undecided on Star Wars Plan," *Globe and Mail*, December 15, 1984.

[87]James Rusk, "PM's Support on Star Wars Pleases U.S.," *Globe and Mail*, February 2, 1985.

[88]Urquhart, "U.S. Friend in Ottawa," *Wall Street Journal*, September 24, 1984.

[89]Thomas Walkom, "NEP Next on Hit List, PM Tells U.S. Group," *Globe and Mail*, December 11, 1984.

[90]Transcript of interview with Pamela Wallin on *W5*, CTV network, December 23, 1984.

[91]L. Ian MacDonald, *Mulroney: The Making of the Prime Minister* (Toronto: McClelland and Stewart, 1984).

[92]Interview on CTV, December 23, 1984.

[93]Jeffrey Simpson, "Clearly of Like Mind," *Globe and Mail*, September 26, 1984.

[94]Richard Burt, assistant secretary for European and Canadian affairs, in Richard Gwyn, "Reagan Wants Special Accord with Canada, Aide Says," *Toronto Star*, September 15, 1984.

[95]Speech from the Throne to open the first session, 33rd Parliament of Canada, November 5, 1984.

[96]Diane Francis, "Oil Takeovers May Test Tory Pledges," *Toronto Star*, October 20, 1984.

[97]Bob Hepburn, "Tories Lift Barriers to Foreign Investment," *Toronto Star*, December 8, 1984.

[98]The Hon. Michael H. Wilson, *A New Direction for Canada: An Agenda for Economic Renewal* (Ottawa: Department of Finance, November 8, 1984).

[99]Livingston T. Merchant and A.D.P. Heeney, "Canada and the United States — Principles for Partnership," *Department of State Bulletin*, August 2, 1965.

[100]"Won't Threaten U.S. on Acid Rain Controls, New Minister Declares," *Globe and Mail*, December 17, 1984.

[101]Bill Walker, "PM Decries Our Record on Acid Rain," *Toronto Star*, February 2, 1985.

[102]James Rusk, "PM's Support on Star Wars Pleases U.S.," *Globe and Mail*, February 2, 1985.

[103]James Bagnall, "New NORAD Deal All Set to be Signed with the U.S.," *Financial Post*, February 2, 1985.

[104]Murphy, Chodos and Auf der Maur, *Mulroney*, p. 212.

[105]Jennifer Lewington, "Canadians Happy with U.S. Trade Bill," *Globe and Mail*, October 11, 1984; "Issue Alert," *Canadian Business Roundtable*, Washington, January 1985.

[106]Jennifer Lewington, "Protectionist Moves Set to Return in Next Congress," *Globe and Mail*, November 20, 1984.

[107]Hufbauer and Samet, *U.S. Receptivity to Bilateralism*, pp. 25-36.

[108]Hyman Solomon, "New Threats to our Exports from U.S. Protectionism," *Financial Post*, February 11, 1984.

[109]The Hon. James F. Kelleher, *How to Secure and Enhance Canadian Access to Export Markets: Discussion Paper* (Ottawa: External Affairs Canada, 1985), pp. 26-28.

[110]Seyom Brown, "The World Polity and the Nation-State System: An Updated Analysis," *International Journal*, vol. xxxix, no. 3 (Summer 1984), p. 524.

[111]Paul Aird, "Tories Deliver Cruelest Cuts to our Wildlife," *Toronto Star*, December 8, 1984.

Index

412

415

continentalism in, 12, 14,
59-60, 61, 62-63, 143, 144,
148, 152
contradictions in, 148, 152
federal paramountcy over
resources, 65-67
industrial benefits from
megaprojects, 67
and market realities, 332,
334-35
self-sufficiency, 61, 63, 149,
361
Enterprise, The, 214, 215
Environmental issues
acid rain, 15, 159, 181,
183-97, 205, 272, 288, 290,
345-47, 362, 366. *See* Acid
rain *for subentries.*
Garrison Diversion Unit, 15,
184, 197-200, 309, 347
Great Lakes Water Quality
Agreement, 15, 184,
200-202, 205, 368
oil spills in Arctic waters,
217-18
Environmental Protection Agency
(U.S.), 187, 188-89, 195, 196,
202, 346
Environment Canada, 190, 194,
195
"Escape clause" relief under
U.S. Trade Act, 118-19
European Economic Community,
29, 125, 136, 139, 160, 250,
281, 292, 330, 331, 348
Evans Research Corporation, 232
Exchange rates, Canada-U.S.,
164, 165, 169, 272
effect of Canadianization
policies on, 177

and interest rates,169, 170,171
and "Nixonomics", 8
Export Administration Act
(U.S.), 348
Exports, Canadian, 115-24
passim, 152-61 passim, 337-40
passim, 353, 364, 366. *See
also* Auto Pact; Free trade;
Protectionism in the U.S.;
Reciprocity.
Exports of energy from Canada,
148-52, 361
controls over, 14, 61, 62, 63
sale of electricity, 159, 305,
323
tax on, 61, 62, 305
Export subsidies, U.S., 121-22
External Affairs, Canadian
Department of, 13, 79, 182,
266, 284, 288, 318, 319, 325,
331, 333, 346, 356, 357-58
and environmental issues in
Canada-U.S. relations, 195,
198
and generation of foreign
strategy, 294-300
problems of morale in, 299
relations with provinces, 304,
306, 307, 308, 309
reorganization of, 296-97, 298,
333
U.S. Bureau of, 298, 299, 300,
319
Extra-territoriality
and branch plants in Canada,
102-3, 177, 230, 231, 291
impact of American pollution,
202
and practices of U.S.
government, 101-3, 121,

416

Foreign Investment Review
Agency (FIRA), 13, 18, 20,
87-89, 234, 271-72
attitudes of provinces to, 305,
306
initial U.S. responses (1970s),
86-87
not expanded in response to
U.S. pressure, 36-37, 41,
42, 45, 83, 104-7, 113
U.S. objections to (1981), 14,
26-48 passim, 53, 90-92, 95,
98-104, 115
weakened and dismantled, 333,
334, 335-36, 358, 360, 361,
366
Foreign investment by U.S.
firms, 90-91, 98. *See also*
Foreign investment in Canada.
Foreign investment in the U.S.
state limitations on, 95, 96-97
U.S. government restrictions
on, 93-95
Foreign ownership and control in
Canada, 6, 7, 336
and economic rents, 153, 154,
161
of the electronics industry, 232
of the forest industries, 156
of mining, 153, 154, 161-62
of the oil and gas industry, 68,
70-71, 75-76. *See also*
Canadianization of the oil
and gas industry.
Foreign policy, Canadian,
278-80, 349-53, 356-68. *See
also* "American strategy" for
Canada.
Forestry industry, and
Canada-U.S. relations, 155-57
Fortune magazine, 37

Fortune 500, 35
Foster, Harold, 158, 185
Fox, Francis, 342-43, 353
Fraser, John, 190, 346
Free trade between Canada and
the U.S.:
in the automotive industry,
126-33, 290
broad approach to, 136-38, 290
for derivative petrochemicals,
135-36
exploration continues
(1984-85), 364-66
in farm machinery, 133-34,
290
NEP and FIRA seen in U.S. as
obstacles to, 28-29, 58, 84,
111
options for Canada, 124-26
sectoral, 126-38, 364-66
Friedman, James, 191

Gallagher, Jack, 18, 72, 311
Ganley, Oswald, 234, 238
Garrison Diversion Unit, 15, 184,
197-200, 309, 347
General Agreement on Tariffs and
Trade (GATT), 29, 34, 37, 47,
104, 119, 120, 124, 138, 292,
330, 336, 339, 353
"Kennedy Round" of
negotiations under, 118
"Tokyo Round" of
negotiations under, *see*
"Tokyo Round" of GATT
negotiations.
Georges Bank, 206, 208, 209,
211, 349
Gillespie, Alastair, 65, 73
Gillespie Guidelines, 67
Globe and Mail, 39, 68, 313-14,

344, 346
Gordon, Walter, 12, 17
Gordon Report, *see* Royal
 Commission on Canada's
 Economic Prospects.
Gotlieb, Allan, 41, 94-95, 229,
 231, 285, 286, 289, 294, 296,
 297, 298, 358
 letter of December 16, 1981,
  44-45, 46, 104
Government procurement policies
 in Canada, 121
 in the U.S., 122
Gray, Colin, 256
Gray, Herb, 19-20, 21, 30, 31,
 34, 36, 47, 101, 108, 131, 132,
 333, 335
 on strengthening FIRA, 88-89,
  105
Gray Report (1972), 12, 20, 85,
 86, 88
Great Lakes Water Quality
 Agreement (1972), 15, 184,
 200-202, 205
Greene, J.J., 59
Green Paper on Energy (1973),
 60
Grenada, U.S. invasion of, 350,
 351, 354, 363
Grey, Rodney, 121, 122-23, 124,
 137, 138, 282
Griffiths, Franklyn, 253
"Group of 77", 215, 216

Haig, Alexander, 22, 25, 29, 30,
 39, 41, 44, 248, 283, 284, 331
 letter of October 9, 1981, 39
Hamre, John, 254
Harbron, John, 282
Harmel Report (1968), 247
Hart, Gary, 249

Head, Ivan, 13, 295
Hedlin, Ralph, 76
Heinbecker, Paul, 99
Heinz, Senator, 140
Herrndorf, Peter, 226
Hibernia oil find, 71, 72, 73, 74,
 334
Hobart Corporation, 25-26
Holmes, John, 251, 254, 264,
 280
Holsti, Kal, 301
Home Box Office, 241, 242
Hormats, Robert D., 46, 95
Horner, Jack, 86
House of Commons Special
 Committee on a National
 Trading Corporation, 125
Howarth, Gorse, 333
Howe, C.D., 6, 14, 310
Hufbauer, Gary, 91, 93, 103,
 141, 365
Husky Oil Ltd., 32
Hyde Park agreement (1941), 259
Hydroelectric projects, 158-59,
 305, 323
Hydro-Québec, 158, 159, 174,
 305

Imperial Oil Ltd., 64, 80, 145
Inco Ltd., 154, 161, 184, 197,
 216
Independent Petroleum
 Association of Canada, 148,
 151
Indexing of taxes, 172, 174
Industrial benefits
 from Alaska pipeline, 148,
  150, 151
 from megaprojects, 67,
  107-13, 151
Industrial strategy, Canadian, 13,

Canadian Mounted Police,
266-67
McDougall royal commission,
299
MacEachen, Allan, 3, 24, 34, 38,
39, 40, 41, 55, 99, 147, 164,
330, 331, 333, 350
MacGuigan, Mark, 16, 25,
210-11, 283, 333
on the Canada-U.S.
relationship, 284, 285, 286,
289, 294
involvement in dispute over
NEP, 39, 40, 41, 44
Mackenzie Valley pipeline, 63,
144, 145, 146
Maclean-Hunter Ltd., 242, 313
Maclean's magazine, 333
McMillan, Charles, 365
MacNaughton, J.D., 259
Magazines, 16, 18, 235, 242
Major Projects Task Force, 18,
109
Malmgren, Harald, 322
Malone, James, 215
Manitoba and Garrison Diversion
Project, 197-98, 199
Manufacturing, *see also*
Industrial benefits; Industrial
strategy.
Canada's position in, 124-25,
176, 177, 308
Marchand, de Montigny, 45, 46
Margin requirements, 27, 33, 34
Massey-Lévesque Report (1951),
223
Maule, Christopher, 242
Medas, James, 332
Media, *see also* Book publishing
in Canada; Broadcasting;
Newspapers; Periodicals;

Radio; Television.
and an American strategy for
Canada, 313-14
Megaprojects
delayed by drop in world oil
price, 81, 113, 177, 287
financing of, 178, 272
industrial benefits from, 67,
107-13
inventory of, 110
tendering on, 30, 31, 40, 42,
108, 111, 112, 115, 122
Meisel, John, 228
Memorandum of Intent on
transboundary air pollution
(1980), 187-88, 196
Merchant-Heeney Report (1965),
6, 7, 102
Middlemiss, Danford, 253
Middle power, Canada as, 292
Military equipment decisions,
Canadian, 256-59, 267, 308
Military policy, Canadian, 7, 8,
244, 252, 260, 273, 341, 363,
364, 367. *See also* North
American Aerospace Defence
Command; North Atlantic
Treaty Organization.
options for Canada, 263-67
Miller, Frank, 365
Mineral incentives plan, 75
Mineral Lands Leasing Act
(U.S.), 26, 27, 33, 103
Mineral rights, differences
between Canadian and U.S.
practices, 73
Mining, 153-55, 161-62
lobbying by U.S. mining
industry, 212, 213, 214, 218
of seabed resources, 213, 214,
218

Mobil Oil Corp., 73, 74, 334
Moffett, Samuel, 241
Mondale, Walter, 57
Monetary policy, and Canadian
  dependency on U.S., 164
Monroe Doctrine, 251
Morin, Claude, 304
Morin, Jacques-Yvan, 303
Moroz, A.R., 138
Movies, 224, 242-43
Moynihan, Patrick, 195
Mulholland, William, 170
Mulroney, Brian, 328, 352,
  353-60
  background, 354-55
  team surrounding, 356-58
  U.S. response to, 360
  views, 356, 358-59, 360, 363
Munton, Don, 185, 189
Music industry, Canadian, 225
Muskie, Edmund, 210
MX missile, 249

National Academy of Sciences
  (U.S.), 192-93
National Energy Board, 59, 62,
  63, 145, 147, 149
National Energy Program (NEP),
  see also Energy policy,
  Canadian.
  aims of, 3, 4, 53, 55, 275, 291
  and the Canada-U.S.
    relationship, 21, 23-48
  passim, 56, 57, 78-83
  passim, 181, 271, 319, 326
  Canadianization aims and U.S.
    corporate interests, 71-78,
    80
  Crown interest under, see
    Crown interest under NEP.
  as development of previous

  energy policies, 68, 73
  and federal-provincial
    relations, 56, 306
  implementation of, 78-82
  megaprojects under, see
    Megaprojects.
  modified, 332, 333, 334,
    352-53, 358, 360, 366
  not developed into industrial
    strategy, 36, 37, 38, 41, 45,
    105-7, 112-13, 161-62, 272
  and petrochemical industry,
    78, 80, 136, 152, 315, 333
  planning of, 20, 67, 68, 297
  price strategy and U.S. national
    interests, 69-71
  response of Reagan
    administration to, 28-35,
    37-44, 68-78, 79, 89, 90,
    316, 332, 334
  short-term economic problems
    caused by, 177-78
National Film Board, 344-45
Nationalism
  Canadian, 17-21, 87,89, 106.
  See also Canadianization of the
    oil and gas industry;
    National Energy Program.
  U.S., 21-22, 116-24. See also
    Protectionism in the U.S.
National Marine Fishery Service
  (U.S.), 208
National Oil Policy, 58, 60, 148
National Planning Association
  (U.S.), 69, 112, 306
National Policy (1879), 116, 138
"National treatment" of foreign
  investors, 24n., 29, 75, 99,
  100, 107, 292, 316
Native people, and northern
  pipeline, 146, 152

New Democratic Party of
Canada, 145, 314. *See also*
Broadbent, Ed.
New England Regional Fisheries
Management Council, 207-8
New International Economic
Order (NIEO), 10, 214, 279
Newspapers, 241, 313
New World Information Order,
236
Nicaragua, 350, 357
Nickel, 153-54, 216
Nixon, Richard, 8, 9, 60, 130,
188, 200, 201, 284, 331
"Nixon Doctrine," 320
"Nixonomics," 8, 10, 271, 286,
315
Non-renewable resources in
Canada, 153-55. *See also*
Petroleum.
Non-tariff barriers, 122-23, 290,
308
North American Aerospace
Defence Command (NORAD),
16, 182, 245, 251-59, 267-68,
341, 367
importance to Canada, 252,
254, 255
reduced significance to U.S.,
254
North American Water and Power
Alliance (NAWAPA), 157
North Atlantic Treaty
Organization (NATO), 16,
182, 245, 246-51, 268, 281,
357, 364
alliance shaken by U.S.
pronouncements, 248-49
importance to Canada, 249-51
Northern Pipeline Act (Canada,
1978), 108-9, 148

Northern Pipeline Agency, 148
Northern Warning radar system,
363
North-South relations, 33, 275,
279
Norton, Keith, 195
Nossal, Kim, 199
Nova Scotia Light and Power
Company, 64
Nuclear weapons, 246, 247, 248,
249

Office of Industrial and Regional
Benefits (OIRB), 111, 112,
113. *See also* Committee on
Industrial and Regional
Benefits.
"Off-oil" policy in U.S., 187,
188, 190
Offshores Supplies Office
(U.K.), 111
Ogdensburg Declaration, 251,
259
Oil, *see* Petroleum.
Oil Import Compensation
Program, 63
Oil spills in Arctic waters, 217-18
Oil substitution program, 70
Ontario government
and acid rain problem, 195-96
exports of electricity, 159
joint action with Ottawa to aid
the auto industry, 131
Suncor shares purchased by, 80
and the U.S. relationship,
307-10
Ontario Hydro, 197
Organization of American States
(OAS), 282, 357
Organization for Economic
Cooperation and Development

426

in cultural matters, 236, 241,
243-44
"linkage," 140, 275, 277,
289, 294
in U.S. trade policy, 138-42,
272, 275, 311
Regan, Donald, 38, 39, 44, 95,
284, 311
Regan, Gerald, 339, 340, 353
Regehr, Ernie, 260
Regional Operations Control
Centres, 257, 258
Reisman, Simon, 127, 133, 284
Relations between Canada and
countries other than the U.S.,
182, 250, 266, 279, 292, 293.
See also Third option.
Renewable resources in Canada,
155-59
Research and development
(R & D)
in the automotive industry, 128
in the electronics industry, 232
low levels in Canada, 125, 176
Resources, and the Canada-U.S.
relationship, 152-59, 162, 272,
287
non-renewable resources,
153-55. *See also* Petroleum.
processed products, 160-61
renewable resources, 155-59
Resource taxes and royalties,
161. *See also* National Energy
Program.
Reston, James, 333
Retaliation by Canada against
U.S. measures, 337, 338, 353
Retaliation by U.S. against
Canadian legislation, 33-39
passim, 47, 48, 120-21, 276,
277-78, 287, 315-16, 319,

324, 327. *See also* Reciprocity.
Retroactivity aspect of Crown
interest provision, 71, 72,
73-74
Richardson, Elliot, 213
Richardson, Robert, 333
Roberts, John, 190, 191, 196
Robinson, Paul, 39, 40, 41, 276,
336, 352
Robinson, Peter, 233
Robinson, Raymond, 345-46
Roosevelt, Franklin Delano, 251
Ross, Douglas, 255
Rotstein, Abraham, 289
Royal Commission on Canada's
Economic Prospects (Gordon
Commission), 75, 84
Royer, Raymond, 18
Ruckelshaus, William, 346

St. Joe Minerals Corporation, 26,
27
Samet, Andrew, 141, 365
Satellites
broadcasting by, 225-28, 237,
238, 239, 241, 343
data communications by, 231
military uses, 258-59
Sauvé, Jeanne, 198
Scarfe, B., 70-71
Schlesinger, James, 147
Schmidt, Helmut, 163
Schwindt, R., 136-37
Seabed mining, 213, 214, 218
Seagram Company Ltd., 23, 26,
27, 32, 77
Securities Exchange Act (U.S.,
1934), 94
Self-sufficiency in oil production,
55, 59, 63, 70, 81, 149, 291
Semiautomatic Ground

427

Takeovers of U.S. businesses by
Canadian companies, 23,
25-27, 28, 32, 38, 48, 57,
77-78, 80
effects on Canadian dollar, 34,
166, 170, 172, 177
Tariff Act (U.S., 1930), 119, 120
Tariffs, Canadian, 7, 125
Tariffs, international agreements
on, 308. *See also* General
Agreement on Tariffs and
Trade (GATT).
Tariffs, U.S., 6, 117, 118-19,
134, 135, 160, 288, 290, 306
Tax cuts in U.S., 167
Tax reform measures (1981), 332
Technology, *see also* Research
and development.
military, 258-59, 267
Tehran hostage incident, 9, 16,
28, 283
Telecommunications, 10, 139.
See also Broadcasting;
Information industries;
Satellites; Television;
Trans-border data flow.
Telecommunications Competition
and Deregulation Act (U.S.,
1981), 140
Telefilm Canada, 343, 344
Telephone communications in
North America, 238
Telesat Canada, 239
Television, 224-28, 291, 343-44,
367-68
cable systems, 140, 225, 226,
227, 241, 242, 342, 343,
344, 345
pay-TV, 226, 227, 344
satellites, 225-28, 237, 238,
239, 241, 343

Telidon, 140, 236
Texas Gulf Corporation, 27
"Third Option," 8, 123, 250,
284, 286, 290, 296
Third World countries, 10, 214,
215, 219, 236, 238, 279, 280,
329, 330, 358-59
Thomson Newspapers Ltd., 313
Time magazine, 16, 18, 235, 242
"Tokyo Round" of GATT
negotiations, 106, 117, 118,
120, 122, 125, 135, 160, 282,
283, 290, 292, 301, 306
Torstar Corporation, 313
Towe, Peter, 24, 30, 31, 37, 41,
73, 94
Tower, John, 26
Trade, *see also* Exports,
Canadian.
diversification of, 290
joint trade commission
proposed, 322
liberalization of, *see* Free trade
between Canada and the
U.S.; "Tokyo Round" of
GATT negotiations.
Trade Act (U.S., 1974), 9, 34,
117, 118-19, 120, 140, 235,
243, 291
use as retaliatory weapon
against Canada considered,
34-35
Trade Agreements Act (U.S.,
1979), 117, 119, 120
Trade balance, Canadian, 176,
292
Trade deficit, U.S., 329, 337,
364, 365
Trade policies, U.S., *see* Free
trade between Canada and the
U.S.; Protectionism in the U.S.